THE OFFICIAL PRICE GUIDE TO AMERICAN

Pottery & Porcelain

BY
DOROTHY ROBINSON
WITH
BILL FEENY

EDITOR
THOMAS E. HUDGEONS, III

D0168661

FIRST EDITION
HOUSE OF COLLECTIBLES, ORLANDO, FLORIDA 32811

ACKNOWLEDGEMENTS

Artwork: Julian Kernes, for the drawings of the Lenox backstamps; Don Rago, for the drawings of the unmarked Lenox items; Bruce Zanar for roughly half of the other backstamps; remaining backstamps by Dorothy Robinson.

Photographers: Cover photo by DeGlau; color photos by DeGlau and Mel Davis; black and white photos by Richard Taylor, Dave Brady, Bruce Gerber, Thomas Mann and others whose names are not know to us.

Contributors of Information, Prices, and/or Photographs: Fran Trout for all the information about the Coxon family and for the photo of Jonathan Coxon; Theresa and Adam Yunger, for many prices and photographs, backstamp information, dimensions, etc.; Mark and Nori Mohr, for photos, prices and backstamp information; Jim Seibert, for the loan of his 1939 Lenox anniversary catalogue; Dennis Clifton, for photographs, prices, and general information; Erma and Harry Brown, for the photograph of the Lenox doll; Morris Rosen, for photographs and prices; and many others who have asked not to be mentioned by name. 1893 *Willets White Ware Catalog*.

NOTE: *This publication is in no way associated with Lenox, Inc., or its subsidiary, Lenox China, Inc., and any opinions expressed herein are those of the authors. Prices listed are for those items being sold on the secondary market, and have no relationship to current retail pricing structures. Furthermore, neither Lenox, Inc., nor Lenox China, Inc., has confirmed any of the specific price or volume figures quoted in this book.*

Every effort has been made to minimize clerical and/or printing errors, and we regret any inconvenience such errors might cause. We have tried to be as precise as possible regarding sizes and shape numbers, and the addition of so very many facts and figures increases the possibility of errors.

Published by The House of Collectibles, Inc.
      773 Kirkman Road, No. 120
      Orlando, FL 32811

Printed in the United States of America

Library of Congress Catalog Card Number: 78-72028

ISBN: 0-87637-010-5

TABLE OF CONTENTS

INTRODUCTION 1
CARING FOR CHINA 3
CONDITION OF CHINA 3
FAKES, FORGERIES, FRAUDS AND FENCES 4
TYPES OF BACKSTAMPS 6
BACKSTAMP REFERENCE GUIDE 7
TYPES OF DECORATION 22
NON-FACTORY ARTISTS 24
VISITING TRENTON 27
COMMENTS ON COLLECTING 28
PRICING GUIDELINES 30
SELLING 30
THE PEOPLE 32
THE COMPANIES (A THROUGH L) 46
LENOX 75
    BACKSTAMPS 78
    ARTWARE AND GIFTWARE 95
    DINNERWARE 186
    LENOX AND METAL ITEMS 257
    FIGURINES 300
    LIMITED AND SPECIAL EDITIONS 325
    SPECIAL ORDER CHINA 328
THE COMPANIES (L THROUGH Y) 330
MISCELLANEOUS 388
BIBLIOGRAPHY 389

COVER PHOTO:

(1) OTT & BREWER, ewer, raised gold paste cattail pattern, two turtle figurines applied to side of piece, turtles and coral handle decorated in green and gold, small fleck on one of the turtles, mark I 700.00

(2) OTT & BREWER, vase, bulbous bottom with long narrow square neck, green background with raised gold paste trim done in at least five different shades ranging all the way from a silver color to a bronze, mark I 750.00

(3) OTT & BREWER, chocolate pot, green bottom section, top section has raised gold paste trim in several shades of gold, gold trim on dragon handle and spout and on finial and rims, mark I 600.00

(4) OTT & BREWER, vase, beautiful hand-painted orchid, raised gold paste work, openwork handles, raised on small openwork feet, one of which is damaged, probably had a lid at one time, mark K 325.00

(5) OTT & BREWER, vase, calla lily shape on rustic base, applied leaf on side helps support the lily, pearlized ivory interior, leaf is pale lavender, gold trim on rim and on base section, a few small rough spots, mark I, 7" high 600.00

(6) OTT & BREWER, shoe, hand-painted small flowers in scatter pattern, gold trim, marks I and J, 5" long 325.00

(7) WILLETS MANUFACTURING, vase, shape number unknown, two-handled, gold paste on beige matte finish, gold wear on handles, mark B in red, 6" high 175.00

(8) WILLETS MANUFACTURING, vase, shape #481, (or possibly 487), beautiful portrait of a woman, elaborate raised gold work, unfortunately no artist signature, mark B in brown, 12" high 600.00

(9) WILLETS MANUFACTURING, loving cup, shape #456, three-handled, raised blue enamel flowers with gold paste trim, mark B in red 175.00

(10) WILLETS MANUFACTURING, chocolate pot, shape #210-1/4, gold paste on matte finish, mark B in red, 10" high 275.00

INTRODUCTION

We have written this book primarily for the beginning collector, and hope that it will provide some basis for the beginner to make informed choices regarding his/her collection. Toward this end, we have tried to remember back to when we were just starting out, and to those things we found the most confusing. Although we may not make our readers into instant authorities on the subject, we can possibly help them avoid some expensive mistakes.

Perhaps the two most commonly asked questions about antiques are how old is it and how much is it worth. If an item was made in Trenton, by the time you finish this book you should have the answers. Although many people frown upon the idea of price guides, they are an invaluable aid to people who have no earthly idea whether a given item is worth $1, $10, $100, or $1,000. Price guides are not "the law" and they should never be used in that fashion, but they certainly can be used to establish whether a given item is junk or treasure.

From this book you should learn not that a particular item is worth precisely $100, but that it is worth more or less than other items in its class. By this we mean that if Morley fish plates are selling for $100 in your part of the country, you should expect to pay more for the rarer Morley bird plates.

For the most part, our prices are the actual selling prices for those items, and we have been careful to note the exceptions. In obtaining the prices we did not use publications which advertise antiques for sale, for we felt that in all too many cases the items advertised never actually sold at the price listed. In addition, some of the other price guides use these sources of information and we felt we would not care to list items which have appeared in print elsewhere. Instead, we obtained our prices from a variety of sources, including auctions, flea markets, antique shops, and yard sales.

Roughly one-third of the prices listed came from the greater Trenton area, with the remainder coming from all over the country. Since Trenton collectors are knowledgeable as a group, the prices from this area tend to be "correct," i.e., not too high for the more common items and very high on the rarer ones.

This started out as a book on Lenox, and for a variety of reasons ended up being about the Trenton ceramics industry as a whole. Perhaps the primary reason was that after we were well into the book it became obvious that we could not separate Lenox from the others without leaving some curious gaps. Lenox was one of the surviving companies, and in a sense it is the sum total of all those that didn't make it.

Without looking very hard we have come up with better than 130 companies which at one time or another were involved with the manufacture of ceramics in the city of Trenton. The decision as to which ones to cover at great length was not easy, and was finally based on three considerations: (1) Founding date of the company — the earlier the better; (2) Types of items produced — many of the companies just never produced anything of great interest to today's collector; and (3) Availability of information.

The final result was to endeavor to give at least a few sentences to any company that operated out of Trenton, and to cover at some length the "big three" — Ott & Brewer, Willets, and C.A.C./Lenox. Lack of information about some of the companies was the primary reason for their rather brief coverage. Companies which were started fairly recently were not covered in great depth partly because they were not a part of the basic time period we wanted to cover and partly because the two biggest ones, Boehm and Cybis, already have books out on them.

Space will not allow us to include every item made in Trenton, and we have tried to concentrate on those items which are of the greatest interest to the average collector. Photographs of items in museums have been deliberately excluded in favor of showing items within reach, and everything pictured in our book is currently in the possession of people of ordinary means.

As already stated, this book is primarily for the beginning collector. Since it is our feeling that the beginner should not have to learn a foreign language in order to buy a few small items, we have eliminated all but one of the foreign terms commonly used in the ceramics field. Although the result could be called simplistic, we felt it better to be sure that all the readers could understand the book than to cater to the elite few.

Like most collectors, we have our own opinions and biases concerning the china of Trenton, and our feelings unavoidably creep into our writing. The field is new enough that there is lots of room for dissenting opinion. We welcome your comments, questions and criticisms, and they may be sent to:

Dorothy N. Robinson
Post Office Box 180
Trenton, New Jersey 08608

As a final note, we would like to point out that we are dealers and collectors, not professional writers, and to ask that we be judged on the contents of our book rather than on its literary merit.

NOTES ON PRICES

1. An offer by a dealer of one half or more of any of the prices listed in this book would be considered fair.
2. Prices tend to be the highest in the Northeast and in California. Adjust your thinking accordingly.
3. The prices for the lower-level items, such as the Lenox dinnerware, are averages from many sales.
4. Hand-painted items are, of course, one of a kind items. Each price listed is the actual selling price of that item during the past year. The price will be an average one only in the event that a particular item was sold more than once during the year.

GENERAL INFORMATION

CARING FOR CHINA

1. Don't use hand-painted or early transfer-decorated items as planters if the soil and/or plants will come in contact with the artwork. The color can actually be pulled right out of the design.

2. Don't hang plates with metal spring-type hangers, for they can wear the trim off the rim. In addition, they are not all that safe and the springs have been known to come loose. There are frames specifically designed to hold plates which are available in frame and gift shops. Custom-made frames, although more expensive than the ready-made variety, are very effective both in protecting the plate and in showing it off to good advantage.

3. Don't put hand-painted items in a dishwasher, for the heat and strong detergents can be devastating to the trim.

4. Don't alter items in any fashion. The possible exceptions to this would be lamps (which may have to be rewired for reasons of safety) and clocks (which are infinitely more interesting if they work.) Save all old parts if any alteration is made.

5. Don't do anything drastic in an attempt to clean a stained or discolored item. If a good soaking in lukewarm water and mild detergent doesn't help, take it to a professional.

6. Never stack cups one inside another. On those patterns which have gold or platinum handles, the trim will eventually wear on the spot where the top cup rests on the bottom one. In addition, this is one of the easiest ways to crack a handle if the cup is put down too hard.

7. Always keep protective liners between flat items. Vibrations caused by normal household activities will cause the plates to move back and forth ever so slightly. This results in minute surface scratches, and over a period of years can remove the glaze in spots.

8. Rotate your china so that the ones on top are not getting all the wear and tear. This is especially important with older patterns that have a lot of color in them, since fading of the pattern will occur.

9. Fine china does not belong in the oven, but if you insist on doing it anyway, the following information may be helpful: Put the item in before turning the heat on, so there is a gradual increase in temperature. When the item comes out of the oven, do not put it down on a cool surface, since it will crack if you do. Make sure that all underplates and serving utensils are warmed beforehand, since a cold silver serving spoon can also cause the item to break.

CONDITION OF CHINA

The condition of an item is of some importance in determining its value. To be considered in mint condition, the following must apply:

(1) No worn or missing spots on gold trim;
(2) Decoration not faded or discolored;
(3) No chips, cracks, or repairs;
(4) No noticeable scratching of surfaces.

Damage is more acceptable on some types of items than others. For example, an eggshell-thin Belleek bowl with a ruffled rim is almost expected to have a few rough spots on the rim, and such flecks really do not affect the value to a substantial degree. On ironstone, however, less than perfect condition is not acceptable, for there is an ample supply of perfect samples.

Crazing (the appearance of tiny lines covering the surface of items) is considered normal for many types of lower-level wares. Lenox and the other better porcelains usually are not crazed, and the rare item that shows up with this type of flaw should be examined for possible repairs. Crazing is caused by unequal expansion of bisque and glaze, and the companies spent a great deal of time and money developing formulas that would expand at the same rate. When an item is repaired, the repairer has no idea of the precise formula a company used and the result can be crazing.

Firing cracks do not affect the value as much as other cracks. Certain types of items, figurines in particular, suffer from firing cracks to a great extent.

Whether to repair a damaged item or not is a very individual decision, since in some cases the cost of the repair can exceed the value of the item (especially in the $100 and down range.) Items which have been heavily damaged can almost never be restored to original condition. In addition, if the repair is easy to spot, the value of the item will be down in the range of an unrestored piece. Repairs on undecorated Belleek-type items tend to be particularly easy to spot, since the repairer can never match the color of the china exactly.

The Lenox figurines should be left alone instead of being repaired, since the repairs tend to be on the clumsy side. Much of the appeal of the figurines is in their needle-thin fingers, and it is better to have fingers damaged than to have a heavy-looking mitt replace it.

The best items to have repaired are ones which are covered with hand-painting, since the person doing the repair work can cover over the repair with paint. These repairs are hard to see and such items are frequently sold as perfect. (Sometimes the fingers can feel what the eye can't see, so always run your hands over an item to feel for subtle differences in thickness of the china or in the texture of the glaze. Look for differences from one part of an item to another—for example, see if both hands on a figurine are the same color, texture, and degree of fineness.)

FAKES, FORGERIES, FRAUDS AND FENCES

As any type of collectible item increases in value, it is virtually certain that sooner or later reproductions and forgeries will follow. The various Trenton companies are still relatively safe, and the fact that Lenox is alive and well makes their china one of the safest. (The company quite naturally has an interest in protecting its trademarks and patents, and if the Lenox mark appears on an item, the buyer can be assured that it was indeed made by Lenox.)

One of the more interesting schemes we have heard of involves not adding the Lenox mark to an item but removing it instead. The idea was then to add another mark, presumably that of the Ott & Brewer Company, thereby at least doubling the value of the item. Except for removing a Lenox item from the collecting market, this idea does not affect the value of Lenox but Ott & Brewer collectors will no doubt get a trifle nervous after reading of this. To the best of our knowledge, these plans have never been implemented, but it points out the growing interest in Trenton ceramics. (The party did not explain how he was going to remove the Lenox mark, but if it is ground off there should be a shallow dimple where the mark had been.)

Since many of the Trenton companies used raw materials from the same sources and workmen traveled from one company to the next taking their production secrets with them, there is a great deal of similarity from one company's products to the next. Many of the shapes are identical (or close to it), and it is often difficult if not impossible to say whether a particular unmarked item was made, perhaps, by Lenox or one of the more expensive companies. (No matter how convincing the seller may be, it is probably a good idea to mentally price such unmarked items as if they were unmarked Lenox.)

Another potential area of deception would be the addition of an artist's name to a previously unsigned item. The price differential between a hand-painted vase signed by a well-known artist and one not signed can be substantial, so it is only a matter of time before some clever individual starts taking the unsigned pieces and adding an appropriate signature. Collectors must familiarize themselves with a particular artist's style as well as the years he was employed at a given factory. By this we mean that a portrait vase with the C.A.C. "wreath only" mark signed by W. H. Morley might well be considered a forgery—Morley is not noted for his portrait work, and he did not start working at C.A.C. until around four years after that mark was dropped. We have not yet seen any forgeries of this type.

Pieces decorated long after the item left the factory turn up now and then, some with the paint barely dry before being put on antique shop shelves. Cold-decorated items (those which are painted but not fired in the kiln) are usually very easy to spot. Those items which were decorated and then fired, however, are sometimes harder to spot, but a careful examination of the item will generally expose the misrepresentation. For example, old items will invariably have at least a few surface scratches from the many years of use, and on the recently-decorated items these cannot be found. Sometimes if such an item is held to the light it can be seen that the new paint actually fills in old scratch marks. The people who do this decorating apparently feel they are smarter than the rest of the world, but they are not taking into account the long memory of Trenton collectors, and we are just naturally suspicious when a pair of undecorated urns is sold at a local auction and an identical pair of matching urns (now decorated) turns up two months later in a local shop.

Items that are supposed to be around a century old will invariably have some minor signs of wear, and absolutely mint items should be examined for possible embellishment or repair. Sometimes new art work or gilding will show up under an ultraviolet light and sometimes it will not—it depends on how close the decorators can come to using the same ingredients as were used on the original item. (The type of ultraviolet light used by most collectors is a small, hand-held affair. Presumably larger, stronger lights made for industrial use would pick up some of the minor variations the smaller ones can't.)

Look at the gold to see if it matches other gold elsewhere on the item. An otherwise magnificent repair on the base of a Willets vase gave itself away by having a bright band of gold around it—all the other gilding on the item showed minor wear. Lenox and most of the other better Trenton companies always used 24K gold on their factory-decorated wares. Commercial grades of gold will often have a brassy look to them and finding that brassy look on a supposedly factory-decorated item would be curious to say the least.

Marriages are as old as the first cave man who got the bright idea to take a perfect lid off a broken pot and put it on another base. In the long history of Trenton ceramics, many strange looking combinations came off the assembly line so it is not always possible to go on appearance alone. An ill-fitting lid does not necessarily mean a marriage either, since such items did sometimes escape the quality control inspectors.

It is also difficult to always tell whether an item without a lid originally had one or not. (For reasons which are easily understood, sellers generally insist the items never had them and buyers insist they did.) With the exception of items which appear in some of the catalogues, usually there is no way to prove whether there was ever a lid or not. The judgment is generally based on gut reaction to an item—does it look out of kilter, is the decoration off center and possibly could have been continued up onto a lid, etc. There are no hard and fast rules, and the only advice we can offer is to study china from a design point-of-view. Both in books and in real life, stop looking at the pretty art work and see only the outline of the item instead. Follow the item's outline from top to bottom, and do this over and over again with every china item you see. Hopefully you can eventually develop a feel for the way china is designed.

The best overall approach is to assume that every item you see is repaired, recently decorated, and has a forged mark. Then examine the item closely to try to prove yourself wrong. Mentally go through your checklist: (1) Does the item have the right styling and look for items of a given period? (2) Is it complete? (3) Is the mark strange looking in any way, and is it the right mark for that type of item? (4) Does it pass the ultraviolet light test? (5) Is the artist known to have done whatever subject is on an item? (6) Is everything else as it should be? Etc., etc., etc. This should take about thirty seconds after you get used to doing it.

Although most people who deal in antiques are honest and aboveboard, every now and then you will run into a few who are not. It is not possible to protect yourself 100 percent of the time, but you can be careful about your transactions.

Rule #1 is to deal only with people you know or with people who are highly recommended to you, and keep alert to signs that they are of questionable character. As a group, antique dealers love to talk and in the course of talking with them it is sometimes possible to pick up little tidbits of information. Pay attention, since through these little chats you can find out whose checks are bouncing all over the place, who is having items repaired and then selling them as perfect, who is fencing hot goods, etc.

Rule #2 is to pay for everything by check or insist upon a signed receipt. Pottery and porcelain items are not popular with burglars since it takes time to properly wrap china. Every now and then, however, hot goods will appear on the market. The cancelled check or receipt is your proof that you did not personally steal the item, and can also be protection against the visitor who comes in and shrieks, "That's my mother's vase, it was taken last month in a robbery!" If your receipt is dated before that time, your vase cannot possibly be the stolen one.

TYPES OF BACKSTAMPS

Applied Molded Marks: A separate piece of china is applied to an item. The maker's mark is impressed into the added section. The only known version of this type of mark in Trenton ceramics is the so-called chewing gum mark used on Belleek-type baskets by Willets and possibly other companies. Some marks which might look like applied molded marks are in fact cast in as part of the original molding process.

Impressed Marks: The mark is stamped onto items by means of a metal die before the item is fired or decorated. Many of the Trenton ironstone companies used this type of mark, and it is also seen many times on bisque or parian items.

Incised Marks: Incised marks are similar to impressed ones, except that they are written in by hand rather than being stamped in. As was also the case with impressed marks, this must be done before the item is fired. Isaac Broome marks are usually incised.

Painted Marks: Painted marks are just that—marks which are painted on either underglaze or overglaze.

Printed Marks: These are by far the most common marks seen on china, and can be applied by engraved copper plate, rubber stamp, or other such processes. Most of the Lenox marks are printed.

As a rule, the impressed and incised marks are the hardest to fake, indeed practically impossible.

BACKSTAMPS REFERENCE GUIDE

American Art China Works-Mark A,
page 50

American Art China Works-Mark B

AMERICAN CHINA

A . C. Co.

American Crockery Company, *page 51*

ANCHOR POTTERY

J. E.N.

Anchor Pottery-Mark A,
page 52

Anchor Pottery-Mark B

Broome-Mark A,
page 54

Broome-Mark B

Broome-Mark C

B–M

Burroughs & Mountford Co.-Mark A,
page 55

Burroughs & Mountford Co. Mark B

B-M

Mark C

HONITON
B. & M. Co.

Burroughs & Mountford Co.-Mark D

C. P. Co.

City Pottery-Mark A, *page 56*

Mark A

Columbian Art Pottery   Mark B
page 57

Mark A

Mark B
Cook Pottery Co., *page 59*

Mark C

Cook Pottery Company
Mark D

Cook Pottery Company·
Mark E

Coxon & Company,
page 60

Delaware Pottery, *page 62*

Enterprise
Pottery Co

Enterprise Pottery Co.,
page 64

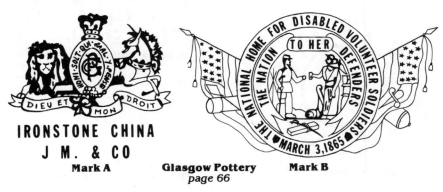

IRONSTONE CHINA
J M. & CO

Mark A

Glasgow Pottery
page 66

Mark B

U.S.M.C. Q.M.D.

Mark C　　**Glasgow Pottery**　　**Mark D**

**Glasgow Pottery-
Mark E**

Glasgow Pottery-Mark F

SAPPHO
J.M.&S. CO.

Glasgow Pottery-Mark G

GLASGOW CHINA

**VITRIFIED
TRENTON, N.J.**

Glasgow Pottery-Mark H

Glasgow Pottery-Mark I

Glasgow Pottery-Mark J

**Greenwood Pottery-
Mark A,** *page 68*

GREENWOOD CHINA
TRENTON, N. J.

Greenwood Pottery-Mark B

G.P.
Co.

**Greenwood Pottery-
Mark C**

N O•LA.
GREENWOOD

Greenwood Pottery-Mark D

GREENWOOD CHINA
—| |—
M.GOLDBERG
CONEY ISLAND
N. Y.

Greenwood Pottery-Mark E

Greenwood Pottery-Mark F

GREENWOOD CHINA

I

Greenwood Pottery-Mark G

GREENWOOD CHINA

TRENTON, N. J.

Greenwood Pottery-Mark H

PATENTED
OCT. 27-25
Greenwood
WM AKERS JR. Co.
PHILA. PA.
china

PATAPPLIED FOR

Greenwood Pottery-Mark I

GREENWOOD CHINA
COOK'S
HOTEL & RESTAURANT
SUPPLY Co
NEW YORK

Greenwood Pottery-
Mark J

1862
GREENWOOD CHINA
TRENTON, N.J.
1876
REG. U.S. PAT. OFF.

Greenwood Pottery-Mark K

B-C
WILTON

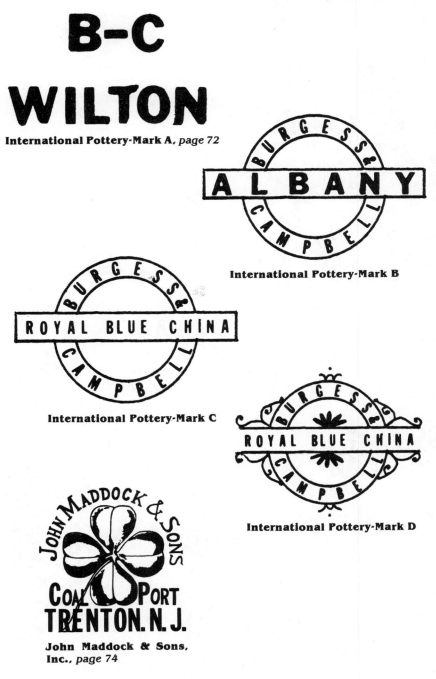

International Pottery-Mark A, *page 72*

International Pottery-Mark B

International Pottery-Mark C

International Pottery-Mark D

John Maddock & Sons,
Inc., *page 74*

POTTERS and DECORATORS

Lenox-Mark A, *page 75*

Lenox-Mark B

Lenox-Mark C

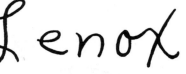

Lenox-Mark D

Lenox-Mark E

BELLEEK

Lenox-Mark F

Lenox-Mark G

LENOX

Lenox-Mark H

BELLEEK

Lenox-Mark I

LENOX

Lenox-Mark J

Lenox-Mark K

Lenox-Mark L

LENOX

Lenox-Mark M

M
CHINA
L

Maddock Pottery, *page 330*

Mercer Pottery-Mark A, *page 331*

Mercer Pottery-Mark B

Mercer Pottery-Mark C

Mercer Pottery-Mark D

MERCER POTTERY
TRENTON, N.J.

Mercer Pottery-Mark E

Mercer Pottery-Mark F

Millington, Astbury & Poulson-Mark A, *page 332*

Millington, Astbury & Poulson-Mark B

Ott & Brewer-Mark A,
page 333

O. – B.
CHINA

Ott & Brewer-Mark B

Ott & Brewer-Mark C

Ott & Brewer-Mark D

O. & B.

Ott & Brewer-Mark E

MANUFACTURED BY
OTT&BREWER
TRENTON, N.J. USA

Ott & Brewer-Mark F

O & B

Ott & Brewer-Mark G

Ott & Brewer-Mark H

Ott & Brewer-Mark I

Ott & Brewer-Mark J

Ott & Brewer-Mark K

Ott & Brewer-Mark L

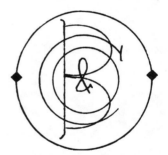

Ott & Brewer-Mark M

Star Porcelain Company, *page 344*

Thomas Maddock & Sons, *page 346*

TRENTON CHINA CO.

TRENTON, N.J.

Trenton China Company, *page 347*

THE TRENTON POTTERIES CO

HOTEL CHINA

Trenton Potteries-Mark A, *page 347*

TRENTON POTTERIES CO

T R E N T O N, N E W J E R S E Y

U S A

Trenton Potteries-Mark B

Trenton Potteries-Mark C

Trenton Potteries-Mark D

Trenton Potteries-Mark E

Trenton Potteries-Mark F

Trenton Potteries-Mark G

Trenton Potteries-Mark H

Trenton Potteries-Mark I

T. P. Co.

CHINA

Trenton Pottery, *page 349*

Willets-Mark A, *page 351*

Willets-Mark B

Willets-Mark C

Willets-Mark D

WILLETS

CHINA

Willets-Mark E

TYPES OF DECORATION

Decoration can be either hand-done or transfer, and sometimes two will be combined on a single item. The decoration can also be applied either before the item is glazed or after. The glaze firing is the hottest of all the firings, so any color put on underneath the glaze must be able to withstand those high temperatures. The "hard fire" colors are blue, brown, green and yellow, and these colors will predominate in underglaze work. Do not make the mistake, however, of automatically assuming that these colors are always underglaze just because they can be underglaze.

Overglaze decoration allows for a wider variety of decoration, and most of the Trenton items being collected today are of the overglaze type. Part of this was due to the decorating styles of the day, and part of it was due to economic reasons. Any time an item is fired, there is the risk that it will not come out of the kiln in satisfactory condition. The two chief firings are the *bisque* firing and the *glost* (glaze) firing. The glost firing is particularly tricky, since minor variations in temperature can cause the glaze to become very runny. If there happens to be artwork already on an item when this happens, the artwork will move when the glaze starts to run. The many long hours spent on the artwork are then a total loss. Overglaze work, on the other hand, is fired at a much lower temperature and accidents of this type are less likely to happen.

There is no price differential between underglaze and overglaze artwork where Trenton ceramics are concerned, and most of the collectors of Trenton items could not tell the difference if their lives depended on it. The trend among them is to call all fired artwork underglaze and to use the overglaze label only for cold-painted items (those which are painted but never fired.) Since so many people have this notion in their little heads, it is probably best not to even bring up the topic.

Transfer decoration can be applied in any number of ways, and some of the designs used were very clever and innovative. The Trenton potteries frequently used transfer decoration which was then touched up by hand. The end results can be quite pleasing, and such items are to be preferred to badly done totally hand-painted ones. Depending on the type of transfer work done, a magnifying glass will sometimes show the design as being made up of series of tiny dots and lines.

Gold trim is of three main types: (1) Flat gold, which is merely applied by brush. (2) Etched gold, which is applied by coating the sections not to be etched with a protective substance and then giving the item a bath in hydrofluoric acid. The unprotected sections are then etched by the acid. The gold is applied over the area, and the final result is some type of design in the gold. (3) Raised gold paste work, which is accomplished by applying a paste-like substance called sizing in the desired design. The gold goes on the sizing, and the result is a raised-up gold design. Different shadings of gold can be used on the same piece to give very striking effects. All of the different types of gold work must be fired.

Applied decorations must be molded and fired and then affixed to the main item and fired again. Samples of this type of work would be the Willets basket with applied flowers on the rim and the Ott & Brewer ewer with turtles climbing up it, both of which are shown in the color section. Applied work must be distinguished from decorations which are molded in as an original part of the casting process, and there is usually no trouble telling them apart since the molded-in designs can never be as finely done as the applied ones.

Molded-in designs are usually referred to as embossed designs, and although some of them are quite original and lovely, this type of work really cannot be called "decoration."

Pate-sur-pate work is extremely rare in Trenton ceramics and since most of the collectors have never seen a piece of true pate-sur-pate they tend to corrupt the term and use it for embossed designs. Real pate-sur-pate is done by painstakingly building up a design with slip (liquid porcelain) until the desired effect is achieved.

Although all of the above may or may not have been interesting to you, the real breakdown of decoration of Trenton ceramics (as determined by the people who have been collecting it) is into three categories: undecorated, factory-decorated, and nonfactory-decorated. As it usually works, factory-decorated is the best to have, with undecorated and nonfactory-decorated less desirable. Although this can vary somewhat depending on the type of item, factory-decorated is always at the top and this is not likely to change.

Factory-decorated quite literally means any item decorated at the factory and this could include all the different types of decorating. The term as it is commonly used, however, applies to items which were *hand-painted* at the factory. Some of these items will be artist-signed and some will not. Non-factory-decorated means any item decorated away from the factory, by artists ranging from unskilled amateurs to talented professionals who decorated china for a living.

If we loosely group art work into three categories, excellent, mediocre, and bad, the factory artwork invariably falls into the first two categories. Non-factory, however, can include all three and this is where the problems begin for the novice collector. With this in mind, we will go into a brief discussion of good art work vs. bad. Although we cannot turn the novice into an art critic overnight, we can offer a few hints concerning ceramic art work.

Subject Matter: The subject matter should be in keeping with the piece of china, i.e., a formal shape vase should be painted in a formal style. The design should fit on the china nicely, being neither too large nor too small. This is something the professional artist seemed to do almost automatically, whereas the amateur would often make their central design too large for the item.

Use of Color: The professional artist by instinct and by training knows which color to use in combination with the others on his item. We will use as our example a vase with large pink roses on it. The professional artist knows in advance that using a particular shade of green for a leaf will make the pink rose look washed out, something an amateur never seems to grasp. (To better see what we mean, paint 10 squares of the same color pink on a piece of paper. Next to each square of pink place 10 different shades of green. The pink will appear to change color from block to block depending on the shade of green next to it.)

On the leaves of our example vase, the amateur used only shades of green. The professional, on the other hand, frequently would use different colors to enhance a leaf, such as Marsh's use of turquoise to highlight each leaf. The casual observer may never even see that there is blue in the leaf, yet the presence of these colors makes a vast difference in the overall effect.

Use of Gold: The amateur artist apparently viewed gold as something to use when he/she didn't know what else to do. The amateurs also tended to use cheaper commercial grades of gold decoration. The overall effect is usually rather garish, and can be the first clue that a piece is badly done for those of you who will never learn to otherwise tell good from bad artwork. Gold frequently covered bases, lids, handles and anything else that didn't move.

Lenox and other fine china companies employed gilders whose only function was to take an item and apply the gold as an enhancement rather than a cover-up. The factory gilders, instead of doing a whole handle gold, would sometimes use a filigree design, or perhaps a speckled effect. On an item such as a Lenox whisky jug, the factory-decorated items will have only the inside of the spout done in gold, whereas the home-decorated items will have inside and outside of the spout done as well as the handle.

Information on some of the nonfactory artists follows. The factory artists are covered in Part II of this book.

NON-FACTORY ARTISTS

The art of china painting flourished throughout America (and the world, for that matter) during the latter part of the 19th-century and on into the first quarter of the 20th-century. So extensive was this pastime that the Trenton collector will find a wealth of items to select from this category, as opposed to the relative scarcity of factory-done items. To be sure, most of the worst examples of art work are to be found here, some so poor that it might be a kindness to break them.

This leads to a distrust among collectors of the value in collecting nonfactory wares, which is somewhat unfortunate since there are many beautiful pieces which were done by nonfactory decorators.

It is our hope that the following discussion of the nonfactory artists will serve today's collector and/or dealer in realizing that there are several fine points in determining value for this category. To a large extent some of the best bargains are available in the nonfactory field. Unfortunately, this category is also prone to some of the worst examples of overpricing, due in part to the fact that the value is in the artistic content as much as in the piece of porcelain itself. Often the evaluation of that artistic merit is at best a guess based on subjective feelings.

In an effort to broaden the scope of knowledge needed by today's collector and to allow the home-decorated market to take on a more cohesive form, we have divided nonfactory artwork into three categories:

(1) Amateur
(2) Studio
(3) Professional

Amateur Artists: This category encompasses the majority of nonfactory items seen today, perhaps as much as 50 to 75 percent. The amateur artist viewed ceramics decorating as an interesting hobby and perhaps never did more than a few items. Many of them failed miserably in their artistic endeavors, but others produced items which, if not exactly fine art, are at least not objectionable. (These items are known in the trade as "Dear Aunt Martha's Niceties.)

Studio Artists: The term "studio artist" would include all those ceramics decorators with some degree of talent and training who were capable of producing accomplished and sometimes innovative works of art. (In all probability, he/she had a studio in which to work, hence the choice of the word to describe the category.)

Some of these amateur studio artists were as talented as the professionals mentioned later, but their credentials are usually less well publicized. Many of these artists were quite prominent in their own time, and either taught ceramic art or belonged to various ceramic clubs around the country. Following are a few of the better-known studio artists from the first quarter of this century.

Henrietta Barclay Paist — Mrs. Paist began decorating china in 1889 and continued until after World War I. She was best known in the Midwest and West as a teacher of ceramic art. In 1896 she received the first place medal in a national exhibition in Chicago (best of 108 entries), and an honorable mention in the 1900 Paris Exhibition. She was president of the Twin City Keramic Club and founder of the ceramic department for the St. Paul Institute of Art. She also worked in pottery, leather, wood block printing, and oil and water colors.

Mrs. Dorothea Warren O'Hara — Mrs. O'Hara was a Kansas City resident who had studied at the Royal College of Art in London. She learned ceramic decorating under Bischoff, Fry, and Robineau. After moving to New York, she was awarded life membership in the National Arts Club of New York as well as a gold medal in the Panama Pacific Exposition. Two of her vases were in the National Museum in Tokyo. She was president of the Keramic Society of Greater New York.

Miss Maud M. Mason — Miss Mason was president of the Association of Women Painters & Sculptors, and received a gold medal at the Panama Pacific Exposition for some of her work. She taught at the Fawcett School of Industrial Art in Newark, NJ.

Mrs. Kathryn E. Cherry — Mrs. Cherry studied under Robineau and Fry, and was a gold medal recipient in St. Louis in 1904. She was a Master Craftsman of the Boston Society of Arts & Crafts, and received honorable mention for the Armour prize at the 1917 exhibition by the Art Institute of Chicago.

Mrs. Vernie Lockwood Williams — Mrs. Williams had studied at the Pratt Institute in Brooklyn, and was an instructor of porcelain decoration at the University of Pittsburgh, as well as an officer of the Duquesne Ceramic Club.

Below is a list of other studio artists about whom little or nothing is known except for the fact they were all teachers in this field:

Miss Fannie M. Scammell — Chautauqua, NY
Mr. Vance Phillips
Miss Jeanne M. Stewart — Portland, OR and Toledo, OH
Mrs. A. A. Frazee — Chicago, IL
Mrs. C. C. Filkins — Buffalo, NY
F. G. Coover, Alice L. Brown, and Edw. F. Christian, all of Coover Studios in Minneapolis, MN

Many of the studio artists founded or were members of the various ceramics clubs. The purpose of these clubs was to bring together talented artists with the idea of improving the state of the art. Many of these clubs came and went quickly while others lasted for a long time and were the forerunners of art leagues still in existence. Information on most of them is sketchy or unavailable, but we can supply the following:

Twin City Keramic Club — This club was based in the Minneapolis-St. Paul area, and was apparently academically oriented. It is known that the Atlar Prize for ceramic art was awarded to this club on at least three occasions. Members included Mrs. Henrietta Paist, Miss Florence Huntington, Etta Beede, Mrs. Arch Coleman, Mrs. Laval, and Mrs. Reed.

Kansas City Ceramic Club — The Kansas City club was a rather large and prosperous one. Club members included: Mrs. J. W. Smith, Mrs. Gibbons, Mrs. M. Barker, Miss Bartholdt, Miss Barker, Miss Halbert, Miss Bayha, Mrs. E. E. Smith, Miss Smith, Miss Borch, Mrs. Alys M. Binney, Mrs. Burney, Mrs. J. H. Daly, Mrs. W. T. Timlin, Mrs. Moore, Mrs. Lynval Davidson, Mrs. G. H. Bilheiner, Mrs. J. E. McFadden, Mrs. Pauline James, Mrs. Maude E. Nutter, Mrs. Estelle McDougal, Mrs. Twyman, Robert D. Haire, Mrs. Kate Ward, Mrs. A. E. Findley, Mrs. Hannah Cuthbertson, Mrs. Gleason, Miss Vic Harris.

Duquesne Ceramic Club — Membership was primarily within a 50 mile radius of Pittsburgh. Instruction for this group was provided by Professor Herbert Kniffin of the University of Pittsburgh. Regular members included: Mrs. V. L. Williams, Miss Anne McIntyre, Mrs. Ray E. Motz, Albert J. Rott, Mrs. L. S. Price, Miss Maud Chapin, Mary C. Walters, Mrs. Anna McIntyre, Ella Faber, Edith Sillaman, Sadie Kier, Mrs. Kolgel, Nettie Davis, Jeannette Negley, Alice McQuade, Leda Harrison, Mrs. D. Horton Lutz, and Mrs. Byron Mitchell.

Keramic Society of Greater New York — Two of the principal members of this club were Marshall Fry, Jr., and Dorothea Warren O'Hara. Other members included Lillian C. Smith, Miss Dalmore, Mrs. Nina Hatfield, Esther A. Coster, Georgia Pierce Unger, Cornelia P. Nelson, Anna E. Fitch, Alice M. Hurd, Marguerite Cameron, Mary E. Harrison, Sarah A. C. Draegert, Annie S. Tardy, Alma P. Kraft, and Frances White Wilcox. This club is known to have been a driving force in spreading the latest of decorative motifs to the home ceramics market. Their styles were always the latest and most stunning available, and their work is highly collectible in its own right.

Chicago Ceramic Art Association — The Chicago group began sponsoring ceramic exhibits as early as 1892, and was in the forefront with the New York club when it came to promoting the art of ceramic decoration. The A. H. Abbott prize was offered for best collection of pieces by one decorator; the Burley & Co. prize went for the best design on tableware; and the Hasburg Gold prize was conferred for the best use of gold in decoration. Members included: Mrs. Anne T. Brown, Mary E. Hipple, Mrs. Isabelle C. Kissinger, Miss Ione Wheeler, Mrs. George E. Emmons, Miss Marie B. Bohmann, Miss Grace E. Minister, Mrs. Rena O. Patterson, Mrs. Grace Bush, Miss Amanda E. Edwards, Mrs. Valla Ramey, and Mrs. Marie Sparks.

Professional Artists: Professional artists would be those who were able to earn most or all of their income from decorating china, and as one might imagine this took a great deal of talent. The work of many of them should be considered equal to that of the factory artists.

Marshall Fry, Jr. — decorator from New York City, also instructor in china painting.

Mrs. Adelaide Alsop Robineau — Mrs. Robineau was born in Middletown, CT, in 1865. She was married to Samuel E. Robineau, and they lived in Syracuse, NY, where she died in 1929. The Robineaus published a magazine called *Keramic Studio* which in addition to giving instructions in various painting techniques also served as source for news about the various clubs and organizations.

Mary F. Overbeck — Ms. Overbeck was one of the founders of Overbeck Pottery of Cambridge City, IN, and was a frequent contributor to national magazines devoted to china painting. She introduced various designs and decorating techniques in her articles and was well-known in pottery and porcelain circles.

Lycett — Edwin Lycett was known as "the father of American china painting", and his son, William, opened a decorating shop in Atlanta, GA. Pieces are usually marked with "Lycett, Atlanta, Ga." in a powder blue diamond on the base.

Mary Nourse — Ms. Nourse was at one time an artist at Rookwood Pottery, and her name has been noted on some C.A.C. lavender palette mark items.

Bischoff — a leading American decorator of the day.

Joseph Yeschek — Pickard artist

Schindler — decorated for D'Arcy Studios.

Curtis Marker — Pickard artist

Mr. Messino — Pickard artist

Since these artists and the decorating firms for whom some of them worked did not limit themselves to Trenton blanks, their names will turn up on a variety of different chinas. What the Trenton collector must realize is that examples by these people and firms usually carry a premium in value. This does not mean that the artwork is better, but that the items are sought by more than one type of collector.

As must be obvious from this section, most of the nonfactory artists were women while most of the factory ones were men. This breakdown by sex had little to do with talent but rather reflects the spirit of the times. For the most part, the men started painting as professionals (even apprentices were paid), while the women made the slow progression from rank amateur to studio to professional.

VISITING TRENTON

Most collectors of Trenton ceramics probably sooner or later get the notion to visit the City of Trenton and, of course, the whole greater Trenton area is a happy hunting ground for both collector and researcher. Like most of the cities on the East Coast which go back a couple of centuries, Trenton grew up around a small original area. This willy-nilly growth makes it difficult to find your way, and a map of the city is an absolute must.

State Street, the main thoroughfare through the city, has been paved over for a few crucial blocks and made into a "pedestrian mall." This, combined with one-way streets and no-turn signs, makes navigating around the city a little difficult, but it can be done. Parking can be something of a problem but patience is almost always rewarded. (Author Robinson has long been tempted to drive her car up over the curb and leave it parked dead smack in the middle of the pedestrian mall.)

As a rule, run-of-the-mill Trenton ceramics will be cheaper in Trenton than in other parts of the country, while top of the line items will be more expensive. Trenton people are very knowledgeable about what was made there, so don't count on finding a bargain there. What you will find is variety. It would be easy enough to say to buy lesser items in Trenton and finer items away from Trenton, however, there is a catch — many of the finer items never left the Trenton area.

Don't waste your time advertising in a Trenton newspaper that you are seeking Lenox or other Trenton chinas, for this has been done many times over. We deliberately left out house numbers when discussing addresses for the early workers, for fear large numbers of collectors, dreaming of finds in basements and attics, might descend upon the current residents of these houses. This avenue of approach has already been pretty well covered, as has the idea of calling people with the same last names as the workers. Sorry, you're about twenty-five years too late.

Following is a brief description of things to do or places to visit:

Museums (for those who like to torture themselves by seeing things they can't buy): The New Jersey State Museum on West State Street has a nice assortment of Trenton ceramics. This includes the Brewer Collection, photographs of which are used in many books on ceramics. Displays are changed frequently, so it might be best to check with the museum before making a special trip. The staff is courteous and helpful, and the building is laid out to allow for wheelchairs.

The Trenton museum is located in Cadwalader Park in a Victorian mansion that until recently had been used as the monkey house. It is near the bear pits, and although not everybody will be able to show you where the museum is, most of them can direct you to the bear. The city museum is now open to the public on a regular basis and they are rapidly expanding their collection of Trenton ceramics.

Showrooms: The Lenox showroom is off of Olden Avenue, and although their collection is lacking in some areas, they do have a nice assortment of items. This includes samples of their Presidential and other special order china, figurines. and early hand-painted wares. The early items are not for sale, and there is no discount on the current production items which are for sale. Parking is a problem if the company parking lot is full.

Boehm maintains a showroom in their Fairfacts Avenue complex. It can be reached from Calhoun Street via North Willow Street, and while still on Calhoun Street you can see the backs of the white buildings across the field. There is no discount on items purchased at the showroom. The staff is exceptionally polite and helpful. Parking is ample. For security reasons, the door is always locked and you must ring a bell to get in.

Cybis also maintains a showroom, and we are embarrassed to admit we have never been there. All we can supply is the information that it is open Monday through Friday, and the items are only for display and not for sale. They suggest not coming during the lunch hour.

Libraries: The Trenton Public Library on Academy Street has a wealth of information about the pottery industry. Although there is some overlapping, the New Jersey State Library on West State Street also has a large amount of information.

Old Buildings: Looking for the old potteries is rather frustrating work, since many have been torn down and others are not recognizable due to changes in their appearance. The easiest one to find is the old Thomas Maddock pottery on Carroll Street. From State Street, turn down Ewing Street and go all the way to the end at Perry Street, turn left onto Perry Street for one block and then left onto Carroll. Some of the buildings are on Ewing and the main part is on Carroll. Except for ascertaining that most of the old potteries were made of brick, there really isn't much point to looking for them.

SOME CASUAL COMMENTS ABOUT COLLECTING

Most collections begin in a rather willy-nilly fashion with the purchase of a few small items. By the time collectors realize they are collectors, their collection has already taken form and is unlike any other collection in the world. The choice of what to buy and what not to buy is, of course, a very individual thing.

For optimum happiness, a collection should reflect the owner's personal tastes and life style. People who like clean, modern lines probably do not buy ornate Victorian urns and if they do buy them, they will probably never be quite satisfied with them. If a collection does not fit in with a given way of life, the items become unless extravagances.

Very few of us have unlimited funds to spend on our collections, and for some each purchase must be carefully squeezed in between the grocery bills and mortgage payments. A certain amount of self-discipline is necessary if a collection is to fit into the general economic scheme. The ideal situation is for the collector to figure out how much can be spend in a given time period and to spend only that amount. (The only problem with this is that interesting collectibles always seem to turn up in feast-or-famine style.)

As a group, Trenton items tend to be underpriced when compared against similar items made elsewhere. This is, of course, good news for the collector since it means that money spent now could in time turn out to be money well-spent. If compared against the American art pottery field, the underpricing of Trenton items becomes very apparent since they were being made during the same time period. Pottery items with little or no workmanship can outdistance a comparable size Lenox item by 10 to 20 times.

Some Trenton items will probably increase in price quicker than others, and in our opinion they are those items which:

(1) are not likely to ever be produced again;
(2) are underpriced when compared to comparable current retail items;
(3) are not questionable in any way.

Artists' salaries being what they are, it is unlikely that anyone will ever duplicate the older hand-painted items. Hand-painted fish and bird plates can be had today for less than the current transfer-decorated Boehm bird plates by Lenox. Silver overlay work and china liners in silver holders are also very underpriced compared to current standards and they are not likely to be copied.

The prices on some of the Art Deco items are way beyond the cost of reproducing them today, and there is nothing to prevent the Lenox Company from doing so. The new items would, of course, have current markings so they could be distinguished from the old, but the market for the old ones would be affected because some percentage of collectors will be satisfied with the reproduction and no longer look for the original. This was the case when the Hawthorn tea set was reproduced as a limited edition a few years back, and the prices on the originals dropped down to the level of the reproduction pieces.

Don't pay premium prices for damaged, repaired, unmarked and/or incomplete items unless you have a very good reason for doing so, such as completing a set. A vase by a top Lenox artist is currently making the rounds in the New Jersey area, with an asking price well over $2,000. The item is not marked, although it is definitely a Lenox shape, and the reason it is not marked is because the piece was never finished. Although the portrait was finished, the gilding was for some reason left undone — perhaps the item was borrowed by a workman or perhaps some flaw was discovered and it was considered unworthy of completion. While at a lower price this item might be interesting, the money might better be invested in a set of 12 gorgeous game plates, or perhaps four less opulent but completed vases.

The problem with incomplete or repaired items is that they open the door just a little for misrepresentations and fakes, and it is against the fakes that these questionable items will eventually be compared and possibly lose in value rather than going up. A century from now, it will be the easily authenticated items which will command top prices. By being just a trifle choosy about what we will buy and how much we will pay, we can help correct pricing inconsistencies and at the same time make life a little more difficult for the forgers.

None of the above statements should be interpreted as meaning that you should only buy items which are absolutely mint, but rather that you should keep an eye on the price differential between mint items and those less than mint. At the time of this writing, there is perhaps $25 difference between an absolutely perfect Lenox figuring and one with maybe a finger missing. For the extra $25, the perfect one is a better investment. (This assumes, of course, that you can find any figurines at all.)

A collection should be expanded upward instead of laterally. This can take some of the fun out of collecting, since instead of a weekly $25 purchase, it means saving up the money to buy one $200 item. If necessary, sell off lesser items to finance the purchase of a single fine item. You can never have the largest or best collection, for there are people in Trenton who have a 30 year head-start on you. Strive instead for quality and uniqueness. Collecting crazes come and go, and the whole idea is not to be the one to be left with undesirable items at the end.

A rather general collection is probably the best idea, since it offers the best protection against price variations. Keep in mind if you collect, for instance, small teapots, that if you dump them all on the market at one time it can have a devastating effect on prices. Whereas a single small teapot at an auction might bring a good price, a hundred of them at one auction might have the effect of making them look common.

PRICING GUIDELINES

Estimating the value of an item is usually done for one of three reasons: (1) insurance purposes; (2) possible sale; (3) idle curiosity. One very common practice used by people looking for a free appraisal is to call in a local antique dealer and ask for offers on items. In additon to wasting the dealer's time, they are taking an awful chance that the dealer is stupid, crazy, dishonest, or all three. The money spent on obtaining an accurate appraisal will turn out to be a good investment.

Another increasingly popular technique is to send photos to a far-distant auction house, asking them what they think the items will bring at auction. The results obtained will depend to a large extent on the auctioneer's familiarity with a given category and on the owner's honest description of condition.

Dinnerware can be compared to comparable current items, with deductions for wear or damage. Also, keep in mind that certain items are very hard to sell and they will bring nowhere near their appraised value should you go to sell them. Included in this category would be bouillon cups and saucers, after dinner coffees, and non-essential serving pieces, and many of the rather quaint items which were once considered an integral part of dinner sets. Most people can get along very well without baked apple dishes, individual chocolate pots, egg cups and the like, and they simply will not pay a premium on them. This is, of course, a reversal of the trend in the used silver market, where customers will pay handsomely for asparagus tongs, strawberry forks, and other strange implements with limited applications. It is really only the highly-collectible Lenox patterns which can command top dollar for obscure items, and the collectors of these patterns will cheerfully kill each other for them. Where dinnerware is concerned, it is important to keep in mind that you are selling a used set of china and not the Meissen "Swan Service."

In general, an offer by a dealer of one half or better of the prices listed in this book should be considered fair. If you would rather try to retail the item yourself, see the following section.

SELLING

Auctions: Putting items in an auction can be an anonymous and sometimes profitable way of disposing of them. Some auctions will allow you to put the items on reserve, that is to say they will not allow the item to be sold for less than a specified price. The seller, however, must still pay the auctioneer for time and trouble and this fee can vary somewhat from place to place.

Auctions are ideal if secrecy is important, since except for the auctioneer no one will know who owns the items. They are also the traditional dumping ground for questionable items, since would-be buyers don't always have a chance to carefully examine things.

The "big" auction houses traditionally have turned up their noses at Lenox, but this seems to be slowly changing. The auctioneer who perhaps has handled more Lenox than anyone is located in Trenton, and can be contacted as follows: Lester & Robert Slatoff, Inc., 777 W. State Street, Trenton, NJ, 08618.

Consignment: Some antique dealers will take items on consignment, taking some percentage when the item finally is sold. Pay attention to the terms of the agreement, since some shops automatically start marking items down after a certain time period unless you go and retrieve the item first.

Direct: Advertising locally that you have items for sale will no doubt attract some attention, both from potential customers and from criminals. We suggest that instead of doing it this way, it would be better to take the items to a flea market rather than having strangers coming into your home. The few extra dollars gained by selling direct are not worth the hassle and possible trouble that can result.

Mail Order: There are several publications which take advertisements for antiques, and there are a good source of potential customers. Most of these publications require references before taking an ad.

Selling this way will eventually mean packing and shipping the items. United Parcel Service has a good record for getting things there in one piece, but the post office is better at paying claims for damage. UPS tends to be faster and cheaper.

The following magazines and newspapers may be of some help to the collector in: (1) checking current prices; (2) buying through the mail; (3) finding other people with similar interests; (4) selling items. For the most part, advertising rates are quite reasonable.

American Art & Antiques
1515 Broadway
New York, NY 10036

American Collector
Post Office Box A
Reno, NV 89506

The Magazine Antiques
551 Fifth Avenue
New York, NY 10017

Antiques & The Arts Weekly
Newtown Bee
Bee Publishing Company
Newtown, CT 06470

Antique Collecting
(American Antique Collector)
Post Office Box 237
Ephrata, PA 17522

Antiques Journal
Post Office Box 1046
Dubuque, IA 52001

Antique Monthly
Post Office Drawer 2
Tuscaloosa, AL 35401

Antique Trader
Post Office Box 1050
Dubuque, IA 52001

Antiques World
Post Office Box 990
Farmingdale, NY 11737

Collectibles Monthly
Post Office Box 2023
York, PA 17405

Collector Editions Quarterly
170 Fifth Avenue
New York, NY 10010

National Antiques Courier
Post Office Box 500
Warwick, MD 21912

Nineteenth Century
60 Fifth Avenue
New York, NY 10011

THE PEOPLE

For the most part, the important people in the history of the Trenton ceramics industry were white Anglo-Saxon Protestant men. Women, Catholics, Jews, and those who were less than lily white had rather a rough go of it. Perhaps the primary exception to this rule would be the Japanese artists who worked at many of the Trenton companies — it was the "in" thing for a company to have at least one Oriental artist. Although most of the discrimination took the form of giving a good job to a friend's son rather than some outsider, it was very definitely thought that the newcomers were lazy, stupid, or worse yet, labor organizers.

The company owners were, by most accounts, hard-working, industrious, and devoted family men. They played an active role in the affairs of the city, and were frequently active in church and fraternal organizations as well. (There were a few flaming exceptions to these generalizations; however, we are saving these stories for a novel.)

They were not above "borrowing" ideas or workers from each other, and it was not unknown for an officer of one company to stand outside of a competitive business as workmen left for the day and offer them better pay and working conditions. Accusations of stolen formulas were common, since many of the workers never shared their secrets with their employers but instead took them along from company to company. Often these secrets would be written down in coded notebooks, and these notebooks became prime targets of Victorian corporate espionage. We have heard one story of a plant superintendent staying late every day for thirty years hoping that a certain foreman would forget his notebook. The foreman died and apparently took the notebook with him since the company folded soon after his death.

Many of the partnerships which were formed disintegrated quickly due to disagreements over a variety of topics, but others lasted for a long time and in at least a few instances, partners were buried next to each other. Many of the pottery managers were related by blood or marriage, and family gatherings must have been interesting considering some of the feuds that developed. (Imagine the problem of serving dinner to several guests each of whom firmly believed he developed the glaze formula for the china being used.)

Information about some of the people is very sketchy, a situation we hope to be able to correct in the future. Official versions of stories are often at odds with local hearsay, probably due to the fact that the victors got not only the spoils but most of the newspaper coverage as well.

Allan: Partner in Yates, Bennett & Allan.

Allen, W. B.: Secretary-treasurer of the Mercer Pottery.

Alpaugh: Co-founder of Empire Pottery. Helped to run Coxon & Company after Charles Coxon died.

Astbury, John: One of the founders of Millington, Astbury & Poulson and associated companies.

Baker, Charles H.: Co-founder of Egyptian Pottery 1891, Fidelity 1902.

Baker, George: Lenox factory records indicate Baker was employed as an artist there from 1904 to 1908, and that he returned much later to do gilding for them from 1942 to 1946. Since these were the war years, it is likely he was called back to replace younger men who had been drafted. Pieces by him are not common but they include fish plates.

Barlow: The name Barlow appears as a partner in Wood & Barlow, as having been connected with the Empire Pottery, and as a co-founder of Crown Porcelain Works in 1890. Since there is no first name, it is not certain if these are all the same person.

Bayne, David K.: Involved with Trenton Potteries Company.

Bedson, Samuel: Co-founder of Elite Pottery in 1901.

Bennett: Partner in Yates, Bennett & Allan.

Bloor, William: Bloor was a successful East Liverpool, OH, potter who came to Trenton and provided financial assistance to Taylor & Speeler. In 1359 he went back to Ohio, and when he returned to Trenton in 1863 he helped start the Etruria Pottery (Ott & Brewer). Later he went back once again to Ohio, where he died.

Boch, N. W.: Founder of the Artistic Porcelain Company in 1893 and the American Porcelain Works in 1895.

Boehm, Edward Marshall: Born 1912, died 1969, founder of the company bearing his name.

Booth: One of the founders of the Etruria Pottery, and prior to that the owner of a stationery business in Trenton.

Boullemier/Boullimer/Bullimer: Antonin Boullemier was born in France in 1840. He went to England where he decorated for Mintons, and was later self-employed at Stoke-on-Trent where he continued to paint for Mintons and for other companies as well. That at least one of his sons worked in Trenton is verified, and that Antonin might have visited the son in Trenton is not unlikely. It would also be possible that the son might have prevailed upon Antonin to do up a few items for Lenox, and there are supposedly a few pieces of Lenox bearing his signature. He died April 25, 1900, at Stoke-on-Trent.

Lucien Boullemier, the son of Antonin, was employed at Lenox from 1900 to 1906, and is best known for his figures in the English style.

An Edgar Bullimer/Boullimer/Boullemier also worked at Lenox as an artist, from 1890 to 1896, and there is no indication that he was related to Antonin. There is at least some possibility that Edgar's name was originally Bullimer, and that either on his own initiative or with the encouragement of the company he changed the spelling of his name at least once and possibly twice.

Bowman: The Trenton Fire Clay & Porcelain Company was founded in 1893 by O. O. Bowman, R. K. Bowman, and W. J. J. Bowman. O. O. Bowman also founded the Trenton Terra-Cotta Company.

Bradbury, William H.: Founder of the Economy Pottery in 1900 and the Resolute Pottery in 1903.

Brearly: First president of Greenwood Pottery.

Brewer, John Hart: John Hart Brewer was born in Hunterdon County, NJ, on March 29, 1844. He was descended on his mother's side from John Hart, a signer of the Declaration of Independence. During the Civil War he served on the U.S.S. Huntsville, and after the war returned to New Jersey and bought an interest in the Etruria Pottery (Ott & Brewer). In 1875 he was elected to the New Jersey House of Assembly as a Republican, and was also in the 47th and 48th Congresses. It is not clear whether he continued with his interest in the pottery while being involved in politics, but in all probability he continued to be active to at least some degree. From 1889 to 1892 he was co-owner of the Fell & Throp business, and in 1895 he founded the Hart Brewer Pottery Company, which manufactured sanitary wares. Brewer died in Trenton on December 21, 1900.

Brewer, William P.: William was the father of John and the brother-in-law of Joseph Ott. William Brewer and Ott had been in the livery business in Trenton prior to the start of the pottery business.

Brian, John: Co-founder of the Enterprise Pottery in 1879 and the Keystone Pottery in 1892.

Brian, Richard, James and George: Co-founders of the Brian Pottery Company in 1898.

Britton, Dr. Charles: Trenton druggist who was a co-founder of Star Porcelain in 1899.

Bromley: John Hart Brewer brought William Bromley, Jr., to Trenton from the Irish Belleek factory to help Ott & Brewer develop their Belleek ware. William, Jr., called for his brother, John, and his father, William, Sr., to join him in Trenton.

One of the Bromleys (probably William, Jr.) was the head of the art department at Ott & Brewer, and later head of the art department at Willets. Other information about the Bromleys is sketchy.

A William Bromley who was part of the Ohio ceramics industry is presumed not to be one of the Trenton Bromleys because of noncorrelation of dates.

Broome, Isaac: Broome was born in Valcartier, Quebec, Canada, on May 16, 1835. He came to Trenton in 1875 to work for Ott & Brewer as a modeller and designer, and many of his pieces were exhibited at the Centennial Exhibition in Philadelphia that year. His employment history includes the following: Self-employed c. 1880; Harris Manufacturing Company (Trent Tile) c. 1883; Providential Tile Works c. 1886; Beaver Falls Tile Company (in Pennsylvania) c. 1890; and finally at the Lenox Company. Although his term of employment at Lenox is uncertain, it is known that a bust of John A. Roebling done in 1909 was one of his last works.

(Note: Some sources give his date of birth as 1836 instead of 1835, and his term of employment at Ott & Brewer as beginning in 1876 instead of 1875.)

Burgess, John W.: Co-founder of Burgess & Campbell (International.)

Burgess, William: President of International Pottery.

Burroughs, Garret S.: Burroughs bought Booth's interest in Bloor, Ott & Booth in 1864, and a year later sold that interest to John Hart Brewer due to ill health. We do not know if this is the same Burroughs who later co-founded Burroughs & Mountford in 1879.

Callowhill, Scott: Callowhill came to America from England in 1885. While in England he had worked both at Royal Worcester and at the Doulton pottery. While in Trenton, he worked at Providential Tile Works where he decorated some of their tiles in a Royal Worcester cloisonne effect.

Campana, Dominic: This Venetian-born artist was employed at Pickard in Illinois around 1900, and worked for Lenox for only one year (1904). He was later a very successful self-employed china decorator and had a large studio on Wabash Avenue in Chicago, where he did his painting and also wrote books on the subject. The name Campana was shortened to Camp on some of his Pickard items, and it is possible that the name will appear that way on Lenox items also.

Campbell, John A.: Campbell was one of the founders of Burgess & Campbell and was with the company from 1879 to 1895.

Carr, James: Carr was born in Hanley, England in July, 1820, and upon coming to America was employed at the Jersey City Pottery for eight years.

He was very active in the pottery industry in New York and New Jersey for a long time, and had interests in several of the Trenton firms.

Challinor, Edward Stafford: Challinor was born in England and was the grandson of a well-known Staffordshire potter. He studied at the Royal Academy in London, and apprenticed at Royal Doulton when he was seventeen. An uncle in Canada induced him to come to America, and he eventually found his way to Trenton where he was employed for a brief while at Willets as an artist. He went to Chicago in 1902 and worked for Pickard for many years.

Clark, Edward: Co-founder (with James Carr) of the Lincoln Pottery.

Clayton, William H.: Clayton was apprenticed to Walter Lenox to learn the art of decorating china, and was employed as an artist at Lenox from 1891 to 1908, at which time he became head of the art department. He was later to become a corporate officer at Lenox.

Clifford, John: Co-founder of the Monument Pottery in 1896.

Cochran, Andrew: Co-founder of Equitable Pottery in 1888, and of Cochran-Drugan pottery in 1907.

Cogill, J. Harris: Co-founder of Fidelity Pottery in 1902.

Collear, Moses: Part-owner of the Maddock Pottery Company.

Connelly, Thomas: Irishman involved with Belleek experimentation at Delaware Pottery. Formerly of the Irish Belleek Company. He died in 1890.

Cook, Charles Howell: Cook was a co-founder of the Crescent Pottery in 1881, and president of Cook Pottery Company in 1894.

Cook, William: Co-founder of the Excelsior Pottery Company in 1905.

Coughley: Coughley entered the Millington, Astbury & Poulson concern after Poulson died, and Coughley himself died in 1869.

Coxon, Charles: Charles Coxon was born in England, and after coming to the United States he was employed at the Edwin Bennett Pottery Company where he stayed about 12 years. He is generally credited with having modelled the "Rebekah at the Well" teapot which is so well-known.

He was a co-founder of Coxon & Thompson, probably in 1863, and this company eventually became Coxon & Company. He died in 1868 and is buried in Greenwood Cemetery in Trenton.

(Note: He is possibly the father of Jonathan Coxon, q.v.)

Coxon, Jonathan and Family: Jonathan Coxon was born in Longton, Staffordshire, England, and emigrated to the United States at about the age of seven in May 1844. He lived in Jersey City, NJ until 1857, when he went to South Amboy, NJ to work in a pottery. It was in South Amboy that he met his future wife, Miss Hanna Joshua, who was from Nantiglow, Wales. When Coxon was 22, he and Miss Joshua were married at the Methodist Church in South Amboy. Around 1860, the Coxons went back to Jersey City and remained there until 1863, at which time Jonathan enlisted in the 21st New Jersey Volunteers, Company A.

Following the Civil War, the Coxons came to Trenton where Jonathan was a foreman at the Coxon & Thompson Pottery. He left Coxon & Thompson in 1868 to seek employment with the Mercer Pottery Company which was founded that year. The **Daily State Gazette** of October 22, 1872, gives an interesting account of a party given for Jonathan by his subordinates at Mercer on the occasion of his leaving his job there.

After leaving Mercer, he was next employed at Greenwood Pottery Company, again as a foreman. He and Mr. Tams, the president of Greenwood, came from the same town in England. His term of employment at Greenwood is uncertain.

Jonathan Coxon

Following Greenwood, he was employed at International Pottery as a foreman. Since International was founded in 1878, we can be safe in saying he did not start there before then.

After leaving International, he was employed at Ott & Brewer where he eventually became superintendent after Bromley left to go to Willets. It was at Ott & Brewer that he and Walter Lenox probably met for the first time.

In 1888, Coxon was co-founder of the Equitable Pottery Company which manufactured sanitary wares. Equitable was eventually merged into the Trenton Potteries Company in which W. S. Hancock had an interest. It may very well be the case that it was Coxon and not Lenox who obtained the $4,000 loan from Hancock with which C.A.C. was started. We don't know if Coxon kept his interest in Equitable while he was also involved with the Ceramic Art Company.

His partnership with Walter S. Lenox in the Ceramic Art Company began in 1889 and ended in 1896, and after that he became first the superintendent of Anchor Pottery and later the Crescent Pottery, where he remained until his final retirement. (W. S. Hancock was one of the founders of Crescent, which gives more weight to the notion that it was Coxon who arranged the loan.)

Coxon was always active in community affairs. He served on the Trenton Common Council for three years, having been elected as a Republican from the First Ward. Later he spent four years on the Mercer County Board of Chosen Freeholders, was twice director of that group, and was given a diamond pin upon his retirement from the board. He spent 13 years on the Park Board and was its president for two terms.

In addition, he was a past master of Loyal Lodge #131 of F. and A. M., past regent of Capital City Council, Royal Arcanum, past commander Aaron Wilkes Post #23 G. A. R., and a member of Crescent Temple, Mystic Shrine.

The Coxons lived on Hillcrest Avenue in Trenton for many years with their eight children. George Evans, later of Rittenhouse and Evans China, was a nephew of Jonathan Coxon and lived in the Coxon home for some time. Coxon always claimed that George stole the formula for making Belleek from a dresser drawer, and the outcome of the family feud is not known.

The Coxon's eight children were:

(1) William G. — known to have worked at and/or started the Great Western Pottery, Kokomo, IN. He had four children: Nellie, Jonathan, Hanna and Adele.

(2) Edward T. — foreman of Great Western Pottery. Edward had a son, Edward, Jr.

(3) George H. — known to have stayed on at Ceramic Art Company for at least a short while after his father left, then went on to become superintendent of an electrical porcelain plant in Peru, IN. He had two daughters, Ruth and Audrey.

(4) John Frederick — superintendent of Great Western's branch in Tiffin, OH. He is also known to have operated a small pottery in Fredericksburg, OH, and to have lived in Wooster, OH, He was the youngest of the Coxon children.

(5) Frank — known to have worked at Prospect Hill Pottery in Trenton.

(6) Theodore — nothing known except that he died in Tiffin, OH.

(7) Mrs. Joseph B. Erskine — of Pittsburgh and Aspinwall, PA. She had two children, Harold and Florence.

(8) Mrs. Hugh D. Trout — remained in the Trenton area.

William and Edward together started Sanitary Pottery, which was later bought out by Standard Sanitary Corporation. In 1926, Frederick, Edward, Sr., and Edward, Jr., started Coxon Belleek in Wooster, OH. The Depression caused the concern to fail in 1930.

Cybis, Boleslaw: Polish-born founder of Cybis Porcelain. He worked at Cordey for awhile after coming to this country and designed some of their more collectible items.

Dale: With Isaac Davis, established Prospect Hill Pottery in 1880.

Dale, James J.: Established a sanitary pottery with Thomas Davis. Although this might be the same party who was involved with Prospect Hill, it would appear from the dates that possibly Dale and Davis each had a son, and that the sons also ended up as partners.

Davis, Issac: Davis was born in England, and came to Trenton in 1862 where he worked for William Young & Sons. He was involved at various times with Glasgow Pottery, Taylor & Speeler, and Prospect Hill Pottery.

Davis, Thomas: Co-founder of Dale & Davis pottery for sanitary wares.

Dean, Jesse: Trenton decorator.

Deasy, S. P.: Co-founder of Acme Sanitary Pottery Company in 1901.

Deihl, Louis J.: Co-founder of Elite Pottery in 1901.

DeLan, Eugene A.: Not much is known about this Spanish artist except that Lenox company records place him at the factory from 1900 to 1915. A transition-mark tobacco jar dated 1899 would indicate that he was there at least a year earlier, however, and a tankard with the C.A.C. wreath mark would put him there earlier yet. It is possible that he had two terms of employment at Lenox, although this cannot be documented. At some point he had his own decorating firm in Trenton with a partner named McGill.

Des: This name has appeared once, on a transition-mark/Glen-Iris Lenox vase, and we don't have the slightest idea who this might be. From the way the name is written, it might be that the artist started signing his name and then stopped abruptly. The artwork is virtually identical to that on a vase done by Marsh, and it is possibly the case that "Des" was an apprentice who was given a Marsh piece to copy.

DeVegh, G.: Modeller of many of the Lenox Art Deco figurines and busts, later worked for Scammell.

Donoher, Thomas P.: Part-owner of the Maddock Pottery Company c. 1893.

Dorety, James A.: Co-founder of Acme Sanitary Pottery Company in 1901.

Drugan, Samuel: Co-founder of Cochran-Drugan Pottery in 1907.

Eakin, Patricia J.: Modeller of the Lenox American Costume figurine series, later worked for Boehm and Cybis. For more information about her, see the section on Lexon figurines.

Edge, W. H.: Modeller from Trenton.

Evans, George: Evans was a nephew of Jonathan Coxon and a co-founder of the American Art China Works (Rittenhouse & Evans.)

Fauji, Gazoo: Fauji was one of two Japanese artists employed at Lenox in the early years and he worked there from 1890 to 1893. Signed works by him are virtually unknown. An artist with a very similar name was employed at Roseville Pottery in Ohio some time later, and could very well be the same person if we allow for differences in the transliteration of the name from the Japanese to English.

Fay, Charles: Co-founder of Delaware Pottery.

Fenzel, F.: This German artist was employed at Lenox from 1937 to 1946 (doing mainly orchids and roses) and he also later worked at Boehm.

Forman, J. G.: Helped to run Coxon & Company after Charles Coxon died.

Fort, Howard: Lenox artist.

Foster, J. W.: Secretary/treasurer of the Eagle Pottery.

Gallimore: William Gallimore, an Englishman, was an engraver and designer in the English pottery industry and worked for Wedgwood and other English concerns. His son, William Wood Gallimore, was a modeller who worked first in the English industry and then later at the Belleek factory in Ireland. It was in Ireland that he lost his right arm in a gun accident. He retrained himself to model with his left arm, and eventually came to Trenton.

In 1886 he became a designer and modeller for Trent Tile, and was later employed at Lenox where he designed some of their more important vases.

William Wood Gallimore's children (William, Jesse, Flora and Marian) were apparently also talented and all found a place in the ceramics industry. A Victor Gallimore was a modeller for a pottery in Connecticut, but the relationship (if any) between Victor and the others is uncertain.

Gasper, P. Paul: This Pickard artist is known to have done much of the Delft-type decoration at Cook Pottery and may have worked for other Trenton companies as well.

Geyer, Bruno: There is very little information about Geyer except that a turn-of-the-century city directory lists him as living on East Hanover Street. He did magnificent portrait plates for Lenox.

Goodwin, John: Goodwin was a partner in Taylor & Goodwin (Trenton Pottery Company) from 1870 to 1872, and sold his interest in the latter year and went to East Liverpool, OH. He was from Burselm, England, and died in East Liverpool in 1875.

Greenberg, Harry: Greenberg is the founder of Cordey, and is from Philadelphia.

Gruessner, Robert: With Fell & Thropp c. 1892-4.

Hancock, W. S.: Co-founder of Crescent Pottery in 1881 and later involved with the Trenton Potteries Company.

Harris: Founder of Harris Manufacturing Company (later called Trent Tile.)

Hattersley, Charles: Founded Hattersley Pottery in 1852.

Healy, Owen: Co-founder of Standard Sanitary Pottery Company in 1901.

Heidrich, Antonie: This German artist worked at Lenox for around ten years beginning in 1890. His specialty was figures, and many of his items are elaborately enhanced with silver overlay or gold paste work.

Hendrickson, W.: Trenton decorator.

Hicks, Richard: The Barber book lists Hicks as one of C.A.C.'s top artists, and goes on to describe a vase done by him which depicts Orpheus descending into Hades.

Hill, Charles C.: Co-founder of Interstate Pottery in 1909.

Hoelscher, J. M.: Co-founder of Monument Pottery in 1896.

Houdayer, John F.: Partner in Taylor & Speeler c. 1860-1870, co-founder of Taylor & Houdayer in 1883.

Houghton, George Yarnold: Houghton was born in Bromsgrove, Worcestershire, England, on February 1, 1856, and came to the United State in 1884. He was employed at Willets as an artist, and later worked at Lenox until his retirement in the early 1930's. He died in Trenton on January 11, 1942, and is buried in Riverview Cemetery there.

Family pets were frequent models for Houghton's artwork. A black and white St. Bernard named Grover appears on many of his pieces, and a large brown and white mixed-breed dog named Rover (who had only three legs) was also immortalized.

Houghton was a well-rounded artist, and in addition to animals did portraits, flowers, and on at least one occasion a nude. He was also capable of intricate gold work and should be given credit for many of the Willets items with floral motifs delicately outlined in gold. His animals and humans have an almost photographic quality and can easily be mistaken for transfer-decorated items at first glance. His best work will be found on Willets and what he did at Lenox all those years remains something of a mystery.

Houghton, Oliver: Oliver was George's brother, and he was also employed at Willets as an artist. He stayed only a brief while before leaving to become a bricklayer, and was eventually a successful contractor.

Hutchinson: Co-founder of Cochran-Drugan Pottery in 1907.

Jones, Josiah: Jones was born in 1801, and worked first at the Greenpoint pottery in Brooklyn until 1856, and then went to Kaolin, SC to work for the Southern Porcelain Company. Around the time of the Civil War, Jones went to Trenton where he was a modeller at Millington, Astbury & Poulson, and probably for other companies. He died in 1887.

Judnak, Stephen: Co-founder of General Porcelain in 1939.

Kelly, John: Co-founder of Standard Sanitary Pottery Company in 1901.

Kimble, Warren: Founder of the Warren Kimble Pottery.

Kuhn: Miss Kuhn's first name was written on a tiny scrap of paper which has unfortunately been lost. She was from Philadelphia and worked as an artist at Lenox from 1897 to 1900.

Laurence, Sturgis: The reknowned Rookwood Pottery artist is known to have worked at Lenox as well. His work has appeared on several pieces with the C.A.C. wreath mark, and one piece in particular is dated 1894. Lenox records indicate he was there from 1893 to 1898, which conflicts with other information that he was at Rookwood from 1895 to 1904. While at Rookwood he did make several lengthy trips to New York City for that company, so perhaps he decorated for both companies at the same time. He is also known to have worked for the Jefferson Lamp Company. On Lenox items, his specialty was monochrome cobalt work.

Lawton, George: A partner of I. Davis.

Lee: Trenton decorator.

Walter Scott Lenox

Lenox, Walter Scott: Lenox was born in Trenton, NJ in 1859. His father, Hiram, had a hardware business in Trenton, and his grandfather, Samuel, had a river trade with boats and warehouses. Samuel Lenox had been born in County Antrim, Ireland, in 1784, although he was Scottish and not Irish. Samuel, who was 22 when he came to America, arrived first in Baltimore and then proceeded from there to Philadelphia, and eventually to Trenton. His brother, James, joined him in the river trade.

Although he had been named for Sir Walter Scott, the young Walter S. Lenox took little interest in writing and even less interest in hardware. He had been fascinated as a child by the pottery he passed on the way to school, and eventually became an apprentice at the Ott & Brewer factory in Trenton, where he rose to become head of the art department.

Although his early training was in sculpting as opposed to decorating china, he developed his skill as a decorator in his spare time as a hobby. There are no known signed samples of his artwork, however. (There was an amateur artist by the name of Lenox in the Trenton area, and some perfectly horrible samples of this party's work turn up now and then. They are definitely not the work of Walter Lenox, for they are usually marked with the Lenox palette mark, not in use until long after Walter Lenox had gone blind.)

Lenox left O&B to be art director at the Willets Company, and although we do not have an exact date for when he started at Willets, the indications are that he was there only a few years.

In 1889 he formed the Ceramic Art Company with Jonathan Coxon as his partner. Lenox fulfilled the responsibilities of being both art director and secretary/treasurer of the young company.

In 1895 Lenox was afflicted with locomotor ataxia which was to eventually leave him blind and paralyzed. He continued in his work with the help of Harry Brown, who became corporate secretary after Lenox became president. Lenox called Brown by the name of "Dominie", a Scottish word meaning schoolmaster, pastor or minister. It is a variant of "domine" which means lord or master. Exactly why Lenox chose this form of address is a puzzle, for it would have made more sense for Brown to use it when addressing Lenox.

Old Trenton city directories list Lenox as living on Jackson Street, then a very fashionable section of the city and currently the site of a restoration project which has unfortunately not gotten far enough down the street to include the Lenox home. He apparently also lived on Broad Street for awhile before returning to Jackson Street where he resided with his sister and her family.

Lenox, who never married, enjoyed a rather flamboyant life style. He always dressed in the height of fashion no matter how poorly the company was doing, and was a frequent guest in the best homes of New York and Philadelphia society. It was from his wide circle of friends that he frequently borrowed money to keep the company going, and at one point he had sort of a round robin going where he would borrow from one friend to pay back another, while at the same time borrowing more from a third party to meet the payroll or other expenses.

He was a nice-looking man, and apparently had a charming way about him. Lenox was somewhat egotistical and, among other things, liked to ride at the head of parades in Trenton. He died in Trenton on January 11, 1920, and is buried in Riverview Cemetery with his family.

Leukel, John: Co-founder of Equitable Pottery in 1888.

Lynch, James and Thomas: The Lynch brothers ran the Hattersley Pottery in the 1850's.

Lyons, James H. and J. W.: Co-founders of the Keystone Pottery in 1892.

Mackenzie, Dr. Thomas H.: Trenton doctor who was a co-founder of Star Porcelain Company in 1899.

Maddock, Thomas: Maddock was born in April 1818, into a family of English potters. He learned to decorate at the Davenport works in England, and he was to later use a variation of the Davenport anchor backstamp on his own china. In 1847 he came to America, and he and his friend, William

Leigh, opened a decorating studio on Spruce Street in New York City. They were the first American china decorating shop, and in 1853 they decorated a dinner service for use in the White House.

Maddock next had a retail pottery business in Jersey City, NJ, and was an agent for Millington, Astbury & Poulson. He eventually purchased a share of M.A.P., and finally owned the entire company.

Maddock, John: John was the son of Thomas Maddock, and was the founder of John Maddock & Sons c. 1884. John had four sons: Thomas, A. W., W. B., and H. E.

Magowan: Co-founder of Empire Pottery in 1884.

Marsh: Co-founder of Crown Porcelain Works.

Marsh, Walter: Most of the examples of Marsh's work seen thus far have been on Lenox items with the transition mark/Glen-Iris backstamp, and they have all been floral motifs. His name is also seen on Willets blanks, suggesting that he either worked for them as well or else had a decorating studio at one time or another. The Willets pieces are also decorated with flowers. Some of the gilding on the Willets pieces looks rather amateurish, which gives weight to the theory that he worked out of his own studio and did his own gilding. Be alert to the fact that Marsh sometimes signed his name in a rather careless fashion and it can look like "Mansby" or some other variation. He worked at Lenox from 1903 to 1910, and nothing is known about his personal life.

Martell: Martell was an artist at the Lenox factory in 1904.

May, C. A.: Part-owner of the Maddock Pottery Company c. 1893.

Mayer, Joseph: Proprietor of Mayer Pottery Manufacturing Company and the Arsenal Pottery.

McGill: Trenton decorator.

McPherson, Joseph: An officer in Trenton Terra-Cotta.

Meagher, John: Co-founder of Acme Sanitary Pottery Company in 1901.

Mellor, F. G.: Vice-president of Cook Pottery Company in 1894.

Millington, Richard: One of the founders of Millington, Astbury & Poulson, and later of the Eagle Pottery in 1876.

Moona, P. H.: Co-founder of Standard Sanitary Pottery Company in 1901.

Morley, George and William: The Morleys are perhaps the best-known of the Lenox factory artists. They had worked in the British ceramics industry until 1891 when they were brought to East Liverpool, OH, by the Knowles, Taylor and Knowles factory. At some point in the 1890's, they left K.T.K. and it is not clear where they went next. It is conjectured that the Morley whose name appears as an artist on reverse painted glass lampshades by the Pairpoint Corporation of Massachusetts is one (or perhaps both) of them. Lenox company records indicate both came there in 1900. Although William was George's uncle, they were not that far apart in years leading many to believe they were brothers.

William is perhaps best known for his fish and game sets, which he produced in great numbers. He is reported to have been a trifle difficult to work with at times, and he apparently preferred the company of a pet mouse to that of his co-workers.

He died after two months of illness with pneumonia on March 1, 1935. Other literature suggests a death date of 1934, but our date of 1935 can be proven by newspaper obituaries and the date on his tombstone in Greenwood Cemetery in Trenton. Lenox records have him stopping work there in 1934, but a co-worker of his has told us that he continued working on plates until practically the day he died.

George's work is encountered less frequently than William's, due no doubt to fewer years of employment at Lenox. He stayed only a short time during his first term with them, returning a second time in 1930 and leaving for good in 1939.

Lenox items signed by a "C. Morley" turn up now and then, and to the best of our knowledge this is George's careless signature and not that of yet another Morley. The artwork of George and William is so very similar that it is difficult to tell them apart without checking signatures.

Morris, W. T.: Morris had worked at Royal Worcester and the Irish Belleek Company, and was a decorator at Ott & Brewer after coming to Trenton. He was one of the founders of Columbian Art Pottery, also known as Morris & Willmore.

Moses, James: This American potter was the founder of Mercer Pottery Company in 1868 or 1869.

Moses, John: John Moses was born in County Tyrone, Ireland, in 1832, and came to the United States at the age of 20. He started the Glasgow Pottery in 1863, and died in 1902.

Mountford: co-founder of Burroughs and Mountford, and a general manager at Eagle Pottery.

Mulheron, James J.: Secretary of Cook Pottery in 1894.

Naylor, H. Roger: Naylor was the first Trenton-born artist to be hired at the Lenox Company, and he worked there from 1890 to 1893. We have no other information about him except that he is buried in Riverview Cemetery.

Norris, James E.: Founded Anchor Pottery c. 1894.

Nosek, Hans (John): Nosek was born in Czechoslovakia, and emigrated to America in 1903 to work in Trenton. His first term of employment at Lenox was from 1903 to 1907 (some say 1908), and he also worked at Willets for a brief time. Some time after coming to the United States he Americanized his name fron Hans to John, leading many to think there was more than one Nosek at Lenox.

After leaving Lenox in 1907(8), he tried his hand at many endeavors including photography and chicken farming. In 1939 he returned to the Lenox factory and stayed until his retirement in 1954 at the age of 77. Nosek lived in Ringoes, NJ, which is several miles north of Trenton. His name also appears on at least one piece of English china, so it is possible he worked in England at one point.

There are persistent rumors of trouble between Nosek and one or both of the Morleys. George Morley did leave Lenox about the time Nosek came there in 1903, and he left again in 1939 when Nosek returned there. This does not necessarily prove they disliked each other but could be taken instead to mean that the company twice hired Nosek to replace a departing Morley.

Oliphant, General: Oliphant owned the Delaware Pottery 1884-1895, and prior to that time was connected with the Enterprise Pottery. He had three sons (Sidney, Robert and Hughes) who founded the Bellmark Pottery in 1893.

Ott, Joseph: One of the founders of Ott & Brewer. He was the uncle of John Hart Brewer, and prior to going into the pottery business he had livery stables in Trenton in partnership with J. H. Brewer's father, William.

Page, G. W.: Co-founder of the Excelsior Pottery Company in 1905, and of the Elite Pottery in 1901.

Phillips, Henry D.: Co-founder of Hart Brewer Pottery in 1895.

Plantier, Arthur: Co-founder of Sanitary Earthenware Specialty Company in 1897.

Poole: Trenton decorator.

Pope: Trenton decorator.

Potts, Richard T.: Co-founder of Standard Sanitary Pottery Company in 1901.

Poulson: One of the founders of Millington, Astbury & Poulson. Died in 1861.

Przechacki: Joseph: Co-founder of General Porcelain in 1939.

Renelt: Willets factory artist.

Rhodes: Rhodes came to Trenton in 1859 and helped to found the City Pottery in that year. He left the company in 1865.

Riley, John B.: President of Eagle Pottery.

Rittenhouse: Co-founder of American Art China Works (Rittenhouse & Evans.)

Robinson, James H.: Co-founder of Providential Tile Works in 1885.

Rolege, Herman: In the 1860's was the only person in Trenton who knew how to decorate china and worked for all 10 potteries in operation at that time, including Ott & Brewer.

Rouse: Maker of modern-day parian pieces.

Saunders, Harry: Saunders was from Trenton and did pate-sur-pate work at Ott & Brewer.

Sears, Kate: Nothing is known about Ms. Sears except that she was one of the earliest recorded sculptors at Lenox. Her specialty was a type of sculpture done by carving still-wet porcelain with a jackknife. Chariot scenes, cherubic little children, life-like lilies and other such items were the subjects she favored. She sometimes took the show on the road and worked in public at fairs and exhibitions. This no doubt accounts for the scarcity of signed and backstamped samples of her work.

Sinclair, Herbert: Founder of Star Porcelain Company in 1899.

Skirm, Charles H.: Co-founder of Enterprise in 1879.

Speeler, Henry: Co-founder of Taylor & Speeler in 1853 and International Pottery in 1860.

Stangl, J. M.: A ceramic engineer at Fulper Pottery and later established the dinnerware line which bears his name.

Stephens: Co-founder of Greenwood Pottery in 1861.

Stockton: Trenton decorator.

Sully: The name Sully appears on one Lenox factory-decorated item.

Swalk: Lenox factory artist.

Swetman, Thomas: Co-founder of Sanitary Earthenware Specialty Company in 1897.

Tams, James: Tams was from Longton, Staffordshire, England, and was a co-founder of Greenwood Pottery in 1861.

Tatler, Elijah: Outstanding porcelain artist, died January 12, 1876.

Tatler, W. H.: W. H. was Elijah's son and the president of W. H. Tatler Decorating Company in Trenton.

Taylor: Co-founder of Taylor & Houdayer.

Taylor, James: Taylor once worked at the Harker Pottery in Ohio, and in 1853 he was part of Taylor & Speeler and later of Taylor, Speeler & Bloor. He died c. 1890. (It is not certain if James Taylor and the Taylor listed above are one and the same.)

Tekauchi, M.: Tekauchi was one of the Japanese artists employed at Lenox in the early years. He worked there from 1890 to 1891 and his specialty was underglaze cobalt work.

Thompson, J. F.: Co-founder of Coxon & Thompson in 1863.

Thropp, Samuel E.: Co-founder of Fell & Thropp.

Till, A.: Willets factory artist.

Titus: Partner in Yates & Titus.

Tscheuden: Founder of Bay Ridge Specialty Company.

Tunnicliffe, George: Had a decorating studio in Trenton.

Turford, Cornelius: Co-founder of the Egyptian Pottery in 1891.

Umpleby, W. H.: Co-founder of Enterprise Pottery in 1879 and of Keystone in 1892.

Walton, Benjamin, Jr.: Co-founder of Interstate Pottery in 1909.

Walton, C. B.: Founder of C. B. Walton Company in 1900.

Weeden, Frank E.: Co-founder of Interstate Pottery Company.

Whitehead, C. Louis: Co-founder of Providential Tile in 1885.

Willets, Joseph, Daniel and Edmund R.: Co-founders of Willets Manufacturing Company.

Willmore: Co-founder of Columbian Art Pottery (Morris & Willmore) and prior to that a decorator at Royal Worcester and Ott & Brewer.

Wirkner S.: Lenox records indicate Wirkner was there from 1900 until the 1920's although there are very few signed samples of his work available today. His portrait pieces are particularly desirable.

With, A.: With was a Willets factory artist, and nothing else is known. Due to hard-to-read signatures, this artist may very well be the same one who appears below as Witte.

Witte: Name appears once on a Lenox factory-decorated item.

Wolff, L. and J. M.: Co-founders of Monument Pottery in 1896.

Wood: Co-founder of Wood & Barlow and also connected with Empire Pottery.

Yates: Co-founder of the City Pottery (Rhodes & Yates) 1859; of Yates & Titus 1865; of Yates, Bennett & Allen 1871; City Pottery 1875.

Young, William, Sr.: Young originally worked for the John Ridgway Pottery in Hanley, England. In 1853 he opened a pottery in Trenton on the Hattersley pottery site. In 1857 he built a new pottery, the Excelsior Pottery Works. He retired from the company in 1870 and died in 1872. His sons, Edward, John and William, Jr., eventually sold out to Willets.

THE COMPANIES

BACKGROUND INFORMATION

To understand why the United States lagged so far behind in the production of china, we have to go back to Colonial days. England's policy regarding its colonies all over the world as well as in America was that the colonies existed to provide raw materials for the industries located in the mother country. Colonies were not allowed to develop any industry which would either interfere with the flow of raw materials to England or compete directly with an English product. They accomplished these ends with laws expressly forbidding certain activities or with tax structures so unfavorable that competitive colonial industry could not survive.

The English ceramics industry was protected in this fashion, and from the beginning the American colonies were discouraged from entering into the production of anything other than very ordinary household items. Although many American companies tried to enter the china market at one time or another, it was to take the better part of a century before the American pottery industry reached full stride.

Trenton, NJ, was the home of many of the early companies due to easy access to transportation lines and the raw materials used in making china. The exact number of Trenton potteries will perhaps never be known. Businesses started up overnight and died just a quickly, as the companies competed both for the buying public's attention and for the services of top designers, artists, and technical people.

The companies all engaged to at least a minimal extent in copying each others wares, which would be only natural as workmen left one place for another taking their designs and technical know-how with them. Ceramic experts were imported, primarily from England and Ireland. European designs were copied, and to some extent the European backstamps were duplicated on Trenton wares.

It has been frequently stated that American potters used the European backstamps in order to sell their wares because the American public would not buy china made in the United States. Although there is probably some truth to this, it is vastly overstated. A casual inspection of the known marks of Trenton potteries shows 12 percent to be flagrant copies of European marks, 20 percent to be American in styling, and 68 percent to be nondescript. (Marks were counted as copies of European ones if they were the same as or very similar to existing European ones. They were counted as American marks if they used symbols such as the American eagle or if they included the words Trenton, New Jersey, or U.S.A.)

The Trenton companies which used the European backstamps were primarily those owned by Englishmen, and it was usually the English marks which were copied. Rather than being a way of tricking the public into buying Trenton wares, it might have been a simple case of continuing to mark wares as they always had.

In any event, the European companies whose marks were being copied were not sufficiently alarmed by the competition to do anything about it. The only known exception to this was the Irish Belleek Company. For nearly half a century, Trenton companies had used the term Belleek at will, until the late 1920's when the Irish company sued in a successful effort to gain total rights to the name. (Wherever possible throughout this book, we have used the term Belleek-type to avoid confusion with the Irish product. It is impossible, however, to discuss Trenton ceramics without using the word Belleek.)

Labor strikes forced many of the businesses to go under, although it must be mentioned that unionization brought stability to the Trenton pottery industry. Once pay scales were established, there was no longer any reason for workers to jump from one pottery to the next. In addition, many of the unsafe conditions were eliminated and fewer workers died from handling toxic chemicals or from lung problems associated with the ever-present dust in the potteries.

The economic depression of the 1890's forced several of the borderline operations to go out of business, and others were consolidated into larger companies at that time. The companies that started up after this time were, for the most part, involved in the manufacture of sanitary wares rather than decorative items or dinnerware.

Following World War II, many of the Trenton potteries were unable to compete with cheap foreign imports and either closed their doors forever or else moved elsewhere and consolidated with other companies. Lenox was the last of the major potteries to leave Trenton.

Some of the confusion over founding dates and the like is due to the way in which many of the companies were formed. If two men formed a partnership in 1879, built a pottery in 1880, and finally produced their first piece of china in 1881, any one of those dates could be used as the founding date. In other cases the companies deliberately added years to their history in many different ways. If a pottery operated out of a building which had been built several years before, it was common to claim the date of the erection of the building as the founding date of the current pottery on that site. Similar sounding names add to the confusion — i.e., Trenton Pottery Company, Trenton Potteries Company, Trenton Pottery Works.

If we chart the Trenton pottery industry year by year beginning with 1852 and ending with 1910, a certain growth pattern can be seen:

1852 — Hattersley
1853 — M.A.P.; Taylor & Speeler; Wm. Young & Sons
1854 — none
1855 — none
1856 — none
1857 — none
1858 — none
1859 — City Pottery; Trenton China Company
1860 — International
1861 — Stephens, Tams, & Company (later called Greenwood)
1862 — none
1863 — Coxon & Thompson; Glasgow; Ott & Brewer
1864 — none
1865 — Taylor & Company; Trenton Pottery Company
1866 — none
1867 — none
1868 — Mercer
1869 — New Jersey Pottery
1870 — none
1871 — none
1872 — none
1873 — none
1874 — none
1875 — none
1876 — American Crockery Company; Eagle Pottery
1877 — none
1878 — none

1879 — Burroughs & Mountford; Enterprise; Willets
1880 — Prospect Hill
1881 — Crescent
1882 — Trent Tile
1883 — Taylor & Houdayer; Trenton Pottery Works
1884 — Delaware
1885 — Providential
1886 — none
1887 — none
1888 — East Trenton; Equitable
1889 — Fell & Thropp; Ceramic Art Company (Lenox)
1890 — Crown Porcelain
1891 — American Art China Works; Egyptian
1892 — Trenton Potteries Company; Dale & Davis; Keystone; Columbian
1893 — Artistic Porcelain; Bellmark Pottery; Maddock Pottery; Trenton Fire Clay
1894 — Anchor Pottery; Cook Pottery; John Maddock & Sons
1895 — American Porcelain Works; Hart Brewer Pottery Company
1896 — Monument
1897 — Sanitary
1898 — Brian Pottery
1899 — Star Porcelain
1900 — C.B. Walton; Economy
1901 — Acme; Elite; Standard Sanitary
1902 — Fidelity
1903 — Resolute
1904 — none
1905 — Excelsior
1906 — National
1907 — Bay Ridge; Cochran-Drugan
1908 — none
1909 — Interstate
1910 — none

Our chart has the following flaws: (1) many of the starting dates are unknown so those companies are not listed; (2) there are companies that are totally unknown to us; (3) some of the companies had many incarnations and it was difficult to choose the "proper" one. Even allowing for all these variables, certain trends can be noted.

The 1870's had the lowest growth rate (five new companies), even lower than the very beginning years. The 1890's had the greatest growth, with 20 new companies. This is very surprising, since this decade had a serious depression beginning with the Panic of 1893. The 1860's had nine new companies, the 1880's had 11, and the early 1900's had 12. (The "unknowns" were probably evenly spread throughout the 1852-1910 period under discussion, so all of the above numbers can easily be doubled.) For 22 of the 58 years covered, no new companies were started, with the longest stretch being the six-year period from 1870 through 1875.

We will not make any serious attempt here to rate the companies, but will make some casual comments regarding their relative merits in various categories.

(1) Rarity — Many of the companies that made sanitary wares and other mundane products seemed unable to resist the temptation to make a quality product at one time or another. Some of them failed miserably and never made more than a few prototype items. Although such items are extremely hard to find today, they are frequently viewed merely as curiosities and do not always have a premium price tag on them.

It seems there is somehow a subtle difference between rare and obscure, and for our purposes here we will ignore the obscure and concentrate on the "name" makers of Belleek and porcelain items — Ott & Brewer; Rittenhouse & Evans; Morris & Willmore; Greenwood; Cook; Willets; and C.A.C. (Lenox). Cook and Greenwood are perhaps the rarest, followed by R.&E.. and M.&W., then by Ott & Brewer, by Willets, and finally C.A.C. Although there is some connection between rarity and price, Ott & Brewer is still king where prices are concerned.

(2) Translucency — All of the above-mentioned companies were capable of putting out a fine porcelain, but the single thinnest piece of Trenton Belleek we have seen was made by Rittenhouse & Evans. The overall lightweight champion, however, is probably Ott & Brewer who consistently put out a very thin ware.

(3) Design — Since all the companies copied so much from themselves and from European companies, it is very difficult to choose a winner. (Keep in mind we are only including pre-1906 Lenox.) Cook and Greenwood are too scarce to be considered for this category. Morris & Willmore put out one spectacular tea set and not much else. Rittenhouse & Evans put out little that hadn't been seen before. Ott & Brewer wares look like the Irish Belleek catalogue revisited. We suppose Willets and C.A.C. are the winners by default.

(4) Decoration — We don't think we can get into too much trouble giving the gold paste award to Ott & Brewer. For variety of artwork and for consistently high quality on factory-decorated hand-painted items, C.A.C. is our choice.

(5) Quality Control — Judging by what we see, C.A.C. had the pickiest inspectors in all of Trenton.

In the following section, listed are many obscure companies whose wares we have never seen. Since we have never seen them we cannot give accurate selling prices, and so have given estimates based on comparable prices from other known companies. Many of these lower-level wares, however, are still available at flea markets and auctions at $1 for the whole box. To a collector living, perhaps, in Kansas who is trying to assemble a collection of one piece by each company listed in this book, these lower-level wares assume a greater importance.

There are no doubt many readers who have never heard of some of these companies before. Don't feel badly for until we started the book, we had never heard of a few of them either. Now that their names are up in lights, rises in prices for them can be expected. Much of the attractively decorated ironstone type of ware is already disappearing from the marketplace as the Belleek type products become difficult or impossible to find. Much of the Trenton "junk ware" is in the true antique class, i.e., over 100 years old, and this fact seems to have escaped many people.

Although the glory days are gone, it is not possible to drive through Trenton without being constantly reminded of the once-great industry. Many of the old buildings are still there, and several of the industry's founders had streets named for them. Little is being done to preserve this part of Trenton's history, however, and as time goes on more and more landmarks are being lost to general lack of care and the never-ending urban renewal.

In the following section about the companies, they are listed in alphabetical order as the name actually appears. (For example, John Moses & Company is listed under "J" and not under "M".)

ACME SANITARY POTTERY COMPANY

Acme was founded in 1901 by Messrs. James A. Dorety, John Meagher, and S. P. Deasy. They produced sanitary wares.

Marks: *Not known*
Prices: We have never seen any of Acme's products sold on the open market and it is possible they never made anything but sanitary wares. A miniature three-piece bathroom set by them would be valued at a minimum of $50.

ALPAUGH & MAGOWAN

See Coxon & Company.

AMERICAN ART CHINA WORKS

In December 1891, Rittenhouse and Evans formed the American Art China Works for the production of a Belleek-type ware which was sold both decorated and undecorated. The company was located in what had previously been the Washington Pottery. Their china tends to have a slightly whiter appearance than many of the other Trenton wares. The company was not in business long and items by them are rare. Few people know the company by its proper name and it is generally called Rittenhouse & Evans.

Marks: Mark A is the most common one, and appears primarily (but not always) on factory-decorated items. Mark B can also appear on both factory and home-decorated items. Marks A and B are usually printed in blue. Variations of the marks occur.

Mark A  **Mark B**

☐ Bonbon dish, 5" round, ruffled top, pearlized pink interior, gold trim on rim, factory decorated, mark B	**125.00**
☐ Pin tray, 4" x 3", scalloped rim, home-decorated with flowers and gold trim, mark B	**75.00**
☐ Salt dip, 2-1/2" diameter round, ruffled top, pearlized lavender interior, sponged gold on exterior, mark A	**65.00**
☐ Shell, 6" diameter, raised on two small almond-shaped feet, gold paste trim, mark B	**295.00**
☐ Vase, 13" high, handles, gold paste and hand-painting, mark A	**340.00**

AMERICAN CHINA COMPANY

American China Company produced stone china, and may have been a part of the American Crockery Company. The company should not be confused with a company of the same name in Toronto, Canada.

Marks: *Not known*
Prices: We have never seen any products from this company. If you come across a quality procelain or Belleek-type item by them, it can be compared to a comparable Willets item. Their stone china can be figured roughly as follows:

Bowls, $10 to $20 depending on size, $5 for dessert or soup size; Cups and saucers, $5 to $10; Dinner plates, $5 to $20; Mugs, $5 to $25; Platters, $10 to $30 depending on size; Smaller plates, $2 to $5.

AMERICAN CROCKERY COMPANY

Although the founding date of this company is uncertain, it is known that they exhibited at the 1876 Centennial Exposition in Philadelphia. They manufactured white granite and bisque items, frequently decorated with American historical scenes.

Marks: American Crockery marks include the British coat of arms with IRON STONE CHINA above and A.C.Co. underneath, and an American eagle on top of the initials ACCO, which are intertwined. A third mark is shown below. All three marks were printed in black.

AMERICAN CHINA

A.C.Co.

Prices: We are totally unfamiliar with this company's products, so the following prices are estimates:

Bisque items — if interesting, compare against comparable Lenox items; if boring, divide Lenox prices in half.

Centennial items — a minimum of $50 for any backstamped sample Graniteware or stoneware:

Bowls, $10 to $20 for serving size, $5 for soup or dessert size; Cups and saucers, $5 to $10; Dinner plates, $5 to $20; Mugs, $5 to $25; Platters, $10 to $30 depending on size; Smaller plates, $2 to $5.

AMERICAN PORCELAIN WORKS

This company was founded in 1895 by N. W. Boch. No other information available.

Marks: *Not known*
Prices: Not only are we unfamiliar with American Porcelain Works' products, we're not even sure what they made. If something respectable turns up, compare against comparable Lenox items. Lower-level wares can be rated against a company like Greenwood.

AMISON POTTERIES

No information available.

Marks: *Not known*
Prices: Without knowing what Amison made we cannot list any prices. Compare against comparable items from known companies.

ANCHOR POTTERY

Anchor was established in 1894 by James E. Norris. Fulper Pottery took over the plant at a later date.

Marks: A British coat of arms with the words IRONSTONE CHINA and the word WARRANTED underneath was the first mark. The initials AP were inside the shield. Other company marks include the ones shown and numerous other variations.

ANCHOR POTTERY

J. E. N.

Price: Vase, 15" high, two handles, orange lustre finish, transfer decoration of pink roses which are touched up by hand, gold trim on handles, very possibly the ugliest piece of china to ever come out of Trenton, $20.

The above price is fairly representative for Anchor products of this type. Following are some estimates on dinnerware type items:

Bowls, $10 to $20 for serving bowls, $5 for desserts or soups; Cups and saucers, $5 to $10; Dinner plates $5 to $10; Mugs, $5 to $25; Platters, $10 to $30 depending on size.

ARSENAL POTTERY

This relatively obscure Trenton company supposedly made fine Toby jugs, majolica and decorated porcelain. It was part of the Mayer Pottery Manufacturing Company, which is equally obscure. The proprietor was Joseph Mayer.

Marks: *Not known*
Prices: We have never seen any of their "fine Toby jugs, majolica and decorated porcelain," and will have to take it on faith that they do indeed exist somewhere. Since they are obviously rare, we would estimate a minimum of $100 on one of their Toby jugs. The decorated porcelain and the majolica would be anyone's guess.

ARTISTIC PORCELAIN COMPANY

Artistic was founded in 1893 by N. W. Boch.

Marks: *Not known*
Prices: Artistic is even more obscure than Arsenal (if that is possible), and we will offer the advice to compare their items against comparable items by other companies.

ARTON STUDIOS

Original name of Cordey, q.v.

ASTBURY & MADDOCK

See Thomas Maddock & Sons

ASTBURY & MILLINGTON

See Millington, Astbury & Poulson

BAY RIDGE SPECIALITIES
This still-existing company was founded in Brooklyn, NY, c. 1907 by a Mr. Tscheuden. The company moved to Stokes Avenue in Trenton c. 1910. Their output included bath accessories, beer mugs, and decorative items sometimes embellished with applied flowers. When the Fairfacts Company went out of business, Bay Ridge bought their machines and designs.

Marks: Many items unmarked, others marked with company name in one fashion or another.

Prices: Since this company is still functioning, prices for their wares will probably be a little lower than for those which have closed their doors forever. Their items will, of course, still have interest for those trying to complete a one-from-each company collection.

☐	Beer mugs, *undecorated*		**5.00**
☐	Beer mugs, *decorated*..............................	**5.00**	**50.00**
☐	Items with applied flowers, *a minimum of*		**10.00**

BELLMARK POTTERY COMPANY
Bellmark was founded in 1893 by Sidney, Robert and Hughes Oliphant. They manufactured plumbers' and druggists' items.

Marks: A bell with the words VITREOUS CHINA.

Prices: We can only conjecture about what their plumbers' and druggists' items were, but if their line included something like a mortar and pestle, we would estimate $50 for such a set. (Keep in mind that "druggists' supplies" in those days did not necessarily mean a piece of porcelain or pottery. Some of the concoctions sold by druggists in those days were made up of the ingredients which go into ceramics, and many of the companies sold these compounds to druggists.)

BOEHM
Edward Marshall Boehm founded a studio pottery in Trenton in 1949. His first workshop was on Stokes Avenue, and he later moved to Fairfacts Avenue. Following Mr. Boehm's death, his wife Helen took over the company. Studios have now been opened in England as well as in Trenton, so the Trentoniana collector might go to special pains to select an item which was made in Trenton rather than in England.

Both authors have to confess to a lack of knowledge about Boehm porcelains, and all of the information here, including the prices listed below, is secondhand material gleaned from trade journals and Boehm advertising material. Their items are beautifully made and show a great deal of time and attention to detail. Considering the amount of work that must go into them, the current prices seem fair.

Prices: Following are selected auction results for items which are no longer being made. Because they are all pre-1971 items, it is assumed they were made in Trenton although we are not certain of this.

☐	Blue Grosbeak	**750.00**
☐	Bobolink..	**800.00**
☐	Boxer, large size	**850.00**
☐	Carolina Wrens	**4,350.00**
☐	Catbird	**1,400.00**
☐	Crested Flycatcher	**1,800.00**
☐	Downy Woodpecker	**1,100.00**

☐	Fledgling Blue Jay	120.00
☐	Fledgling Canada Warbler	1,200.00
☐	Fledgling Goldfinch	140.00
☐	Fledgling Magpie	550.00
☐	Fledgling Red Poll	130.00
☐	Green Jays	3,600.00
☐	Lazuli Bunting Paperweight	100.00
☐	Mourning Doves	3,750.00
☐	Nuthatch	200.00
☐	Oven-Bird	1,100
☐	Parula Warbler	2,000.00
☐	Polo Player	3,000.00
☐	Prothonotary Warblers	350.00
☐	Road Runner	3,500.00
☐	Rufous Hummingbirds	1,500.00
☐	Scottish Terrier	400.00
☐	Standing Poodle, *apricot-colored*	1,200.00
☐	Thoroughbred and Exercise Boy, *decorated*	5,500.00
☐	Towhee	1,600.00
☐	Tufted Titmice	900.00
☐	Varied Buntings	3,800.00
☐	Whippets	2,700.00

Current items range all the way from an $18 cup and saucer to a $35,000 Prince Rudolph's Blue Bird of Paradise.

BRIAN POTTERY COMPANY

Brian was founded in 1898 by Richard, James and George Brian. They manufactured sanitary items.

Marks: *Not known*
Prices: A miniature three-piece bathroom set by this company would be valued at a minimum of $50.

BROOME

Isaac Broome, who is perhaps best known for his work at the Ott & Brewer pottery, at one point went out on his own for a brief time c. 1880. The items made while on his own were primarily small vases.

Marks: Mark A is the one used on the items he made on his own. Marks B and C are more likely to appear on items he did for other companies. All three marks are incised. A European modeller named Tebo used a mark similar to mark A, and the two should not be confused.

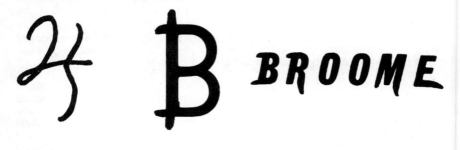

Prices: No known recent sales for items made by Broome while on his own. Our estimate wuld be a minimum of $1,000 for any perfect, signed specimen. (Note: See the other companies where Broome worked for additional listings on Broome items.)

BLOOR, OTT & BOOTH
See Ott & Brewer.

BURGESS & CAMPBELL
See International Pottery.

BURROUGHS & MOUNTFORD COMPANY
Burroughs & Mountford is somewhat more interesting than many of the other Trenton companies making similar wares, for B&M apparently paid a little more attention to the fine details of manufacturing and decorating.

The company was founded in 1879 in what had formerly been the Eagle Pottery. Wares included the usual assortment of granite and cream-colored wares, and they also made a limited amount of porcelain, little of which is seen today. They employed a Japanese artist who did gold paste work for them. Tiles with both printed and embossed designs were also produced at B&M.

Marks: All of the marks shown were used on various types of decorated cream-colored and granite ware items. It is not known which of these marks was used on their porcelain and tiles.

☐ Pitcher, *6-1/4" to top of spout, transfer decoration with hand-coloring and sponged gold, mark B, (see photo)* **75.00**
☐ Pot, *chocolate, 10" high, decoration similar to above, mark C* **75.00**
Note: Nearly all B&M items suffer from crazing of the glaze, and this is generally not held against them where price is concerned.

Pitcher, *hand-colored, 6-1/2"*

Lower-level Burroughs & Mountford items can be estimated as follows:

☐ Bowls, *dessert or soup* **5.00** **10.00**
☐ Bowls, *serving size* **10.00** **20.00**
☐ Cups and saucers **5.00** **10.00**
☐ Dinner plates **5.00** **10.00**
☐ Mugs.. **5.00** **25.00**
☐ Platters, *depending on size* **10.00** **30.00**
☐ Smaller plates **2.00** **5.00**

C. B. WALTON COMPANY
This company was founded in 1900 by C. B. Walton for the manufacture of sanitary items.
Marks: *Not known*
Prices: A three-piece miniature bathroom set would be estimated at a minimum of $50. If this company made any other wares, compare them against comparable products from other companies.

CERAMIC ART COMPANY
See Lenox.

CITY POTTERY
The City Pottery was formed by Rhodes & Yates in 1859 in the old Hattersley Pottery. Although they were primarily concerned with making cream-colored wares and white granite, they were known to have also made some parian and to have done some applied flower work. The name City

Pottery did not appear until 1875 and prior to that time the company was known first as Rhodes & Yates, then as Yates & Titus, and finally as Yates, Bennett & Allan. They went out of business c. 1880.

Marks: As shown.
Prices: We have no known sales for City Pottery items, but considering its early founding date and closing date, anything by them should have a premium on it. Compare their cream-colored and other lower-type wares to similar Ott & Brewer products. Their parian and applied flower pieces would probably rate a little lower than Ott & Brewer's. If they made anything for the Centennial, it is probably worth a minimum of $75.

CLARK & CARR
See International Pottery.

COALPORT WORKS
See John Maddock & Sons.

COCHRAN-DRUGAN SANITARY MANUFACTURING COMPANY
This company was founded in 1907 by E. C. Hutchinson, Andrew Cochran, and Samuel Drugan. They manufactured sanitary items.

Marks: *Not known*
Prices: A three-piece miniature bathroom set would be worth a minimum of $50. Compare anything else they made against similar items listed under other companies. Since this company came along rather late, there should be no premium on any of their products.

COLUMBIAN ART POTTERY
Columbian Art Pottery was founded late in 1892 by Morris and Willmore, and was so named for the Chicago World's Columbian Exposition at that time. Although they did make some opaque wares, they are best known for their very fine Belleek-type items. The company is usually referred to as Morris & Willmore rather than as Columbian Art Pottery.

Perhaps their most famous item is the Belleek Liberty Bell shown on the next page. Other items include a nice assortment of transfer-decorated mugs and tankards which are touched up by hand and which have hand-painted shaded backgrounds.

Marks: Mark A appears usually on Belleek-type items regardless of type of decoration. Mark B is usually found on opaque type items regardless of type of decoration. Exceptions occur.

Mark A

COLUMBIAN
TRENTON
N. J.
ART POTTERY

Mark B

☐ Creamer, *gold paste trim, mark A*................................. **150.00**
☐ Liberty Bell, *transfer cobalt decoration, Mark A*.................. **225.00**
**Note: The lettering on Liberty Bell varies considerably, and the $225
price is for one with clear lettering. An unreadable one would be
worth about $25 less.**

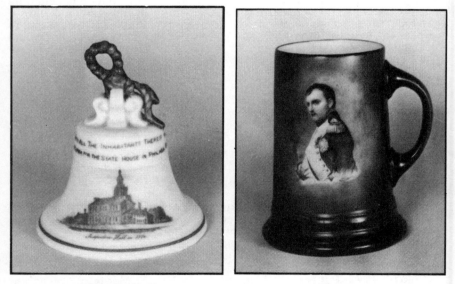

Liberty Bell   **Mug**

☐ Mug, *5-1/2" high, transfer decoration of Napoleon, mark A* **70.00**
☐ Plate, *opaque, transfer decorated with red cross-hatching, mark B* .. **5.00**
**Note: Their opaque items are usually unattractive and are primarily
purchased for the backstamp rather than for the item. Most of the
Columbian items of this type can be compared against Table X.**

COOK & HANCOCK
See Crescent Pottery.

COOK POTTERY COMPANY

Following the demise of the Ott & Brewer Company, the Cook Pottery Company was formed February 14, 1894, to manufacture china on that site. Products included semi-vitreous ware, porcelain dinnerware, Belleek-type items, and Delft-type items.

The Cook Delft was marked with a backstamp similar to that of The Porcelain Bottle, a noted Dutch company. Production of the Delft began c. 1897 and continued for an unknown number of years. The Cook glaze contained no tin as would be found in original Delft glazes, but other than this the Cook items were excellent reproductions.

Cook Belleek is extremely rare, and production of it probably did not last for very long. It is possible that Cook inherited O&B molds as well as the building.

Perhaps the best known Cook item is their Admiral Dewey pitcher, which commemorated Dewey's victory at Manila in 1899.

Marks: Marks include variations on the British coat of arms, with the words Mellor & Co. underneath. The name of Mellor, who was vice-president of Cook, was used to avoid confusion with Cook & Hancock items. A four-leaf clover mark, again with the name Mellor & Co., was used on semi-vitreous wares. Marks A and B were used on porcelain dinnerwares. Marks A and C were used on Belleek items. Mark D, a copy of the mark of The Porcelain Bottle, was used on Delft items. Mark E is found on the Admiral Dewey pitcher. Variations of all the marks are seen, and frequently the Mellor & Co. will be replaced by "C.H.C." and the word Belleek.

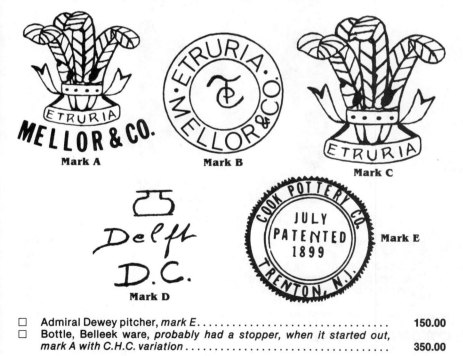

Mark A   Mark B   Mark C

Mark D   Mark E

☐	Admiral Dewey pitcher, *mark E*..	150.00
☐	Bottle, Belleek ware, *probably had a stopper, when it started out, mark A with C.H.C. variation*..	350.00

☐ Delft pitcher, *tall and narrow, polychromatic decoration, backstamp is a variation of mark D, Paul Gasper's initials on bottom* **25.00**
Note that even though the Delft piece sold for only $25 that the current owner would not sell it for 12 times $25. This is the perfect example of underpricing on items so rare that nobody appreciates them for what they are.

CORDEY

Cordey is frequently (and erroneously) referred to as "early Cybis". The company was in existence before Cybis came to Trenton and is still very much alive in the same location. The company was founded in the 1930's as Arton Studio by Harry Greenberg of Philadelphia, and is located in a building which may be the old Enterprise Pottery.

Greenberg met Cybis at the New York World's Fair, where Cybis was working in the Polish Pavilion. Cybis came to Trenton to work at Cordey, where he designed many of the items being collected today.

The company is now officially Schiller/Cordey, Inc., and is a part of Instrument Systems Corporation, which is a division of Litron Corporation. They are primarily engaged in making table lamps.

Marks: The word Cordey, either impressed or written in gold.

Bust of woman

☐ Bust of woman, *16" high* **125.00**
☐ Figurine of lamb, *8" high* **25.00**
☐ Figurine of woman, *14" high* **125.00**
☐ Figurines, man and woman, *11" high, pair* **60.00**
☐ Figurines, man and woman, *8" high, pair* **60.00**
☐ Figurines, man and woman, *14" high, pair* **150.00**
☐ Wall plaque, *12", woman in center* **45.00**

COXON & COMPANY

Coxon & Company was founded in 1863 as Coxon & Thompson, and they produced cream-colored and granite wares. The founders were Charles

Coxon and J. F. Thompson. At some point Coxon acquired Thompson's interest in the company and re-named it Coxon & Co. After Charles Coxon died in 1868, the company was run by his wife and sons. S. M. Alpaugh and J. G. Forman helped the Coxon family run the pottery, and in 1884 Alpaugh & Magowan acquired the company, which was merged into the Trenton Pottery Company.

Marks: The one shown is the only known mark for Coxon & Company, although there must have been at least one other mark when the company was Coxon & Thompson.

☐ Centennial cup and saucer, *transfer decoration of the U.S. exhibition, rivals the Anchor Pottery vase as being the ugliest piece of Trenton china, very heavy and unattractive* **90.00**

Items by Coxon & Company are very rare, and they are also vital to a collection of Trenton items. Expect to pay a minimum of $25 for any item by them.

COXON & THOMPSON
See Coxon & Company.

CRESCENT POTTERY
The Crescent Pottery manufactured cream-colored wares and sanitary specialties. The company was established in 1881 by Charles Howell Cook and William S. Hancock. In 1892, they were consolidated with four other companies into the Trenton Potteries Company.

Marks: At least 13 different marks were used by Crescent, most of which incorporated either the word Crescent or the names of the founders, Cook & Hancock.

Prices: The following prices are estimates:

☐ Bowls, *serving*	10.00	20.00
☐ Bowls, *soup or dessert*		5.00
☐ Cups and saucers	5.00	10.00
☐ Dinner plates	5.00	10.00
☐ Mugs...	5.00	25.00
☐ Platters, *depending on size*	10.00	30.00
☐ Smaller plates	2.00	5.00
☐ Three-piece minature bathroom set		50.00

CROWN PORCELAIN WORKS
In 1890 partners by the names of Barlow and Marsh started the Crown Porcelain Works to make faience.

Marks: *Not known*
Prices: We are not familiar with this company's products. Compare their wares to other similar items in this book.

CYBIS PORCELAIN
Cybis was started by Polish-born Boleslaw Cybis and his wife Marja after he left Cordey. They specialize in a wide range of sculptures. The company is too new to be covered in depth here.

DALE & DAVIS
See Prospect Hill Pottery for first partnership by this name. In 1892 James J. Dale and Thomas Davis manufactured sanitary wares under the Dale & Davis name.

Prices: A three-piece minature bathroom set by this company would be worth $50 or more. All other wares they might have made should be rated against comparable items elsewhere.

DELAWARE POTTERY
A group consisting of Mr. Oliphant, his three sons, Mr. Charles Fay, and Mr. Thomas Connelly (formerly of the Irish Belleek Company) got together in 1884 and formed Oliphant & Company for the purpose of operating the Delaware Pottery.

The company experimented with a Belleek-type formula around 1886 and supposedly produced an exceptionally high-quality china. The ware was never manufactured on anything other than an experimental basis, however, and we have not seen any samples. Other products included sanitary items and druggists' supplies. Delaware was merged into the Trenton Potteries Company in 1892.

Marks: The mark shown here can be either impressed or printed. Variations of the mark occur.

Prices: Belleek-type items (you should be so lucky as to ever fine one!) — compare to Ott & Brewer prices.

All other wares — compare to similar items elsewhere.

DOWNS POTTERY
We have no first-hand information about this pottery but have been informed that they operated during the 1930's. The one sample at hand is a 6" vase, very attractive in form, and decorated with a lovely blue glaze. Right now things by Downs are still inexpensive, but considering how rare they are and how attractive, we would expect to see sharp increases in value shortly.

Marks: "Downs Pottery" incised in the bottom.

☐   Vase, *as described above* **20.00**

DUGAN'S POTTERY
Dugan is possibly a misspelling of Drugan (see Cochran-Drugan), and the only information we have about "Dugan" is that the building burned to the ground, was rebuilt, and then burned again.

Marks: *Not known*
Prices: Since we don't know what they made, we really can't be of much help with prices.

EAGLE POTTERY
Eagle was founded in 1876 by Richard Millington, and at a later date, the pottery's officers included: John B. Riley, President; J. W. Foster, Secretary/Treasurer; and Elijah Mountford, General Manager. The pottery eventually had four biscuit kilns and four glost kilns and employed 250 people. First Burroughs & Mountford in 1879 and eventually Cook Pottery took over the building.

Marks: *Not known*
Prices: Their products are unknown to us; compare against similar items appearing elsewhere in this book.

EAST TRENTON POTTERY COMPANY
East Trenton Pottery produced white granite ware, and was founded in 1888. Their most interesting items had the pictures of Presidential candidates printed on them.

Marks: Presidential campaign items were marked with the New Jersey state seal and the initials "E.T.P.Co." White granite was marked with the British coat of arms with the company's initials underneath. Variations occur.
Prices: The following prices are estimates.

☐ Bowls, *serving*	10.00	20.00
☐ Bowls, *soup or dessert*	5.00	6.00
☐ Cups and saucers	5.00	10.00
☐ Dinner plates	5.00	10.00
☐ Mugs..	5.00	25.00
☐ Platters, *depending on size*	10.00	30.00
☐ Presidential campaign items, *a minimum of*		50.00
☐ Smaller plates	2.00	5.00

ECONOMY POTTERY COMPANY
Economy was founded in 1900 by William H. Bradbury for the production of sanitary wares.

Marks: *Not known*
Prices: A three-piece miniature bathroom set by this company can be valued at a minimum of $50. All other items they might have made can be rated against comparable items appearing elsewhere.

EGYPTIAN POTTERY
Egyptian was founded in 1891 by Charles H. Baker and Cornelius Turford for the production of sanitary items.

Marks: *Not known*
Prices: A three-piece miniature bathroom set by this company can be estimated at no less than $50. Any other items can be compared to similar items appearing elsewhere in this book.

ELI POTTERY
No information available, unless Eli is a shortened version of Elite, q.v.

Marks: *Not known*
Prices: If a pottery by this name did indeed exist, compare their items to similar ones elsewhere in this book.

ELITE POTTERY
Elite was founded in 1901 by G. W. Page, Samuel Bedson, and Louis J. Deihl for the production of sanitary wares.

Marks: *Not known*
Prices: A three-piece miniature bathroom set by this company is worth no less than $50. All other wares they might have produced can be compared to similar items elsewhere in this book.

EMPIRE POTTERY
When the Coxon family gave up the Coxon & Co. pottery, it was taken over by Alpaugh & Magowan, who renamed it as the Empire Pottery. Later the company ownership passed to Wood & Barlow and eventually it became part of the Trenton Potteries Company. Wares included granite ware, sanitary items, and (supposedly) a very fine grade of porcelain.

Marks: The first mark was the British coat of arms with the words Empire Pottery above and the initials A&M below. During the Wood & Barlow period the term "Imperial China" was used, and the last mark was a wreath with the word "Empire" above, "Trenton, N.J." below, and the initials TPCO intertwined inside a wreath.
Prices: The following prices are estimates.
Porcelain items — compare to similar items elsewhere in this book.

☐ Miniature bathroom set, *three pieces, no less than*		**50.00**

Granite ware can be estimated as follows:

☐ Bowls, *serving*	**10.00**	**20.00**
☐ Bowls, *soup or dessert size*	**5.00**	**6.00**
☐ Cups and saucers	**5.00**	**10.00**
☐ Dinner plates	**5.00**	**10.00**
☐ Mugs...	**5.00**	**25.00**
☐ Platters, *depending on size*	**10.00**	**30.00**
☐ Smaller plates	**2.00**	**5.00**

ENTERPRISE POTTERY COMPANY
Enterprise was founded c. 1879 by W. H. Umpleby, John Brian, and Charles H. Skirm. General Oliphant was also connected to the company. The company made sanitary items and later became part of the Trenton Potteries Company.

Enterprise Pottery Co

Mark: *Only one known mark*
Prices: A three-piece miniature bathroom set is worth no less than $50. Anything else they might have made can be compared to similar items appearing elsewhere in this book.

EQUITABLE POTTERY COMPANY
Equitable was founded in 1888 by Andrew Cochran, John Leukel, and Jonathan Coxon. They made sanitary wares and later became part of the Trenton Potteries Company.

Marks: *Not known*
Prices: A three-piece miniature bathroom set by Equitable is worth no less than $50. All other items should be rated against similar items elsewhere in this book.

ETRURIA POTTERY
See Ott & Brewer and Cook Pottery.

EXCELSIOR POTTERY COMPANY
Excelsior was founded in 1905 by G. W. Page and William Cook. They made sanitary wares.

Marks: *Not known*
Prices: A three-piece miniature bathroom set by Excelsior should be worth no less than $50. All other items can be compared to similar items elsewhere in this book.

EXCELSIOR POTTERY WORKS
See William Young & Sons.

FAIRFACTS COMPANY
Fairfacts manufactured bath accessories. After they went out of business Bay Ridge bought their machines and designs and Star bought the building.

Marks: *Not known*
Prices: A soap dish or similar item should probably be worth no less than $5.

FELL & THROPP COMPANY
Samuel E. Thropp and J. Hart Brewer were co-owners of the Fell & Thropp Company c. 1889-1892. The company, which was located in the old Taylor & Speeler pottery, manufactured white granite and cream-colored wares. They made sanitary wares 1892-1894 when the company was under Robert Gruessner.

Marks: Marks include both the New Jersey and the British coats of arms as well as a circular mark with a cougar's head inside of it. All three marks have the initials "F&T" with them.
Prices: White granite items are estimated as follows:

☐ Bowls, *serving*	10.00	20.00
☐ Bowls, *soup or dessert*	5.00	7.00
☐ Cups and saucers	5.00	10.00

☐	Dinner plates	**5.00**	**10.00**
☐	Mugs..	**5.00**	**25.00**
☐	Platters, *depending on size*........................	**10.00**	**30.00**
☐	Smaller plates	**2.00**	**5.00**

FIDELITY POTTERY COMPANY

Charles H. Baker and J. Harris Cogill founded Fidelity in 1902 to manufacture sanitary items.

Marks: *Not known*
Prices: $50 for a miniature bathroom set. Since the company came along rather late, anything else they might have made would be of minimal value, less than comparable earlier items.

FORTUNE COMPANY

Manufacturers of bath accessories.

Marks: *Not known*
Prices: $3 and up for any item by this company.

FULPER POTTERY

Fulper was founded in Flemington, NJ, in 1805, and is mentioned here only because in 1926 they took over the old Anchor Pottery in Trenton and operated there for some time, both under the Fulper name and later under the Stangl name. Both companies will be covered at greater length in future volumes.

GENERAL PORCELAIN

This company is located on Pennsylvania Avenue in Trenton, and was founded in 1939 by Stephen J. Judnak and Joseph Przechacki. Products include porcelain forms for the rubber industry and lamp bases. Their Just-Rite subsidiary makes bathroom accessories.

Marks: *Not known*
Prices: $5 and up.

GLASGOW POTTERY

The Glasgow Pottery was founded in 1863 by Mr. John Moses and the company engaged in the manufacture of white granite, semi-porcelain, opaque wares, ironstone and cream-colored items. Other names for the pottery included John Moses & Company and John Moses & Sons Company.

Marks: Numerous marks, including those shown.

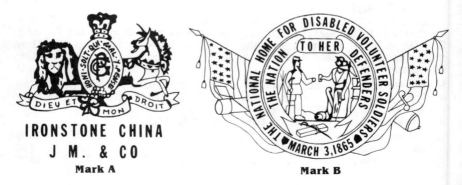

IRONSTONE CHINA
J M. & CO
Mark A

Mark B

U.S.M.C.
Mark C

Q.M.D.
Mark D

Mark E

TRILBY
J.M.&S.CO.
TRENTON, N.J.
Mark F

SAPPHO
J.M.&S. CO.
Mark G

Mark I

GLASGOW CHINA
VITRIFIED
TRENTON, N.J.
Mark H

GLASGOW POTTERY
— CO. —
TRENTON
N. J.
Mark J

Prices: The only actual sale we have for a Glasgow item is $20 for a berry dish decorated with the inscription "Martha Washington Tea Party, Millville, N.J., Feb. 22, 1874". In the center of the bowl is a circle with "1776 - Centennial - 1876". Although there is no backstamp, Glasgow is known to have created this set of china. The little dish is quite the worse for wear since both the lettering and the gold trim on the rim are worn.

Since Glasgow was a very early company, prices for most of their wares will be higher than for other similar wares. Following are estimates:

☐	Bowls, *dessert or soup*	15.00	20.00
☐	Bowls, *serving*	25.00	50.00
☐	Cups and saucers	20.00	25.00
☐	Dinner plates	10.00	15.00
☐	Mugs	5.00	15.00
☐	Platters, *depending on size*	50.00	75.00
☐	Smaller plates	5.00	10.00

GLOBE
Manufacturers of bath accessories.

Marks: *Not known*
Prices: $5 for a sample item.

GREENWOOD ART POTTERY COMPANY
See Greenwood Pottery Company.

GREENWOOD POTTERY COMPANY
In 1861, James Tams and James P. Stephens organized Stephens, Tams, & Company. In 1868, the company was incorporated under the name of Greenwood Pottery Company, with Tams as its president and Stephens as secretary/treasurer. The company made white granite ware, stone china, vitrified and translucent china, and a wide assortment of electrical and hardware items.

Greenwood also made a fine porcelain art line, typically decorated in the Royal Worcester style, which is very rare today. The names of those who developed this line and the artists who decorated them are not known.

Mark A

GREENWOOD CHINA
TRENTON, N. J.
Mark B

G.P.
Co.

Mark C

N O. LA.
GREENWOOD

Mark D

GREENWOOD CHINA
M. GOLDBERG
CONEY ISLAND
N. Y.

Mark E

GREENWOOD CHINA
VICTORY
L BARTH & SON
NEW YORK
DESIGN PATENTED

Mark F

GREENWOOD
CHINA
I

Mark G

GREENWOOD CHINA

TRENTON, N. J.

Mark H

Marks: In addition to the marks shown there are countless others, usually incorporating the name or initials of the company in one fashion or another.

Belleek and Porcelain Items

Any of their finer wares can be rated at a hint less than the comparable Ott & Brewer items. Although these items are very rare, the demand for them is not quite as great as for the Ott & Brewer.

Ironstone and Other Lower-Level Wares

☐ Bowl, *round, 9" diameter, plain white*	15.00
☐ Bowl, *round, 10" diameter, green banding*	15.00
☐ Bowl, *round, 6" diameter, cereal size, hotel insignia*	5.00
☐ Bowl, *round, 6" diameter, cereal size, undecorated*...............	2.00
☐ Bowl, *round, 6" diameter, cereal size, gold trim*	2.00
☐ Bowl, *round, 5" diameter, military insignia*	3.00
☐ Bowl, *round, 4" diameter, undecorated*...........................	2.00
☐ Butter pat, *undecorated*	1.00
☐ Cup and saucer, *undecorated*..................................	4.00
☐ Cup and saucer, *cobalt blue banding on both pieces*	5.00

☐ Cup and saucer, *hotel insignia* **6.00**
☐ Cup and saucer, *after dinner size, undecorated, very cute shape* **9.00**
☐ Cup and saucer, *full size, undecorated* **5.00**
☐ Cup and saucer, *West Point Military Academy insignia* **20.00**

Jar, *women's head handles, cobalt blue trim*

☐ Cup and saucer, *Blue Onion trim* **10.00**
☐ Jar, *women's head handles, cobalt blue trim, mark C* **35.00**
☐ Jar, *identical to above but undecorated and unmarked* **3.00**
☐ Plate, *10" diameter, undecorated* **3.00**
☐ Plate, *10" diameter, cobalt blue bands on border* **4.00**
☐ Plate, *10" diameter, Blue Onion pattern* **10.00**
☐ Plate, *10" diameter, hotel insignia on rim* **7.00**
☐ Plate, *9" diameter, undecorated* **3.00**
☐ Plate, *9" diameter, maroon trim* **3.00**
☐ Plate, *8" square, cobalt decoration, mark D variation* **70.00**
☐ Plate, *8" diameter, hotel crest* **3.00**
☐ Plate, *8" diameter, undecorated* **1.00**
☐ Plate, *6" diameter, hotel insignia* **2.00**
☐ Plate, *6" diameter, gold trim* **1.00**
☐ Plate, *6" diameter, green gadroon trim* **1.00**
☐ Plate, *5" diameter, blue floral design on rim* **1.00**
☐ Platter, *10" oval, undecorated* **15.00**
☐ Platter, *10" oval, maroon border* **20.00**
☐ Platter, *12" oval, undecorated* **25.00**
☐ Platter, *13" oval, undecorated* **25.00**
☐ Platter, *13" oval, hotel insignia* **30.00**

- ☐ Platter, *14" oval, hotel insignia* **32.00**
- ☐ Platter, *14" oval, green and black trim, hotel insignia in center, marks A and B* **35.00**
- ☐ Pot, *mustard, 3¼" high, undecorated, very cute* **15.00**
- ☐ Shell dishes, *undecorated, mark A, pair* **25.00**

HAMILTON DECORATING COMPANY

This very obscure Trenton decorating company did very competent work that equalled that done at the Lenox Company. The one sample we have at hand is a bouillon cup and saucer tastefully decorated with a banding of lime green and hand-painted pink roses. The gold trim is restrained and well done. Although we have no hard information about this company, if we had to take a guess, it would be that a former Lenox dinnerware decorator set up shop on his/her own.

Marks: "Decorated by Hamilton Decorating Co., Trenton, NJ" in reddish-brown.

Prices: The above-mentioned cup and saucer was priced at about $15 which is probably a little low for such a scarce item.

HARRIS MANUFACTURING COMPANY

See Trent Tile.

HART BREWER POTTERY COMPANY

In 1895, John Hart Brewer and Henry D. Phillips took over the Fell & Thropp operation. The company manufactured sanitary specialties.

Marks: *Not known*

Prices: Since John Hart Brewer was associated with this company, their items would have perhaps a greater interest than other similar wares. A three-piece miniature bathroom set by this company would perhpas be valued at around $100 instead of the usual $50.

HATTERSLEY POTTERY

The name Hattersley Pottery probably refers to a building rather than a company, and it is doubtful that a company by that name existed. Charles Hattersley erected the building in 1852 and possibly ran a company by that name for a short while. William Young & Sons were tenants in the building, as were the City Pottery and Maddock & Company. The building was located on Perry Street.

I. DAVIS

See Prospect Hill Pottery.

IDEAL POTTERY

See Trenton Potteries Company.

IMPERIAL PORCELAIN WORKS

No information available.

INTERNATIONAL POTTERY COMPANY

International was founded in 1860 by Henry Speeler. In 1868 his two sons entered the firm and the name was changed to Speeler & Sons. The business was purchased by Edward Clark and James Carr, who renamed it as the Lincoln Pottery Company, or as Carr & Clark. Burgess & Campbell were the next to own the property.

The name International probably refers to the building itself rather than to a company. One of the owners did use the name International as a backstamp, however.

Products included semi-porcelain and white granite ware.

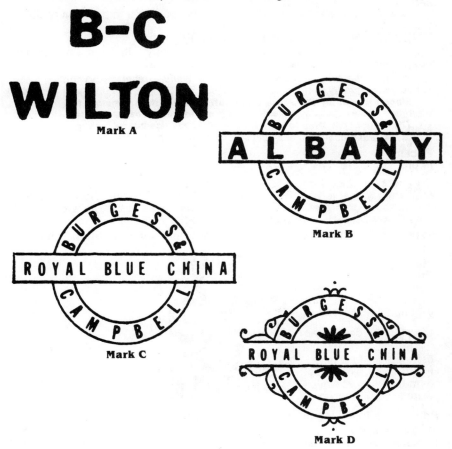

Mark A

Mark B

Mark C

Mark D

Marks: Backstamps include those shown plus many others. Most of the marks use either the initials "B&C" (for Burgess & Campbell) or "I.P.Co." (for International Pottery Company.)

Prices: The following listings are estimates.

☐	Bowls, *serving*	10.00	20.00
☐	Bowls, *soup or dessert*	5.00	6.00
☐	Cups and saucers	5.00	10.00
☐	Dinner plates	5.00	10.00
☐	Mugs	5.00	25.00
☐	Platters, *depending on size*	10.00	30.00
☐	Smaller plates	2.00	5.00

INTERSTATE POTTERY COMPANY

This sanitary ware company was founded in 1909 by Frank E. Weeden, Benjamin Walton, Jr., and Charles C. Hill.

Marks: *Not known*

Prices: A three-piece miniature bathroom set would be in the area of $50.

JESSE DEAN DECORATING COMPANY

The name of this Trenton decorating company will sometimes appear along with that of the manufacturers of the china.

☐ Plate, *9" diameter, transfer decoration of William Jennings Bryant, very poor quality work* **10.00**

Since samples by the Jesse Dean outfit are not that common, this figure is low especially considering it is a Presidential campaign item. The thought occurred to us to tamper with the price but we managed to restrain ourselves. We would estimate its worth at more like $25 to $40.

JOHN MADDOCK & SONS, INC.

John Maddock & Sons was founded in 1894 or 1895 to make earthenware and sanitary specialties. They operated out of the Coalport Works. The company was incorporated in 1905. John Maddock was in charge, aided by his sons (Thomas, A.H., W.B., and H.E. Maddock.)

Marks: Backstamps include the one shown and some variations on it.

Prices: The following prices are estimates.

☐ Bowls, *serving*	10.00	20.00
☐ Bowls, *soup or dessert*	5.00	6.00
☐ Cups and saucers	5.00	10.00
☐ Dinner plates	5.00	10.00
☐ Mugs	5.00	25.00
☐ Platters, *depending on size*	10.00	30.00
☐ Smaller plates	2.00	5.00

JOHN MOSES & COMPANY

See Glasgow Pottery.

JOHN MOSES & SONS COMPANY

See Glasgow Pottery.

JUST-RITE

See General Porcelain.

KEYSTONE POTTERY COMPANY

Keystone made vitreous china and sanitary specialties beginning c. 1892. Company officers included James H. Lyons, J. W. Lyons, Joseph Umpleby, and John Brian.

Marks: A keystone within a wreath
Prices: The following prices are estimates.

☐	Bowls, *serving*	10.00	20.00
☐	Bowls, *soup or dessert*	5.00	6.00
☐	Cups and saucers	5.00	10.00
☐	Dinner plates	5.00	10.00
☐	Mugs	5.00	25.00
☐	Platters, *depending on size*	10.00	30.00
☐	Smaller plates	2.00	5.00
☐	Three-piece miniature bathroom set		50.00

LAMBERTON WORKS

Site of John Maddock & Sons and later of Scammell China.

LENOX

Lenox China was founded on May 18, 1889, by Jonathan Coxon, Sr., and Walter Scott Lenox, who had met when both were employed at Ott & Brewer. The original name of the new company was the Ceramic Art Company, and Coxon was its president with Lenox as secretary/treasurer and art director.

The partnership did not last long, due both to personality conflicts and to disputes over company management. Most sources give us 1894 as the date when the partnership was dissolved, but the *State Gazette* of August 31, 1916, states that Coxon was associated with C.A.C. for seven years, which would make 1896 the date of departure.

The early years were lean ones for the young company, and it was only with great difficulty that the original loan of $4,000 from William Hancock was repaid. We quote from *The Story of Walter Scott Lenox:* "The flame of a zealot glowed in the heart of Lenox. Not so in the hearts of some of his backers, who stipulated that the factory he erected at the corner of Meade and Prince Streets in Trenton should be so constructed as to be converted into a tenement should the pottery fail."

Company activities in the early years included production of both decorated and undecorated wares. By the end of the C.A.C. period, they were producing around 600 different shapes decorated both in standard and original fashion. The emphasis was on giftware instead of dinnerware, and many of the more interesting Lenox collectibles date from this time.

With the formation of Lenox, Inc., in 1906, the company started taking more direction. Dinnerware production was expanded greatly and hand-painting, although it would continue for another half-century, started taking a back seat to more and more transfer decoration. World War I perhaps gave the company the chance it had been waiting for, since foreign-made china became impossible to obtain. President Wilson's order of Lenox for the White House helped to establish their fine reputation for dinnerware. The Lenox shapes and designs took on a look of their own rather than being copies of European items, and the Lenox Company was among the first to bring a 20th-century look to porcelain.

By the time of World War II, the company had produced more than 3,000 different shapes decorated with any of thousands of different designs. During the war, the Lenoxite Division was started to produce steatite as a radio-radar ceramic insulating material. The same product was used to make cylinders for the manufacture of penicillin. The standard Lenox porcelain was used to make marine dials for Navy vessels.

Since World War II, the company has added crystal, bone china, and oven-proof ware to their list. The china is now made in Pomona, NJ, and new corporate headquarters were recently opened in Lawrenceville, NJ. The Lenox corporate umbrella now covers a diversified group of companies making everything from school rings to candles.

MARKINGS ON LENOX CHINA

The various marks used on Lenox china down through the years can cause considerable confusion for both beginning and advanced collectors, and these marks are frequently the subject for debate (not always polite) among them. It is possible to garner a wealth of information concerning a particular item by examining the sometimes cryptic little marks on the back or bottom. This information might include any or all of the following:

(I) Approximate date of manufacture (from design and/or color of backstamp);

(2) Shape number (very important if a collector is trying to assemble, perhaps, a set of cups and saucers);

(3) Pattern number (vital to matching old china);

(4) The store that retailed the item (can occasionally be interesting);

(5) Whether an item was decorated at the factory or elsewhere (often the deciding factor in purchasing an item);

(6) The name of any other company that was involved in making an item (for example, the name of a silver company that did overlay work, or the name of a decorating studio).

As we proceed with this discussion of the marking system, we have made the assumption that the marks do indeed mean something, and were not put on in some slaphappy fashion, and that each new mark was introduced to indicate either a particular type of item or a change in the company's status. Although this assumption may appear self-evident to some readers, we found it necessary to keep reminding ourselves of it as we delved into the marking system, particularly the backstamps.

Although we will introduce information on markings which to the best of our knowledge cannot be found elsewhere, we will also be adding to the general confusion concerning Lenox because what was previously considered a fairly cut and dried area becomes a tangle of contradictions and inconsistencies.

We will try to be as specific as possible regarding sources for our information, items used as examples, etc., and hope that as more samples come to light some of the problem areas can be cleared up.

Although the beginning collector may find this section moderately uninteresting, he/she will no doubt profit the most from this information. Since beginners lack the experience to buy wisely based on other considerations, the various markings can be of great importance to them. The advanced collector, on the other hand, really only uses the marks to verify initial impressions of an item.

RETAIL STORE NAMES

Many Lenox items will bear the mark of the retail outlet which sold it. No particular importance should be attached to these marks except in the case where the information can be used to help date an item. For example, if a Lenox green wreath mark item should carry the name of a store that went out of business in 1908, we can accurately date the item from 1906 to 1908. In addition, a store name on a hand-painted item generally can be taken as an indication that the item was factory-decorated.

There is some dispute over which store mark was the earliest, and we feel this distinction belongs to Bailey, Banks & Biddle in Philadelphia or Davis Collamore & Co. of New York City. Both store names have appeared on red C.A.C. palette mark items, which would mean they were certainly early customers. We have not seen any other store names with this mark, although such items may exist, and base our conclusion on this fact.

The Tiffany Company, often thought of as the first store to order Lenox, apparently did not really begin their long association with Lenox until a little later. Ott & Brewer items have been seen with the Tiffany mark, and it is possible that they had an existing contract with O&B when C.A.C. was formed. Since O&B went out of business in 1893, it would be likely that the first Tiffany orders date from around that time. The Tiffany Company did have the distinction, however, of displaying the first complete set of Lenox dinnerware.

ITEM NUMBERS, PATTERN NUMBERS AND COLOR CODES

Item numbers (shape numbers) rarely if ever appear on C.A.C. items, perhaps because there was little need for them. The 1891 C.A.C. catalogue lists only 132 items, so it would have been fairly simple to keep them straight without actually putting a number on the bottom of an item. (In the catalogue they are, of course, numbered.) It was with the expansion of the company that it became necessary to begin marking the items with the appropriate number.

Item numbers can be impressed and/or handwritten, and in some cases do not appear on an item at all (even on later Lenox items). Once an item received a number, it kept that number throughout the entire time it was in production. When a shape was discontinued, no new item was matched up with that number.

When an item number is handwritten it is generally followed by a slash and then another number (e.g., 1830/P44.) The item number is always the first number, and any numbers appearing after the slash are always decorating (pattern) numbers. The above code would properly be interpreted as a shape 1830 dinner plate decorated with the pattern P44 etched gold banding. Those of you with a keen interest in decoding pattern numbers are referred to the dinnerware section where this information is discussed at greater length. We will mention, however, that those patterns with no letter in front of them (e.g., 70, 86-1/2, 338, etc.) were originally C.A.C. patterns even though they might have been in production for many years after the Lenox takeover.

A letter at the end of a shape and pattern designation refers to the color of the rim. For example, 1830/P44C would be the same shape 1830 dinner plate with the same P44 etched gold rim but with cobalt blue trim on the rim.

Body colors (the color actually in the china itself) are achieved by adding dyes to the liquid porcelain early in the production process. The Lenox body color codes are:

X- 9 Goeblin Blue	X-17 Dawn Blue	X-31 Ivory
X-10 Egyptian Blue	X-19 Primrose Yellow	X-34 Gray
X-11 Lenox Green	X-24 Ivory	X-39 Green
X-12 Gazelle	X-26 Ashes of Roses	X-40 Yellow
X-14 Sky Blue	X-27 Malachite Green	(Black came along at
X-15 Coral	X-28 Buff	a much later date as
X-16 Fawn	X-30 Celadon	a china body color.)

Overglaze groundlay colors are done by putting sizing on the area to be covered and then carefully dusting powdered dyes onto the space. When the china is fired the color fuses to the surface. (If a piece of overglaze groundlay is broken, the color will be only on the very edge, while a body color item will have the color throughout.) The groundlay color codes follow, but keep in mind that the codes were adopted by Lenox in 1918, and they only apply to patterns beginning with code letters R to Z, numbers 1 to 299, and on all patterns with numbers higher than 300. Those patterns designed prior to 1918 had individualized color designations. (For example, O-46F is pink, not turquoise gray.)

A. Ivory	J. Salmon	S. Leather Brown
B. Cobalt Blue	K. Brown	T. Night Green
C. Chinese Blue	L. Shading Green	V. Russian Green
D. Yellow	M. Turquoise Blue	W. Red
E. Pink	N. Ecru	X. Dark Green
F. Turquoise Grey	O. Violet	Y. Pearl Grey
G. Lettuce Green	P. Deep Plum	Z. Black
H. Old Rose	R. Maroon	

BACKSTAMPS

Several of the backstamps used by Lenox Company through the years are shown on the following two pages. Many of these marks can be found in more than one color, and there are variations on the shape as well. The table is in no particular order, and we have used letters instead of numbers to designate the marks, since we felt that giving a mark number 1 might establish an undue importance for that mark. These marks have in many cases been given nicknames by collectors, which will be listed below.

Mark A—written-out C.A.C.	Mark G—Indianhead
Mark B—written-out double	Mark H—transition mark
wreath C.A.C.	Mark I—L palette
Mark C—C.A.C. wreath	Mark J—L wreath
Mark D—script Lenox	Mark K—L porcelain
Mark E—metal mark	Mark L—L opaque
Mark F—C.A.C. palette	Mark M—gold wreath

Additional comments may be made to further describe a mark, such as "L" wreath, no U.S.A." or "C.A.C. lavender palette".

Although there are other Lenox marks, we have listed those most likely to be encountered by the collector or those marks which cause the most confusion. Some of the marks not shown in the table will be mentioned at the end of the backstamp section.

Minor variations of the marks shown do occur, and can include the lettering and/or the squiggles in the wreaths. The palette marks have been seen both with and without the circle extending through the palette.

All of the colors listed in the text can vary from pale to dark, and it can be difficult at times to distinguish light brown from gold, for example, or to tell the pinkish-red from light lavender.

Table I lists some comments about the various marks which have appeared in other publications. As becomes immediately obvious, there is quite a bit of conflict concerning when and why some of the marks were used. It is not our intent to prove that any of the other sources are right or wrong, but rather to add to and expand existing knowledge. Some of the marks are just too obscure for accurate conclusions, and in making our statements about these marks we wonder if we are like a Martian who lands in Yellowstone Park and declares that Earthlings are shaggy and ferocious.

In attempting to understand the backstamp situation, particularly in the early years, we rearranged Table I into a year-by-year account of the marks according to the other sources, and this appears here as **Table II.**

Table III lists backstamps by the factory artists whose names have appeared on items with certain marks. Since employment dates for some of the artists are questionable, we cannot use a particular artist's signature as proof positive concerning backstamps, but when taken with all the other available information they can certainly help establish possibilities.

Table IV shows the type of decoration which has appeared with the various backstamps, and although it was not a big help in piecing together the backstamp puzzle, we have included it as an aid to the beginner in assembling a collection. By sticking to those marks listed as factory decorated, the collector can be relatively certain of obtaining items which have at least an acceptable level of artistic merit. This, of course, means that they will be passing by some beautiful examples of hand-painting on palette mark items, but it is probably better to be safe than sorry. (The beginner can tell that he/she is no longer a beginner when he/she is able to walk past a transition mark Morley-signed item with a comment about how it is not the best sample of Morley's work.)

Table V is the Robinson/Feeny version of the dating for Lenox backstamps, based on the text which follows and relying heavily on assumptions and theories. Although our version may be no more correct than any of the others, we have tried to give a date and use for each mark. As we stated earlier, it is likely that each mark and the color variations within marks had a meaning at the time it was introduced. In the course of our investigation, we have made genuine pests of ourselves by going into friends' homes and turning over their china or by calling them at inconvenient times to ask which artist signed which item.

In spite of our efforts, we are still somewhat in the dark concerning some of the marks, and particularly about the color variations. For example, we are still unable to explain why some transition mark items have the mark in lavender and other times it will be green. As is possibly the case with all the marks, this may have been an internal factory code of some sort, relating perhaps to inventory or quality control.

It was previously reported in an article about Lenox steins that the color of the backstamp is coordinated with the color of the stein, but we have found this not to be true. Most of the steins are monochromatic brown, green, or blue, and since the backstamps in use at the time were the same colors, by happenstance you will find many blue steins with a blue backstamp. Identical steins can also be found, however, with other color backstamps, and we suppose the color coordination theory is another Yellowstone Park assumption.

Double-marked items are always interesting, and from them we can assume that the marks involved were in use at about the same time. They also tend to bear out our feeling that on occasion items were taken from the white ware pile to be decorated at the factory. (Double-marked items always seem to have a premium value on them.)

Palette-mark items with a known factory artist's signature on them do not necessarily prove that things were taken from the white ware pile for factory decoration, since so many of the artists are known to have decorated on their own time and a few actually set up shop as decorators.

Dated items can be a help in that we know what year a piece was decorated, but dates cannot tell us when an item was actually manufactured. Remember that an item could have been on a shelf for a long time before someone actually got around to painting on it, or that a date might be put on

TABLE I   Backstamps (According to Other Sources)

Mark	1891 Catalogue	Other Lenox Co.Sources	Mohr T.A.T. Article	Barber Book
Written-out C.A.C. (Mark A)	Not mentioned	Not mentioned	Gives date of 1891 for lavender color, indicates for special orders	No date given, lists as special decorative work for the trade
Written-out C.A.C. double wreath (Mark B)	Not mentioned	Not mentioned	Listed same as above	Listed as a special mark for decorators used in 1897
C.A.C. wreath (Mark C)	Not mentioned	Not mentioned	Not mentioned	Not mentioned
Script Lenox (Mark D)	Not mentioned	Not mentioned	Not mentioned	Not mentioned
Metal mark (Mark E)	Not mentioned	Not mentioned	Not mentioned	Not mentioned
C.A.C. palette (Mark F)	Shown on every page, no mention of color	Decorated ware 1889-1896, white ware 1889-1906, no mention of color	1894-1896 in lavender for factory decor.; 1897-1898 green or gold for undecorated; 1898-1906 black for undecorated	1893 part of book lists red from 1889 (see p. 413); later section lists lavender and other colors for undecorated ware but gives no dates.
Indianhead (Mark G)	Shown on every page, no mention of color	Not mentioned	Not mentioned	Undecorated ware prior to 1895
Transition (Mark H)	Not applicable	Decorated	1894-1896 in lavender; 1896-1906 green or gold; all decorated	Lists only as being on decorated ware, no mention of dates or colors.
L palette (Mark I)	Not applicable	1906-1924 for undecorated ware	1906-1924 green on undecorated ware	Not applicable
L wreath (Mark J)	Not applicable	Decorated stamp 1906-1924, for both decorated and undecorated 1924-1930. No mention of color. "Made in U.S.A." added in 1930	1906-1930 in green on factory decorated ware "Made in U.S.A." added in 1931.	Not applicable
L Porcelain (Mark K)	Not applicable	Not mentioned	Circa 1930 in black, rare mark used on specialty items and lamps	Not applicable
L opaque (Mark L)	Not applicable	Not mentioned	Not mentioned	Not applicable
Gold wreath (Mark M)	Not applicable	Not mentioned specifically by color	1953, all factory decor.	Not applicable

TABLE II
Backstamps by Year
of Possible Use
(According to Other Sources)

1889 — C.A.C. palette mark, Indianhead mark
1890 — C.A.C. palette mark, Indianhead mark
1891 — C.A.C. palette mark, Indianhead mark, both written-out marks
1892 — C.A.C. palette mark, Indianhead mark, both written-out marks
1893 — C.A.C. palette mark, Indianhead mark, both written-out marks
1894 — C.A.C. palette mark, Indianhead mark, transition mark, both written-out marks
1895 — C.A.C. palette mark, Indianhead mark, transition mark, both written-out marks
1896 — C.A.C. palette mark, transition mark, both written-out marks
1897 — C.A.C. palette mark, transition mark, both written-out marks
1898 — C.A.C. palette mark, transition mark, both written-out marks
1899 — C.A.C. palette mark, transition mark, both written-out marks
1900 — C.A.C. palette mark, transition mark, both written-out marks
1901 — C.A.C. palette mark, transition mark, both written-out marks
1902 — C.A.C. palette mark, transition mark, both written-out marks
1903 — C.A.C. palette mark, transition mark, both written-out marks
1904 — C.A.C. palette mark, transition mark, both written-out marks
1905 — C.A.C. palette mark, transition mark, both written-out marks
1906 — phase-out of C.A.C. palette, start of L palette, phase-out of transition mark, start L wreath mark, phase-out of written-out marks (apparently not replaced by another mark)
1906 to 1924 — L palette and L wreath
1924 — L wreath only
1930 — "Made in U.S.A." added to L wreath mark
1930's and 1940's — L wreath/Made in U.S.A., L opaque and L porcelain
1947 — unnecessary lines removed from wreath to make clearer and more modern
1953 — gold wreath, used to present day

TABLE III
Backstamps/Factory
Artist Comparison

Baker—Lenox wreath
Boullemier—transition mark
Boullimer/Bullimer—no known signed samples
Campana—transition mark, L palette
Clayton—transition mark
DeLan—C.A.C. wreath, transition, L palette
Fauji—no known signed samples
Fenzel—L wreath
Geyer—transition
Heidrich—C.A.C. wreath
Hicks—uncertain
Kuhn—transition mark
Laurence—C.A.C. wreath
Lenox—no known signed samples
Marsh—transition mark, L palette
Martell—transition
Mayer—no known signed samples
Morley (George)—transition, Lenox wreath, Lenox wreath/U.S.A.
Morley (William)—transition, Lenox wreath, Lenox wreath/U.S.A.
Naylor—no known signed samples
Nosek—transition mark, L wreath, L wreath/U.S.A., gold wreath
Sully—transition mark
Swalk—transition mark
Tekauchi—no known signed samples
Wirkner—transition mark
Witte—transition mark

TABLE IV
Backstamps by Type of Decoration

Usually Factory-Decorated
Mark A, written-out wreath in lavender
Mark C, all colors C.A.C. wreath
Mark E, metal mark
Mark F, red C.A.C. palette
Mark H, all colors transition
Mark J, Lenox wreath
Mark K, L porcelain
Mark L, L opaque
Mark M, gold wreath

Always Non-Factory Decorated
None of the marks are exclusively non-factory, but the following come the closest:

Mark A, written-out wreath in green
Mark F, green C.A.C. palette
Mark I, green L palette

Either Factory or Non-Factory
Mark F, C.A.C. palette, in lavender—about evenly divided
Mark F, C.A.C. palette, brown, gold and black—usually non-factory but many exceptions seen

Too Few Samples Seen
Mark B, double wreath written-out
Mark D, script Lenox
Mark G, Indianhead

TABLE V
Backstamps Dates and Uses (According to Robinson and Feeny)

Mark	Color	Date	Primary Use
Written-out C.A.C. (Mark A)	Lavender	1891-1906	Special orders
	Green	No later than 1906	Uncertain
Written-out C.A.C. double wreath (Mark B)	Probably green	1897	Decorating contest
C.A.C. wreath (Mark C)	Blue, green, brown, lavender	1892-1896	Factory-decorated with original artist designs
Script Lenox (Mark D)	Not applicable	Uncertain	Uncertain
Metal mark (Mark E)	Not appicable	No later than 1906	Items with bronze fittings
C.A.C. palette (Mark F)	Red	1889-1896	Factory-decorated in standard designs
	Lavender	No later than 1906	Both factory decorated and white ware
	Green	No later than 1906	White ware
	Gold	No later than 1906	White ware
	Black	No later than 1906	White ware
Indianhead (Mark G)	Unknown	1889-1895	White ware
Transition (Mark H)	Lavender, green, brown, black, gold	1896 1906	Factory-decorated, all types
L palette (Mark I)	Green & others	1906-1924	White ware
L wreath ● (Mark J)	Green & others "Made in U.S.A."	1906-1930 1930-1952	Factory-decorated items Factory-decorated items
L porcelain (Mark K)	Black	1930's & 1940's	Lamps
L opaque (Mark L)	Black	1930's & 1940's	Non-porcelain items
Gold wreath (Mark M)	Gold	1906-1930's 1952-present	Special items All wares

an already decorated item when it was presented as a gift. This would be particularly true of the items which have silver on them, since the item would have gone from Lenox to the silver company to a jewelry store to a retail customer, which might have taken some time.

A date does not even necessarily prove the latest date when an item could have been made, for it is possible that an artist pre-dated an item for reasons we will never know.

We look forward to a time when enough early items have been examined for someone to make definitive statements about backstamps, and will not mind at all if we are proven wrong in our assumptions.

MARK A—C.A.C. WRITTEN OUT

This mark was possibly one of the earlier ones in use at the Ceramic Art Company. The Mohr article lists a date of 1891 for the lavender version of this mark, and Barber, while he gives us no dates or colors, concurs with Mohr in the use of the mark—for special order items. On page 26 of the 1891 catalogue the company states, "We are also prepared to manufacture special forms of articles for private parties who may desire to control an exclusive and uncommon line." This would indicate a willingness on the company's part to make special order items, and it would seem likely that they might have had a special mark for these items. The catalogue, however, does not tell us what that mark was.

It would be very possible that the Mohr date of 1891 for this mark is correct, for it would be unlikely that a customer would give a special order to a company without having seen their regular line. The company was two years old in 1891, which would have given them enough time to establish production of standard items which could serve as samples of their work. (The same page of the catalogue goes on to tell us that they maintained a show room for display of their wares.)

POTTERS and DECORATORS

We have seen enough non-catalogue shapes to verify that C.A.C. probably did produce special-order items, and most of the items with Mark A are indeed distinctive. Two of these items, however, create problems for us since they bring up the likelihood that C.A.C. did, on at least a few occasions, decorate on products which were not of their own manufacture. The first item is a cup and saucer, decorated primarily with transfers, and double-stamped with "Limoges, France" and the C.A.C. written-out mark. (Two of these have been seen.) The second item is the clock shown elsewhere in this book which is double-stamped with Mark A and the German letters N.A. inside a wreath. The German mark might be taken to mean that the clockwork was made in Germany and the china part by C.A.C., but the clockwork was American. The china is much heavier than most Lenox of the day, but is the proper creamy color.

A brief examination fo the economic situation in the 1890's shows a depression beginning with the Panic of 1893. Perhaps it was necessary for the company to take such orders to stay afloat. We can place only four artists at C.A.C. in 1895, down from seven in 1893, so perhaps the theory is correct.

Other items with the written-out wreath mark include a loving cup decorated for an Irish-American fraternal organization and dated March 17, 1898, and a mug decorated with a picture of Admiral Dewey. Although the mug is not dated, it is no doubt in honor of his victory at Manila in 1898.

Another mug with Mark A is additionally marked as being made for Theodore Starr, a New York silver company which began operating in 1900. This mug, although not artist-signed, could very well be the work of Walter Marsh who began working at C.A.C. in 1903. It is possible that this mark was in use up until 1906, when all C.A.C. marks were dropped.

Mark A can be either green or lavender, and the items already discussed have been with the lavender mark. Green appears primarily on what appear to be home-decorated items, and unless these items are somehow related to Mark B, we are at a loss to explain them. It is always possible that Mark A in green was used for white ware, but it is unlikely considering how few samples turn up.

This mark is sometimes seen with the words "Potters and Decorators" and sometimes not. Variations in the basic lettering also occur, but we consider this to be meaningless in terms of usage and date. There are simply too few samples of Mark A to draw any definite conclusions.

MARK B—C.A.C. WRITTEN OUT DOUBLE WREATH

Merely by looking at Mark B we are able to determine that it is somehow connected to an art competition held in 1897. What we do not know for sure is if the contest were held by C.A.C. with artists submitting pieces to them or if the C.A.C. artists sent their items to a contest held elsewhere. The first possibility seems more likely and fits in nicely with rumors we have heard concerning just such a contest.

The story has the Lenox Company sponsoring a decorating contest in an effort to find talented artists. The company has no record of this event, unlike the soap carving contest which they can verify—the winning sculpture was eventually produced in porcelain. We have heard of the decorating contest from two widely-separated individuals, both of whom said Walter Lenox had given the items to their families along with the tale that they were the non-winning entries in a decorating contest. Neither of the items had a backstamp, and both were earthenware rather than porcelain. Excluding the possibility that they are the long-missing Indian China, it would seem likely that the contestants used whatever blanks they had at hand. The items, one a large round platter signed Callowhill (a noted ceramics artist) and the other a pitcher signed Boullemier, were both beautifully decorated with hand-painting and gold. It is interesting to note that Boullemier did indeed later come to work at Lenox. (Somehow we can't help but wonder who the winner might have been if Callowhill and Boullemier were the losers.)

We have never actually seen Mark B on an item, but reliable sources tell us they have and we will acknowledge the existence of items so marked. Our sources indicate that it appears mainly on bowls. The Barber book tells us this mark was a special one for decorators used in 1897, and nothing more.

Since the bottom wreath is left empty, we feel perhaps that only the best entries received the mark and the bottom half of it was filled in with "First Place", "Honorable Mention" or some such notation. Non-winning entries would have presumably been marked with only the top half of the mark, and this would account for the green mark pieces mentioned under Mark A. All of this is, of course, only theory until such time as a sample shows up with the bottom wreath filled in.

MARK C—C.A.C. WREATH

The C.A.C. wreath mark is not mentioned by any of our quoted sources, yet several items with this mark appear in our book. The small blue vase shown later in the book, and a similarly decorated one which is not shown both have this mark, although one mark is green and the other blue. There is no artist signature on either to help us date them. The jug with silver overlay by Heidrich, shown later, also has this mark and is engraved on the silver with the date 1896. The Sturgis Laurence vase, also shown later, is dated 1894 and has Mark C in blue. There also exists a tankard by DeLan with this mark in brown, which gives us headaches since we cannot otherwise place DeLan at the factory earlier than 1899.

It is rather obvious that this mark was in use for factory decorated items prior to the introduction of the transition mark, and was probably not used after 1896 despite the DeLan piece. What we do not know is when it was first used, and we will have to guess that it was 1892 or 1893. We know that the red C.A.C. palette mark was in use from 1889 until at least 1894, and it is possible that the C.A.C. wreath replaced the red palette mark during the period 1894-1896 on factory-decorated items. It is equally possible, however, that the two marks co-existed at least for a while, with the red palette mark indicating dinnerware type decoration or patterns and the C.A.C. wreath being used on more individualized items.

Returning once again to the 1891 catalogue we find on page 34 the following statement: "One of the strongest claims that we can possibly make for the originality of our decorations is that, *with the exception of the after-dinner coffees, teas, and plate services,* our decorations are never duplicated. This is effected mainly by the varied schools of art pursued by our artists, who are allowed the fullest latitude in the display of their special talents." (The emphasis is ours, not the catalogue's.)

We can see from this that even at this early date the company was already making a distinction between frequently repeated designs, such as those on dinnerware, and original works of art. It would not seem unlikely that at some point they decided to differentiate between the two types of decoration by giving the artistic creations their very own mark. Since the catalogue shows the palette mark but not the wreath mark, we assume that this differentiation was not made in 1891 but perhaps a few years later. The pieces we have seen thus far seem to bear out our theories concerning both dating and usage.

MARK D—SCRIPT LENOX

Our reason for placing this mark with the earlier ones is based on the fact that the only known sample of the incised version of this mark was on a Kate Sears type item. Since Kate Sears was apparently at C.A.C. only a short while during the earlier years, her work should not appear on a piece so marked. The only explanation we can offer is that this might have been done by Walter Lenox himself, either while at C.A.C. or at one of the other companies where he worked. Since he started out as a sculptor, a Kate Sears type item would not have been too much of a problem for him. The general appearance of the mark is that of a signature rather than a backstamp.

$$\mathcal{L}enox$$

A very similar mark, impressed rather than incised, appears on some very special pieces of Lenox, including the doll shown in the color section.

The mark is altogether too rare to draw any concrete conclusions regarding it.

MARK E—METAL MARK

This mark appears on the metal portions of urns such as the bronze and Lenox one in the metals section. When this mark appears on the metal, the china never seems to be marked. All of these items should be considered extremely rare.

MARK F—C.A.C. PALETTE

The Barber book lists this mark in red from 1889, and goes on to inform us that lavender and other colors were used at a later date. The Mohr article gives us the dates 1894-1898 in green or gold on undecorated ware, and 1898-1906 in black for undecorated. The 1891 catalogue shows a palette mark on every page, and from what little text appears in this catalogue we can perhaps ascertain that this mark was certainly used on white ware and probably on factory-decorated items as well. Other Lenox sources indicate this mark was used on decorated ware from 1889-1906. Unfortunately, only Barber mentions which color was being used when for what type of item.

BELLEEK

Our personal observations of this mark would indicate the following:

The red is virtually always factory-decorated. The fern pot shown on page 122 bears this mark, and additionally has the Davis Collamore store mark. Many items with this red backstamp are decorated in a fashion similar to the fern pot, leading us to believe that this red palette mark was used on items decorated in a more or less standard fashion. The "red" is more often that not actually a pink, and can be easily confused with the lavender mark.

It is the other colors of C.A.C. palette mark which cause us the most problems, since they are not actually documented anywhere. From our quoted sources and from our own observations, we have this mark in lavender, green, gold, black and brown as well as the above-mentioned red or pinkish-red. This gives us a total of six colors to be fitted in somehow into the 18-year period everyone agrees they covered.

We can fairly well document the red for factory-decorated items from 1889 to 1894 or 1896, but have a problem deciding what color they were using during that same period for non-factory items. If we look at Table II we see that the three marks available for use would have been the written out one, the red palette one, and the Indianhead mark. Having already established that the red palette and written out marks were not used for the white ware and considering that the Indianhead mark is virtually non-existent, we can possibly surmise that the palette mark in some other color was used for non-factory items.

The lavender palette mark seems about evenly divided between factory and non-factory items. The bouillon cup and saucer shown elsewhere is obviously factory-done, since almost all of this type of gold paste work was factory. The ramekin shown is one of a set of six, five of which have lavender transition mark and one of which has lavender C.A.C. palette mark, yet all are identical. Although samples of fully-decorated items such as vases have been seen which are apparently factory-done, many very poor examples of artwork are also seen with this backstamp. We think it is equally possible that the lavender palette mark was (1) for some amount of time a very definite factory-decorated mark, or (2) primarily for home-decorated items but items were frequently pulled from the white ware pile to fill orders for factory-decorated wares.

The green C.A.C. palette mark seems to be almost always in the province of the amateur artist, and that this mark would appear on a factory-done item only in the instance listed above, where they used items from the white ware inventory in an emergency.

The gold C.A.C. palette mark mentioned by others has not been seen by us, and we can conjecture that it is perhaps a faded version of the brown mark. If it does indeed exist, we have no idea of its age or use. The brown pallette mark appears on at least two items shown in this book—the Hawthorn cup and saucer on page 223 and the inkwell on page 285, which also bears the transition mark in green. We theorize that the brown pallette mark was intended for the non-factory artist, but cannot date it accurately. The Hawthorn cup and saucer on which it appears was produced first in 1889 and was made for many years thereafter, so it is no real help to us, except to note that it is eggshell thin and possibly a very early piece. The inkwell on which it appears places the uses of the brown mark in the same time frame as the transition mark.

A true black C.A.C. palette mark would be very rare, and we do not recall ever seeing one. Many of these so-called black palette marks are probably either a very dark green or brown. As was the case with the gold one, we cannot help with the dating of the black mark if it indeed does exist.

MARK G—INDIANHEAD

In the marks section of the Barber book he lists this as being for undecorated ware prior to 1895, and in the part of the text written in 1893 he tells us that C.A.C. produced "Belleek and Indian China." The 1891 C.A.C. catalogue also lists Belleek and Indian China, so from these sources it is possible to say that this Indian China was not the Belleek-type china we generally associate with Lenox, and that it was undecorated.

It must be pointed out that to the best of our knowledge this mark simply does not exist. We have never seen it on an actual item, and none of our collector friends have seen it either. If this mark had indeed been used from 1889 to 1895, surely samples would have materialized by now. If we accept the idea that it was not a Belleek-type product, we have the inevitable question: what was it? We can only theorize:

(1) It was a heavier type of china, perhaps of the type known as hotel ware, and it was not marked because the company was not particularly proud of it. It could very well have been the case that in the earlier years this type of ware

had to be made in order to meet expenses while they experimented around with the finer ware. This would allow for the possibility that we are all walking right past Indian China items without knowing it.

(2) It was so easily broken that no samples remain. This is unlikely considering the number of years it was supposed to be in production.

(3) The white porcelain that later received the same marks as the creamy was originally designated as Indian China, but the earlier versions were not marked because the company wanted to be known for the Belleek-type ware and not an inferior version of European white porcelains. The idea may have some merit to it, since even in the early years their Belleek ware was the equal of other similar chinas, while this white china suffers from many imperfections as a rule. Even in the early years, imperfect items were a no-no, so not marking this white china might appear to make sense. Although the 1891 catalogue does not actually so state, it would seem from the use of the Indianhead mark on every page that the items appearing on those pages would have been available in either the Belleek or the Indian China. In this case, the Indian China was probably a porcelain rather than an earthenware or hotel ware, since many of the items shown could really only have been done in porcelain.

(4) After having spent a great deal of time explaining Indian China and the use of the various colors of the palette mark, we now with some hesitation offer the suggestion that Indian China and Belleek were one and the same, with factory-decorated items receiving the red palette mark, special orders receiving the written-out mark, and undecorated ware for the amateur artist receiving no mark. This very nicely solves the problem of which color palette mark was used on undecorated items during the earliest years. As to why undecorated items received no backstamp, we can only suggest that the company wanted no association with home-decorated items. The Indianhead mark itself might very well have been used on advertising literature without ever actually appearing on the items.

Choose whichever explanation you like, for until a marked item turns up no one can say you are wrong. We ourselves are accepting explanation #4 as the most reasonable.

MARK H—TRANSITION

This mark is perhaps the least confusing of all the early marks, since everyone agrees that it was used on factory-decorated items, although there is some disagreement about whether it was first used in 1894 or 1896. It is called by this name because it relates to the transitional period when Lenox was taking over control of the company and Coxon was bowing out, and it is perhaps the confusion over precisely when Coxon left that gives us this minor discrepancy in the beginning date for the mark.

An additional minor point is the use of three different colors—gold, green and lavender. Gold is very rare, but the green and lavender seem about evenly divided. If we attempt to date the colors by known dates of employment for various artists, we are still somewhat confused since we have signed Morley items (both Morleys 1900 and later) on green transition mark, and yet we have the signed Marsh items primarily on lavender even though he was also after the turn of the century.

We next made what we felt was a logical conclusion—that the two colors were not meant as dating distinctions, but rather to identify different types of items. Once again, we were quickly proven wrong by an examination of several items. Items with silver overlay are about evenly divided between the two color marks, as was also the case with liners for silver holders. Artist-signed vases and other large items also turned up with both colors. Small type items such as salt dips are seen with both.

Perhaps if we could gather together in one place a couple hundred examples of these transition marks we could make more conclusive statements regarding the color variation in the mark, but as it is now we cannot explain why some pieces are green, some are lavender, and a few others marked in gold.

The transition mark has a rather interesting variation which is seen only on rare occasions. The mark itself is the same as other transition marks, but underneath are the words "Glen-Iris." All of the items with this mark apparently were done with floral motifs, and most were signed by Walter Marsh. Although we have no hard facts concerning this mark, we can theorize that Marsh came to Lenox to develop this particular line. For years we had no first name for Marsh, and were very disappointed to finally determine that it was Walter and not Glen as we had hoped, for this would have solved the problem for us. Since an alternate meaning for iris is rainbow, this "Glen-Iris" could have then been loosely translated as "Marsh's Rainbow." Since the words marsh and glen conjure up somewhat the same image, perhaps our little theory still holds true.

Items bearing this mark are done in a tri-color fashion in only two known variations: (1) orange, yellow, and lavender; and (2) green, purplish-red, and yellow. The flowers themselves would seem to be almost secondary to the use of color, unlike other hand-painted items where the flower would be the focusing point. The black and white photograph of the Glen-Iris vase in the artware section, however, brings out the flowers for reasons we can't explain.

A quick examination of the five Glen-Iris pieces which are readily accessible to us shows they all have the lavender transition mark, but we do not exclude the possibility of the green version of the mark showing up.

MARK I—LENOX PALETTE OR L PALETTE

In 1906, the familiar C.A.C. palette mark was changed slightly by the substitution of an L for the C.A.C. inside the palette. This new mark took over the function of the former one, i.e., indicating that an item was not factory-decorated. Most of the examples we have seen of this mark were in the green color, although black and others are not unknown. The Lenox palette mark was in use until 1924, at which time the white ware part of the business was discontinued.

Although we would like to be able to state unequivocably that at this stage the company has finally managed to separate out their white ware and decorated ware, this is unfortunately not the case. We offer at least one item

BELLEEK

as proof that this Lenox palette mark was occasionally factory decorated, and that item is a small ramekin decorated in a common Lenox pattern, with numbers on the bottom to match the proper decorating codes for that pattern. There is just no way this can be a home-decorated item. A second less-convincing offering would be a lovely DeLan vase, among the best we have seen by him, with this green L palette mark. We cannot prove, however, that he did this vase while employed at the factory.

MARK J—LENOX WREATH OR L WREATH

This mark was used on factory-decorated items from 1906 until 1930, usually in green but also occasionally in blue, red, black, and even sometimes gold. (We will delay discussion of this early use of the gold wreath mark until we get to Mark M.) Most of the giftware items from this period will have the green version, but others do turn up. Dinnerware had the full range of wreath mark colors, some of which might appear to correspond to the color of the pattern (i.e., the use of a rose-colored wreath on Lenox Rose), but this was probably coincidence.

LENOX

Lenox wreath mark is virtually 100 percent factory decorated, and the collector must be wary only of the occasional item which was embellished after leaving the factory.

In 1930 the words "Made in U.S.A." were added to this mark, and the mark continued to be used on factory-decorated and intentionally undecorated items. Green remained the predominant color for this mark.

MARK K AND L—L PORCELAIN AND L OPAQUE

These two marks date from the 1930's and 1940's. The L porcelain mark is often found on lamp bases, and on rare occasions on standard giftware. The L opaque mark is a very obscure one sometimes noted on what we will call hotel type ware, for the items are not porcelain.

MARK M—GOLD WREATH

Mark M is actually a continuation of Mark J, the Lenox green wreath, and we originally planned to include it in the discussion of Mark J. Since it is the current mark, however, we decided to give it a letter and discussion of its very own.

Gold wreath made its appearance as the standard mark for all types of Lenox items in the early 1950's, and it continues to the present day. To the best of our knowledge, there are no plans to change it.

The only problem with this mark is that is sometimes turns up on items done by artists long-since gone from this world. Morley and DeLan fish plates are examples of this discrepancy, and the most plausible explanation for this is that the gold mark was in use much earlier than the 1950's for particular types of items. Since the transition mark can also be gold, it seems reasonable that a gold mark continued to be used on occasional items, or that the gold wreath mark was used to indicate a special order after the written-out C.A.C. mark was dropped. (The other explanation for the use of the gold wreath mark on these items is that items were discovered in some cranny of the warehouse at a much later date and stamped then. We think this is about as likely as the story that the company still has boxes of figurines stashed away somewhere.)

Variations of the gold wreath mark include the addition of the word "Special" under the regular mark. This indicates nothing more than the item was specially done for the sale Lenox holds at regular intervals. Another variation is the substitution of "Trenton, New Jersey" for "Made in U.S.A.", for no apparent reason.

OTHER BACKSTAMPS

Perhaps the chief mark not shown is the impressed LENOX one, primarily used on bisque Art Deco figures but also seen on other items. It can appear by itself or with other impressed information such as the year of copyright.

This mark is interesting because it is the only one that appears on the visible portion of items, usually on the back, instead of being on the bottom like most backstamps.

Another mark, perhaps a variation of the current gold wreath one, has the word Lenox spelled out. From the general appearance of the items and the mark, it would seem this is a fairly recent mark.

Lenox crystal is marked on the bottom with a few different marks, all of which include the word LENOX in block letters. Oxford Bone China is marked as such, with the addition of the letter L in script form. Temperware is marked with that word and additional information.

CONFUSING MARKS

(1) Dinnerware bearing the Lenox wreath mark and the added words "The White House" turns up now and then. This should not be confused with Presidential china, for "The White House" was a store in San Francisco. Apparently someone objected to the use of the White House name, for some items can be found where the words have been rubbed out (but still readable).

(2) There were two Ceramic Art Companies in England. The first dates from 1893 to 1903. Godden's book lists them as decorators located on Stoke Road, Hanley, Staffordshire. Their mark is:

THE CERAMIC ART
CO. LTD. HANLEY
STAFFORDSHIRE
ENGLAND

Another Ceramic Art Company in England was in business from 1905 to 1919, and they are listed as manufacturers of earthenware. Their mark is:

CERAMIC ART CO.
LTD. CROWN
POTTERY
STOKE-ON-TRENT
MANUF. OF FAIENCE

(3) Lenox Silver, Inc., New York, is listed in the Rainwater book as manufacturers of sterling silver around 1950. There is no connection between this silver company and the Lenox china company.

(4) China liners for silver holders sometimes have a mark which very much resembles the Lenox green wreath mark. Instead of having the word Lenox underneath the wreath, however, the word "Excelsior" appears there. In addition, the "L" inside the wreath will have a small "X" through the middle. Items with this mark do bear a resemblance to Lenox, although they are generally heavier, and one of the decorations commonly used is a version of Lenox pattern #86. The manufacturer who used this mark is not known to us.

UNMARKED ITEMS

Certain items, because of their shape or intended use, are rarely marked with a Lenox backstamp. Included in this grouping are pens, thimbles, door knobs, sherbert liners, cane handles, knife handles, etc. Virtually every other item that left the Lenox factory through legitimate channels will have the Lenox mark on it somewhere.

Unmarked items do appear with some frequency, however, and for the most part these are items that were taken by workmen before the manufacturing process was completed. Many of the unmarked items were rejects that were scheduled for destruction before being given a reprieve, and such items are often referred to as "back door" Lenox.

We consider most of the back door items to be a poor investment for the following reasons:

(1) There is an ample supply of marked pieces.

(2) They are usually flawed in some fashion. One of the great joys of owning Lenox is, of course, having such a perfect china.

(3) Unmarked items might not be Lenox.

Our advice would be to purchase only those unmarked items which fall into one of the following categories:

(1) Items which are never or rarely marked.

(2) Items which were usually marked but which suffered such a high attritiongrate that samples, marked or unmarked, are very hard to find. Included in this group would be picture framch a high attrition rate that samples, marked or unmarked, are very hard to find. Included in this group would be picture frames, watering cans and the like.

(3) Prototype items which were never put into general production. These items always seem to come with a lengthy tale of how Walter Scott Lenox himself gave the item to the owner. (There is a stale old story in the Trenton area that Walter Lenox gave away precisely 2,245 such unmarked prototype items, some 6,000 of which can still be found in Trenton.)

ADDITIONAL INFORMATION ON MARKS

(1) Professional decorating firms sometimes added their own mark to Lenox blanks they were painting. These companies include Pope and Lee, Poole and Stockton, DeLan and McGill, Tatler, W. C. Hendrickson, Jesse Dean, D'Arcy, Stouffer, and Pickard.

(2) The letter C in a circle, of course, means that the design is copyrighted. We only include this here because we actually heard a dealer telling a would-be customer that this mark indicated the piece was done by Jonathan Coxon.

(3) In addition to shape and pattern numbers written in gold on items, there will sometimes be small numbers somewhere on the bottom. These marks were probably internal Lenox numbers, used to identify decorator or gilder. Since in years past factory workers might have been paid "by the piece," this seems logical. They could also represent quality control numbers of one type or another. In any event, they give the collector no practical information.

(4) On bisque items where the green wreath mark appears instead of an impressed mark, the wreath mark will frequently have a rather strange appearance, as if someone had dabbed brown shellac over the mark. The appearance of this mark has to do with production problems with putting a mark on a bisque item and having it stay there, and does not mean the item is questionable.

ARTWARE AND GIFTWARE

Although some of the more advanced collectors reading this book may be disturbed to find undecorated giftware mentioned in the same breath as fine samples of hand-painting, we have grouped them together in this section for this reason: Many readers are novice collectors, and we felt it was important to show them how the same undecorated vase valued at $25 can be worth $100 by the addition of some fair art work by an amateur artist, and can also be worth $300 if it is beautifully decorated and signed by a Lenox factory artist.

This section will include the vases, cigarette boxes, candy dishes and the like that Lenox has produced down through the years. Dinnerware items such as plates and cups and saucers will be found in this section only if they are hand-painted in something other than a standard Lenox pattern.

Since age is one of the determining factors, we have included the backstamp which appeared on the items listed. Item numbers (shape numbers) are given in most cases as well to aid in proper identification.

Sets or groupings were broken down into their constituent parts since this is the way they are sometimes found, and we felt it was a no-harm way of helping the novice identify items. Since there is not yet a premium placed on completed sets, separating the items does not affect the pricing scheme.

Names of amateur artists have been omitted since they are not important to the value. Factory artists matter a great deal, however, and we will give the next several pages to some discussion of the Lenox art department.

Table VI lists by year the artist who might have been employed at Lenox at that time. Even allowing for a few unknown artists wandering in and out during a given year, we still arrive at what we consider to be plausible figures. It would appear that except for the founding year there would have been an ample supply of artists on hand to take care of orders, and that the company would not have had to seek outside help in filling them. Additionally, it would seem that the art department did not suffer from overcrowding at any particular time.

If we take the year 1900 as an example, we have eight known artists: Heidrich (portraits), Clayton (monochromes), Kuhn (portraits), DeLan (animals and scenics), L. Boullemier (figures), Wirkner (portraits), George and William Morley (animals, fruit, flowers.) Even in 1895, where we have only four known artists, there would have been enough diversification of talent to negate stories about pieces being sent outside to be done.

To be sure, our chart suffers from some flaws:

(1) We have taken the liberty of listing Lenox and Mayer as working artists, with nothing more to back us up than the notion that those who could probably did. (For those of you who are wondering who Mayer might be, see Table VII.)

(2) Employment dates for some of the artists are questionable, and others are mere guesses on our part. Those artists whose employment dates are completely unknown were placed in a year corresponding to the backstamps seen on their work.)

(3) We simply do not know how many other artists might have been there at one time or another.

In addition to the artist-signed items already discussed, the collector will find many samples of factory-decorated items (as determined by backstamps) which are not artist signed. The reason for this could be any of the following:

TABLE VI
Lenox Artists

1889 — Lenox
1890 — Lenox, Fauji, E. Boullimer, Heidrich, Tekauchi, Naylor
1891 — Lenox, Fauji, E. Boullimer, Heidrich, Tekauchi, Naylor, Clayton
1892 — Lenox, Fauji, E. Boullimer, Heidrich, Naylor, Clayton
1893 — Lenox, Fauji, E. Boullimer, Heidrich, Naylor, Clayton, Laurence
1894 — Lenox*, E. Boullimer, Heidrich, Clayton, Laurence
1895 — E. Boullimer, Heidrich, Clayton, Laurence
1896 — E. Boullimer, Heidrich, Clayton, Laurence, Hicks
1897 — Heidrich, Clayton, Laurence, Kuhn, Sully
1898 — Heidrich, Clayton, Laurence, Kuhn, Swalk
1899 — Heidrich, Clayton, Kuhn, DeLan, Des, Witte
1900 — Heidrich, Clayton, Kuhn, DeLan, L. Boullemier, Wirkner, George Morley, William Morley
1901 — Clayton, DeLan, L. Boullemier, Wirkner, George Morley, William Morley
1902 — Clayton, DeLan, L. Boullemier, Wirkner, George Morley, William Morley
1903 — Clayton, DeLan, L. Boullemier, Wirkner, George Morley, William Morley, Nosek, Marsh
1904 — Clayton, DeLan, L. Boullemier, Wirkner, William Morley, Nosek, Marsh, Mayer, Campana, Martell, Baker, Geyer
1905 — Clayton, DeLan, L. Boullemier, Wirkner, William Morley, Nosek, Marsh, Baker, Geyer
1906 — Clayton, DeLan, L. Boullemier, Wirkner, William Morley, Nosek, Marsh, Mayer, Baker, Geyer
1907 — Clayton, DeLan, Wirkner, William Morley, Nosek, Marsh, Mayer, Baker
1908 — Clayton, DeLan, Wirkner, William Morley, Nosek, Marsh, Mayer, Baker
1909 — DeLan, Wirkner, William Morley, Marsh
1910 — DeLan, Wirkner, William Morley, Marsh
1911-1915 — DeLan, Wirkner, William Morley
1916-1925 — Wirkner, William Morley
1926-1929 — William Morley
1930-1935 — William Morley, George Morley
1936 — George Morley
1937-1938 — George Morley, Fenzel
1939 — George Morley, Fenzel, Nosek
1940-1946 — Fenzel, Nosek
1947-1954 — Nosek

(All hand-painting was discontinued in 1954) (The 1891 C.A.C. catalogue pictures the art department with eight people. At this late date we have no way of knowing if this has any basis in fact or whether it was some engraver's idea of what an art department should look like, but it does fit in nicely with our list of seven artists and one gilder for the year 1891.)

* We assume Lenox did not continue painting after going blind.

TABLE VII

Heads of the Lenox Art Department
Walter Lenox—1889 to 1904
Mayer—1904 to 1908
Clayton—1908 to 1950
Hedt—1950 to 1955

Enamelers
G. Heufel, Germany—1894 to 1906
Mrs. Bradberry—1918 to 1930
Minnie Swan, Mamie Dougherty, Elizabeth Eggert—all 1920's and 1930's
Bertha Walton—1930
Jane Eardley—1941

Gilders
Alfred Powner—1890 to 1891, later returned to Mintons
Pholes (Tholes??) did the gold work on the Wilson china
Otto Barr—dates unknown
Alice van der Griff—1920's
Bertha Walton—1933
George Baker—1940's
Howard Ford—still employed at Lenox
Eleanor Peters—1946
Joan Guy—1952 to 1959
Lillian Kolb—1950's

(1) More than one artist worked on some items. (We know this to be true in at least one case—an urn signed by both Morley and Boullemier, with one artist (probably Morley) doing the flowers and background and the other (probably Boullemier) doing the figure of a little girl. If this were done with top-of-the-line items such as this, it could have been done on lesser pieces as well.)

(2) Such items were parts of sets, only one item of which was signed. (For example, a teapot might be signed but not the matching sugar and creamer. If the pieces to the set were separated, there would be no way to ever prove who painted the sugar and creamer.)

(3) When they were very busy, the artists didn't bother signing their work.

(4) They were done by apprentice artists who were not allowed to sign their work.

Whatever the reason, these unsigned works of art just do not command the same prices as those which are artist-signed, although in many cases they are at least the equal of the signed items.

ASHTRAYS

Ashtrays are not particularly popular among collectors, and this is reflected in the prices.

- ☐ Ashtray, shape #2030, *5" x 1-3/8" high, undecorated, Lenox wreath mark* **8.00**
- ☐ Ashtray, shape #2030, *5" x 1-3/8" high, Lenox Rose pattern, Lenox wreath mark* **20.00**
- ☐ Ashtray, shape #2030, *5" x 1-3/8" high, Ming pattern, Lenox wreath mark* **25.00**
- ☐ Ashtray, shape #2030, *5" x 1-3/8" high, solid green, Lenox wreath mark* **18.00**
- ☐ Ashtray, shape #2030, *5" x 1-3/8" high, solid green, Lenox wreath mark* **18.00**
- ☐ Ashtray, shape #2030, *5" x 1-3/8" high, solid coral, Lenox wreath mark* **14.00**
- ☐ Ashtray, shape #2030, *5" x 1-3/8" high, white with gold trim, monogram in center, Lenox wreath mark* **15.00**
- ☐ Ashtray, shape #2399, *2-1/8" x 3-3/4" x 1-7/8" high, undecorated, Lenox wreath mark* **5.00**
- ☐ Ashtray, shape #2399, *2-1/8" x 3-3/4" x 1-7/8" high, Lenox Rose pattern, Lenox wreath mark* **14.00**
- ☐ Ashtray, shape #2399, *2-1/8" x 3-3/4" x 1-7/8" high, pale pink outside, white inside, gold trim on rim, Lenox wreath mark* **15.00**
- ☐ Ashtray, shape #2399, *2-1/8" x 3-3/4" x 1-7/8" high, cobalt, Lenox wreath mark* **9.00**
- ☐ Ashtray, shape #2427, *2-5/8" x 4-1/4" x 3/4" high, undecorated, Lenox wreath mark* **5.00**
- ☐ Ashtray, shape #2427, *2-5/8" x 4-1/4" x 3/4" high, green with gold trim, Lenox wreath mark* **8.00**
- ☐ Ashtray, shape #2427, *2-5/8" x 4-1/4" x 3/4" high, yellow with gold trim, Lenox wreath mark* **12.00**
- ☐ Ashtray, shape #2427, *2-5/8" x 4-1/4" x 3/4" high, coral, Lenox wreath mark* **6.00**
- ☐ Ashtray, shape #2997, *coral and white apple blossom design, Lenox wreath mark* **15.00**
- ☐ Ashtray, shape #2997, *blue and white apple blossom design, Lenox wreath mark* **15.00**
- ☐ Ashtray, shape #3003, *5-1/8" x 1-1/2" undecorated, Lenox wreath mark* **10.00**

☐ Ashtray, shape #3003, *5-1/8" x 1-1/2" gold trim, Lenox wreath mark* **15.00**
☐ Ashtray, shape #3008, *5-1/8" x 1" high, undecorated, Lenox wreath mark* **10.00**
☐ Ashtray, shape #3032, *3-3/8" x 1" high, white, Lenox wreath mark* . **10.00**
☐ Ashtray, shape #3032, *3-3/8" x 1" high, coral, Lenox wreath mark* . **13.00**
☐ Ashtray, shape #3032, *3-3/8" x 1" high, green, Lenox wreath mark* . **16.00**
☐ Ashtray, shape #3066, *3-3/8" x 1" high, undecorated, Lenox wreath mark* **10.00**
☐ Ashtray, shape #3066, *3-3/8" x 1" high, blue, Lenox wreath mark* . . **15.00**
☐ Ashtray, shape number unknown, *has knob in center for tapping tobacco out of pipe, white with royal blue knob, raised laurel wreath design on outside, Lenox wreath mark* **30.00**
☐ Ashtray, shape number unknown, *approximately 7" diameter, full-color pheasant scene, Lenox wreath mark* **35.00**
☐ Ashtray, shape number unknown, *coat of arms shape and decoration, gold trim* **25.00**
☐ Ashtray, shape number unknown, *green with gold trim* **15.00**
☐ Ashtray, shape number unknown, *pheasant scene, gold trim* **20.00**

BONE DISHES

Lenox made one style of bone dishes, shape #263, in a four-inch long size with a vague S-shape to it. Bone dishes were very common items around the turn of the century, and we cannot explain why so few Lenox bone dishes are seen today. A marked sample would be in the $50 range for an undecorated one, up to around $100 for one that is decorated.

BOUILLON CUPS

Bouillon cups are two-handled soup cups which come with an underplate and, on rare occasions, with a lid. The underplate can be either a saucer type, with an indentation where the cup rests, or else can resemble a bread and butter plate with no indentation. (We refer to both types as saucers.)

☐ Bouillon cup and saucer, shape #104, *dimpled surface, ring handles, cover also has a ring for finial, C.A.C. brown palette mark, raised on ball feet* **35.00**
☐ Bouillon cup and saucer, shape #104, *dimpled surface, ring handles, cover missing, C.A.C. green palette mark* **25.00**
☐ Bouillon cup and saucer, shape #175, *scalloped rim and fancy handles, undecorated, Lenox palette mark raised on ball feet* **15.00**
☐ Bouillon cup and saucer, shape #175, *scalloped rim and fancy handles, hand-painted tiny roses, C.A.C. lavender palette mark* **50.00**
☐ Bouillon cup and saucer, shape #175, *scalloped rim and fancy handles, gold trim on handles and rim, gold monograms, Lenox palette mark* **15.00**
☐ Bouillon cup and saucer, shape #557-1/2, *squared-off handles, plain shape, undecorated, Lenox palette mark* **10.00**
☐ Bouillon cup and saucer, shape #557-1/2, *square-off handles, single large red rose, Lenox palette mark* **20.00**
☐ Bouillon cup and saucer, shape #628, *transfer decorated with vegetables, gold trim, Lenox palette mark* **18.00**
☐ Bouillon cup and saucer, shape #628, *undecorated, Lenox wreath mark* **12.00**
☐ Bouillon cup and saucer, shape #633, *undecorated, Lenox wreath mark* **10.00**
☐ Bouillon cup and saucer, shape #757, *gold trim, Lenox palette mark* . **15.00**

Bouillon cup and saucer, *shape number unknown*

☐ Bouillon cup and saucer, shape #839-1/2, *undecorated, Lenox wreath mark*. **13.00**

☐ Bouillon cup and saucer, shape #846-1/2, *undecorated, Lenox wreath mark*. **10.00**

☐ Bouillon cup and saucer, shape number not known, *had lid, raised gold paste work, gold trim on twig type handles and lid finial, C.A.C. lavender palette mark* **60.00**

BOWLS

☐ Bowl, shape #11, *3-1/2", lotus leaf style, very early and thin, undecorated, C.A.C. brown palette mark, some small flecks on ruffles*. . **125.00**

☐ Bowl, shape #11, *3-1/2", lotus leaf style, top part coral, base white, Lenox wreath mark* **60.00**

☐ Bowl, shape #11, *3-1/2", lotus leaf type, top part white, base blue, Lenox wreath mark* **60.00**

☐ Bowl, shape #11, *3-1/2", pearlized finish with gold trim on rim and base, Lenox palette mark* **110.00**

☐ Bowl, shape #23, *3-3/4" x 6-1/2", ruffled rim, hand-painted small wildflowers, artist signed and dated, C.A.C. lavender palette mark* . . . **67.00**

☐ Bowl, shape #23, *3-3/4" x 6-1/2", ruffled rim, hand-painted with Cupids and hearts, gold trim, several flecks on ruffles, Lenox palette mark*. **100.00**

Bowl shape #43 is shown in catalogues with a 10" round underplate which was not present with either of the above two samples.

☐ Bowl, shape #37, *6-1/4" high, lotus leaf type, white base with coral top section, Lenox wreath mark* **90.00**

☐ Bowl, shape #37, *6-1/4" high, lotus leaf type white base with yellow top section, Lenox wreath mark* **110.00**

☐ Bowl, shape #37, *6-1/4" high, early and very thin, pearlized lavender finish inside, speckled gold trim on outside and rims, C.A.C. red palette mark, Bailey, Banks & Biddle store mark* **160.00**

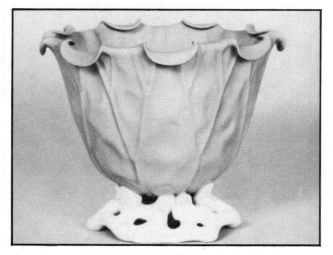

Bowl, *shape #37, coral top*

Note: All of the lotus leaf bowls listed here are commonly referred to as "cabbage leaf" bowls by collectors. The early catalogues, however, list them as lotus leaves.

☐ Bowl, shape #53, *3-1/2", lotus leaf type, top section done in pearlized pink, whole base covered with gold, artist signed and dated, C.A.C. green palette mark* 60.00

☐ Bowl, shape #53, *3-1/2", lotus leaf type, undecorated, Lenox palette mark* 70.00

☐ Bowl, shape #54, *6-1/4" high, lotus leaf type, sponged gold trim, C.A.C. lavender palette mark* 110.00

☐ Bowl, shape #54, *6-1/4" high, lotus leaf type, undecorated, Lenox wreath mark* 75.00

☐ Bowl, shape #65, *6-1/2" high, lotus leaf type, top part white, base yellow, Lenox wreath mark* 100.00

☐ Bowl, shape #92, *2-1/2" x 5", ruffled top, hand-painted butterflies, gold trim, blue glaze inside bowl, C.A.C. green palette mark* 40.00

☐ Bowl, shape #92, *2-1/2" x 5", ruffled top, undecorated, C.A.C. brown palette mark* 35.00

☐ Bowl, shape #92, *2-1/2" x 5", ruffled top, hand-painted small pink roses, gold trim on rim, part of one ruffle missing, C.A.C. red palette mark* 70.00

☐ Bowl, shape #92, *2-1/2" x 5", hand-painted with elves and rabbits, gold trim, nicely done, C.A.C. green palette mark* 100.00

Note: Bowl shape #92 originally came with a 6-3/4" underplate and was perhaps intended to be a mush set. None of the bowls we have seen have had the underplate, however.

☐ Bowl, shape #96, *5-1/2" high, lotus leaf type, very early and thin, no decoration, C.A.C. brown palette mark* 125.00

☐ Bowl, shape #512, *10-1/4" diameter, hand-painted chrysanthemums, signed Morley, transition mark* 250.00

☐ Bowl, shape #512, *10-1/4" diameter, undecorated, Lenox palette mark*   30.00

☐ Bowl, shape #512, *10-1/4" diameter, hand-painted inside and out with badly done red and pink roses, gold trim on rim, artist signed and dated, small fleck on base, C.A.C. green palette mark* **50.00**

☐ Bowl, shape #512, *10-1/4" diameter, hand-painted fruit on inside, outside covered with gold, artist signed and dated, Lenox palette mark* . **45.00**

☐ Bowl, shape #512, *10-1/4" diameter, hand-painted small pink roses in scatter pattern, gold trim on rim, C.A.C. lavender palette mark* **80.00**

☐ Bowl, shape #512, *10-1/4" diameter, gold pencil-line trim, Lenox wreath mark* **60.00**

☐ Bowl, shape #513, *8" x 3-1/2", hand-painted fruit on outside, pearlized orange inside, gold trim, artist's initials and date, C.A.C. green palette mark* **50.00**

☐ Bowl, shape #513, *8" x 3-1/2", hand-painted fruit on outside, inside plain, gold trim on rim, transition mark, beautifully done* **160.00**

☐ Bowl, shape #513, *8" x 3-1/2", geometric enamel pattern inside and out, Lenox palette mark*.. **30.00**

☐ Bowl, shape #513, *8" x 3-1/2", undecorated, Lenox wreath mark* **40.00**

☐ Bowl, shape #527, *8-3/4" x 4", hand-painted garlands of flowers outside, gold trim, small chip on rim, transition mark* **100.00**

☐ Bowl, shape #527, *8-3/4" x 4", hand-painted pansies on outside, single large pansy inside on bottom, gold trim, shaded background inside and out, C.A.C. green palette mark*...................... **75.00**

☐ Bowl, shape #527, *8-3/4" x 4", transfer decorated with medallion portraits in four places, inside pearlized pink, gold trim on rim, Lenox palette mark* **40.00**

☐ Bowl, shape #553, *6" x 2-1/2", hand-painted berries and leaves on outside, gold trim, artist signed and dated, C.A.C. green palette mark* **60.00**

☐ Bowl, shape #553, *6" x 2-1/2", undecorated, Lenox palette mark* **15.00**

☐ Bowl, shape #553, *6 x 2-1/2", hand-painted scattered flowers, set of six, each marked with what are apparently dogs' names, one cracked, occasional chips on others, artist signed and dated, C.A.C. green palette mark (and we thought we had seen everything!), each*.. **15.00**

☐ Bowl, shape #575, *5-1/2" diameter, hand-painted bees and flowers, gold trim, Lenox palette mark*................................... **25.00**

☐ Bowl, shape #575, *5-1/2" diameter, hand-painted flowers inside, pearlized blue exterior, gold trim, artist's initials, Lenox palette mark* **20.00**

☐ Bowl, shape #586, *10" handle to handle, 3" high, undecorated, Lenox palette mark* **35.00**

☐ Bowl, shape #586, *10" handle to handle, 3" high, gold trim, Lenox palette mark* **40.00**

☐ Bowl, shape #586, *10" handle to handle, 3" high, hand-painted harvest scene, very professisonal looking, Lenox palette mark* **160.00**

☐ Bowl, shape #586, *10" handle to handle, 3" high, all over black with white Art Nouveau florals, outlined in gold, not badly done but a poor choice of design for this type of bowl, Lenox palette mark*.......... **30.00**

☐ Bowl, shape #586, *10" handle to handle, 3" high, gold trim, Lenox wreath mark* **50.00**

☐ Bowl, shape #587, *5-1/2" x 1-1/4", undecorated, Lenox palette mark* .. **10.00**

☐ Bowl, shape #589, *9" x 2-5/8", hand-painted asters on shaded background, artist signed, Lenox palette mark* **90.00**

☐ Bowl, shape #590, *5-1/8" diameter, undecorated, Lenox palette mark*. **8.00**

☐ Bowl, shape #644, *(mayonnaise bowl), undecorated, Lenox palette mark*.. **25.00**

☐ Bowl, shape #644, *(mayonnaise bowl), hand-painted single small pink roses, green leaves, raised gold work, Lenox wreath mark* **75.00**

☐ Bowl, shape #690, *(listed in catalogue as finger bowl), pencil line gold trim, Lenox wreath mark* **15.00**

☐ Bowl, shape #690, *(listed in catalogue as finger bowl), hand-painted daffodils on outside, gold trim, artist signed and dated, not badly done, Lenox palette mark, set of six* **90.00**

☐ Bowl, shape #715, *8-1/2" diameter, hexagon shape, footed, undecorated, Lenox wreath mark*.............................. **35.00**

☐ Bowl, shape #715, *8-1/2" diameter, hexagon shape, footed, covered all over with brown glaze as if intended for silver overlay, Lenox palette mark* **50.00**

☐ Bowl, shape #715, *8-1/2" diameter hexagon shape, footed, hand-painted geometric pattern, Lenox palette mark* **40.00**

☐ Bowl, shape #730, *10-1/2" x 3-1/8", undecorated, Lenox palette mark* . **25.00**

☐ Bowl, shape #730, *10-1/2" x 3-1/8", hand-painted fruit on outside, lustre finish inside, gold trim, artist signed and dated, Lenox palette mark*.. **65.00**

☐ Bowl, shape #730, *10-1/2" x 3-1/8", rainbow striped effect outside, pale pink-inside, Lenox palette mark* **30.00**

☐ Bowl, shape #730, *10-1/2" x 3-1/8", gold and silver bands alternating with narrow strips of black, unusual looking but neatly done, inside of bowl done entirely in gold, artist's initials and date, Lenox palette mark*.. **75.00**

☐ Bowl, shape #730, *10-1/2" x 3-1/8", apple green exterior, white inside, pencil line of gold on rim, Lenox wreath mark* **75.00**

☐ Bowl, shape #730, *10-1/2" x 3-1/8", outside glazed in purple, hand-painted lilacs in bottom of bowl, gold trim on rim, artist signed and dated, very nicely done, Lenox palette mark*..................... **110.00**

☐ Bowl, shape #730-1/2, *same as above but with salamander handles, plain white with gold trim on rim and on salamanders, Lenox palette mark*.. **65.00**

☐ Bowl, shape #730-1/2, *same as above, transfer decoration with Oriental scenes in bright colors, salamanders done in burnt orange color, same color on rim and base, overall effect very pleasant, Lenox palette mark* **95.00**

☐ Bowl, shape #730-1/2, *same as above, hand-enameled flowers separated by bands of black, artist's initials and date, Lenox palette mark* **45.00**

☐ Bowl, shape #730-1/2, *same as above, overall light green glaze, salamanders darker green with speckles of gold on them, tastefully done, dated on bottom, Lenox palette mark* **100.00**

Bowls #730 and 730-1/2 are frequently referred to as console bowls.

☐ Bowl, shape #778, *mayonnaise, hand-painted berries on outside, pink lustre inside, gold trim, Lenox palette mark* **35.00**

☐ Bowl, shape #778, *mayonnaise, raised gold and blue dot work, home decorated but not bad, Lenox palette mark* **50.00**

☐ Bowl, shape #778, *mayonnaise, undecorated, Lenox wreath mark* ... **30.00**

☐ Bowl, shape #778, *mayonnaise, 1/2" gold trim, etched, Lenox wreath mark*.. **35.00**

☐ Bowl, shape #779, *mayonnaise, with underplate, gold trim and gold initial on front and on plate, Lenox palette mark* **37.00**

☐ Bowl, shape #780, *small scattered hand-painted violets, gold trim, artist's initials and date on bottom, Lenox palette mark* **50.00**

☐ Bowl, shape #781, *mayonnaise, cobalt covering bowl, gold trim, Lenox wreath mark* **60.00**

☐ Bowl, shape #781, *mayonnaise, undecorated, Lenox palette mark* ... **15.00**

☐ Bowl, shape #782, *mayonnaise, hand-painted small pink roses on rim, gold trim, Lenox palette mark* **35.00**

☐ Bowl, shape #783, *mayonnaise, hand-painted lemons and oranges on shade background, gold trim, artist's initials, Lenox palette mark* ... **45.00**

☐ Bowl, shape #784, *mayonnaise, pencil-line gold trim, Lenox wreath mark* **30.00**

☐ Bowl, shape #785, *mayonnaise, hand-painted butterflies on shaded background, gold trim, Lenox palette mark* **50.00**

Although many of the bowls listed above had other uses, we are referring to them all as mayonnaise bowls.

☐ Bowl, shape #796, *9" diameter, 4-1/4" high, hand-painted forget-me-nots, gold trim, artist signed and dated, Lenox palette mark* **75.00**

☐ Bowl, shape #811, *2-1/4", hand-painted in rainbow swirls, interior of bowl done in pink, gold trim on rim, artist's initials and date, Lenox palette mark, tiny chip on base of one, set of six* **90.00**

☐ Bowl, shape #811, *2-1/4", tiny raised gold teardrops covering exterior, gold trim on rim, Lenox palette mark* **40.00**

☐ Bowl, shape #823, *4" x 10", hand-painted exterior with fruit and vines, gold trim on rim and base, artist signed and dated, nicely done, Lenox palette mark* **80.00**

☐ Bowl, shape #823, *4" x 10", pencil-line gold trim on rim, exterior done in shaded greens, inside plain, Lenox palette mark* **75.00**

☐ Bowl, shape #823, *4" x 10", undecorated, Lenox palette mark* **37.00**

☐ Bowl, shape #823, *4" x 10", scattered hand-painted tiny flowers inside and out, gold trim, artist's initials, Lenox palette mark* **65.00**

☐ Bowl, shape #824, *5-1/2" diameter, undecorated, Lenox wreath mark* . **8.00**

☐ Bowl, shape #824, *5-1/2" diameter, pencil-line gold trim on rim, Lenox wreath mark* **12.00**

☐ Bowl, shape #940, *5-3/8" diameter, fruit saucer type, solid coral, Lenox wreath mark* **10.00**

☐ Bowl, shape #961, *5-1/2" diameter, transfer decorated with baby's picture in bottom, gold trim on rim, Lenox palette mark* **13.00**

☐ Bowl, shape #971, *2-5/8" high, pale pink with raised gold in floral design and gold trim on rim, home-decorated but tastefully done, artist signed and dated, several flea bite flecks on bottom, Lenox palette mark* **18.00**

☐ Bowl, shape #1254, *9-1/2" x 3", scalloped rim, hand-painted small roses on each scallop connected by garlands of blue dot enamel work, possibly intended to be a liner for a sterling holder but quite usable on its own, Lenox wreath mark* **100.00**

☐ Bowl, shape #1376, *coral exterior, plain inside, Lenox wreath mark* .. **35.00**

☐ Bowl, shape #1667, *5-1/2" x 9", hand-painted grapes on exterior, green inside, the same green from the inside comes up over the rim and down the outside shading eventually to a pale ivory, beautifully done, no artist signature, Lenox palette mark* **130.00**

☐ Bowl, shape #1929, *double-handled fruit bowl, decorated in shades of pink and coral, gold handles, rather garish, Lenox palette mark* ... **50.00**

☐ Bowl, shape #1929, *two-handled fruit bowl, gold trim on handles and rim, Lenox wreath mark* **55.00**

☐ Bowl, shape #1929-1/2, *same shape as 1929 but without handles, hand-painted with holly berries and leaves with Christmas inscription in center of bowl, rather nice overall effect, artist signed, Lenox palette mark, tiny chip on base* **60.00**

BRUSHES, COMBS, MIRRORS AND OTHER VANITY ITEMS

All of these items are in the rare category, probably because they were the type of thing which would have been picked up frequently and, therefore, were likely to be broken. In addition, the marks can be hidden by the looking glass or brush, making positive identification difficult unless such items are parts of larger sets which have other marked items.

Vanity items

Those vanity items which were factory-decorated tend to be done either with little roses or with violets, both usually in a scatter pattern.

The smaller unmarked pieces would have a starting price of $50 undecorated, going up to perhaps $150 for decorated and marked items.

BUTTER PATS

Butter pats are not common Lenox items. Item #178 is perhaps the most available of them. We have included #176 as a butter pat since it is rather shallow to be a salt or nut dish and it appear sequentially in catalogues with the other butter pats.

- ☐ Butter pat, item #176, *3", hand-painted little pink roses with gold trim, Lenox wreath mark* **25.00**
- ☐ Butter pat, item #176, *3", gold trim, C.A.C. lavender palette mark* **15.00**
- ☐ Butter pat, item #177, *3-1/4" round, scalloped rim similar to that of item #178, undecorated, Lenox palette mark* **10.00**
- ☐ Butter pat, item #178, *3-1/4", hand-painted with small pink roses, gold trim, transition mark* **25.00**
- ☐ Butter pat, item #178, *3-1/4", gold trim, Lenox palette mark* **15.00**
- ☐ Butter pat, item #178, *3-1/4", undecorated and unmarked* **5.00**

BUTTONS

Lenox supposedly made some buttons in the early days, but we have never seen any sold on the open market. A backstamped button would be worth at least $100 undecorated, and perhaps $150 or $175 decorated.

Butterpat, *item #178, pink roses*

CANDLESTICKS

☐ Candlesticks, shape #147, *10-1/2" high, embossing, undecorated, Lenox wreath mark, pair* **75.00**

☐ Candlesticks, shape #147, *10-1/2" high, brushed gold trim, Lenox wreath mark, pair* **80.00**

☐ Candlesticks, shape #147, *10-1/2" high, embossing, undecorated, C.A.C. green palette mark, pair* **100.00**

☐ Candlesticks, shape #147-1/2, *same styling as #147 but much shorter, undecorated, Lenox wreath mark, pair* **45.00**

☐ Candlesticks, shape #147-1/2, *light blue, Lenox wreath mark, pair* ... **40.00**

☐ Candlesticks, shape #156, *1-3/4" high, attached underplate with ring handle, ruffled rim, undecorated C.A.C. green palette mark* **55.00**

☐ Candlesticks, shape #156, *1-3/4" high, attached underplate with ring handle, ruffled rim, hand-painted tiny pink roses, gold trim, few small flecks on ruffled rim, C.A.C. red palette mark* **15.00**

☐ Candlesticks, shape #156, *1-3/4" high, attached underplate with ring handle, ruffled rim, hand-painted flowers on light blue background, gold trim, Lenox palette mark* **80.00**

☐ Candlesticks, shape #220, *8" high, hand-painted green vines on yellow background, gold trim, C.A.C. green palette mark, pair* **80.00**

☐ Candlesticks, shape #220, *8" high, undecorated, Lenox palette mark, one only* **20.00**

☐ Candlesticks, shape #220, *8" high, gold trim, artist signed and dated, C.A.C. lavender palette mark, pair* **60.00**

☐ Candlesticks, shape #250, *5-1/8" high, hand-painted violets on green background, gold trim, artist signed and dated, C.A.C. green palette mark, pair* **100.00**

☐ Candlesticks, shape #250, *5-1/8" high, undecorated, Lenox palette mark, pair* **40.00**

- ☐ Candlesticks, shape #250, *5-1/8" high, gold trim, Lenox wreath mark, pair*.. **55.00**
- ☐ Candlesticks, shape #300, *6-1/4" high, one side of base comes up high to form shield against drafts, handle, hand-painted blue floral design on rim, blue handle, Lenox palette mark*.................. **50.00**
- ☐ Candlesticks, shape #300, *6-1/4" high, one side of base comes up high to form shield against drafts, handle, small violets in scatter pattern, gold trim on rims and handle, small chip on base, C.A.C. red palette mark*... **150.00**
- ☐ Candlesticks, shape #353, *6" high, same type as #300 above but with scalloped rim, undecorated, C.A.C. green palette mark* **125.00**
- ☐ Candlesticks, shape #930, *8-1/4" high, hexagon shape, undecorated, Lenox palette mark, pair* **30.00**
- ☐ Candlesticks, shape #930, *8-1/4" high, hand-painted roses and blue enamel ribbons, gold trim top and bottom, artist signed and dated, Lenox palette mark, pair* **75.00**
- ☐ Candlesticks, shape #930, *8-1/4" high, gold pencil-line trim, Lenox wreath mark, pair*.. **30.00**
- ☐ Candlesticks, shape #930, *8-1/4" high, hand-painted roses in scatter pattern, Lenox palette mark, one only* **30.00**
- ☐ Candlesticks, shape #973, *8-1/2" high, hand-painted in Art Deco style, gold trim, artist signed and dated, Lenox palette mark, pair* ... **30.00**
- ☐ Candlesticks, shape #973, *8-1/2" high, hand-painted with flowering vines, artist's initials on bottom, Lenox palette mark, pair* **55.00**
- ☐ Candlesticks, shape #973, *8-1/2" high, undecorated, Lenox palette mark, one only* **15.00**

Candlesticks, *shape #2029, holes for electrification*

- ☐ Candlesticks, shape #973, *8-1/2" high, wide flat gold trim, Lenox wreath mark, pair*.. **50.00**
- ☐ Candlesticks, shape #974, *8-1/4" high, undecorated, Lenox palette mark, one only* **10.00**
- ☐ Candlesticks, shape #974, *8-1/4" high, hand-painted bees and butterflies, gold trim on top and bottom, artist signed and dated, small fleck on base of one, Lenox palette mark, pair* **100.00**

☐ Candlesticks, shape #975, *2" high, attached underplate with handle, gold trim on all rims and handle, Lenox palette mark* **50.00**

☐ Candlesticks, shape #975, *2" high, pencil-line gold trim, Lenox wreath mark* **40.00**

☐ Candlesticks, shape #1992, *tall, undecorated, Lenox wreath mark, pair*... **35.00**

☐ Candlesticks, shape #1992, *tall, gold trim, Lenox wreath mark, pair* .. **45.00**

☐ Candlesticks, shape #2029, *deep greenish-blue, ornate gold trim, factory-drilled holes for electrification, Lenox wreath mark, pair*.. **40.00**

CANE AND UMBRELLA HANDLES
Handles are usually unmarked, and those which were not broken are probably lying somewhere in a junk shop unnoticed and unpurchased. We have no sales for handles during the past year, but feel that an authenticated shape would be worth in the $75 to $100 range.

CHOCOLATE POTS
☐ Chocolate pot, shape #26, *10" high, mask spout, embossed aquatic figures on bottom half of pot and on lid, shaded from green to lavender to almost white, gold trim highlighting embossed sections and handle, 1/8" high on spout, C.A.C. wreath mark* **225.00**

☐ Chocolate pot, shape #26, *10" high, mask spout, embossed aquatic figures on bottom half of pot and lid, undecorated, C.A.C. lavender palette mark* **140.00**

☐ Chocolate pot, shape #107, *8" high, hand-painted cabbage roses, pink on one side of pot, yellow on other, shaded blue background, gold trim on spout, handle, rims and lid, C.A.C. green palette mark, artist signed and dated* **125.00**

☐ Chocolate pot, shape #107, *8" high, beautifully done floral design on shaded background, gold trim, signed W. H. Morley, transition mark* . **300.00**

☐ Chocolate pot, shape #107, *8" high, brushed gold trim on handle, spout, and lid, single yellow tea rose on either side, very nice for home decoration, C.A.C. lavender palette mark* **125.00**

☐ Chocolate pot, shape #107, *8" high, undecorated, Lenox palette mark* **70.00**

☐ Chocolate pot, shape #842, *11" high, plain design, gold trim on handle, rim and lid finial, gold initials on front, Lenox palette mark* **50.00**

☐ Chocolate pot, shape #842, *11" high, plain shape, hand-painted scattered violet design, gold trim, although home decorated it is a good copy of the basic factory pattern of violets and was possibly an attempt to replace a missing piece to a set, artist signed on bottom, Lenox palette mark* **75.00**

☐ Chocolate pot, shape #842, *11" high, undecorated and unmarked* ... **20.00**

☐ Chocolate pot, shape #842, *11" high, undecorated, Lenox wreath mark*... **45.00**

☐ Chocolate pot, shape #905, *11" high, hexagon shape, hand-painted spring flowers on shaded background, gold trim, really messy looking, Lenox palette mark*....................................... **65.00**

☐ Chocolate pot, shape #905, *11" high, hexagon shape, hand-painted Delft-type scene in monochromatic blue, nice work for a home artist, artist signed and dated, Lenox palette mark, small chip on base* **125.00**

CIGAR JARS

- ☐ Cigar jar, shape #346, *3-1/2" x 3-1/2", gold trim and monogram, Lenox palette mark* **25.00**
- ☐ Cigar jar, shape #346, *3-1/2" x 3-1/2", hand-painted tiny roses, C.A.C. palette mark* **50.00**

CIGARETTE BOXES

- ☐ Cigarette box, shape #2424, *plain green, Lenox wreath mark* **22.00**
- ☐ Cigarette box, shape #2424, *white with Lenox Rose trim, Lenox wreath mark* **32.00**
- ☐ Cigarette box, shape #2424, *white with Ming trim, Lenox wreath mark* **35.00**
- ☐ Cigarette box, shape #2996, *feather finial, coral and white, Lenox wreath mark* **25.00**
- ☐ Cigarette box, shape #2996, *feather finial, green and white, Lenox wreath mark* **25.00**
- ☐ Cigarette box, shape #2996, *feather finial yellow and white, Lenox wreath mark* **30.00**
- ☐ Cigarette box, shape #2996, *feather finial, green with gold on finial, Lenox wreath mark* **35.00**
- ☐ Cigarette box, shape #2996, *feather finial, white with gold trim, Lenox wreath mark* **25.00**
- ☐ Cigarette box, shape #3006, *relief floral design on top section, plain white, Lenox wreath mark* **23.00**
- ☐ Cigarette box, shape #3006, *relief floral design on top section, plain coral, Lenox wreath mark* **25.00**
- ☐ Cigarette box, shape #3006, *relief floral design on top section, yellow and white, Lenox wreath mark* **40.00**
- ☐ Cigarette box, shape #3006, *relief floral design on top section, Lenox Rose design on bottom section, Lenox wreath mark* **20.00**
- ☐ Cigarette box, shape #3006, *relief floral design on top section, gold tracing on flowers, Lenox wreath mark* **24.00**
- ☐ Cigarette box, shape #3006, *relief floral design on top section, large single rose design on bottom, Lenox wreath mark* **24.00**
- ☐ Cigarette box, shape #3006, *relief floral design on top section, Ming pattern on bottom section, Lenox wreath mark* **30.00**
- ☐ Cigarette box, shape #3018, *rounded corners, ribbing, relief apple blossom design, Lenox wreath mark* **24.00**
- ☐ Cigarette box, shape #3018, *rounded corners, ribbing, relief apple blossom design, green with white flowers, Lenox wreath mark* **35.00**
- ☐ Cigarette box, shape #3018, *rounded corners, ribbing, relief apple blossom design, coral and white, Lenox wreath mark* **34.00**
- ☐ Cigarette box, shape #3018, *rounded corners, ribbing, relief apple blossom design, white with gold tracing on flowers and finial, Lenox wreath mark* **30.00**
- ☐ Cigarette box, shape #3018, *rounded corners, ribbing, relief apple blossom design, green with gold trim on handle and flowers, Lenox wreath mark* **40.00**
- ☐ Cigarette box, shape #3033, *rounded corners, Lenox Rose pattern, Lenox wreath mark* **35.00**
- ☐ Cigarette box, shape #3033, *rounded corners, solid green, Lenox wreath mark* **28.00**
- ☐ Cigarette box, shape #3033, *rounded corners, solid yellow, Lenox wreath mark* **40.00**

Cigarrette box, *shape #3018, apple blossom design*

☐ Cigarette box, shape #3033, *rounded corners, full-color clipper ship motif, Lenox wreath mark* **50.00**

☐ Cigarette box, shape #3033, *rounded corners, Blue Ridge pattern, Lenox wreath mark* **30.00**

☐ Cigarette box, shape #3033, *rounded corners, Rhodora pattern, Lenox wreath mark* **30.00**

☐ Cigarette box, shape #3033, *rounded corners, Fairmount pattern, Lenox wreath mark* **30.00**

☐ Cigarette box, shape #3033, *rounded corners, Caprice pattern, Lenox wreath mark* **30.00**

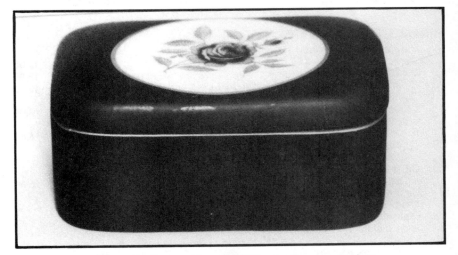

Cigarette box, *shape #3033, single rose design*

Cigarette box, *shape #3033, floral design*

☐ Cigarette box, shape #3033, *rounded corners, laurel wreath in gold around outer rim of top, Lenox wreath mark* **24.00**
☐ Cigarette box, shape #3033, *rounded corners, maroon with gold trim and single rose design, Lenox wreath mark* **40.00**
☐ Cigarette box, shape #3033, *rounded corners, pale blue with gold floral design on top, Lenox wreath mark* **30.00**
☐ Cigarette box, shape #3165, *bird finial, undecorated, Lenox wreath mark* **50.00**
☐ Cigarette box, shape #3165, *bird finial, coral and white, Lenox wreath mark* **55.00**
☐ Cigarette box, shape #3165, *bird finial, blue and white, Lenox wreath mark* **57.00**

CIGARETTE HOLDERS AND JARS

☐ Cigarette holder, shape #2614, *3" high, white with gold trim, Lenox wreath mark* **10.00**
☐ Cigarette holder, shape #2614, *3" high, coral, Lenox wreath mark* ... **13.00**
☐ Cigarette holder, shape #2614, *3" high, blue, Lenox wreath mark* **13.00**
☐ Cigarette holder, shape #2619, *2-7/8" high, gadroon base, coral, Lenox wreath mark* **14.00**
☐ Cigarette holder, shape #2619, *2-7/8" high, gadroon base, blue, Lenox wreath mark* **15.00**
☐ Cigarette holder, shape #2619, *2-7/8" high, gadroon base, yellow, Lenox wreath mark* **17.00**
☐ Cigarette holder, shape #2629, *3" high, fluted base, coral, Lenox wreath mark* **13.00**
☐ Cigarette holder, shape #2629, *3" high, fluted base, coral and white, Lenox wreath mark* **14.00**
☐ Cigarette holder, shape #2629, *3" high, fluted base, blue, Lenox wreath mark* **14.00**
☐ Cigarette holder, shape #2635, *3" high, relief laurel wreath on base, coral, Lenox wreath mark* **15.00**

☐ Cigarette holder, shape #2635, *3" high, relief laurel wreath on base, blue, Lenox wreath mark* **15.00**

☐ Cigarette holder, shape #2635, *3" high, relief laurel wreath on base, green, Lenox wreath mark* **15.00**

☐ Cigarette holder, shape #2635, *3" high, relief laurel wreath on base, white with gold trim, Lenox wreath mark* **13.00**

☐ Cigarette holder, shape #2643, *yellow and white, Lenox wreath mark* . **15.00**

☐ Cigarette holder, shape #2643, *undecorated, Lenox wreath mark* **10.00**

☐ Cigarette holder, shape #2643, *gold trim, Lenox wreath mark* **12.00**

☐ Cigarette holder, shape #2646, *yellow and white, Lenox wreath mark* . **17.00**

☐ Cigarette holder, shape #2646, *gold laurel wreath trim, Lenox wreath mark* **12.00**

☐ Cigarette holder, shape #2646, *undecorated, Lenox wreath mark* **7.00**

☐ Cigarette holder, shape #2656, *2-1/4" high, shape with fluting on base, plain white, Lenox wreath mark* **11.00**

☐ Cigarette holder, shape #2656, *2-1/4" high, oval shape with fluting on base white with gold trim, Lenox wreath mark* **13.00**

The above-listed cigarette holders are small, urn-shaped items and not something through which to smoke a cigarette.

☐ Cigarette jar, shape #347, *2-1/2" x 2-1/2", undecorated, Lenox wreath mark* **15.00**

☐ Cigarette jar, shape #347, *2-1/2" x 2-1/2", blue lustre exterior, gold trim, Lenox palette mark* **13.00**

COFFEEPOTS

☐ Coffeepot, shape #108, *8" high, hand-painted scattered wild flowers, nicely done gold trim, artist signed and dated, C.A.C. lavender palette mark* **95.00**

☐ Coffeepot, shape #108, *8" high, hand-painted yellow daffodils on shaded green background, gold trim all over the place, in addition to being bad artwork it is also very messy, artist's initials, C.A.C. green palette mark* **50.00**

☐ Coffeepot, shape #108, *8" high, floral design in monochromatic green, speckled gold trim, chip on end of spout, C.A.C. green palette mark* **100.00**

☐ Coffeepot, shape #108, *8" high, undecorated, C.A.C. lavender palette mark* **70.00**

☐ Coffeepot, shape #365, *8-1/2" high, Turkish shape demitasse pot, undecorated, Lenox palette mark* **65.00**

☐ Coffeepot, shape #365, *8-1/2" high, Turkish shape demitasse pot, portrait medallion, remainder of pot decorated in aqua with gold trim, artist signed, C.A.C. green palette mark* **150.00**

☐ Coffeepot, shape #365, *8-1/2" high, Turkish shape demitasse pot, gold trim over brown glaze, raised gold paste pseudo-Arabic lettering, C.A.C. lavender palette mark, tiny fleck on end of spout* **150.00**

☐ Coffeepot, shape #371, *10" high, square pedestal base, hand-painted single yellow rose on front, rosebud on back, gold trim on handle, base and top, appears to be a variation of pattern #82, transition mark* **15.00**

☐ Coffeepot, shape #371, *10" high, square pedestal base, hand-painted floral garlands, on shaded pale turquoise background, elaborate gold trim, finial repaired, C.A.C. lavender palette mark* **75.00**

☐ Coffeepot, shape #371, *10" high, square pedestal base, undecorated, Lenox palette mark* **45.00**

☐ Coffeepot, shape #371, *10" high, square pedestal base, transfer portrait surrounded by blue and gold dot work, smaller blue dots covering rest of pot, gold trim on handle and rim, nice for its type, C.A.C. green palette mark* **150.00**

☐ Coffeepot, shape #371, *10" high, square pedestal base, bunch of violets on front and back, small violets on lid, gold trim, well-done, artist signed, Lenox palette mark* **135.00**

☐ Coffeepot, shape #521-1/2, *7-3/4" high, hand-painted pink and red cabbage roses on both sides, lots of gold trim, artist signed and dated, C.A.C. green palette mark* **100.00**

☐ Coffeepot, shape #521-1/2, *7-3/4" high, transfer decorated with Oriental scene in cobalt, coffeepot shades from white around decal to dark cobal on end of spout and on handle and lid, well-executed, Lenox palette mark* **90.00**

☐ Coffeepot, shape #521-1/2, *7-3/4" high, decorated all over with disc-shaped enamel work in different shades of pink, rather resembles anemic-looking blood cells, gold trim on handle, spout, rim and lid, artist's initials and date, Lenox palette mark* **60.00**

☐ Coffeepot, shape #542-1/2, *6-1/2" high, angular modernistic shape, gold trim on handle and spout, gold initial on front, Lenox palette mark* **35.00**

☐ Coffeepot, shape #542-1/2, *6-1/2" high, angular modernistic shape, hand-painted black rose on front, black handle and trim, Lenox palette mark* **30.00**

☐ Coffeepot, shape #542-1/2, *6-1/2" high, undecorated, Lenox wreath mark* **25.00**

☐ Coffeepot, shape #579, *6-1/2" high, hand-painted group of roses on pale beige background, gold trim on handle and finial, good for its type, Lenox palette mark* **75.00**

☐ Coffeepot, shape #579, *6-1/2" high, all cobalt, no trim, Lenox palette mark* **24.00**

☐ Coffeepot, shape #579, *6-1/2" high, pale pink with raised gold work, artist's initials and date, Lenox palette mark* **60.00**

☐ Coffeepot, shape #660, *8" high, hexagon shape, panels of small flowers separated by maroon and raised gold bands, spout is maroon with scattered flowers, handle and lid maroon with gold trim, the pattern would make beautiful drapery material, Lenox palette mark* **100.00**

☐ Coffeepot, shape #660, *8" high, gold trim and monogram, Lenox palette mark* **35.00**

☐ Coffeepot, shape #692, *9" high, decorated with enamel ribbons and hearts, gold trim, artist signed and dated, Lenox palette mark* **90.00**

☐ Coffeepot, shape #692, *9" high, gold geometric design top and bottom, gold handle, Lenox palette mark, small chips on rim opening and bottom of lid* **25.00**

☐ Coffeepot, shape #699, *7" high, undecorated, Lenox wreath mark* . . . **25.00**

☐ Coffeepot, shape #699, *7" high, hand-painted pansies on shaded green background, gold trim, artist's initials and date, Lenox palette mark* **75.00**

☐ Coffeepot, shape #731, *10-5/8" high, hexagon shape, undecorated, Lenox palette mark* **40.00**

☐ Coffeepot, shape #731, *10-5/8" high, beige pearlized finish with gold trim and gold initials on front, Lenox palette mark* **35.00**

☐ Coffeepot, shape #731, *10-5/8" high, hand-painted bunch of wildflowers, gold trim, artist signed, Lenox palette mark* **100.00**

☐ Coffeepot, shape #741, *10" high, hand-painted irises in blue, purple and maroon, green leaves, shaded yellow background, well-done gold trim, artist's initials, Lenox palette mark* **150.00**
☐ Coffeepot, shape #741, *10" high, undecorated, Lenox wreath mark* . . **40.00**
☐ Coffeepot, shape #741, *10" high, powder blue with transfer gold floral decoration, gold trim on handle and rims, gold finial, crack in handle* . . . . : **35.00**
☐ Coffeepot, shape #787, *8-7/8" high, hexagon shape, hand-painted lily of the valley on pale green background, gold trim in appropriate places, Lenox palette mark* **65.00**
☐ Coffeepot, shape #887, *10-1/2" high, undecorated, Lenox palette mark* **50.00**
☐ Coffeepot, shape #933, *5-5/8" high, individual size, solid coral, Lenox wreath mark* **25.00**
☐ Coffeepot, shape #933, *5-5/8" high, individual size, gold trim on handle and rims, gold monogram surrounded by tiny blue forget-me-nots, Lenox palette mark* **60.00**
☐ Coffeepot, shape #933, *5-5/8" high, individual size, blue dot enamel work and small hand-painted little pink roses, artist's initials and date on bottom; Lenox palette mark, two small chips on rim and several flecks on bottom* **50.00**
☐ Coffeepot, shape #933, *5-5/8" high, undecorated, Lenox palette mark* **15.00**

COMPORTS

☐ Comport, shape #441, *9-3/4", open ornate handles, tall base, undecorated, C.A.C. green palette mark* **95.00**
☐ Comport, shape #441, *9-3/4", open ornate handles, tall base, hand-painted roses, yellow on one side, pink on other, gold trim on rims and handles, artist signed and dated, C.A.C. lavender palette mark* . . **85.00**

COVERED BOXES *(EXCLUDING CIGARETTE BOXES)*

☐ Box, shape #60, *1" x 3", embossed design, ribbon finial, undecorated, C.A.C. lavender palette mark* **50.00**
☐ Box, shape #128, *2" x 3", gadroon border, hand-painted roses on blue background, artist signed and dated, C.A.C. green palette mark* **55.00**
☐ Box, shape #146, *3-1/4", plain with gold trim, C.A.C. green palette mark* . . . . : **45.00**
☐ Box, shape #152, *3-1/2" x 2-7/8", hand-painted white doves on lavender background, gold trim, artist signed, C.A.C. green palette mark* **65.00**
☐ Box, shape #169, *4", gentle scalloping on rim, hand-painted violets in scatter-pattern, gold trim, C.A.C. pink palette mark* **100.00**
☐ Box, shape #170, *3-1/4", embossed design, gentle scalloping to rim, undecorated, C.A.C. brown palette mark* **35.00**
☐ Box, shape #171, *5-3/4", embossed design, gentle scalloping to rim, gold tracings on embossed sections, gold trim on rim, C.A.C. green palette mark* **60.00**
☐ Box, shape #172, *2" x 4", rectangle shape, hand-painted small red roses, gold trim and initial, Lenox palette mark, small chip on under-side of rim* **50.00**
☐ Box, shape #194, *4-1/2" x 3-1/8", heart shaped, embossing on lid and base, undecorated C.A.C. brown palette mark* **75.00**
☐ Box, shape #275, *5", round, plain shape with finial, hand-painted flowers in ring around middle, gold trim on finial and rims, artist signed, Lenox palette mark* **80.00**

☐ Box, shape #278, 2", for rouge, round, embossing on rims, ornate finial, undecorated, C.A.C. green palette mark, spider crack in bottom **25.00**

☐ Box, shape #308, 5-1/4", round, embossed design, finial, solid green with gold trim, Lenox wreath mark **40.00**

Box, *shape #514, Lenox rose pattern*

☐ Box, shape #514, 3-3/4", round, undecorated, Lenox palette mark **30.00**

☐ Box, shape #514, 3-3/4", round, Ming pattern, Lenox wreath mark **80.00**

☐ Box, shape #514, 3-3/4", round, hand-painted flowers and gold trim, artist signed, Lenox palette mark **75.00**

☐ Box, shape #514, 8" x 3-3/4", round, solid coral, Lenox wreath mark .. **50.00**

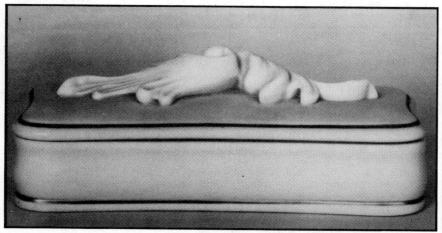

Box, *shape number unknown, white finial*

☐ Box, shape #514, 8" x 3-3/4", round, powder blue with gold trim, Lenox wreath mark **60.00**

☐ Box, shape #514, *8" x 3-3/4", round, yellow, Lenox wreath mark* **70.00**

☐ Box, shape #514, *8" x 3-3/4", round, plain with gold trim, Lenox palette mark* **35.00**

☐ Box, shape #514, *3-3/4", round, Lenox rose pattern, Lenox wreath mark* **75.00**

☐ Box, shape #819, *5-1/2" x 3", finial, round, medium pink with gold trim, gold finial, Lenox wreath mark* **35.00**

☐ Box, shape number unknown, *same as #514 but larger, entire rim covered in etched gold, wide gold banding on bottom section, Lenox wreath mark* **100.00**

☐ Box, shape number unknown, *approx. 3" x 7", rectangle, gray with silver trim, white finial, Lenox gold wreath mark* **35.00**

CUPS AND SAUCERS—COFFEE, TEA AND CHOCOLATE

Numerous listings of cups and saucers decorated with standard dinnerware patterns can be found in the dinnerware section. The following are those cups and saucers which are undecorated or which are hand-painted.

☐ Cup and saucer, shape #2, *2-1/4", ribbed design, fancy handle, eggshell thin, undecorated, C.A.C. brown palette mark* **35.00**

☐ Cup and saucer, shape #2, *2-1/4", ribbed design, fancy handle, eggshell thin, beige matte finish with gold trim, C.A.C. red palette mark* **50.00**

☐ Cup and saucer, shape #2, *2-1/4", ribbed design, fancy handle, gold trim, Lenox palette mark* **25.00**

☐ Cup and saucer, shape #3, *2-1/4", six panels with fish scale design, fancy handle, undecorated, C.A.C. lavender palette mark* **35.00**

☐ Cup and saucer, shape #3, *2-1/4", six panels with fish scale design, handle trimmed in gold and fish scales outlined in gold, handle repaired, small fleck on rim, transition mark* **50.00**

☐ Cup and saucer, shape #4, *2-1/4", fluted design with fancy handle, decorated with hand-painted forget-me-nots and gold, C.A.C. lavender palette mark* **40.00**

☐ Cup and saucer, shape #4, *2-1/4", fluted design with fancy handle, matte finish with raised gold paste in floral design, C.A.C. pink palette mark* **65.00**

☐ Cup and saucer, shape #5, *2", swirled rib design, undecorated, Lenox palette mark* **20.00**

☐ Cup and saucer, shape #5, *2", swirled rib design, gold trim on handle, sponged gold effect on ribs, transition mark* **50.00**

☐ Cup and saucer, shape #6, *2-1/4", swirled rib design, undecorated, Lenox wreath mark* **20.00**

☐ Cup and saucer, shape #8, *2-1/2", seashell design, eggshell thin, undecorated, C.A.C. lavender palette mark* **50.00**

☐ Cup and saucer, shape #8, *2-1/4", seashell design, eggshell thin, gold trim, C.A.C. green palette mark* **55.00**

☐ Cup and saucer, shape #46, *2", square shape with rounded corners, forked handle, narrow ribbed design on cup and saucer, undecorated, Lenox wreath mark* **35.00**

☐ Cup and saucer, shape #46, *2", square shape with rounded corners, forked handle, narrow ribbed design on cup and saucer, gold trim, C.A.C. brown palette mark* **45.00**

☐ Cup and saucer, shape #98, 2-1/4", fluted design with ring handle, saucer comes up very high and resembles a small bowl rather than a saucer, known as the "engagement cup", Lenox wreath mark **25.00**

☐ Cup and saucer, shape #98, 2" x 2-1/4", fluted design with ring handle, deep saucer, hand-painted small pink roses in a scatter pattern on inside of cup and on top side of saucer, outside of cup and bottom part of saucer completely covered in gold, saucer repaired, C.A.C. red palette mark **40.00**

☐ Cup and saucer, shape #105, 3-1/4", melon ribbed with dimpled finish, ring handle, raised on ball feet, C.A.C. brown palette mark.... **50.00**

☐ Cup and saucer, shape #105, 3-1/4", melon ribbed with dimpled finish, ring handles, raised on ball feet, gold trim on handle and rims, small fleck on bottom edge of saucer, C.A.C. pink palette mark **55.00**

☐ Cup and saucer, shape #106, 2-1/4", melon ribbed with dimpled finish, ring handle, raised on ball feet, undecorated, C.A.C. green palette mark **45.00**

☐ Cup and saucer, shape #117, 2-1/8" x 2-7/8", tall thin shape, ribbed design, fancy ring handle, gold trim on handle and rims, C.A.C. green palette mark **45.00**

☐ Cup and saucer, shape #121, 2" x 2-7/8", fluted design, flared rim, saucer very deep, gold trim, artist's initials on bottom of saucer, Lenox, palette mark.. **30.00**

☐ Cup and saucer, shape #162, 1-1/4", double ring handle, wide fluting on cup and saucer, hand-painted with tiny pink roses, sponged gold near rims, gold handle, transition mark......................... **70.00**

☐ Cup and saucer, shape #162, 1-1/4", double ring handle, wide fluting on cup and saucer, undecorated, Lenox palette mark.............. **20.00**

☐ Cup and saucer, shape #163, 1-1/2", double ring handle, square shape with rounded corners, large red roses hand-painted on front and on saucer, gold trim on handle and rim, Lenox palette mark..... **30.00**

☐ Cup and saucer, shape #163, 1-1/2", double ring handle, square shape with rounded corners, small violets in scatter pattern, gold trim on handle and rims, transition mark **65.00**

☐ Cup and saucer, shape #163, 1-1/2", double ring handle, square shape with rounded corners, small violets in scatter pattern, gold trim on handle and rims, transition mark **65.00**

☐ Cup and saucer, shape #164, 2", very plain shape and handle, undecorated, C.A.C. green palette mark **20.00**

☐ Cup and saucer, shape #164, 2", very plain shape and handle, hand-painted with cherries, gold trim, C.A.C. lavender palette mark **38.00**

☐ Cup and saucer, shape #164, 2", very plain shape and handle, hand-painted with small pink roses in scatter pattern and gold trim, transition mark... **65.00**

☐ Cup and saucer, shape #164, 2", very plain shape and handle, undecorated, C.A.C. green palette mark **20.00**

☐ Cup and saucer, shape #164, 2", very plain shape and handle, hand-painted with fruit, gold trim, C.A.C. lavender palette mark **38.00**

☐ Cup and saucer, shape #164, 2", very plain shape and handle, hand-painted with small pink roses and gold trim, transition mark **65.00**

☐ Cup and saucer, shape #174, 2-1/8", ruffled rim and fancy handle, gold trim, Lenox palette mark.................................. **35.00**

☐ Cup and saucer, shape #174, 2-1/8", beige matte finish with raised gold paste floral design, gold trim on rims, C.A.C. red palette mark .. **80.00**

☐ Cup and saucer, shape #174, 2-1/8", ruffled rim and fancy handle, gold trim, Lenox palette mark.................................. **35.00**

☐ Cup and saucer, shape #174, 2-1/8", ruffled rim and fancy handle, beige matte finish with raised gold paste floral pattern, gold trim on handle and rims, C.A.C. red palette mark **80.00**

☐ Cup and saucer, shape #179, 2", slight melon ribbed shape with fancy handle, gold trim on handle and rims and gold monogram on front of cup, Lenox palette mark **25.00**

☐ Cup and saucer, shape #179, 2", slight melon ribbed shape with fancy handle, beige matte finish, raised gold paste design, centers of flowers tinted a pale coral color, transition mark.................. **75.00**

☐ Cup and saucer, shape #180, 2", swirled ribbing, undecorated, C.A.C. green palette mark... **20.00**

☐ Cup and saucer, shape #180, 2", swirled ribbing, rainbow effect with each rib a different pastel color separated by gold, gold speckling on handle, home decorated but nicely done and an interesting decorating concept, C.A.C. green palette mark **60.00**

☐ Cup and saucer, shape #216, 2", flared scalloped rim, fancy handle, undecorated, Lenox palette mark **25.00**

☐ Cup and saucer, shape #216, 2", flared scalloped rim, fancy handle, hand-painted with large roses in pink, gold handle, gold trim, on rims, C.A.C. green palette mark **35.00**

☐ Cup and saucer, shape #247, 2-1/4", ornate handle, hand-painted poppies (badly done), gold trim on handle and rims, Lenox palette mark.. **30.00**

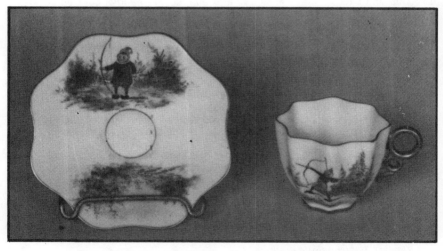

Cup and saucer, *Palmer-Cox brownie decoration*

☐ Cup and saucer, shape #261, *Palmer-Cox brownie decoration, gold trim, C.A.C. lavender palette mark* **80.00**

☐ Cup and saucer, shape #301, 1-7/8", resembles Irish Belleek's "Tridacna" pattern, forked handle, pearl glaze on inside, speckled gold on handle, C.A.C. lavender palette mark.................... **60.00**

☐ Cup and saucer, shape #301, 1-7/8", resembles Irish Belleek's "Tridacna" pattern, forked handle, small, hand-painted roses around inside of rim, pearl glaze on outside, very badly done, Lenox palette mark.. **35.00**

☐ Cup and saucer, shape #309, 2-1/2", *large ribbed design, reverse "C" handle, hand-painted with different fruit designs, gold trim on handle and rims, Lenox palette mark* **35.00**

☐ Cup and saucer, shape #309, 2-1/2", *large ribbed design, reverse "C" handle, undecorated, C.A.C. lavender palette mark* **30.00**

☐ Cup and saucer, shape #402, *shell-shaped, forked handle, white with gold trim, Lenox palette mark* **30.00**

☐ Cup and saucer, shape #448, *plain with squared-off handle, hand-painted flowers, gold trim on handle and rims, Lenox palette mark* ... **30.00**

☐ Cup and saucer, shape #448, *plain shape with squared-off handle, hand-painted fruit, gold trim on handle and rims, Lenox palette mark* **35.00**

☐ Cup and saucer, shape #448, *plain shape with square-off handle, gold trim on handle and rims, gold monogram in front of cup, Lenox palette mark* **20.00**

☐ Cup and saucer, shape #495, *square pedestal base, plain shape with squared-off handle, hand-painted overall floral design, gold trim on handle and rims, Lenox palette mark* **35.00**

☐ Cup and saucer, shape #495, *square pedestal base, plain shape with squared-off handle, hand-painted garlands of flowers, gold trim on handles and rims, Lenox wreath mark* **65.00**

☐ Cup and saucer, shape #551, *plain, undecorated, Lenox palette mark* **18.00**

☐ Cup and saucer, shape #551, *hand-painted roses, gold trim, Lenox palette mark* **30.00**

☐ Cup and saucer, shape #556, *tall and thin, square handle, covered with badly done blue dot enamel work, Lenox palette mark* **25.00**

☐ Cup and saucer, shape #557, *hand-painted small pink roses in a scattered design, gold pencil-line on rim and handle, Lenox wreath mark* . **50.00**

☐ Cup and saucer, shape #595, 2-1/4", *hand-painted with butterflies and flowers, artist signed, Lenox palette mark* **35.00**

☐ Cup and saucer, shape #600, *hand-painted with cherub and flowers, gold trim (worn), Lenox palette mark* **50.00**

☐ Cup and saucer, shape #608, *solid coral outside, cream color inside, Lenox wreath mark* **15.00**

☐ Cup and saucer, shape #610, *hand-painted monochromatic "Blue Willow" type scene, home decorated but nicely done, Lenox palette mark* **60.00**

☐ Cup and saucer, shape #633D, *plain white, Lenox wreath mark* **10.00**

☐ Cup and saucer, shape #633D, *floral transfer design, pink handle, Lenox palette mark* **28.00**

☐ Cup and saucer, shape #654-1/2, *squared-off handle, gold trim and gold flower design, Lenox palette mark* **20.00**

☐ Cup and saucer, shape #664, *all cobalt (probably a piece earmarked for silver overlay that never got that far), Lenox wreath mark* **20.00**

☐ Cup and saucer, shape #665, *hand-painted with little hearts and flowers, Lenox palette mark* **40.00**

☐ Cup and saucer, shape #668, *hand-painted berries, gold trim, Lenox palette mark* **28.00**

☐ Cup and saucer, shape #669, *blue dot enamel work with small pink roses, artist signed and dated, Lenox palette mark* **50.00**

☐ Cup and saucer, shape #670, *hand-painted fruit, gold trim, signed J. Nosek, Lenox wreath mark* **50.00**

☐ Cup and saucer, shape #714, *hexagon shape, hand-painted pink roses on green background, gold trim, Lenox palette mark* **30.00**

☐ Cup and saucer, shape #756, *gold trim with gold initial on front, artist initialed and dated on bottom, Lenox palette mark* **15.00**

☐ Cup and saucer, shape #773, *floral garlands, gold trim, Lenox palette mark*... **30.00**

☐ Cup and saucer, shape #813, *hexagon shape, brown glaze, (probably meant for silver overlay), Lenox palette mark* **17.00**

☐ Cup and saucer, shape #814, *hexagon shape, gold trim and outlining, dreadful artwork, Lenox palette mark* **14.00**

☐ Cup and saucer, shape #815, *hand-painted morning glories on yellow background, Lenox palette mark* **25.00**

☐ Cup and saucer, shape #816, *hand-painted roses on tan background, Lenox palette mark* **30.00**

☐ Cup and saucer, shape #837, *undecorated, Lenox palette mark* **12.00**

☐ Cup and saucer, shape #838, *hand-painted with wildflowers and gold trim, Lenox palette mark* **35.00**

☐ Cup and saucer, shape #839, *undecorated, Lenox palette mark* **15.00**

☐ Cup and saucer, shape #841, *gold trim, Lenox palette mark*......... **15.00**

☐ Cup and saucer, shape #843, *hand-painted with small violets in a scatter pattern, Lenox wreath mark*........................... **60.00**

☐ Cup and saucer, shape #845, *hand-painted with picture of gray cat, silver trim, rather unusual looking but not badly done, Lenox palette mark*.. **50.00**

☐ Cup and saucer, shape #846, *undecorated, Lenox palette mark* **13.00**

☐ Cup and saucer, shape #847, *hand-painted with large pink rose on both sides, pale green background, gold trim, the absolute pits in home decorating, Lenox palette mark* **30.00**

☐ Cup and saucer, shape #852, *hand-painted with pastel enamels in a drippy sort of effect, gold trim, Lenox palette mark* **25.00**

☐ Cup and saucer, shape #852, *undecorated, Lenox palette mark* **15.00**

☐ Cup and saucer, shape #854, *gold trim on handle and rims, Lenox palette mark* **15.00**

☐ Cup and saucer, shape #866, *cup has small knob instead of regular handle, undecorated, Lenox palette mark*....................... **20.00**

☐ Cup and saucer, shape #866, *cup has small knob instead of regular handle, gold trim on handle and rim, Lenox palette mark* **20.00**

☐ Cup and saucer, shape #885, *hand-painted butterflies on tan background, artist signed and dated, Lenox palette mark* **30.00**

☐ Cup and saucer, shape #886, *undecorated, Lenox palette mark* **13.00**

☐ Cup and saucer, shape #895, *hand-painted pansies on cream background, nicely done, gold trim, Lenox palette mark*........... **35.00**

☐ Cup and saucer, shape #943, *solid deep blue-green, Lenox wreath mark*.. **25.00**

☐ Cup and saucer, shape #1006, *undecorated, Lenox palette mark* **15.00**

☐ Cup and saucer, shape #1006, *transfer decoration of Martha Washington, gold trim, Lenox palette mark* **15.00**

DARNING EGGS

Lenox darning eggs are usually unmarked. They were made in two shapes—#217, 6" long, is a full-sized egg, and #287 is a smaller, skinnier one used to repair the fingers on gloves. Both are very rare.

We have no actual selling prices for these two darning eggs, but would estimate their worth from $50 to $100 depending on condition and trim. Although an item this rare would typically be worth more, since they are not marked there is no way to verify they are Lenox.

DESK ITEMS

- ☐ Inkwell, shape #61, 2-1/2" high, beehive-shaped, undecorated, C.A.C. green palette mark **50.00**
- ☐ Inkwell, shape #136, hand-decorated with musical symbols, C.A.C. lavender palette mark, very pretty **75.00**
  The above inkwell came with a ruffled-rim tray originally, but no tray was present with the sample listed.
- ☐ Inkwell, shape #157, underplate 5" diameter, tiny inkwell, hand-painted yellow flower on both parts, gold trim, transition mark **135.00**
- ☐ Inkwell, shape #157, underplate missing, small blue flowers, C.A.C. lavender palette mark **65.00**
- ☐ Inkwell, shape #239, 2-1/4" high, embossed design, cobalt with gold trim, liner missing, C.A.C. brown palette mark **90.00**
- ☐ Inkwell, shape #239, 2-1/4" high, embossed design, undecorated and unmarked, liner present **50.00**
- ☐ Inkwell, shape #239, 2-1/4" high, embossed design, gold trim on embossing, Lenox palette mark **95.00**
- ☐ Inkwell, shape #313, 4" across base, square shape with round lid, undecorated and unmarked **25.00**
- ☐ Inkwell, shape #313, 4" across base, square shape with round lid, hand-painted flowers and gold trim, artist signed and dated, C.A.C. green palette mark **100.00**
- ☐ Inkwell, shape #549, 2-1/2", round, gold trim and initial, Lenox palette mark **75.00**
- ☐ Inkwell, shape #549, 2-1/2", little pink flowers with gold trim, Lenox palette mark **90.00**
- ☐ Inkwell, shape #550, 3-1/4", round, gold quill pen on side and on lid, green all over, artist signed and dated, unmarked **40.00**
- ☐ Three-piece desk set, item numbers unknown, unmarked rolling blotters, two-compartment standing letter holder (6" x 8"), and covered inkwell with 5" underplate, monochromatic blue Delft type scene with houses, children, etc., artist's initials, transition mark and Tiffany & Company mark **450.00**

Three-piece desk set, *item numbers unknown*

DOOR KNOBS AND DRAWER PULLS

Most of the knobs which were sold are probably still in place on the purchaser's furniture or doors. They are usually unmarked, and an identifiable knob would have to be priced at $100 or better.

EWERS

☐ Ewer, shape #33, *8-1/4" high, yellow and orange enamel work, gold handle and rims, C.A.C. purple palette mark* **80.00**

☐ Ewer, shape #33, *8-1/4" high, purple and yellow flowers, mostly pansies, artist signed, Lenox palette mark* . . . .

☐ Ewer, shape #33, *8-1/4" high, undecorated, C.A.C. brown palette mark* **150.00**

☐ Ewer, shape #33, *8-1/4" high, gold trim on handle and brushed gold effect on rims, Lenox green wreath mark* **100.00**

☐ Ewer, shape #36, *10" high, undecorated, Lenox palette mark* **75.00**

☐ Ewer, shape #36, *10" high, hand-painted roses, gold trim on handle and rims, C.A.C. palette mark, artist signed and dated* **125.00**

☐ Ewer, shape #36, *10" high, monochromatic green scenic with gold on handle, not factory done but a very interesting look and not badly painted, C.A.C. palette mark* **150.00**

☐ Ewer, shape #36, *10" high, white with coral handle, Lenox green wreath mark* **75.00**

☐ Ewer, shape #39, *9-1/4" high, twig handle, shaded from rust brown to yellow to lavender, roses painted in tri-colors already mentioned, signed Marsh, transition/Glen-Iris mark* **300.00**

☐ Ewer, shape #39, *9-1/4" high, undecorated, Lenox palette mark* **125.00**

☐ Ewer, shape #39, *9-1/4" high, sponged gold work on upper half, handle gold, home-done but beautiful, C.A.C. green palette mark* **250.00**

☐ Ewer, shape #39, *9-1/4" high, beige matte finish, raised gold trim, gold on handle, C.A.C. wreath mark* **300.00**

☐ Ewer, shape #40, *10" high, undecorated, Lenox palette mark* **100.00**

☐ Ewer, shape #40, *10" high, nasturtiums on shaded brown to tan background, artist signed and dated, C.A.C. green palette mark* **175.00**

☐ Ewer, shape #40, *10" high, enamel flowers, gold trim on handle and rim, Lenox palette mark* **125.00**

☐ Ewer, shape #41, *9" high, shaded from green to pink to lavender, gold work on handle and rims, small repaired spot on rim, transition mark* **175.00**

☐ Ewer, shape #41, *9" high, yellow floral trim, gold handle and rim, artist signed and dated, C.A.C. lavender palette mark* **150.00**

☐ Ewer, shape #41, *9" high, undecorated, C.A.C. brown palette mark* . . . **175.00**

☐ Ewer, shape #42, *10-1/2" tall, beautifully decorated with pale yellow and brown orchids outlined in gold, beige satin background, speckled gold trim on handle and near rim, no artist signature, transition mark* **325.00**

☐ Ewer, shape #42, *10-1/2" high, plain with gold trim, Lenox wreath mark* **100.00**

☐ Ewer, shape #42, *10-1/2" high, hand-painted spray of small roses, gold handle and rims, nicely done, C.A.C. green palette mark* **150.00**

☐ Ewer, shape #43, *10" high, beige satin background, gold work on handle and rims, gold tracings on detailing of ewer, C.A.C. wreath mark* . **250.00**

☐ Ewer, shape #43, *10" high, undecorated, Lenox palette mark* **125.00**

☐ Ewer, shape #44, *10-1/2" high, single yellow rose on front and back, gold trim on handle and rims, Lenox palette mark* **130.00**

☐ Ewer, shape #44, *10-1/2" high, gold handle, no other decoration, C.A.C. palette mark* . . . . : **135.00**

☐ Ewer, shape #45, *shaded from green to lavender, raised gold work, factory done but strangely unappealing, transition mark* **175.00**

☐ Ewer, shape #45, *10-1/2" high, hand-painted spray of autumn leaves on front and back, shaded tan background, C.A.C. palette mark* **200.00**

☐ Ewer, shape #69, 6-1/4" high, shaped like leaf with curly end to form spout and tendril coming up to form handle, white with gold trim, Lenox wreath mark **65.00**

☐ Ewer, shape #69, 6-1/4" high, description as above, solid dark green, Lenox wreath mark **60.00**

☐ Ewer, shape #69, 6-1/4" high, description as above, white with coral tendrils, Lenox wreath mark **50.00**

☐ Ewer, shape #69, 6-1/4" high, hand-painted violets on front and back, tendrils painted green, although not great art work the overall effect is very nice, C.A.C. palette mark **150.00**

☐ Ewer, shape #354, 10-1/4" high, portrait of Victorian woman, raised gold paste and blue dot enamel work, gold handle and pedestal base, artist signed and dated, perfectly dreadful, C.A.C. green palette mark **250.00**

☐ Ewer, shape #354, 10-1/4" high, satin beige background with raised gold floral work, gold handle, gold pencil-line rims, C.A.C. wreath mark **400.00**

☐ Ewer, shape #443, 14-1/2" high, undecorated, C.A.C. green palette mark.. **150.00**

☐ Ewer, shape #443, 14-1/2" high, hand-painted roses, gold handle and rims, C.A.C. lavender palette mark **250.00**

☐ Ewer, shape #444, 12" high, hand-painted peacock on shaded background, artist signed, C.A.C. palette mark **150.00**

FERN POTS AND PLANTERS

☐ Fern pot, shape #154, 2-1/2" high, 8-1/2" diameter, has lift-out liner with several holes in bottom to allow for proper drainage, hand-painted maroon, pink and blue flowers and green leaves, gold trim, C.A.C. pink palette mark, Davis Collamore store mark, liner unmarked **150.00**

Fern pot, shape #154

☐ Fern pot, shape #173, *3" high, bulbous shape, ruffled rim, catalogue picture looks like it might have had a liner like the one in shape #154 but none present with this example, hand-painted small violets in scatter pattern, C.A.C. lavender palette mark* **100.00**

☐ Fern pot, shape #181, *6-1/4", round shape, ruffled rim, speckld gold trim, C.A.C. lavender palette mark, several flecks on rim* **75.00**

☐ Fern pot, shape #182, *6-1/4", same basic shape as #181 but rim is scalloped as well as ruffled, pale lavender exterior, gold trim on rim, C.A.C. pink palette mark* **125.00**

☐ Fern pot, shape #299, *10-1/2" x 13", undecorated, embossed neck, round body, C.A.C. green palette mark* **95.00**

☐ Planter, shape #2400, *white with blue handles, Lenox wreath mark* .. **50.00**

☐ Planter, shape #2441, *plain white, Lenox wreath mark* **25.00**

Planter, *shape #2616, coral handles*

☐ Planter, shape #2616, *white with coral handles, Lenox wreath mark* .. **65.00**

☐ Planter, shape #2616, *all white, Lenox wreath mark* **25.00**

☐ Planter, shape #2616, *yellow with white handles, Lenox wreath mark*. **80.00**

☐ Planter, shape #2634, *similar to #2616, white with pale green handles, Lenox wreath mark* **45.00**

☐ Planter, shape #2637, *similar to #2616, white with blue handles, Lenox wreath mark* **35.00**

☐ Planter, shape #2788, *white with gold trim, Lenox wreath mark* **32.00**

☐ Planter, shape #3010, *undecorated, embossed design, Lenox wreath mark.* **30.00**

☐ Planter, shape #3011, *undecorated, embossed design, Lenox wreath mark.* **30.00**

☐ Planter, shape #3019, *white embossed design on pale peach background, Lenox wreath mark* **65.00**

FRAMES

Although they were made in several shapes and sizes during the early days of the Lenox Company, few picture frames have survived to the present day. They would have been prime candidates for breakage considering that they would have been left out in vulnerable spots like dressing tables and desks.

Both of the sales we have listed for last year were for unmarked specimens. The price for a plain frame was $75., and for an ornate one $110.

HONEY POTS

Item #894, is a 4-1/4" beehive-shaped honey pot with applied bees on the sides and lid. The same shape was used much earlier on a 2-1/2" item, but this one is actually an inkwell and is listed in that section.

- ☐ Beehive honey pot, *undecorated, Lenox palette mark* **30.00**
- ☐ Beehive honey pot, *each bee a different color, red stripe on top and bottom of pot, Lenox palette mark* **45.00**
- ☐ Beehive honey pot, *beige background, multi-colored bees, dark brown banding top and bottom, Lenox wreath mark* **65.00**
- ☐ Beehive honey pot, *gold bees and banding, Lenox wreath mark, top bee glued on* **35.00**
- ☐ Beehive honey pot, *pearlized champagne color, each bee a different color, several wing chips on bees, Lenox palette mark* **25.00**

HORNS OF PLENTY

The horn of plenty was done in five different sizes in an upright position, and a tiny horizontal one is in current production.

- ☐ Horn of plenty, shape #70, *4-1/2" high, plain white, Lenox wreath mark* **22.00**
- ☐ Horn of plenty, shape #70, *4-1/2" high, white with gold trim, Lenox palette mark* **25.00**
- ☐ Horn of plenty, shape #70, *4-1/2" high, solid coral, Lenox wreath mark* **30.00**

Horn of Plenty, *shape #70, hand-painted*

☐ Horn of plenty, shape #70, *4-1/2" high, white with blue handle, Lenox wreath mark* **32.00**

☐ Horn of plenty, shape #70, *4-1/2" high, solid green, Lenox wreath mark*. **35.00**

☐ Horn of plenty, shape #70, *4-1/2" high, hand-painted roses and raised blue enamel work, gold trim, artist signed, C.A.C. lavender palette mark*. **175.00**

☐ Horn of plenty, shape #2442, *10" high, plain white, Lenox wreath mark*. **35.00**

☐ Horn of plenty, shape #2442, *10" high, white with gold trim, Lenox wreath mark* **45.00**

☐ Horn of plenty, shape #2442, *10" high, coral and white, Lenox wreath mark*. **60.00**

Horn of Plenty, *shape #2442, signed J. Nosek*

☐ Horn of plenty, shape #2442, *10" high, hand-painted fall flowers, gold trim, signed J. Nosek, Lenox wreath mark, pair* **425.00**

☐ Horn of plenty, shape #2443, *8-1/4" high, plain white, Lenox wreath mark*. **40.00**

☐ Horn of plenty, shape #2443, *8-1/4" high, gold trim on white, Lenox wreath mark* **50.00**

☐ Horn of plenty, shape #2443, *8-1/4" high, blue and white, Lenox wreath mark* **50.00**

☐ Horn of plenty, shape #2443, *8-1/4" high, floral transfer design, gold trim, Lenox wreath mark* **65.00**

☐ Horn of plenty, shape #2754, *7" high, plain white, Lenox wreath mark* **38.00**

☐ Horn of plenty, shape #2754, *7" high, solid coral, Lenox wreath mark*. **45.00**

☐ Horn of plenty, shape #2754, *7" high, solid green, Lenox wreath mark* **50.00**

☐ Horn of plenty, shape #2754, *7" high, Lenox Rose pattern, Lenox wreath mark* **75.00**

☐ Horn of plenty, shape #2818, *6-1/8" high, plain white, Lenox wreath mark*. **32.00**

INVALID FEEDERS

These are relatively scarce Lenox items, and were made in only one shape.

☐ Invalid feeder, shape number unknown, hand-painted leaves with gold trim, Lenox wreath mark **95.00**

Invalid feeder

JUGS

Although we have several listings for whisky jugs, they should not be considered common items. For the most part they are found only with early marks.

☐ Jug, shape #271, *8" tall, undecorated, Lenox palette mark* **40.00**

☐ Jug, shape #271, *8" tall, badly decorated with wheat stalks on mottled background, artist initialed, Lenox palette mark* **65.00**

☐ Jug, shape #357, *6" tall, gold trim with "Whisky" written across front, C.A.C. palette mark* **75.00**

☐ Jug, shape #357, *6" tall, hand-painted hops and leaves on shaded background, nicely done, C.A.C. palette mark* **130.00**

☐ Jug, shape #357, *6" tall, grapes and blackberries on shaded background, gold handle, Lenox palette mark* **100.00**

☐ Jug, shape #358, *6-1/2" tall, beautifully decorated with spotted hunting dogs, transition mark* **250.00**

☐ Jug, shape #358, *6-1/2" tall, hand-painted ears of corn on shaded background, gold handle, Lenox palette mark, artist signed* **120.00**

☐ Jug, shape #358, *6-1/2" tall, monochromatic blue monk scene, transition mark* **200.00**

☐ Jug, shape #359, *6" tall, monochromatic brown monk scene, transition mark* **175.00**

☐ Jug, shape #359, *6" tall, hand-painted berries with gold trim on spout and handle, C.A.C. lavender palette mark* **125.00**

☐ Jug, shape #359, *6" tall, undecorated, Lenox palette mark* **75.00**

☐ Jug, shape #360, *6" tall, transfer decorated with drunken Irishman and appropriate inscription, Lenox palette mark* **100.00**

☐ Jug, shape #360, *6" tall, monochromatic monk scene in green, transition mark* **160.00**

☐ Jug, shape #361, 7-1/4" tall, monochromatic blue monk scene, C.A.C. wreath mark **250.00**

☐ Jug, shape #361, 7-1/4" tall, hand-painted fruit and berries on shaded background, nicely done, C.A.C. palette mark **200.00**

☐ Jug, shape #362, 6" tall, trimmed in gold with "Papa" written across front, Lenox palette mark **75.00**

☐ Jug, shape #362, 6" tall, hand-painted vines in greens and rusts, C.A.C. palette mark **150.00**

☐ Jug, shape #363, 6-1/4" tall, monochromatic monk scene, transition mark... **150.00**

☐ Jug, shape #363, 6-1/4" tall, hand-painted ears of corn on solid brown background, gold trim on handle and rim, C.A.C. palette mark **100.00**

☐ Jug, shape #364, 6" tall, monochromatic blue monk scene, transition mark... **125.00**

☐ Jug, shape #364, 6" tall, beautifully decorated with fruit and leaves on shaded background, undoubtedly the work of Morley but unsigned, transition mark **200.00**

Jug, shape #534

☐ Jug, shape #364, 6" tall, undecorated, Lenox palette mark **60.00**

☐ Jug, shape #364, 6" tall, blackberries on shaded background and gold trim on spout and handle, artist signed and dated, Lenox palette mark... **100.00**

☐ Jug, shape #364, 6" tall, full-color cavalier drinking a toast, shaded background, C.A.C. palette mark **100.00**

Shape #364 is the most common of the jugs to be found. For picture of shape, see the jug with silver stopper in metal section.

☐ Jug, shape #407, 8-1/4" tall, undecorated, Lenox palette mark **50.00**

☐ Jug, shape #407, *8-1/4" tall, transfer decoration with ear of corn and gold trim, overall effect not bad, C.A.C. palette mark* **95.00**

☐ Jug, shape #417, *5-3/4" tall, hand-painted berries on shaded background, home decorated but nicely done, Lenox palette mark* **125.00**

☐ Jug, shape #417, *5-3/4" tall, hand-painted purple grapes on green shaded background, dreadful, Lenox palette mark, artist signed and dated* **80.00**

☐ Jug, shape #534, *4" tall, hand-painted grapes and leaves on shaded background, gold inside spout, signed G. Morley, transition mark* ... **225.00**

LADLE RESTS

The item most commonly referred to as a ladle rest is in fact a holder for sugar cubes. Since there are so few of the matching creamers, we feel it possible that many home decorators bought only the sugar holder intending to use it as a rest.

☐ Ladle rest/sugar bowl, shape #72-1/2, *4-1/2" diameter, undecorated, Lenox wreath mark* **25.00**

☐ Ladle rest/sugar bowl, shape #72-1/2, *4-1/2" diameter, gold trim, Lenox palette mark* **35.00**

☐ Ladle rest/sugar bowl, shape #72-1/2, *4-1/2" diameter, tiny pink flowers beneath rim, gold trim, artist signed and dated, C.A.C. green palette mark* **40.00**

LOVING CUPS

We have listed as loving cups any drinking vessels which have more than one handle. Those with one handle are listed later as mugs.

☐ Loving cup, shape #258, *three-handled, undecorated, Lenox palette mark*.. **60.00**

☐ Loving cup, shape #258, *three-handled, decorated with fruit on a shaded background, gold handles and rims, C.A.C. lavender palette mark*.. **60.00**

Loving cup, *shape #317, monk scene*

☐ Loving cup, shape #258, *three-handled, monochromatic blue monk scenes, transition mark* **135.00**

☐ Loving cup, shape #259, *three-handled, transfer cavaliers on shaded background, gold handles, C.A.C. lavender palette mark* **65.00**

☐ Loving cup, shape #259, *multi-colored scenic, transition mark* **200.00**

☐ Loving cup, shape #259, *pink roses with blue knotted ribbon bows on cream background, C.A.C. lavender palette mark* **135.00**

☐ Loving cup, shape #260, *undecorated, C.A.C. lavender palette mark..* **60.00**

☐ Loving cup, shape #260, *purple flowers with green leaves and gold trim, dated 1905, very professional artwork, C.A.C. lavender palette mark.* **175.00**

☐ Loving cup, shape #260, *monochromatic green golfing scene, signed W.H. Clayton, transition mark* **225.00**

☐ Loving cup, shape #317, *4-1/4" tall, transfer pictures of horses on hand-painted background, overall effect very nice, Lenox palette mark.* **100.00**

☐ Loving cup, shape #317, *4-1/4" tall, plain with gold trim and monogram, Lenox palette mark* **60.00**

☐ Loving cup, shape #317, *5-1/4" tall, monochromatic blue monk scene, C.A.C. wreath mark* **135.00**

Loving cup, *shape number uncertain, golfing scene*

☐ Loving cup, shape #331, *3-1/2" tall, cherry blossoms on shaded background, artist initialed and dated, C.A.C. lavender palette mark .* **90.00**

☐ Loving cup, shape #331, *3-1/2" tall, raised enamel work with garlands of roses, gold handles, C.A.C. green palette mark* **100.00**

☐ Loving cup, shape #341, *8-1/4" tall, pedestal base, gold trim on handles and rims, gold outlining on body of item, Lenox palette mark* **60.00**

☐ Loving cup, shape #342, *6-3/4" tall, undecorated, C.A.C. green palette mark.* **75.00**

☐ Loving cup, shape #342, *6-3/4" tall, hand-painted with hops on shaded background, nicely done, Lenox palette mark* **130.00**

☐ Loving cup, shape #440, *8-1/4" tall, figural handles, hand-painted monks in full color, C.A.C. transition mark, signed Wirkner, magnificent* **400.00**

☐ Loving cup, shape #446, *8" tall, gold trim on figural handles, brushed gold on rims, Lenox palette mark* **150.00**

☐ Loving cup, shape number uncertain, *similar to #259 but shorter and fatter, monochromatic green golfing scene, signed W.H. Clayton, transition mark* **175.00**

MATCH HOLDERS AND JARS

☐ Match holder, shape #2425, *undecorated, Lenox wreath mark* **30.00**

☐ Match holder, shape #2425, *undecorated and unmarked* **8.00**

☐ Match holder, shape #2425, *gold trim, Lenox wreath mark* **30.00**

☐ Match holder, shape #2426, *undecorated, Lenox wreath mark* **25.00**

☐ Match holder, shape #2426, *floral transfer decoration, Lenox wreath mark* **35.00**

☐ Match holder, shape #2426, *gold trim, Lenox wreath mark* **25.00**

☐ Match jar, shape #348, *1-3/4" x 1-3/4", undecorated, Lenox wreath mark* **12.00**

☐ Match jar, shape #348, *1-3/4" x 1-3/4", hand-painted small pink roses, C.A.C. palette mark* **45.00**

MENU STANDS

Menu stands are extremely scarce. The catalogue lists the one shape as 6-1/4" x 4-3/4". It has a fancy outer rim, which is glazed, and an unglazed inner section which looks like it is framed by the outer section. It would seem likely that the inner portion was left unglazed so that the surface would be easier to write on. We have no sales for this item to list, but would estimate the value of a decorated, signed specimen at around $150. One unmarked sample reportedly sold recently for $65, but we did not personally see this item.

MINIATURES

Most of the Lenox miniatures seen today were probably salesman samples to begin with, but there are a few items which were probably intended just to be cute little collectibles. As a rule, if an item is the same shape as a standard Lenox item only smaller it was probably a sample. If the shape is unfamiliar, it was probably meant for a doll house. (We seem to recall reading somewhere that to be a true miniature, an item must be 1/12th the size of the original.)

Most of the miniatures are priced in the $50 to $100 range, depending both on shape and type of decoration. Lenox Rose pattern seems to be popular on miniatures, and of course plain gold trim can also be found. Most are undecorated.

The little creamer, less than 1" high, is well-liked because it can be worn as a necklace. (Keep the chain short so the china can't fall forward and hit something.) The creamer is part of a little teaset, complete with teapot, sugar bowl, cups and saucers, and tiny tea plates. The teapot and sugar bowl have removable lids.

MUFFINEERS

☐ Muffineer, shape number unknown, *hand-painted flowers, Lenox wreath mark* **48.00**

☐ Muffineer, shape number unknown, *undecorated, gold wreath mark* . **25.00**

MUGS

☐ Mug, shape #251, *4-7/8" high, undecorated, Lenox palette mark* **15.00**

☐ Mug, shape #251, *4-7/8" high, gold trim on handle and rims, gold monogram on front, Lenox palette mark* **30.00**

☐ Mug, shape #251, *4-7/8" high, blue bands top and bottom and blue on handle, mediocre central scenic section, C.A.C. lavender palette mark* **60.00**

☐ Mug, shape #251, *4-7/8" high, Indian brave, full color, shaded background and handle, transition mark* **160.00**

☐ Mug, shape #252, *5" high, undecorated, Lenox palette mark* **25.00**

☐ Mug, shape #252, *5" high, hand-painted grapes on shaded background, gold handle, C.A.C. purple palette mark* **50.00**

☐ Mug, shape #252, *5" high, hand-painted pinecones on plain background, C.A.C. green palette mark* **40.00**

☐ Mug, shape #252, *5" high, monochromatic green monk scene, transition mark* **75.00**

☐ Mug, shape #252, *5" high, transfer monk on hand-painted background, C.A.C. green palette mark* **65.00**

☐ Mug, shape #252, *5" high, monk on green background, artist signed and dated 1901, C.A.C. lavender palette mark* **70.00**

☐ Mug, shape #252, *5" high, blackberries and leaves on shaded background, Lenox palette mark* **50.00**

☐ Mug, shape #252, *5" high, beer taster with German saying on reverse side, nicely done, artist initialed, C.A.C. green palette mark* **85.00**

☐ Mug, shape #253, *5" high, full-color portrait of Indian in headdress, dated 1901, fine artwork, C.A.C. lavender palette mark* **185.00**

☐ Mug, shape #253, *5" high, hand-painted grapes and leaves, off-white background, C.A.C. green palette mark* **80.00**

☐ Mug, shape #253, *5" high, red berries and branches, gold rims and handle, Lenox palette mark* **75.00**

☐ Mug, shape #253, *5" high, monochromatic monk scene, blue, transition mark* **90.00**

☐ Mug, shape #254, *5-1/2" high, monochromatic browns, monk with wine casket, gold rim and handle, no Lenox mark, artist signed DeLan* **95.00**

☐ Mug, shape #254, *5-1/2" high, monochromatic monk scene, very badly done, Lenox palette mark* **28.00**

☐ Mug, shape #254, *5-1/2" high, portrait of a black boy with straw hat, monochromatic green, transition mark* **125.00**

☐ Mug, shape #254, *5-1/2" high, monochromatic blues, monk making sandwich, transition mark* **75.00**

☐ Mug, shape #254, *5-1/2" high, ears of corn on shaded brown background, artist signed, Lenox palette mark* **60.00**

☐ Mug, shape #255, *5-1/2" high, portrait of old woman done in monochromatic browns, C.A.C. green palette mark* **75.00**

☐ Mug, shape #255, *5-1/2" high, seascape (ocean with lighthouse), artist signed and dated 1897, C.A.C. lavender palette mark* **80.00**

☐ Mug, shape #255, *5-1/2" high, multi-colored fruit decoration with gold handle and rims, Lenox palette mark* **75.00**

☐ Mug, shape #255, *5-1/2" high, Dutch scenes, full color, nicely done, C.A.C. lavender palette mark* **80.00**

☐ Mug, shape #255, *5-1/2" high, monochromatic browns, monks seated, standing and drinking, transition mark* **120.00**

☐ Mug, shape #255, *5-1/2" high, full-color, trees on light brown background, Lenox palette mark* **45.00**

☐ Mug, shape #256, 5-3/4" high, plain white with gold trim on handle and brushed gold on top rim, gold initials on front, Lenox palette mark... **50.00**

☐ Mug, shape #256, 5-3/4" high, monochromatic browns, monk drinking wine, transition mark... **100.00**

☐ Mug, shape #256, 5-3/4" high, multi-colored pinecones on shaded background, nicely done, C.A.C. lavender palette mark **80.00**

☐ Mug, shape #257, 6" high, undecorated, Lenox palette mark **20.00**

☐ Mug, shape #257, 6" high, monochromatic monk scene in blue, transition mark.. **125.00**

☐ Mug, shape #257, 6" high, transfer decorated scene, gold trim, Lenox palette mark.. **50.00**

☐ Mug, shape #311, 5" high, monochromatic monk scene in brown, transition mark... **100.00**

☐ Mug, shape #311, 5" high, monochromatic green, three Dickens type characters seated in a pub, transition mark **175.00**

☐ Mug, shape #311, 5" high, monochromatic blue, standing monk, C.A.C. wreath mark **150.00**

☐ Mug, shape #311, 5" high, undecorated, Lenox palette mark **30.00**

☐ Mug, shape #312, 5-3/4" high, undecorated, C.A.C. green palette mark **40.00**

☐ Mug, shape #312, 5-3/4" high, gold trim on handles and rims, Lenox palette mark.. **40.00**

☐ Mug, shape #312, 5-3/4" high, full-color automobile scene, nicely done, Lenox palette mark **125.00**

Shapes #311 and 312 are the same only #312 is taller.

☐ Mug, shape #500, 7" high, decorated with gold insignia and gold trim on handle and rims, Lenox palette mark **50.00**

☐ Mug, shape #500, 7" high, monochromatic monk scene, transition mark... **125.00**

☐ Mug, shape #601, 4" high, raised enamel work and floral design, handwritten on bottom "To Baby Eleanor, June 16, 1915", Lenox palette mark **10.00**

Mug, shape #604, Dickens
type characters

☐ Mug, shape #601, *4" high, undecorated, Lenox palette mark* **25.00**
☐ Mug, shape #604, *4-1/2" high, ear of corn on brown background, Lenox palette mark* **45.00**
☐ Mug, shape #604, *4-1/2" high, berries on shaded background, artist's initials,Lenox palette mark* **60.00**
☐ Mug, shape #604, *4-1/2" high, monochromatic Dickens type characters, transition mark, pair* **225.00**
☐ Mug, shape #754, *no decoration, Lenox wreath mark* **10.00**
☐ Mug, shape #754, *transfer decorated with baby chicks, gold trim, Lenox palette mark* **40.00**
☐ Mug, shape #812, *3" high, gold trim, Lenox wreath mark* **30.00**

Mug, *no shape number*

☐ Mug, shape #812, *3" high, pearlized finish with word "Coffee" written across front, Lenox palette mark* **25.00**
☐ Mug, shape #1313, *no decoration, Lenox wreath mark* **12.00**
☐ Mug, shape #1493, *no decoration, Lenox wreath mark* **14.00**
☐ Mug, *no shape number but similar to #311 and #312, probably a special order, transfer decoration possibly Admiral Dewey framed by laurel wreath, background is off white shading to turquoise, red, white and blue banding at top, written-out C.A.C. lavender mark* **135.00**

PITCHERS, ALL TYPES

Any pitcher-type item which is not a creamer or a ewer will be found in this section.

☐ Pitcher, shape #24, *5" high, undecorated, C.A.C. brown palette mark* . **75.00**
☐ Pitcher, shape #24, *5" high, gold trim on handle and brushed gold near rims, C.A.C. wreath mark, eggshell thin* **15.00**
☐ Pitcher, shape #24, *5" high, green with white handle, Lenox wreath mark* **30.00**
☐ Pitcher, shape #24, *5" high, coral with white handle, Lenox wreath mark* **25.00**
☐ Pitcher, shape #24, *5" high, white with gold trim, Lenox wreath mark* . **25.00**

☐ Pitcher, shape #24, *5" high, solid baby pink with gold trim, Lenox wreath mark* **25.00**
The shape #24 pitcher is a fat-bottomed one with beading at midsection and on handle. It is known as the Colonial pitcher, and is currently being made in a smaller version as a sugar and creamer.

☐ Pitcher, shape #47, *10-1/2" high, bark-type finish on upper portion, rustic handle, covered, undecorated, C.A.C. lavender palette mark* .. **150.00**

☐ Pitcher, shape #47, *10-1/2" high, bark-type finish on upper portion, rustic handle, cover missing, done in shades of green and lavender, C.A.C. lavender palette mark* **200.00**

Pitcher, *shape #352, transition mark*

☐ Pitcher, shape #64, *7-1/4" high, all-over hammered finish, mask spout, eggshell thin, C.A.C. brown palette mark* **175.00**

☐ Pitcher, shape #64, *7-1/4" high, all-over hammered finish, mask spout, pale pink with pearlized finish, Lenox wreath mark* **75.00**

☐ Pitcher, shape #64, *7-1/4" high, all-over hammered finish, mask spout, medium green outside, white inside, Lenox wreath mark* **80.00**

☐ Pitcher, shape #64, *7-1/4" high, all-over hammered finish, mask spout, white with gold trim, Lenox palette mark* **70.00**
Shape #64 is known as the mask pitcher.

☐ Pitcher, shape #71, *4" high, undecorated, hand-painted roses, gold trim, Lenox palette mark* **35.00**

☐ Pitcher, shape #71, *4" high, undecorated, C.A.C. lavender palette mark* **30.00**

☐ Pitcher, shape #184, *4" high, undecorated, C.A.C. green palette mark* **32.00**

☐ Pitcher, shape #184, *4" high, hand-painted with small violets and gold trim, C.A.C. lavender palette mark* **90.00**

☐ Pitcher, shape #184, *4" high, white with gold trim, Lenox palette mark* **50.00**

☐ Pitcher, shape #185, *4" high, tiny red flowers, gold filigree and scroll work, plain background, C.A.C. lavender palette mark* **75.00**

☐ Pitcher, shape #185, *4" high, undecorated, Lenox palette mark* **25.00**

☐ Pitcher, shape #270, *12" high, covered, hand-painted apples and leaves on plain background, gold trim, Lenox palette mark* **90.00**

Pitcher, *tankard, monk scene*

☐ Pitcher, shape #270, *12" high, covered, overall grape decoration on wine-colored background, C.A.C. green palette mark* **100.00**

☐ Pitcher, shape #270, *12" high, covered, overall pearlized orange color, gold trim, perfectly dreadful, Lenox palette mark* **30.00**

☐ Pitcher, shape #337, *14" high, monochromatic brown monk scene, transition mark* **190.00**

☐ Pitcher, shape #337, *14" high, hand-painted red berries and green leaves on cream-colored background, artist signed and dated, C.A.C. green palette mark* **170.00**

☐ Pitcher, shape #352, *5-1/4" high, undecorated and unmarked but verifiably Lenox* **10.00**

☐ Pitcher, shape #352, *5-1/4" high, beautifully decorated with fruit on shaded background, unsigned but possibly the work of Morley, gold trim inside top rim and on handle, transition mark* **250.00**

☐ Pitcher, shape #352, *5-1/4" high, plain with gold trim, Lenox palette mark* **40.00**

☐ Pitcher, shape #352, *5-1/4" high, hand-painted fruit on brown background, artist signed and dated, C.A.C. green palette mark* **125.00**
The above pitcher is generally called a cider pitcher.

☐ Pitcher, shape #456, *13" high, undecorated, Lenox palette mark* **50.00**

☐ Pitcher, shape #456, *13" high, overall grape design on green shaded background, artist signed, C.A.C. green palette mark* **125.00**

☐ Pitcher, shape #456, *13" high, bridal portrait in oval medallion, blue dot enamel work, overall effect so-so, artist signed and dated, C.A.C. palette mark* **150.00**

☐ Pitcher, shape #457, *12" high, overall floral design of roses, baby's breath and daisies on pale blue background, Lenox palette mark* **125.00**

☐ Pitcher, shape #457, *13" high, hand-painted blackberries and flowers on shaded background, C.A.C. green palette mark, signed Fuchs (Pickard artist)* **175.00**

☐ Pitcher, shape #467, *8" high, cherries and blossoms on pale green background, gold trim, the worst in home decorating, C.A.C. lavender palette mark* **75.00**

Pitcher, *shape number unknown, embossed floral design*

☐ Pitcher, shape #467, *8" high, undecorated, C.A.C. green palette mark* **65.00**

☐ Pitcher, tankard shape, *14" high, undecorated, C.A.C. green palette mark* **50.00**

☐ Pitcher, tankard shape, *14" high, hand-painted green and purple on background which is shaded green to yellow, artist signed and dated, nicely done, C.A.C. green palette mark* **175.00**

☐ Pitcher, tankard shape, *14" high, monochromatic green scene of monk holding pig, C.A.C. wreath mark, signed E.A. DeLan* **275.00**

☐ Pitcher, tankard shape, *14" high, hand-painted ears of corn on brown shaded background, artist signed, Lenox palette mark* **125.00**

☐ Pitcher, tankard shape, *14" high, overall grape and hops motif, lavish gold, professional look, C.A.C. green palette mark* **200.00**

☐ Pitcher, tankard, *14" high, floral sprays of mums on green background, artist signed, Lenox palette mark* **160.00**

☐ Pitcher, tankard, *14" high, monochromatic blue monk scene, excellent artwork, C.A.C. wreath mark* **250.00**

☐ Pitcher, tankard, *14" high, monochromatic browns, monk drawing wine from a cask, signed M. Nourse, C.A.C. lavender palette mark* ... **250.00**

☐ Pitcher, tankard, *14" high, monochromatic green monk scene, transition mark* **200.00**

☐ Pitcher, tankard, *14" high, purple and red grapes on cream colored background, artist's initials and date, Lenox palette mark* **150.00**
Note: There were two shapes of tankard pitchers, only slightly different. Our catalogue pictures are not good enough to tell one from the other, so we have omitted shape numbers for this category. The two numbers would be #514 and #519.

☐ Pitcher, shape #526, *6" high, gold trim and initials, Lenox palette mark* **40.00**

☐ Pitcher, shape #526, *6" high, hand-painted berries and fruit on shaded green background, C.A.C. lavender palette mark* **125.00**

☐ Pitcher, shape #526, *6" high, undecorated and unmarked, verifiably Lenox* **20.00**

☐ Pitcher, shape #555, *11" high, covered hand-painted roses with gold trim, artist signed, Lenox palette mark* **100.00**

☐ Pitcher, shape #555, *11" high, covered, hand-painted grapes on both sides, Lenox palette mark* **90.00**

☐ Pitcher, shape #566, *8-1/4" high, covered, undecorated, Lenox palette mark* **40.00**

☐ Pitcher, shape #566, *8-1/4" high, covered, hand-painted ears of corn, Lenox palette mark* **70.00**

☐ Pitcher, shape #566, *8-1/4" high, covered, transfer decorated with French-type scene, gold trim, Lenox palette mark* **40.00**

☐ Pitcher, shape #567, *7-1/2" high, single orchid on either side, Lenox wreath mark* **150.00**

Pitcher, *shape number unknown, modernistic styling*

☐ Pitcher, shape #568, *6" high, undecorated, Lenox palette mark* **30.00**
☐ Pitcher, shape #568, *6" high, hand-painted grapes and leaves on tan background, nicely done, artist signed and dated, Lenox palette mark* **90.00**

☐ Pitcher, shape #666, 8-1/2", high, hand-painted with lemons and oranges, gold trim, Lenox palette mark **100.00**

☐ Pitcher, shape #666, 8-1/2" high, hand-painted with roses and gold trim, Lenox palette mark **50.00**

☐ Pitcher, shape #667, 8-1/2" high, decorated with stylized tulips in panels down the sides in raised enamel work, Lenox palette mark ... **50.00**

☐ Pitcher, shape #667, 8-1/2" high, undecorated, Lenox wreath mark ... **30.00**

Pitcher, *shape number unknown,*
modernistic look

☐ Pitcher, shape #918, 9-1/2" high, hand-painted fruit on brown background, gold trim, artist signed and dated, Lenox palette mark .. **50.00**

☐ Pitcher, shape #918, 9-1/2" high, hand-painted with Dutch type designs in blue, Lenox palette mark **35.00**

☐ Pitcher, shape number unknown, embossed floral design, all white, Lenox wreath mark **30.00**

☐ Pitcher, shape number unknown, modernistic styling with transfer decoration, Lenox wreath mark **30.00**

☐ Pitcher, shape number unknown, modernistic look, gold trim on pink, Lenox wreath mark **30.00**

PLATES

Animals (not including birds and fish). Farm animals are the subject of one of the more famous series of Morley plates. The first set, done from a photograph (black and white in those days) and a description of the colors, was of a prize-winning horse owned by a Pennsylvania farmer. The second set, ordered by the same man, pictured a champion hog and was also done by Morley from photographs. The farmer was to eventually order 18 sets of plates, all with pictures of his winning livestock.

Birds. Bird plates are scarcer than fish, and a well-done bird plate should be priced at around twice the going rate for a comparable fish plate. The birds most often found are:

#1 Pintail duck	#5 Canada goose	#9 Canvasback duck
#2 Snipe	#6 Woodcock	#10 Pheasant
#3 Prairie chicken	#7 Redhead duck	#11 Quail
#4 Partridge	#8 Oyster catcher	#12 Ptarmigan

The following border trims have been noted: B-312, C-317, C-421, D-343, D-345, D-346, E-25, E-35, E-82, E-325, E-414, J-9, J-28, J-57, J-405, J-406, J-407, L-431, M-382, O-15, P-28, R-17, S-71, T-23, V-38, V-39, W-11, W-12, and X-1. The birds can be shown in winter or summer settings, with winter settings being somewhat less common.

Perhaps the most famous set of game birds by Lenox is the exotic pheasant set by William Morley, done in 1927. The man who ordered the plates, Colonel Anthony R. Kuser of Bernardsville, NJ, financed an expedition to the far corners of the world to photograph and sketch pheasants. They are currently owned by a private collector who asks not to be identified by name or location.

A few slightly less impressive copies of the same plates were also made, although the exact number of copies is uncertain. The Lenox Company owns a set of twelve plates which (judging by backstamps) might be made up of parts of two different sets. The owner of the originals also owns a set of the copies. There is also a single plate in the Lenox showroom which might have been part of another set of copies although it is equally possible that it was a single sample.

Matching platters are very much the exception rather than the rule with Lenox game sets. The company owns two of the platters, both decorated with the pheasant. A platter in good condition should be valued in the $500 range.

Bird plate, *Ptarmigan*

☐ Bird plates, *9" diameter, J-57 etched gold borders, signed W. H. Morley, one has ptarmigan in winter plumage, the other has canvasback duck also in a winter setting, Lenox wreath mark, pair* **375.00**

Bird plate, *Canvasback duck*

☐ Bird plates, *9" diameter, 1/2" flat gold border with pencil line gold inside (variation of pattern 86-1/2), gold monogram R.A. at top for Robert Adrian, past president of N. J. Senate, pheasants in snow, misty look to pictures, signed W. H. Morley, Lenox wreath mark, pair.* **150.00**

☐ Bird plates, *10-1/2" diameter, narrow flat gold trim on rims, 12 different game birds, not as detailed as some of the earlier plates, signed J. Nosek, Lenox wreath/Made in U.S.A. mark, set of 12* **600.00**

Fish. Fish plates for the most part saw very little actual use and are often in prime condition. Although William Morley did the majority of them, samples by other artists are not unknown. The 12 fish appearing most frequently are:

#1 Sun fish	#5 Blue fish	#9 Spanish mackerel
#2 Weak fish	#6 Black bass	#10 Striped bass
#3 Salmon	#7 Pike	#11 Porgy
#4 Brook trout	#8 Common mackerel	#12 Yellow perch

The standard sets will typically have the names of the fish hand-printed on the back (as is also the case with the standard bird sets.)

Border trims include: B-312, C-312, C-421, D-343, D-345, D-346, E-25, E-35, E-325, E-82, E-414, J-9, J-38, J-57, J-405, J-406, J-407, K-49, L-431, M-153, M-382, O-15, P-28, R-17, S-71, T-17, T-23, V-38, V-39, W-11, W-12, and X-1.

For reasons we are unable to explain, the sunfish is almost invariably the most attractive in any given set of plates. Since the fish plates were a stock item for many years, anything unusual about a plate increases its value quite a bit.

☐ Fish plate, *9" diameter, central pastel fish, very fine background work, signed E. A. DeLan, Lenox gold wreath mark* **75.00**

Fish plate, K-49 etched border

☐ Fish plate, 9" diameter, fish painted near the borders rather than being centered like most fish plates, good detailing and color, K-49 etched gold borders, Lenox wreath mark, set of six **450.00**

Fish plate, K-49 etched border

☐ Fish plate, 9" diameter, B-312 etched gold borders, well-done fish with good background detailing, gold not quite as bright as it might be, signed W. H. Morley, Lenox wreath mark, Ovington's store mark, set of five **325.00**

☐ Fish plate, 9" diameter, J-57 etched gold borders, large, well-done fish with good color and background details, signed W. H. Morley, Lenox wreath mark and Ovington's store mark, set of four **320.00**

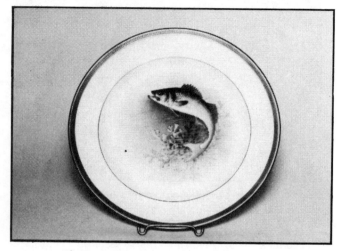

Fish plate, J-57 etched gold border

Fish plate, J-57 etched gold border

Fish plate, *narrow gold trim*

☐ Fish plate, *9" diameter, large, well-done fish, good detailing, narrow flat gold trim, signed W. H. Morley, Lenox gold wreath mark, set of four* **300.00**

Fish plate, *narrow gold trim*

☐ Fish plate, *9" diameter, fish average as to size and detailing, color fair, 3/4" etched gold border in J-28 pattern, gold very bright and new looking, plates in absolutely mint condition, signed W. H. Morley, Lenox wreath mark and Gilman Collamore & Co. store mark, complete set of 12* **800.00**

☐ Fish plate, *9" diameter, fish done in dull greens and grays with washed-out appearance, gold pencil-line trim, coupe shape plate instead of standard shape, signed W. H. Morley, Lenox wreath mark, set of 12, two had tiny flecks on rim* **300.00**

Floral. Perhaps the most spectacular set of flower plates we have seen were by W. H. Morley. Each plate had a different rose, beautifully done, and the entire rim had an etched gold floral design (the same rim which appears on the Nosek portrait plate).

Similar plates with orchids instead of roses were sold at auction in 1978, and brought in the area of $200 each. They no doubt would have gone higher except that there were 54 of them at the auction, all apparently purchased by the same party.

Less-ornate floral plates than these seem to fluctuate quite a bit. Recently, a set of 12 Morley floral plates (not the best, to be sure) sold at a Trenton auction for $18 each. The problem with this particular set was that it had changed hands a few times too often, and had become "jinxed". The plates first showed up at a Trenton auction about six years ago, and made several appearances in the area. They actually went down in value with each auction, from $50 or so six years ago to the recent $18.

Floral plate, *orchid*

Comparable plates, however, typically sell in the $50 and up range. Nicely done but not ornate orchid plates are probably worth a minimum of $100, more if they have the scalloped rims. Nosek did a decent series of floral plates, and these can bring anywhere from $50 to $150, depending on workmanship and luck.

Transfer-decorated floral plates which were filled in by hand are not yet particularly desirable and might well be considered as dinnerware rather than artware. They can bring up to around $25 for the prettier ones. Rim decorations include O-433, O-434, O-435, O-436, O-438, O-450, O-451, O-452, R-302, R-303, R-334, R-429, and R-449. Plate shapes include #2020, #1881, #2803, and #2249.

Fruit. Hand-painted fruit plates from the Morley period are quite lovely, and are actually fully-detailed still life paintings of the fruit. Frequently, the design did not fill the entire center, but rather took up about a 5" diameter, with the rim color coming down into the well to meet the artwork. Plates such as these should probably be valued at $100 minimum.

Later fruit plates have only the fruit in the center of the plate, with no background at all. The subjects became more standardized, and most sets consisted of the following:

#1 Apples	#5 Grapes	#9 Peaches
#2 Cherries	#6 Raspberries	#10 Gooseberries
#3 Strawberries	#7 Apples	#11 Blackberries
#4 Plums	#8 Grapes	#12 Pears

They were available on more than one shape, and rim decorations included D-341, P-359, P-420, X-5, Y-21, Y-78, and Z-66. These plates, sometimes by Morley and other times by Nosek, are usually priced in the $50 range.

Nautical. Morley is known to have hand-painted at least one set of clipper ship plates, but for the most part the nautical plates were transfers filled in by hand. They are all attractive to see and sell particularly well in the New England area. The transfer-done series included the following clipper ships:

#1—Black Prince; Boston MA; 1856	#7—Young America; NY; 1853
#2—Junenta; Thomaston, ME; 1953	#8—Galetea; Charleston, MA; 1854
#3—Aracle; ME; 1853	#9—Great 'Republic; Boston, MA; 1853
#4—Sweepstakes; NY; 1853	#10—Northern Light; Boston, MA; 1851
#5—Ringleader; Medford, MA; 1853	#11—Golden West; Boston, MA; 1852
#6—Red Jacket; Rockland, ME; 1853	#12—John Wade; Boston, MA; 1851

Rim decorations included F-355A, F-395A, F-405B, F-406B, L-352A, and O-333B.

The Yacht Defender plates included some combination of the following yachts:

Volunteer	America	Resolute
Defender	Madeleine	Rainbow
Columbia	Ranger	Enterprise
Puritan	Sappho	Mischief
Vigilant		

Rim for the yacht plates included J-410B, J-411, J-413A, J-414B, J-415B, and L-398B.

Both types of plates typically sell in the $50 to $100 each range, with prices being the highest in sailing-oriented parts of the country.

Portraits. Hand-painted Lenox portrait plates are extremely scarce and desirable. Those by Geyer are absolutely divine and very much in that area of Lenox collecting where it is foolish to quibble over prices. The Nosek portraits, although not quite up to the Geyers, should also be considered as prize pieces of Lenox. The owner of the Nosek recently rejected an offer of $300, and we cannot find much fault with his decision.

Portrait plate,
Geyer

Portrait plate, *Nosek*

Scenics. Perhaps the most famous Lenox scenic plates are known as the European garden set for the scenes they depict or as the Scammell plates for the woman who commissioned them. They were done from black and white photographs of the gardens, with the woman describing to Morley the colors in each photograph. (This is supposedly the only time Morley allowed anyone to look over his shoulder while he was working.) The plates have wide acid-etched gold borders, and are stunning. They are currently owned by a private collector.

Another series of plates had views of 18 bridges built by a Trenton firm, the owner of which commissioned the plates. Although we have not seen these plates, we gather that they were photographic transfers which were filled in by hand. The set is in private hands.

PUNCH BOWLS

C.A.C. made a large punchbowl, 12-1/2" x 16-3/4", with an embossed design. We have heard that at least one does indeed exist but we have never seen it. Undecorated, it would be in the $150 to $200 range. A beautifully decorated one by perhaps one of the better known factory artists would be in the $500 to $1,000 range.

Lenox later made several good-sized bowls which could pass for small punch bowls. Typically, they are about 12" in diameter and 8" high. For the most part, they are under $100 undecorated.

RING TREES

Two types of ring trees were made by Lenox. The tree part of both is pretty much the same, but the earlier one has a ruffled rim around it while the later one has a plain base.

- ☐ Ring tree, shape #161 *small hand-painted roses with gold trim, C.A.C. lavender palette mark* **110.00**
- ☐ Ring tree, shape #161, *undecorated and unmarked* **15.00**
- ☐ Ring tree, later shape, *undecorated, Lenox wreath mark* **45.00**

SALT SHAKERS AND DIPS

- ☐ Salt dip, shape #103, *1-3/4" across bottom, undecorated, Lenox palette mark* **6.00**
- ☐ Salt dip, shape #103, *1-3/4" across bottom, covered all over with gold, Lenox palette mark* **8.00**
- ☐ Salt dip, shape #103, *1-3/4" across bottom, pink roses and gold trim, Lenox palette mark* **10.00**
- ☐ Salt dip, shape #103, *1-3/4" across bottom, tiny pink roses, gold trim, transition mark* **13.00**
- ☐ Salt dip, shape #103, *1-3/4" across bottom, brushed gold on rim, transition mark* **11.00**
- ☐ Salt dip, shape #103, *1-3/4" across bottom, violets with gold trim, C.A.C. wreath mark* **15.00**
- ☐ Salt dip, shape #236, *2-1/4" across, pale green with gold trim and gold on feet, C.A.C. green palette mark* **12.00**
- ☐ Salt dip, shape #236, *2-1/4" across, undecorated, Lenox palette mark* **10.00**
- ☐ Salt dip, shape #236, *2-1/4" across, pink roses with gold trim, transition mark* **25.00**
- ☐ Salt dip, shape #236, *2-1/4" across, small violets and gold trim, C.A.C. pink palette mark and Bailey, Banks and Biddle store mark* **25.00**
- ☐ Salt dip, shape #236, *2-1/4" across, covered all over with gold, Lenox palette mark* **12.00**

☐ Salt dip, shape #806, 2-1/2", hexagon shape, gold inside and out, Lenox palette mark **12.00**

☐ Salt dip, shape #806, 2-1/2", hexagon shape, gold rims, and gold initial, Lenox palette mark **12.00**

☐ Salt dip, shape #807, 1-5/8", hexagon shape, solid cobalt, apparently meant to have silver overlay, Lenox palette mark **8.00**

☐ Salt dip, shape #807, 1-5/8", hexagon shape, lavender lustre finish outside, gold rim, Lenox palette mark **10.00**

☐ Salt shaker, shape #215, 2-1/2" high, pink roses and gold trim, no mark **10.00**

☐ Salt shaker, shape #215, 2-1/2" high, brushed gold trim, no mark **10.00**

☐ Salt shaker, shape #215, 2-1/2" high, undecorated, no mark **5.00**

(Shape #215 shaker is usually not marked because the hole for the cork takes up most of the bottom. It frequently was paired with the #103 salt dip to make a set, or with the smallest swan. In pairs, the #215 was meant to be a salt and pepper shaker set.

☐ Salt shaker, shape #531, 3" high, undecorated, Lenox wreath mark, pair **15.00**

☐ Salt shaker, shape #531, 3" high, hand-painted with roses and gold trim, Lenox palette mark, pair **15.00**

☐ Salt shaker, shape #531, 3" high, gold initial and trim, Lenox palette mark, pair **15.00**

☐ Salt shaker, shape #584, 2-3/8" high, pearlized blue finish with gold trim, Lenox palette mark, pair **12.00**

☐ Salt shaker, shape #584, 2-3/8" high, hand-painted violets and gold trim, Lenox wreath mark, pair **27.00**

☐ Salt shaker, shape #584, 2-3/8" high, undecorated and unmarked, pair **8.00**

☐ Salt shaker, shape #585, 3-1/2" high, hand-painted in a gaudy geometric fashion, Lenox palette mark, pair **12.00**

☐ Salt shaker, shape #585, 3-1/2" high, hand-painted with roses and gold trim, Lenox palette mark, pair **14.00**

☐ Salt shaker, shape #585, 3-1/2" high, undecorated, Lenox wreath mark, pair **12.00**

☐ Salt shaker, shape #882, 5" high, undecorated, Lenox wreath mark, pair **15.00**

☐ Salt shaker, shape #882, 5" high, hand-painted with Art Deco type design in raised enamel effect, Lenox palette mark, pair **18.00**

SHAVING MUGS

Lenox shaving mugs are extremely rare, and they were made in only the one shape, pictured below.

☐ Shaving mug, shape #201, 4" tall, hand-painted violets on shaded background, C.A.C. palette mark **125.00**

☐ Shaving mug, shape #201, 4" tall, undecorated, C.A.C. palette mark . **100.00**

Shaving mug, *shape #201, hand-painted*

SHERBET CUPS AND PUNCH CUPS

These two types of cups are listed together because it is difficult, if not impossible, to tell them apart just by appearance. In general, they are footed cups with one or two handles and no underplate. A few of them came with small trays, apparently for cookies. We would suppose that those cups with ruffled rims are sherberts, since drinking out of them would have been tricky. In the price guide, we are just calling them all cups.

☐ Cup, shape #12, *two-handled, ruffled rim, undecorated, Lenox palette mark* **30.00**

☐ Cup, shape #12, *two-handled, ruffled rim, matte finish with raised gold work, C.A.C. lavender palette mark* **60.00**

☐ Cup, shape #12, *two-handled, ruffled rim, small hand-painted roses, gold trim on handles and rims, transition mark* **100.00**

☐ Cup, shape #13, *same size and shape as #12 but only has one handle, blue dot enamel work and gold trim, C.A.C. palette mark* **75.00**

☐ Cup, shape #13, *undecorated, C.A.C. green palette mark, several flecks on ruffled rim* **25.00**

Cup #13 is shown in catalogues with the shape #14 tray, a small square item with ruffled rim also. None of the listings we have for this cup had the tray with them.

☐ Cup, shape #197, *footed, fancy handle, undecorated, C.A.C. green palette mark* **15.00**

☐ Cup, shape #197, *footed, fancy handles, decorated with gold trim and monograms, C.A.C. green palette mark* **25.00**

☐ Cup, shape #198, *footed, same shape as #197 except base is shorter, undecorated, Lenox palette mark* **15.00**

☐ Cup, shape #198, *footed, gold trim and single large pink rose, Lenox palette mark* **35.00**

☐ Cup, shape #264, *two-handled, plain shape, undecorated, C.A.C. brown palette mark* **30.00**

☐ Cup, shape #264, *two-handled, plain shape, all-over fruit decoration, gold handles, Lenox palette mark* **35.00**

☐ Cup, shape #274, *two-handled, with underplate, gold trim on handle and rims, C.A.C. brown palette mark* **30.00**

SMALL DISHES

The following items are small dishes meant to be used for candy, olives, nuts, and other type items. Since they were multiple-purpose items, we are grouping them all together under this one heading.

☐ Dish, shape #9, *5" x 7-1/4", free-form shape, ruffled rim, undecorated, C.A.C. palette mark* **30.00**

☐ Dish, shape #9, *5" x 7-1/4", hand-painted butterflies and flowers on blue background, gold trim on ruffled rim, C.A.C. green palette mark, several flecks on rim* **35.00**

☐ Dish, shape #10, *5" x 7-1/4", free form, scalloped rim, pale pink pearlized finish with gold trim, Lenox palette mark* **25.00**

☐ Dish, shape #10, *5" x 7-1/4", free form, scalloped rim, hand-painted tiny violets in bunch, gold trim, C.A.C. green palette mark* **50.00**

☐ Dish, shape #10, *5" x 7-1/4", free form, scalloped rim, undecorated and unmarked* **5.00**

☐ Dish, shape #19, *10-1/2", rolled rim with ruffles in four plates, undecorated, C.A.C. lavender palette mark, several flecks on rim* **24.00**

☐ Dish, shape #51, *3", shell shape on footed base, solid coral, Lenox wreath mark* **25.00**

☐ Dish, shape #51, *3", shell shape on footed base, white with gold trim, Lenox palette mark* **23.00**

Dish, shape #91, Lenox wreath mark

☐ Dish, shape #91, *3-1/2" x 6-1/4", leaf shape with erose edges, rolled handle, undecorated, very early and eggshell thin, C.A.C. lavender palette mark* **42.00**

☐ Dish, shape #91, *3-1/2" x 6-1/4", leaf shape with erose edges, rolled handle, plain with gold trim, Lenox wreath mark* **25.00**

Dish, *shape #91, pale pink*

☐ Dish, shape #91, *3-1/2" x 6-1/4", pale pink with white handle, Lenox wreath mark* **24.00**

☐ Dish, shape #91, *3-1/2" x 6-1/4", green with gold trim, Lenox wreath mark*.. **27.00**

☐ Dish, shape #91, *3-1/2" x 6-1/4", Lenox Rose design with gold trim, Lenox wreath mark* **32.00**

☐ Dish, shape #91, *3-1/2" x 6-1/4", blue with gold trim, Lenox wreath mark*.. **26.00**

☐ Dish, shape #95, *5-1/2" x 9-1/4", leaf shape with erose edges, rolled handle, exceptionally thin with fine detailing, brushed gold trim, on handle and raised sections of leaf, C.A.C. red palette mark* **100.00**

☐ Dish, shape #95, *5-1/2" x 9-1/4", leaf shape with erose edges, rolled handle, solid coral, Lenox wreath mark*.......................... **35.00**

☐ Dish, shape #95, *5-1/2" x 9-1/4", leaf shape with erose edges, rolled handle, exceptionally good detailing, solid gold outside, little scattered flowers inside, beautiful, C.A.C. lavender palette mark* **125.00**

☐ Dish, shape #102, *1-1/4" x 4-1/2", swirled ribbing, undecorated, lenox palette mark* **15.00**

☐ Dish, shape #112, *3-1/2" x 6-1/4", (shape #91 with feet), gold trim, C.A.C. brown palette mark* **52.00**

☐ Dish, shape #113, *5-1/2" x 9-1/4", (shape #95 with feet), pale pink pearlized finish inside, gold trim, on outside, C.A.C. green palette mark*.. **95.00**

☐ Dish, shape #133, *3-1/4" x 3-3/4", shallow, vertical bands of fluting, undecorated, unmarked* **3.00**

☐ Dish, shape #134, *3-1/4" x 3-3/4", cross-hatching and fluting, pale pink, Lenox wreath mark*.. **17.00**

☐ Dish, shape #135, *3-1/4" x 3-3/4", fluting and embossed design around bottom, white with gold trim, Lenox palette mark* **18.00**

☐ Dish, shape #307, 5-1/2", heart shaped with embossed shell motif at top, gold trim, C.A.C. green palette mark **47.00**

☐ Dish, shape #307, 5-1/2", heart shaped with embossed shell motif at top, hand-painted large pink rose in center, artist signed, Lenox palette mark **60.00**

☐ Dish, shape #324, 5", heart shaped with embossed shell motif at top, small pink roses in scatter pattern, C.A.C. red palette mark **95.00**

Dish, *shape number uncertain, heart shape*

☐ Dish, shape number uncertain but possibly #977, 5-1/2", heart shape, embossing on rim, hand-painted child with garlands of roses, gold trim on embossed sections shows some wear, artist signed, very well done, C.A.C. green palette mark **95.00**

SPOONS

Lenox made two spoons, one for demitasse coffee and the other for salt. Both are typically unmarked and are extremely scarce. We have no listings on spoons for this past year, but would estimate their value at around $100.

SUGARS AND CREAMERS *(ALL PRICES ARE FOR THE PAIR)*

- ☐ Sugar and creamer, shape #38, *creamer 4", sugar 4-1/2" diameter, raised gold paste trim, C.A.C. lavender palette mark* **125.00**
- ☐ Sugar and creamer, shape #38, *creamer 4", sugar 4-1/2" diameter, pale blue inside bowl, reversed on creamer so that the blue is on the outside, brushed gold trim on rims, several flecks on ruffled rim of sugar, C.A.C. red palette mark* **115.00**
- ☐ Sugar and creamer, shape #38, *creamer 4", sugar 4-1/2" diameter, undecorated, very thin, C.A.C. brown palette mark* **100.00**
- ☐ Sugar and creamer, shape #72 and 72-1/2, *creamer 4-1/", sugar 4-1/4", small blue flowers, gold trim, C.A.C. green palette mark* **75.00**
- ☐ Sugar and creamer, *shaer 4-1/4", sugar 4-1/4", small blue flowers, gold trim, C.A.C. green palette mark* **75.00**
- ☐ Sugar and creamer, shape #72 and 72-1/2, *creamer 4-1/4", sugar 4-1/4", hand-painted work outlining the embossed work in the china, C.A.C. green palette mark* **50.00**

Sugar and creamer, *shape #38, lavendar palette mark*

- ☐ Sugar and creamer, shape #89 and 90, *sugar bowl 5", creamer 4", ribbed seashell effect, pale pink pearlized finish, speckled gold trim, C.A.C. lavender palette mark* **125.00**
- ☐ Sugar and creamer, shape #89 and 90, *sugar bowl 5", creamer 4", ribbed seashell effect, undecorated, Lenox wreath mark* **65.00**
- ☐ Sugar and creamer, shape #183 and 183-1/2, *melon-ribbed, creamer 4", sugar 3-1/2", undecorated, very thin, C.A.C. lavender palette mark* **85.00**
- ☐ Sugar and creamer, shape #213 and 214, *sugar 4-5/8", creamer 3-1/2", hand-painted forsythia, gold trim, C.A.C. palette mark* **100.00**
- ☐ Sugar and creamer, shape #213 and 214, *sugar 4-5/8", creamer 3-1/2", hand-painted small violets in scatter pattern, gold filigree trim, C.A.C. red palette mark, Bailey, Banks and Biddle store mark* **110.00**
- ☐ Sugar and creamer, shape #213 and 214, *sugar 4-5/8", creamer 3-1/2", undecorated, Lenox palette mark* **40.00**

☐ Sugar and creamer, shape #366 and 367, *Turkish shape, gold trim over brown glaze, raised gold paste pseudo-Arabic lettering, C.A.C. lavender palette mark* **150.00**

☐ Sugar and creamer, shape #366 and 373, *square pedestal bases, square handles, orange lustre finish with gold trim and gold monogram, badly done, Lenox palette mark* **25.00**

☐ Sugar and creamer, shape #372 and 373, *square pedestal bases and square handles, yellow rose on front of each and rosebud on backs, gold trim on handle, base and top, appears to be a variation of pattern #82, transition mark* **125.00**

☐ Sugar and creamer, shape #372 and 373, *square pedestal bases and square handles, gold trim and monogram, Lenox palette mark* **60.00**

☐ Sugar and creamer, shape #523 and 524, *transfer-decorated with Oriental scene in cobalt, items shade from white around decal to dark cobalt on end of handles and lids, well-executed, Lenox palette mark* **90.00**

☐ Sugar and creamer, shape #523 and 524, *hand-painted small pink roses in scatter pattern, gold filigree trim, transition mark* **150.00**

☐ Sugar and creamer, shape #523 and 524, *undecorated, Lenox wreath mark* **30.00**

☐ Sugar and creamer, shape #523 and 524, *groups of violets, gold trim, unsigned but nicely done, Lenox palette mark, chip on inside rim of sugar* **65.00**

☐ Sugar and creamer, shape #543 and 544, *angular modernistic shape, hand-painted black rose on fronts, black handles and trim, Lenox palette mark* **30.00**

☐ Sugar and creamer, shape #543 and 544, *angular, modernistic shape, undecorated, Lenox wreath mark* **40.00**

☐ Sugar and creamer, shape #580 and 581, *small hand-painted roses, gold trim, Lenox palette mark* **50.00**

☐ Sugar and creamer, shape #598 and 599, *undecorated, Lenox palette mark* **25.00**

☐ Sugar and creamer, shape #662 and 663, *hexagon shape, gold trim and monogram, Lenox palette mark* **35.00**

☐ Sugar and creamer, shape #662 and 663, *deep aquamarine with nicely done gold trim, Lenox palette mark* **60.00**

☐ Sugar and creamer, shape #697 and 698, *hand-painted pansies on shaded green background, gold trim, artist's initials and date, Lenox palette mark* **75.00**

☐ Sugar and creamer, shape #733 and 734, *hexagon shape, undecorated, Lenox palette mark* **35.00**

☐ Sugar and creamer, shape #733 and 734, *hexagon shape, hand-painted mixed flowers, gold trim, Lenox palette mark* **75.00**

☐ Sugar and creamer, shape #733 and 734, *hexagon shape, gold trim, Lenox palette mark* **40.00**

☐ Sugar and creamer, shape #743 and 744, *gold trim over a pale tan background, overall effect attractive, Lenox palette mark* **65.00**

☐ Sugar and creamer, shape #788 and 789, *hexagon shape, hand-painted flowers (possibly bachelor buttons), gold trim, Lenox palette mark* **50.00**

☐ Sugar and creamer, shape #935 and 936, *individual size, solid coral, Lenox wreath mark* **25.00**

☐ Sugar and creamer, shape #935 and 936, *individual size, hand-painted floral spray, gold trim, artist signed and dated, Lenox palette mark, very pretty* **80.00**

It is not always easy to tell if a Lenox sugar bowl had a lid or not, and we will solve the problem by listing, from old catalogue pictures, those sugars which did **not** have lids.

#38	#366	#598	#1183	#1948*
#72-1/2	#543	#935	#1516	#2101
#183	#580	#1062		

* *This sugar bowl, in addition to having no lid, also had no handles.*

TEA BALLS

Lenox only made one type of tea ball, and this is unfortunately not marked as a rule. It has a swirled rib effect and holes to let the tea brew. The top one fourth of the ball twists off to allow the tea to go in.

There are no verified examples of this tea ball to the best of our knowledge, and,therefore, there can be no prices. We would estimate the value of one at $50 to $100.

TEAPOTS

☐ Teapot, shape #88, *5-1/4", ribbed seashell effect, pale pink pearlized finish, speckled gold trim, C.A.C. lavender palette mark* **125.00**

☐ Teapot, shape #88, *5-1/4", ribbed seashell effect, gold trim, Lenox wreath mark* **75.00**

☐ Teapot, shape #88, *5-1/4", ribbed seashell effect, undecorated, Lenox palette mark* **50.00**

☐ Teapot, shape #101, *4-1/4" high, swan shape, very early and thin, un-decorated, C.A.C. brown palette mark, lower half of swan's beak has 1/8" chip* **95.00**

☐ Teapot, shape #101, *4-1/4" high, swan shape, very early and thin, gold tracing on feathers and handle, unmarked* **100.00**

☐ Teapot, shape #167, *5" high, hand-painted red roses front and back, finial, handle and spout done in same red with gold highlighting, art-ist signed and dated, C.A.C. green palette mark* **125.00**

☐ Teapot, shape #167, *5" high, hand-painted bouquet of flowers on shaded brown background, gold trim on handle, spout and finial, C.A.C. lavender palette mark* **75.00**

☐ Teapot, shape #167, *5" high, hand-painted chrysanthemums in several colors, tiny flowers on lid, gold trim on spout, handle and finial, artist's initials and year, C.A.C. green palette mark* **60.00**

☐ Teapot, shape #167, *5" high, gold trim on handle, spout and finial, Lenox palette mark* **50.00**

☐ Teapot, shape #167, *5" high, small hand-painted violets in scatter pattern, brushed gold trim, C.A.C. red palette mark and Davis Col-lamore store mark, fleck on spout, crack in handle* **100.00**

☐ Teapot, shape #167, *5" high, undecorated, Lenox palette mark* **25.00**

☐ Teapot, shape #476, *7-1/4" spout to handle, square pedestal base, square handle, hand-painted roses and blue dot enamel work, the perfect example of an otherwise beautiful item ruined by messy gilding, artist signed, C.A.C. green palette mark* **125.00**

☐ Teapot, shape #476, *7-1/4" spout to handle, square pedestal base, square handle, hand-painted orchid, delicate gold filigree trim, un-signed but probably the work of W. H. Morley, transition mark* **175.00**

☐ Teapot, shape #476, *7-1/4" spout to handle, square pedestal base, square handle, undecorated, C.A.C. brown palette mark* **65.00**

☐ Teapot, shape #476, *7-1/4" handle to spout, square peddstal base, squad, C.A.C. brown palette mark* **65.00**

☐ Teapot, shape #476, 7-1/4" handle to spout, square pedestal base, square handle, orange lustre finish with gold trim and gold monogram, badly done, Lenox palette mark........................... **25.00**

☐ Teapot, shape #476, 7-1/4" spout to handle, square pedestal base, square handle, delicate gold filigree work on base, spout, midsection, handle and lid, transition mark **75.00**

☐ Teapot, shape #522 7-1/2", infuser type base, spout, midsection, handle and lid, transition mark................................ **75.00**

☐ Teapot, shape #522, 7-1/2", infuser type, overall brown glaze, Lenox wreath mark **75.00**

☐ Teapot, shape #522, 7-1/2", infuser type, hand-painted fruit on shaded tan background, gold trim, beautiful artwork, infuser cracked, spider crack in bottom of pot, artist signed and dated, C.A.C. green palette mark **75.00**

☐ Teapot, shape #522, 7-1/2", infuser type, undecorated, Lenox palette mark.. **60.00**

☐ Teapot, shape #522, 7-1/2", infuser type, hand-painted roses, gold trim, infuser missing, Lenox palette mark......................... **45.00**

☐ Teapot, shape #522, 7-1/2", infuser type, geometric gold work, Lenox palette mark **75.00**

☐ Teapot, shape #522, 7-1/2", infuser type, hand-painted small pink roses in scatter pattern, gold filigree trim, transition mark.......... **150.00**

☐ Teapot, shape #522, 7-1/2", infuser type, single yellow rose on front, bud on reverse side, gold trim, neatly done, Lenox palette mark **100.00**

☐ Teapot, shape #522, 7-1/2", infuser type, hand-painted Oriental dragons in green, gold highlights on dragon, gold trim on handle, spout, and lid, one of the more original designs we have seen, Lenox palette mark **130.00**

Note: The infuser teapots sell somewhat higher than other types since they are avidly sought by tea drinkers as well as Lenox collectors. If the infuser is missing or unusable, the value drops below that of comparable teapots which are not the infuser type. The lid will not fit properly if the infuser is gone.

☐ Teapot, shape #542, 3-1/4", angular shape, undecorated, Lenox palette mark **25.00**

☐ Teapot, shape #542, 3-1/4", 3-1/4", angular shape, gold trim, Lenox palette mark **35.00**

☐ Teapot, shape #579-1/2, 4-1/2", small hand-painted roses, gold trim, Lenox palette mark **50.00**

☐ Teapot, shape #661, 4-1/2", hexagon shape, three small rosebuds on front, one bud on back, gold handle and trim, Lenox palette mark.... **65.00**

☐ Teapot, shape #661, 4-1/2", hexagon shape, undecorated, Lenox wreath mark **30.00**

☐ Teapot, shape #708, 5-3/8", hexagon shape, raised gold paste dots, artist signed, Lenox palette mark................................ **35.00**

☐ Teapot, shape #732, 6-1/4", hexagon shape, hand-painted leaves (possibly teagleaves) on both sidark **35.00**

☐ Teapot, shape #732, 6-1/4" hexagon shape, hand-painted leaves (possibly tea leaves) on both sides, gold trim, rather attractive all things considered, artist signed, Lenox palette mark **50.00**

☐ Teapot, shape #732, 6-1/4", entire outside covered with a crudely done silver lustre effect, Lenox palette mark **65.00**

☐ Teapot, shape #742, 6-1/8", hand-painted morning glories on ivory background, gold trim, tiny fleck on spout, Lenox palette mark...... **75.00**

☐ Teapot, shape #742, 6-1/8", hand-painted pink and yellow roses, gold trim, not artist signed but similar to work done by Marsh, Lenox palette mark **100.00**

☐ Teapot, shape #742, 6-1/8", hand-painted white roses surrounded by blue dot work, very professional look, gold trim, Lenox palette mark . **150.00**

☐ Teapot, shape #786, 5", tiny floral sprays, gold trim, artist's initials, Lenox palette mark **65.00**

☐ Teapot, shape #786, 5", undecorated, Lenox palette mark **15.00**

☐ Teapot, shape #786, 5", pencil-line gold trim and monogram, Lenox wreath mark **25.00**

☐ Teapot, shape #888, 6-1/2", stylized tulips on black background, red trim, Lenox palette mark **18.00**

☐ Teapot, shape #888, 6-1/2", transfer-decorated with Oriental scene, gold trim, Lenox palette mark **35.00**

☐ Teapot, shape #888, 6-1/2", undecorated, Lenox palette mark **15.00**

☐ Teapot, shape #934, 4-3/4", individual size, undecorated, Lenox palette mark **20.00**

☐ Teapot, shape #934, individual size, solid coral Lenox wreath mark .. **25.00**

☐ Teapot, shape #934, 4-3/4", individual size, hand-painted small pink roses in scatter pattern, gold trim, Lenox wreath mark **100.00**

☐ Teapot, shape #934, 4-3/4", individual size, hand-painted berries and leaves, artist signed and dated, gold trim, not bad, Lenox palette mark.. **75.00**

☐ Teapot, shape #946, 3-3/4", hand-painted pansies on pale yellow shaded background, very pretty, handle and spout shade to a deeper yellow instead of having the usual gloppy gold, Lenox palette mark .. **85.00**

☐ Teapot, shape #946, 3-3/4", hand-painted roses, pink on one side, red on the other, gold trim, artist signed, Lenox palette mark **45.00**

TEA STRAINERS

Tea strainers are very scarce, perhaps due more to excessive breakage than to limited production. The top half is never marked. All that we have seen have had the C.A.C. marks.

Tea strainer

☐ Tea strainer, shape #339, *hand-painted roses and gold trim, transition mark* **200.00**

☐ Tea strainer, shape #339, *hand-painted and signed by George Morley (both halves artist-signed for some reason), transition mark* **275.00**

☐ Tea strainer, shape #339, *hand-painted flowers, C.A.C. palette mark* . **150.00**

☐ Tea strainer, *top half only, hand-painted violets, obviously factory done*... **100.00**

☐ Tea strainer, *bottom half only, hand-painted violets, C.A.C. palette mark*.. **35.00**

The above two items were never mates—the artwork is very different.

THIMBLES

These are very rare Lenox items and are frequently unmarked. We have no actual listings for any during the past year, but did see one marked at well over $100. The prettiest ones have little pink roses painted on them.

TOBACCO JARS

Lenox made only one true tobacco jar, but biscuit jars can also be considered tobacco jars depending on the style of decoration.

Tobacco jar, *Lenox wreath mark*

☐ Tobacco jar, shape #328, *7-1/2" high, monochrome green, monk smoking cigarette, signed E.A. DeLan, transition mark* **175.00**

☐ Tobacco jar, shape #328, *7-1/2" high, hand-painted ears of corn, C.A.C. palette mark, artist signed and dated* **100.00**

☐ Tobacco jar, shape #328, *7-1/2" high, hand-painted Indian smoking peace pipe, Lenox palette mark* **135.00**

☐ Tobacco jar, no shape number, *5-1/2" high, Canada geese in flight, blue sky, green grass and swamp plants, signed W. H. Morley, Lenox wreath mark* ∴... **350.00**

TRAYS

- [ ] Tray, shape #15, *6-1/2" square, ruffled rim, plain white, Lenox palette mark* **20.00**
- [ ] Tray, shape #15, *6-1/2" square, ruffled rim, matte finish with raised gold paste decoration, C.A.C. red palette mark* **125.00**
- [ ] Tray, shape #15, *6-1/2" square, ruffled rim, hand-painted butterflies on blue background, gold trim on rim, Lenox palette mark* **30.00**
- [ ] Tray, shape #16, *9-3/4" square, ruffled rim, raised on four feet, hand-painted rose in center, gold trim on rim, C.A.C. green palette mark, probably home decorated but nicely done* **100.00**
- [ ] Tray, shape #16, *9-3/4" square, ruffled rim, raised on four feet, plain with gold trim, C.A.C. palette mark, several flecks on ruffled rim* **60.00**
- [ ] Tray, shape #17, *10-1/2" round, ruffled rim, plain, white, a few small flecks on rim, Lenox palette mark* **50.00**
- [ ] Tray, shape #17, *10-1/2" round, ruffled rim, white with gold trim, C.A.C. palette mark* **75.00**
- [ ] Tray, shape #132, *8" round, swirled ribs on rim, undecorated, C.A.C. palette mark* **75.00**
- [ ] Tray, shape #132, *8" round, swirled ribs on rim, undecorated, C.A.C. lavender palette mark* **45.00**
- [ ] Tray, shape #132, *8" round, swirled ribs on rim, gold tracings on scalloping, Lenox palette mark* **60.00**
- [ ] Tray, shape #137, *5-1/4" x 7-3/4", gourd shaped, ruffled rim, gold trim on rim and gold tracings in center, Lenox palette mark* **100.00**
- [ ] Tray, shape #148, *3-1/2" x 8-1/2", for pens, ruffled rim, Delft type scene in monochromatic blue, C.A.C. wreath mark* **130.00**
- [ ] Tray, shape #159, *8-1/4" x 11", ruffled rim, decorated with hand-painted and gold trim, C.A.C. green wreath mark, flecks on ruffles* . . . **100.00**
- [ ] Tray, shape #159, *8-1/4" x 11", ruffled rim, plain white, flecks on rim, C.A.C. lavender palette mark* **50.00**
- [ ] Tray, shape #168, *3-1/4" x 5", ruffled rim, hand-painted fruit in center, Lenox green palette mark, artist signed and dated 1908* **70.00**

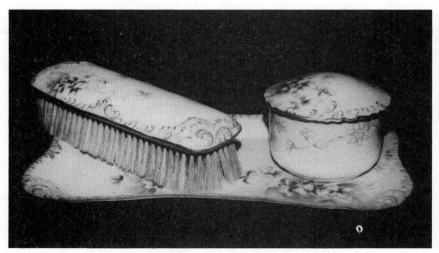

Tray, *shape #323, hand-painted violets*

☐ Tray, shape #323, 7-1/8" x 11-3/8", embossed rim, hand-painted flowers in center and gold trim on rim, gold shows considerable wear, C.A.C. brown palette mark 100.00

☐ Tray, shape #323, 7-1/8" x 11-3/8", embossed rim, hand-painted violets, beautifully done, C.A.C. lavender palette mark 100.00

☐ Tray, shape #323, 7-1/8" x 11-3/8", embossed rim, small hand-painted roses with gold trim, C.A.C. green palette mark 200.00

☐ Tray, shape #616, 6", for pins, plain white, Lenox palette mark 15.00

☐ Tray, shape #616, 6", for pins, small bees and flowers on yellow background, Lenox palette mark 50.00

☐ Tray, shape #616, 6", hand-painted small roses in scatter design, pencil-line gold on rim, Lenox wreath mark...................... 90.00

☐ Tray, shape #617, 7-1/2", for pins, white with gold trim on rim and monogram in center, gold shows wear, C.A.C. green palette mark ... 25.00

☐ Tray, shape #617, 7-1/2", small hand-painted violets with gold trim on edge, C.A.C. pink palette mark and Bailey, Banks and Biddle store mark.. 90.00

☐ Tray, shape #617, pins, 7-1/2", plain white, Lenox palette mark 17.00

☐ Tray, shape #647, 13-1/4" x 7-3/4", orange poppy design, gold trim on rim, Lenox palette mark, artist's initials and date on bottom 90.00

☐ Tray, shape #647, 13-1/4" x 7-3/4", pink roses on green background, nicely done, Lenox palette mark............................... 100.00

☐ Tray, shape #648, 5-1/4" square, plain white, C.A.C. lavender palette mark.. 20.00

☐ Tray, shape #648, 5-1/4" square, small hand-painted roses, transition mark.. 75.00

☐ Tray, shape #648, 5-1/4" square, entire rim done in very sloppy gold trim, Lenox palette mark 25.00

☐ Tray, shape #771, 14-1/2" x 6", gold trim on edges, wedding inscription in middle, slight wear on gold, Lenox palette mark 60.00

☐ Tray, shape #898, 9-1/2" hexagon shape with handles, single large daffodil in center, gold trim on rim, Lenox palette mark, artist's initials 100.00

☐ Tray, shape #898, 9-1/2" hexagon shape, plain white, Lenox palette mark.. 35.00

☐ Tray, shape #898, 9-1/2" hexagon shape, white with gold trim, Lenox wreath mark 50.00

☐ Tray, shape #954, 9", round, handle, plain white, Lenox palette mark . 35.00

☐ Tray, shape #954, 9" round, handled, hand-painted (nicely) with tulips and butterflies, Lenox palette mark, artist's initials and date on bottom.. 125.00

☐ Tray, shape #954, 9" round, handled, hand-painted in geometric enamels, artist's initials, Lenox palette mark.................... 65.00

☐ Tray, shape #955, 12" round, handled, gold trim, Lenox wreath mark . 50.00

☐ Tray, shape #955, 12" round, handled, Art Nouveau enamel work, Lenox palette mark, artist signed and dated 125.00

☐ Tray, shape #956, 14" round, handled, Art Nouveau style hand-painting with water lily design and gold trim, Lenox palette mark, artist initialed and dated 100.00

☐ Tray, shape #956, 14" round, handled, plain white, Lenox palette mark.. 40.00

☐ Tray, shape #957, 9" round, hand-painted with wildflowers design around rim, gold trim, gold handles, Lenox palette mark 65.00

☐ Tray, shape #957, 9" round, gold trim, monogram "C" in center, Lenox palette mark 50.00

☐ Tray, shape #958, *12" round, handled, hand-painted butterflies in center, gold trim, artist signed and dated, dreadful art work, Lenox palette mark* **65.00**

☐ Tray, shape #958, *12" round, handled, hand-painted with stylized tulips and gold trim, Lenox palette mark* **60.00**

☐ Tray, shape #959, *14" round, handled, undecorated, Lenox palette mark* **45.00**

☐ Tray, shape #959, *14" round, handled, gold trim, small chip on underside of one handle, Lenox wreath mark* **40.00**

☐ Tray, shape #983, *11-3/8" x 7-1/8", rounded-off corners, undecorated, unmarked, item number impressed in bottom verifies it's Lenox* **20.00**

☐ Tray, shape #983, *11-3/8" x 7-1/8", rounded-off corners, gold trim, Lenox palette mark* **50.00**

TUMBLERS AND SHOT GLASSES

These items are not especially rare, and can occasionally be found in matched sets both with and without pitchers or whisky jugs.

☐ Shot glass, shape #269, *undecorated, Lenox palette mark* **12.00**

☐ Shot glass, shape #269, *tiny ears or corn hand-painted on front, gold trim, Lenox palette mark* **20.00**

☐ Shot glass, shape #269, *hand-painted plums on green shaded background, C.A.C. green palette mark* **30.00**

☐ Shot glass, shape #269, *gold trim, Lenox wreath mark* **12.00**

☐ Shot glass, shape #394, *hand-painted berries on plain background, gold trim, artist's initials and date* **18.00**

☐ Tumbler, shape number unknown, *4" high, undecorated, Lenox palette mark* **20.00**

VASES AND URNS

We will not attempt to differentiate between urns and vases here, but instead will refer to all the items as vases. The term urn can be loosely applied to any large, ornamental, usually footed vase.

Vase, *item #27, bulbous bottom*

☐ Vase, item #27, 7-1/2" high, bulbous bottom, undecorated, Lenox
wreath mark **15.00**

☐ Vase, item #27, 7-1/2" high, bulbous bottom, white top with coral bot-
tom, Lenox wreath mark, see photo **25.00**

☐ Vase, item #27, 7-1/2" high, bulbous bottom, white bottom with blue
top, Lenox wreath mark **25.00**

☐ Vase, item #27, 7½" high, bulbous, bottom, beige matte finish with
raised gold paste work, lavender palette C.A.C. mark **75.00**

*Item #27 is the only item from the early catalogues to have survived
down to the present day in its original shape and size.*

☐ Vase, item #28, 7-1/2" high, bulbous bottom, one handle, white with
gold trim, Lenox palette mark **30.00**

☐ Vase, item #28, 7-1/2" high, bulbous bottom, one handle, undeco-
rated, Lenox wreath mark **20.00**

☐ Vase, item #28, 7-1/2" high, bulbous bottom, one handle, brushed
gold near rim, gold filigree work on handle, transition mark **75.00**

☐ Vase, item #29, 7-1/2" high, bulbous bottom, two handles, white bot-
tom with blue top and handles, Lenox wreath mark **30.00**

☐ Vase, item #29, 7-1/2" high, bulbous bottom, two handles, undeco-
rated, Levox wreath mark **20.00**

☐ Vase, item #29, 7-1/2" high, bulbous bottom, two handles,
undecorated, Lenox wreath mark **20.00**

☐ Vase, item #29, 7-1/2" high, bulbous bottom, two handles, yellow and
white floral trim, C.A.C. green palette mark **40.00**

☐ Vase, item #29, 7-1/2" high, bulbous bottom, two handles, transfer
decoration on bottom part, gold trim on handles and neck, really bad,
Lenox palette mark **15.00**

☐ Vase, item #30, 6-3/4" high, long neck, two handles, undecorated
C.A.C. green palette mark **40.00**

☐ Vase, item #30, 6-3/4" high, long neck two handles, beige matte finish
with gold trim on handles and inside the rim, C.A.C. lavender palette
mark **100.00**

☐ Vase, item #30, 6-3/4" high, long neck, two handles, Art Nouveau
style grapes with gold trim, C.A.C. brown palette mark **100.00**

☐ Vase, item #31, 6-3/4" high, long neck, two handles, yellow and
orange hand-painted daisies on pale blue background, Lenox palette
mark **60.00**

☐ Vase, item #31, 6-3/4" high, long neck, two handles, transfer decorated with portrait of a woman, gold trim on handles and inside rim,
C.A.C. green palette mark **60.00**

☐ Vase, item #31, 6-3/4" high, long neck, two handles, pink lustre ex-
terior, gold trim on handles, Lenox palette mark **25.00**

☐ Vase, item #32, 6-3/4" high, long neck, two handles, not decorated,
C.A.C. green palette mark **30.00**

☐ Vase, item #32, 6-3/4" high, long neck, two handles, gold grapes with
black outlining, gold trim on handles, C.A.C. lavender palette mark . .   **35.00**

☐ Vase, item #34, 9" high, long neck, two handles, geometric enamel
trim, gold handles and gold trim top and bottom, Lenox palette mark   **50.00**

☐ Vase, item #34, 9" high, long neck, two handles, undecorated, C.A.C.
brown palette mark **60.00**

☐ Vase, item #34, 9" high, long neck, two handles, rainbow shaded
from lavender to yellow, speckled gold over the shading, gold trim on
handles and rims, rather strange-looking but nicely done and in-
teresting, C.A.C. lavender palette mark **150.00**

☐ Vase, item #35, *7-1/2" high, undecorated, C.A.C. green palette mark* . **60.00**
☐ Vase, item #35, *7-1/2" high, hand-painted in center, gold trim, artist signed and dated on bottom, C.A.C. green palette mark* **100.00**
☐ Vase, item #49, *10-1/4" high, bulbous shape with ruffled rim, melon-ribbed effect, white shading to deep turquoise, very nice raised gold paste around middle, transition mark* **225.00**
☐ Vase, item #49, *10-1/4" high, undecorated, Lenox palette mark* **75.00**
☐ Vase, item #52, *10-1/2" high, undecorated, Lenox palette mark* **60.00**

Vase, *item #52, lavendar palette mark*

☐ Vase, item #52, *10-1/2" high, beige matte finish, hand-painted pink flowers and green leaves all outlined with gold tracing, gold handles and trim, C.A.C. lavender palette mark* **200.00**
☐ Vase, item #52, *10-1/2" high, red, white and pink hand-painted roses, gold trim, artist signed, Lenox palette mark* **65.00**
☐ Vase, item #81, *6-1/4" high, Lenox Rose trim with gold, Lenox wreath mark* **30.00**
☐ Vase, item #81, *6-1/4" high, undecorated, Lenox palette mark* **15.00**
☐ Vase, item #81, *6-1/4" high, hand-painted flowers, gold trim, C.A.C. green palette mark* **60.00**
☐ Vase, item #81, *6-1/4" high, undecorated and unmarked* **10.00**
☐ Vase, item #83, *11" high, twisted neck, four side openings and top opening, gold paste trim, C.A.C. lavender palette mark* **200.00**
☐ Vase, item #86, *8-1/2" high, matte finish with brushed gold and tiny blue forget-me-nots on both sides, gold paste leaves, C.A.C. lavender palette mark* **100.00**
☐ Vase, item #86, *8-1/2" high, undecorated, Lenox wreath mark* **25.00**
☐ Vase, item #86, *8-1/2" high, white with gold trim, Lenox wreath mark* . **28.00**

Vase, *item #81, Lenox rose trim*

☐ Vase, item #86, *8-1/2" high, coral, Lenox wreath mark* **32.00**
Note: Item #86 is frequently called the "aorta vase" due to its resemblance to a human heart with arteries coming out from it. It is also sometimes referred to as an "onion vase". Lenox catalogues call it simply "four-part flower holder."

☐ Vase, item #109, *7-3/4" high, two handles, narrow tall neck with ruffled rim, hand-painted roses in pink and red, gold trim on handles and rim, C.A.C. green palette mark* **125.00**

☐ Vase, item #109, *7-3/4" high, two handles, narrow tall neck, hand-painted dog on shaded background, gold trim on handles and rim, C.A.C. green palette mark, artist signed and date, not bad* **150.00**

☐ Vase, item #110, *7-3/4" high, same as #109 except handles different, undecorated, Lenox palette mark* **65.00**

☐ Vase, item #110, *7-3/4" high, same as #109 except handles different, hand-painted jonquils on blue background, gold trim on handles and rim, C.A.C. green palette mark* **135.00**

☐ Vase, item #119, *11-1/4" high, hand-painted lilies with gold trim, artist signed and dated, nicely done, C.A.C. green palette mark* **250.00**

☐ Vase, item #120, *7-1/2" high, undecorated, unmarked* **50.00**

☐ Vase, item #7-1/2" high, hand-painted with morning glories and gold trim, Lenox palette mark* **60.00**

☐ Vase, item #122, *7-3/4" high, same shape as #109 but no handles, hand-painted chrysanthemums on shaded brown background, unsigned but possibly the work of Morley, transition mark* **200.00**

☐ Vase, item #122, *7-3/4" high, hand-painted nasturtium on shaded background, artist signed and dated, C.A.C. green palette mark* **125.00**

☐ Vase, item #126, *7-1/2" high, brushed gold trim near top and bottom, Lenox palette mark* **70.00**

☐ Vase, item #126, *7-1/2" high, hand-painted wildflowers with gold trim, artist signed and dated, C.A.C. green palette mark* **80.00**

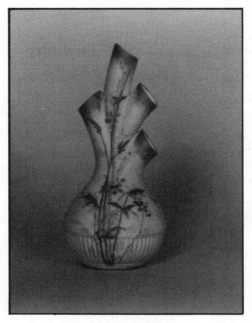

Vase, *Item #86*

☐ Vase, item #129, *7-1/2" high, undecorated, Lenox green wreath mark,
yellow and white* **60.00**

☐ Vase, item #129, *7-1/2" high, cabbage roses in yellow and pink, gold
rims, and handles, C.A.C. palette mark* **75.00**

☐ Vase, item #129, *7-1/2" high, floral spray on cream background,
Lenox palette mark* **100.00**

☐ Vase, item #131, *11-1/4" high, undecorated, C.A.C. palette mark* **125.00**

☐ Vase, covered, item #145, *11-1/2" high, white and pink roses in garlands from the top, cream background, gold trim on handles and rim,
C.A.C. palette mark* **250.00**

☐ Vase, item #199, *8-1/2" high, sponged gold effect on embossed portions of vase, C.A.C. wreath mark* **250.00**

☐ Vase, item #218, *15-1/2" high, trumpet shaped, undecorated, C.A.C.
green palette mark* **50.00**

☐ Vase, item #218, *15-1/2" high, trumpet shaped, green vines coming
down sides, gold trim top and bottom, Lenox palette mark* **125.00**

☐ Vase, item #224, *12-3/4" high, celadon green with gold trim, Lenox
wreath mark* **90.00**

☐ Vase, item #224, *12-3/4" high, yellow roses on pale pink background,
gold trim, C.A.C. green palette mark* **125.00**

☐ Vase, item #265, *7-1/2" high, mottled spongeware type decoration
with gold trim, Lenox palette mark* **40.00**

☐ Vase, item #265, *7-1/2" high, red, white and pink roses, gold trim, artist signed, C.A.C. palette mark* **100.00**

☐ Vase, item #272, *12-1/2" high, undecorated, Lenox palette mark* **175.00**

☐ Vase, item #272, *12-1/2" high, Victorian garden scene with man and woman, pastel colors, unmarked, unsigned but looks very much like the work of Heidrich* **300.00**

☐ Vase, item #289, *3-1/4" high, overall chrysanthemum decoration, excellent color and artwork, C.A.C. palette mark* **60.00**

☐ Vase, item #289, *3-1/4" high, gold rim and base, gold birds in flight on black background, Oriental look, Lenox palette mark* **50.00**

☐ Vase, item #289, *overall design of small pink roses, C.A.C. red palette mark* **70.00**

☐ Vase, item #296, *11" high, tropical seascape with seagulls, moon, sailboat and palm trees, artist signed and dated, Lenox palette mark* **125.00**

☐ Vase, item #296, *11" high, cabbage roses, gold trim on top and bottom, C.A.C. palette mark* **135.00**

☐ Vase, item #297, *8-1/4" high, gold colored vines with black outlining and geometrics, Lenox palette mark* **90.00**

Vase, *item #314, by Sully*

☐ Vase, item #314, *8" high, portrait of young girl standing in a rose garden, gold on rim, signed Sully, transition mark* **225.00**

☐ Vase, item #314, *8" high, outdoor scene of lake and swans, good artwork, artist signed and dated, C.A.C. green palette mark* **225.00**

☐ Vase, item #314, *8" high, overall rose decoration, gold trim on rim, C.A.C. palette mark* **150.00**

☐ Vase, item #314, *8" high, Art Nouveau florals in red, black and gold, gold trim on rim, Lenox palette mark* **75.00**

☐ Vase, item #315, *5-3/4" high, monochromatic blues, male and female pheasant on ground, C.A.C. wreath mark* **175.00**

Vase, item #315, pheasants

☐ Vase, item #315, *5-3/4" high, two finches in flight, monochromatic blue, very similar to above item in general look but not by same artist, C.A.C. wreath mark (decorating style very similar to items done by S. Laurence at Rookwood)*. 175.00

☐ Vase, item #315, *5-3/4" high, undecorated, Lenox wreath mark* 15.00

☐ Vase, item #315, *pink lustre exterior, gold trim on rim, Lenox palette mark*. 18.00

☐ Vase, item #316, *9" high, hand-painted roses, gold trim, Lenox palette mark* 50.00

☐ Vase, item #316, *9" high, yellow daffodils on blue background, artist signed and dated, C.A.C. green palette mark* 100.00

☐ Vase, item #318, *8-1/4" high, portrait of springer spaniel on cream background, back of piece marked "Hunter Arms Co. First Prize", signed Baker, Lenox wreath mark* 225.00

☐ Vase, item #318, *8-1/4" high, hand-painted jonquils on shaded purplish-red and green background, signed "Des", gold trim inside rim, transition mark with Glen-Iris stamp* 225.00

☐ Vase, item #318, *Oriental motif with dragons and geometric design, red, black and gold, artist signed and dated, Lenox palette mark* 125.00

☐ Vase, item #318, *8-1/4" high, seascape signed by DeLan and bearing both the Lenox and DeLan & McGill marks* 300.00

☐ Vase, item #319, *9-1/4" high, top part aqua with raised gold work, bottom half creamy color with garlands of blue dot and gold paste work, C.A.C. lavender palette mark* 90.00

☐ Vase, item #319, *9-1/4" high, hand-painted purple irises on green background, below-average artwork, C.A.C. green palette mark* 50.00

☐ Vase, item #319, *9-1/4" high, overall floral decoration, no artist signature, transition mark* 175.00

Vase, item #318, springer spaniel

☐ Vase, item #320, *10-1/4" high, various shadings of color forming attractive background for raised enamel work in a lattice-work pattern, C.A.C. lavender palette mark* **125.00**

☐ Vase, item #320, *10-1/4" high, gold iris decoration on white shading to turquoise, gold trim on rim, transition mark* **135.00**

☐ Vase, item #326, *9" high, jonquils on purplish-red and green background, no artist signature, gold trim on rim, transition mark and Glen-Iris stamp* **225.00**

☐ Vase, item #326, *9" high, enameled flowers, artist signed and dated, C.A.C. palette mark* **35.00**

☐ Vase, item #326, *9" high, portrait of Victorian woman artist signed, gold trim, C.A.C. green palette mark* **185.00**

☐ Vase, item #355, *8-1/2", yellow, L opaque mark* **60.00**

☐ Vase, item #355, *8-1/2" high, pink, L opaque mark* **55.00**

☐ Vase, item #355, *8-1/2", hand-painted water lilies, fair artwork, artist signed, C.A.C. green palette mark* **130.00**

☐ Vase, item #355, *8-1/2", peacock feathers hand-painted to form panels, gold trim, Lenox palette mark* **105.00**

☐ Vase, item #355, *8-1/2" high, Dutch scene, polychromatic, C.A.C. green palette mark* **175.00**

☐ Vase, item #355, *8-1/2" high, undecorated, Lenox wreath mark* **25.00**

☐ Vase, item #355, *8-1/2" high, pink with gold trim, Lenox wreath mark* . **50.00**

☐ Vase, item #355, *8-1/2" high, Ming pattern, Lenox wreath mark* **110.00**

☐ Vase, item #356, *7" high, bittersweet blossom and berry design, gold trim, C.A.C. green palette mark* **125.00**

☐ Vase, item #356, *7" high, blue and gold Art Nouveau stylized lilies, Lenox palette mark* **60.00**

Vase, *item #318, jonquils*

- [ ] Vase, item #368, *9-7/8" high, hand-painted deep red cabbage roses, gold trim on top and bottom, artist signed and dated, C.A.C. lavender palette mark* **180.00**
- [ ] Vase, item #368, *9-7/8" high, hand-painted poppies on tan background, C.A.C. green palette mark* **150.00**
- [ ] Vase, item #369, *13" high, undecorated, Lenox palette mark* **40.00**
- [ ] Vase, item #369, *13" high, hand-painted morning glories on tan background, artist's initials, C.A.C. green palette mark* **80.00**
- [ ] Vase, item #370, *13" high, yellow crocuses on shaded brown background, gold trim on rim, Lenox palette mark* **125.00**
- [ ] Vase, item #381, *undecorated, Lenox wreath mark* **45.00**
- [ ] Vase, item #409, *8-1/4" high, overall design of small hand-painted violets, gold trim, transition mark* **125.00**
- [ ] Vase, item #412, *9" high, ball-shaped with narrow neck, hand-painted chrysanthemums on brown background, signed W. H. Morley, transition mark* **300.00**
- [ ] Vase, item #412, *9" high, hand-painted cabbage roses, gold trim, artist signed and dated, C.A.C. green palette mark* **125.00**
- [ ] Vase, item #412, *9" high, undecorated, Lenox palette mark* **40.00**
- [ ] Vase, item #416, *5-3/4" high, hand-painted portrait of girl with roses in her hair, badly done, artist signed, Lenox palette mark* **100.00**
- [ ] Vase, item #420, *5" high, hand-painted ivy on off-white background, gold trim, nicely done, artist signed and dated, C.A.C. palette mark* .. **100.00**
- [ ] Vase, item #420, *5" high, hand-painted buttercups on blue background, Lenox palette mark* **30.00**
- [ ] Vase, item #425, *12-1/4" high, hand-painted roses, gold trim on handles and on lid finial, artist signed and dated, not bad artwork for type, C.A.C. lavender palette mark* **250.00**

Vase, item #319, aqua top

☐ Vase, item #426, *11" high, lid missing, monochromatic blue portrait of man, dated 1894 and signed by Sturgis Laurence, C.A.C. wreath mark* **400.00**

☐ Vase, item #427, *11" high, portrait of girl wreathed by raised gold paste work, maroon over rest of urn with more gold paste, gold handles and trim on rim, signed Campana, transition mark, size and type of trim put item into the "pay whatever you have to" category.*

☐ Vase, item #428, *8-1/4" high, orange poppies on shaded green background, gold trim on handles, base and rim, home-decorated but nice, C.A.C. green palette mark* **240.00**

☐ Vase, item #428, *8-1/4" high, pink roses on shaded background, gold handles and rim, C.A.C. green palette mark* **225.00**

☐ Vase, item #429, *13-1/2" high, undecorated, C.A.C. green palette mark* **75.00**

☐ Vase, item #429, *13-1/2" high, gold trim, C.A.C. lavender palette mark* **100.00**

☐ Vase, item #430, *16" high, monochromatic blue Dutch type scene, transition mark* **280.00**

☐ Vase, item #431, *15" high, hand-painted begonias on tan background, gold trim on handles, foot and rim, Lenox palette mark* . **200.00**

☐ Vase, item #433, *15-1/4" high, hand-painted portrait of Victorian woman, blue dot enamel trim, gold on handles and rims, repaired on one handle, C.A.C. green palette mark* **300.00**

☐ Vase, item #435, *16-1/2" high, hand-painted pink roses on one side, yellow roses on other side, shaded background, gold trim, artist signed and dated, C.A.C. lavender palette mark* **300.00**

☐ Vase, item #436, *14" high, hand-painted Grecian temple scene, gold trim, artist signed, home decorated but overall effect rather nice, Lenox, palette mark* **275.00**

☐ Vase, item #437, *12" high, undecorated, unmarked* **75.00**

Vase, item #326, Jonquils

☐ Vase, item #438, *13" high, hand-painted irises in blue and burgundy on off-white background, gold trim on handles and rim, artist signed, C.A.C. green palette mark* **200.00**

☐ Vase, item #439, *11" high, hand-painted chrysanthemums in orange and yellow on shaded tan background, gold trim on handles, Lenox palette mark* **250.00**

☐ Vase, item #442, *17" high, hand-painted cabbage roses on shaded green background, gold trim, Lenox palette mark* **175.00**

☐ Vase, item #445, *16-3/4" high, gold trim, no Lenox mark* **70.00**

☐ Vase, item #451, *10-1/2" high, hand-done with geometric enamel designs, gold trim on rim, artist's initials and date, Lenox palette mark* **60.00**

☐ Vase, item #451 *10-1/2" high, hand-painted tulips and daffodils on pink background, 1/4" chip on rim, C.A.C. palette mark* **75.00**

☐ Vase, item #452, *11-1/4" high, hand-painted pink roses with baby's breath on green background, gold trim on rim, Lenox palette mark* ... **100.00**

☐ Vase, item #452, *11-1/4" high, pink and white peonies on green background, gold trim, Lenox palette mark* **100.00**

☐ Vase, item #452, *11-1/4" high, hand-painted birds on a pine branch, muted effect as if viewed through a mist, artist's initials, C.A.C. palette mark* **230.00**

☐ Vase, item #453, *12" high, hand-painted purple iris on one side and one gold iris on other side, green leaves, neck of vase done in green, gold trim, C.A.C. lavender palette mark, artist signed* **160.00**

☐ Vase, item #454, *9-1/2" high, undecorated, Lenox palette mark* **35.00**

☐ Vase, item #454, *9-1/2" high, hand-painted roses in pink on plain background, gold trim, signed Marsh, transition mark* **300.00**

☐ Vase, item #459, *13" high, hand-painted purple and red grapes, shaded yellow and green background, gold trim on inside of rim, transition mark* **300.00**

☐ Vase, item #470, *18-1/2", high, plain with gold trim, Lenox wreath mark* **115.00**

Vase, item #426

☐ Vase, item #493, *14-3/4" high, hand-painted purple orchid on one side, yellow orchid on other, gold trim on top and bottom, transition mark*. **400.00**

☐ Vase, item #501, *6" high, overall small pink rose design, gold trim on top rim, transition mark*. **90.00**

☐ Vase, item #501, *6" high, hand-painted orange and pink poppies on tan background, Lenox palette mark* **75.00**

☐ Vase, item #501, *6" high, undecorated, Lenox palette mark, small fleck on rim* **15.00**

☐ Vase, item #502, *6" high, bayberry decoration on white background, silver trim on handles, artist signed, Lenox palette mark* **75.00**

☐ Vase, item #502, *6" high, magnolia blossoms on pale green background, Lenox palette mark* **60.00**

☐ Vase, item #503, *8" tall, Siamese cat on tan background, Lenox palette mark*. **150.00**

☐ Vase, item #503, *8" tall, scattered butterflies on blue background, gold trim inside rim, C.A.C. green palette mark* **60.00**

☐ Vase, item #504, *10-1/2" high, monochromatic monk scene, transition mark*. **300.00**

☐ Vase, item #505, *4-1/2" high, black exterior with pencil-line gold trim on rim, Lenox wreath mark* **200.00**

☐ Vase, item #505, *14-1/2" high, red berries and green leaves on shaded brown background, gold trim on rim, C.A.C. green palette mark* **250.00**

☐ Vase, item #506, *14-3/8" high, undecorated, Lenox wreath mark* **60.00**

☐ Vase, item #506, *14-3/8" high, white with gold trim, Lenox palette mark*. **65.00**

☐ Vase, item #507, *6-1/4" high, hand-painted flowering vines down sides, Lenox palette mark* **50.00**

Vase, *item #427, portrait of girl*

☐ Vase, item #508, *12" high, hand-painted Grecian woman with flowing robes in pinkish background, garlands of roses, artist signed, Lenox palette mark* **250.00**

☐ Vase, item #525, *15" high, spray of fall flowers on shaded background, transition mark* **300.00**

☐ Vase, item #525, *15" undecorated, C.A.C. green palette mark* **75.00**

☐ Vase, item #528, *15-1/2" high, bunch of violets, gold pencil-line on rim, Lenox palette mark* **150.00**

☐ Vase, item #528, *15-1/2" high, polychromatic monk scene all the way around, hairline crack about 2" long, transition mark* **125.00**

☐ Vase, item #529, *12" high, metallic gold and copper hand-painted design in geometric pattern, Lenox palette mark* **75.00**

☐ Vase, item #530, *15" high, hand-painted background with transfer decoration of military figures, gold trim on rim, Lenox palette mark* .. **125.00**

☐ Vase, item #559, *3" high, hand-painted scattered rosebud design, gold trim, C.A.C. palette mark* **75.00**

☐ Vase, item #574, *4" high, hand-painted orange berries and brown branches on white background, gold trim on rim, Lenox palette mark* **40.00**

☐ Vase, item #574, *4" high, monochromatic green chrysanthemum design, transition mark* **100.00**

☐ Vase, item #576, *3-1/8" high, enamel panels in different colors separated by gold trim, Lenox palette mark* **15.00**

☐ Vase, item #605, *3-3/4" high, undecorated, Lenox wreath mark* **15.00**

☐ Vase, item #877, *12-1/2" high, gold handles and gold initial on front, Lenox palette mark* **60.00**

☐ Vase, item #877, *12-1/2" high, coral with white handles, Lenox wreath mark* **50.00**

☐ Vase, item #877, *12-1/2" high, undecorated, Lenox palette mark* **45.00**

☐ Vase, item #879, *7" high, hand-painted dog on one side, cat on other, blue background, nicely done, Lenox palette mark* **175.00**

Vase, *item #428, orange poppies*

☐ Vase, item #880 *7-7/8" high, Art Deco style geometric banding in vibrant colors, Lenox palette mark* **25.00**

☐ Vase, item #897, *12-1/4" high, plain with gold trim on feet and rim, Lenox wreath mark* **40.00**

☐ Vase, item #897, *12-1/4" high, hand-painted daisies on pale orange background, gold trim on rim and feet, Lenox palette mark* **50.00**

☐ Vase, item #897, *12-1/4" high, undecorated, Lenox palette mark* **37.00**

Vase, *item #1308, fan shape*

□ Vase, item #919, *blue with white handles, Lenox wreath mark* **45.00**
□ Vase, item #919, *blue with white handles, Lenox wreath mark* **45.00**
□ Vase, item #919, *all coral, Lenox wreath mark* **50.00**
□ Vase, item #922, *10-3/4" high, hand-painted horse head on blue background, artist signed, Lenox palette mark* **125.00**
□ Vase, item #922, *10-3/4" high, undecorated, Lenox wreath mark* **35.00**
□ Vase, item #922, *10-3/4" high, light pink, Lenox wreath mark* **30.00**
□ Vase, item #937, *5-7/8" high, turquoise panels alternating with peacock feathers, gold trim, Lenox palette mark* **25.00**
□ Vase, item #937, *5-7/8" high, gold trim and initial on front, artist signed, Lenox palette mark* **15.00**
□ Vase, item #1025, *8" high, hexagon shape, each panel done in a different enamel color, Lenox palette mark* **17.00**
□ Vase, item #1025, *8" high, undecorated, Lenox wreath mark* **13.00**
□ Vase, item #1036, *8" high, hand-painted berries and leaves on brown background, artist signed, Lenox palette mark* **25.00**
□ Vase, item #1036, *8" high, geometric pattern in American Indian style, artist's initials, Lenox palette mark* **30.00**
□ Vase, item #1053, *15-1/4" high, hand-painted grapes and leaves on pale yellow background, Lenox palette mark* **200.00**
□ Vase, item #1053, *15-1/4" high, undecorated, Lenox wreath mark* **40.00**
□ Vase, item #1063, *5-3/4" high, shaded from light to dark green, Lenox wreath mark* **30.00**
□ Vase, item #1063, *5-3/4" high, Lenox Rose pattern with gold trim* **25.00**
□ Vase, item #1063, *5-3/4" high, gold covering outside of vase, artist's initials, Lenox palette mark* **15.00**
□ Vase, item #1099, *7-1/2" high, hand-painted finch on oak leaf branch, shaded tan background, beautifully done, Lenox palette mark* **125.00**
□ Vase, item #1099, *7-1/2" high, undecorated, Lenox palette mark* **20.00**

Vase, *item #1786, by G. Morley*

- ☐ Vase, item #1185, *10" high, orange blossoms on off-white to blue background, marriage inscription on bottom, Lenox palette mark* ... **100.00**
- ☐ Vase, item #1185, *10" high, celadon green with gold trim on trim, Lenox wreath mark* **50.00**
- ☐ Vase, item #1308, *7" high, slight fan shape, light blue, Lenox wreath mark*. **25.00**
- ☐ Vase, item #1308, *7" high, slight fan shape, dark green with gold trim, Lenox wreath mark* **40.00**
- ☐ Vase, item #1308, *7" high, slight fan shape, Lenox Rose pattern with gold trim, Lenox wreath mark* **32.00**
- ☐ Vase, item #1308, *7" high, slight fan shape, yellow, Lenox wreath mark*. **35.00**
- ☐ Vase, item #1308, *7" high, slight fan shape, undecorated, Lenox palette mark*. **15.00**
- ☐ Vase, item #1309, *4-1/4" high, slight fan shape, undecorated, Lenox palette mark* **18.00**
- ☐ Vase, item #1309, *4-1/4" high, slight fan shape, celadon green, Lenox wreath mark* **24.00**

Vase, *item #2650, undecorated*

- ☐ Vase, item #1309, *4-1/4" high, gold trim, Lenox wreath mark* **18.00**
- ☐ Vase, item #1310, *2-7/8" high, slight fan shape, gold trim, Lenox wreath mark* **15.00**
- ☐ Vase, item #1310, *2-7/8" high, light blue, Lenox wreath mark* **15.00**
- ☐ Vase, item #1311, *2-7/8" high, coral, Lenox wreath mark*............ **16.00**
- ☐ Vase, item #1311, *2-7/8" high, light pink, Lenox wreath mark* **12.00**
- ☐ Vase, item #1311, *2-7/8" high, undecorated and unmarked*.......... **5.00**
- ☐ Vase, item #1312, *8-3/4" high, hand-painted cabbage roses on multi-colored background, artist signed and dated, Lenox palette mark* ... **110.00**
- ☐ Vase, item #1316, *11-3/4" high, apple green, Lenox wreath mark* **75.00**
- ☐ Vase, item #1316, *11-3/4" high, green and brown vines coming down from top, gold trim, Lenox palette mark* **80.00**

☐ Vase, item #1378, *11-3/4" high, pale blue exterior, plain Lenox inside, Lenox palette mark* **75.00**

☐ Vase, item #1378, *11-3/4" high, hand-painted grapes and leaves on tan background, nicely done, artist signed, Lenox palette mark* **175.00**

☐ Vase, item #1479, *bulbous, Ming pattern with yellow banding top and bottom, probably a one of a kind item, Lenox wreath mark* **150.00**

☐ Vase, item #1715, *7-1/4" high, coral, Lenox wreath mark* **50.00**

☐ Vase, item #1717, *11-1/2" high, cylinder shape, white, Lenox wreath mark*. **30.00**

☐ Vase, item #1717, *11-1/2" high, coral, cylinder shape, Lenox wreath mark*. **35.00**

☐ Vase, item #1717, *11-1/2" high, transfer decorated with seahorses and gold trim on turquoise background, Lenox wreath mark* **55.00**

Vase, *swan handles*

☐ Vase, item #1718, *10-1/8" high, powder blue, Lenox wreath mark* **35.00**

☐ Vase, item #1718, *10-1/8" high, coral, Lenox wreath mark* **37.00**

☐ Vase, item #1724, *13" high, bulbous bottom bud vase, Art Deco style banding, Lenox palette mark* **22.00**

☐ Vase, item #1724, *13" high, undecorated, Lenox wreath mark* **20.00**

☐ Vase, item #1724, *13" high, white with gold trim, Lenox palette mark* . **27.00**

☐ Vase, item #1725, *10" high, hand-painted tiny roses and gold trim, Lenox palette mark* **35.00**

☐ Vase, item #1725, *10" high, pale blue exterior, gold pencil-line on rim, Lenox wreath mark* **30.00**

☐ Vase, item #1726, *8" high, 1/2" gold band at top, Lenox wreath mark* . **20.00**

☐ Vase, item #1726, *8" high, hand-painted berries, gold trim on rim, Lenox palette mark* **40.00**

☐ Vase, item #1726, *8" high, undecorated and unmarked* **3.00**

☐ Vase, item #1727, *6" high, hand-painted laurel wreath in green around bottom on lighter green background, gold trim on top and bottom, Lenox palette mark* **25.00**

☐ Vase, item #1733, *15-3/4" high, undecorated, Lenox palette mark* **35.00**

☐ Vase, item #1733, *15-3/4" high, hand-painted picture of French poodle, pale green background, not artist signed but very nicely done, Lenox palette mark* **200.00**

☐ Vase, item #1734, *12" high, plain white, Lenox wreath mark* **40.00**

☐ Vase, item #1734, *12" high, green exterior, gold trim on rim, Lenox wreath mark* **65.00**

☐ Vase, item #1743, *6-7/8" high, hand-painted bees and butterflies, Lenox palette mark* **45.00**

☐ Vase, item #1786, *6" high, hand-painted orchid on both sides, gold trim, band of green near bottom, signed by Morley, Lenox wreath mark* **130.00**

☐ Vase, item #1786, *6" high, hand-painted roses on both sides, gold trim, one signed G. Morley the other identical but unsigned, Lenox wreath mark, pair* **425.00**

☐ Vase, item #1786, *6" high, undecorated, Lenox wreath mark* **16.00**

☐ Vase, item #1786, *6" high, Lenox Rose pattern, Lenox wreath mark* . . **60.00**

☐ Vase, item #1786, *6" high, deep blue, Lenox wreath mark* **60.00**

☐ Vase, item #1786, *6" high, gold trim, Lenox wreath mark* **30.00**

Vase, *portrait of David Teniers by S. Wirkner*

☐ Vase, item #1798, *undecorated, Lenox wreath mark* **25.00**

☐ Vase, item #2078, *undecorated, Lenox wreath mark* **60.00**

☐ Vase, item #2081, *8-1/2" pedestal base, gold trim, Lenox wreath mark* **50.00**

☐ Vase, item #2118, *7-5/8" high, coral with small white handles, Lenox wreath mark* **45.00**

☐ Vase, item #2118, *7-5/8" high, undecorated, Lenox wreath mark* **35.00**

☐ Vase, item #2155, *8-1/8" high, undecorated, Lenox wreath mark* **28.00**

☐ Vase, item #2261, *10" high, Lenox Rose trim, Lenox wreath mark* **65.00**

☐ Vase, item #2261, *10" high, white with gold trim, Lenox wreath mark* . **60.00**

☐ Vase, item #2262, *8-1/2" high, swan handles, undecorated, unmarked* **20.00**

☐ Vase, item #2263, *10-3/8" high, swan handles, light green and white, Lenox wreath mark* **75.00**

☐ Vase, item #2263, *10-3/8" high, swan handles, solid coral, Lenox wreath mark* **60.00**

☐ Vase, item #2317, *7" high, pedestal base, two small handles, undecorated, Lenox wreath mark* **27.00**

☐ Vase, item #2317, *7" high, pedestal base, white with blue handles, Lenox wreath mark* **30.00**

☐ Vase, item #2317, *7" high, two small handles trimmed in gold, Lenox Rose pattern in center, Lenox wreath mark* **50.00**

☐ Vase, item #2317, *7" high, pedestal base, green with white handles, Lenox wreath mark* **40.00**

☐ Vase, item #2318, *10" high, Grecian styling, swan handles, oxblood with ornate gold trim, Lenox Rose pattern in center, Lenox wreath mark*... **95.00**

☐ Vase, item #2318, *10" high, Grecian styling, swan handles, blue with white, Lenox wreath mark* **60.00**

☐ Vase, item #2318, *10" high, Grecian styling, swan handles, plain white, Lenox wreath mark* **45.00**

Vase, *item number unknown, picture of woman*

☐ Vase, item #2334, *10-1/2" high, Grecian styling, handles, blue with white, Lenox wreath mark* **40.00**

☐ Vase, item #2338, *14" high, Grecian styling, handles shaped like women's heads, plain white, Lenox wreath mark* **60.00**

☐ Vase, item #2338, *14" high, Grecian styling, handles shaped like women's heads, coral and white, Lenox wreath mark* **70.00**

☐ Vase, item #2338, *14" high, Grecian styling, handles shaped like women's heads, Lenox Rose pattern, Lenox wreath mark* **90.00**

☐ Vase, item #2338-1/4, *10-1/8" high, Grecian styling, handles shaped like women's heads, green and white, Lenox wreath mark* **65.00**

Vase, *item number unknown, cabbage roses*

☐ Vase, item #2338-1/4, *10-1/8" high, Grecian styling, handles shaped like women's heads, white with gold trim, Lenox wreath mark* **60.00**

☐ Vase, item #2360, *5-1/2" high, pedestal base, small handles, white with coral, Lenox wreath mark, small chip on one handle* **32.00**

☐ Vase, item #2370, *8" high, Grecian styling, small handles, white with gold trim, Lenox wreath mark* **50.00**

☐ Vase, item #2409, *8-1/4" high, pedestal base, small handles, gold and white, Lenox wreath mark* **40.00**

☐ Vase, item #2419, *9-7/8" high, Grecian styling, small handles, undecorated, Lenox wreath mark* **45.00**

☐ Vase, item #2429, *7" high, Grecian styling, small handles, undecorated, Lenox wreath mark* **35.00**

☐ Vase, item #2458-1/2, *9-1/8" high, elaborate drape base, small handles, undecorated, Lenox wreath mark* **75.00**

☐ Vase, item #2459, *11" high, large pedestal base, Grecian styling, small handles, undecorated, Lenox wreath mark* **75.00**

☐ Vase, item #2497-1/2, *10-1/2" high, pedestal base, thin shape, undecorated, Lenox wreath mark* **37.00**

☐ Vase, item #2568, *12" high, Grecian style draping, white and yellow, Lenox wreath mark* **100.00**

☐ Vase, item #2568, *12" high, Grecian style draping, undecorated, Lenox wreath mark* **65.00**

☐ Vase, item #2568-1/2, *10-1/2" high, Grecian style draping, green and white, Lenox wreath mark* **75.00**

☐ Vase, item #2585-1/2, *7-1/2" high, flaring top, undecorated, Lenox wreath mark* **30.00**

☐ Vase, item #2587-1/2, *7-1/8" high, embossed flamingo with reeds, undecorated, Lenox wreath mark* **75.00**

☐ Vase, item #2605, *8-1/4" high, bulbous bottom to narrow top, undeco-*
rated, Lenox wreath mark **15.00**

☐ Vase, item #2606, *6" high, bulbous bottom to narrow top, undeco-*
rated, Lenox wreath mark **12.00**

☐ Vase, item #2650, *8-5/8" high, square pedestal base, fluting, flared*
rim, undecorated, Lenox wreath mark **32.00**

☐ Vase, item #2650, *8-5/8" high, square pedestal base, fluting, flared*
rim, pink and white, Lenox wreath mark **40.00**

☐ Vase, item #2650, *8-5/8" high, square pedestal base, fluting, flared*
rim, green, Lenox wreath mark **35.00**

☐ Vase, item #2650, *8-5/8" high, square pedestal base, fluting, flared*
rim, green with gold trim, Lenox wreath mark **40.00**

☐ Vase, item #2650, *8-5/8" high, square pedestal base, fluting, flared*
rim, white with gold trim, Lenox wreath mark **35.00**
Vase #2650 is known as the Regal vase, and although it is a fairly
common shape it remains popular because its shape is perfectly
designed to hold a dozen roses or other flowers.

☐ Vase, item #2709-1/2, *7-5/8" high, Chinese styling, handles, round*
shape, undecorated, Lenox wreath mark **60.00**

☐ Vase, item #2710-1/2, *8-1/2" high, Chinese styling, square openwork*
handles, relief floral design on round body, Lenox wreath mark **90.00**

☐ Vase, item #2723, *10-3/8" high, wide flaring rim, undecorated, Lenox*
wreath mark **50.00**

☐ Vase, item #2757-1/2, *9-3/4" high, cylinder shape with slight flare at*
top and bottom, relief Oriental design (Pagoda pattern), undeco-
rated, Lenox wreath mark **65.00**

☐ Vase, item #2763, *10-3/4" high, relief gadroon pattern around mid-*
section, wide flaring top, undecorated, Lenox wreath mark **40.00**

Vase, *item number unknown, blue dot*

- ☐ Vase, item #2833, *10-5/8" high, classical styling, small rolled handles, coral and white, Lenox wreath mark* **40.00**
- ☐ Vase, item #2833, *10-5/8" high, classical styling, small rolled handles, yellow and white, Lenox wreath mark* **75.00**
- ☐ Vase, item #2834-1/2, *10-1/4" high, cylinder shape, relief design, undecorated, Lenox wreath mark* **45.00**
- ☐ Vase, item #2842-1/2, *8-1/2" high, rounded bottom to 4-1/2" mouth, swirled wide ribs, undecorated, Lenox wreath mark* **30.00**
- ☐ Vase, item #2876, *10" high, pedestal base, no handles, undecorated, Lenox wreath mark* **38.00**
- ☐ Vase, item #2898-1/2, *11" high, round body, relief pattern, undecorated, Lenox wreath mark* **125.00**
- ☐ Vase, item #2902-1/2, *13" high, floral relief work, undecorated, Lenox wreath mark* **60.00**
- ☐ Vase, item #2902-1/2, *13" high, floral relief work, yellow and white, Lenox wreath mark* **115.00**
- ☐ Vase, item #2908, *11" high, narrow with slight flare on top and bottom, fluting, small chip on rim, Lenox wreath mark* **30.00**

Vase, *item number unknown, landscape in oval*

- ☐ Vase, item #2908-1/4, *8" high, narrow with slight flare top and bottom, fluting, undecorated, Lenox wreath mark* **24.00**
- ☐ Vase, item #2908-1/2, *9-1/2" high, narrow with slight flare top and bottom, fluting, undecorated, Lenox wreath mark* **25.00**
- ☐ Vase, item #2913, *10" high, square pedestal base, swan handles, green and white, Lenox wreath mark* **60.00**
- ☐ Vase, item #2913-1/2", *8-1/2" high, square pedestal base, swan handles, all white, Lenox wreath mark* **35.00**
- ☐ Vase, item #2914, *10-1/4" high, round pedestal base, slight flare at rim, undecorated, Lenox wreath mark* **32.00**
- ☐ Vase, item #2920, *high, round pedestal base, undecorated, Lenox wreath mark* **34.00**

Vase, *item number unknown, white roses*

☐ Vase, item #2920-1/2, *8" high, round pedestal base, undecorated, Lenox wreath mark* **30.00**

☐ Vase, item #2929, *11-1/4" high, round base, fluting, undecorated, Lenox wreath mark* **28.00**

☐ Vase, item #2930, *12-1/2" high, fluted, slight flare to rim and base, undecorated, Lenox wreath mark* **35.00**

☐ Vase, item #2937, *12" high, square pedestal base, round shape, draping and reeding, undecorated, Lenox wreath mark* **60.00**

☐ Vase, item #2938, *7-1/8" high, shaped like large egg cup, relief work, undecorated, Lenox wreath mark* **50.00**

☐ Vase, item #2939, *10-3/4" high, square pedestal base, ribbon and garland embossing, undecorated, Lenox wreath mark* **50.00**

☐ Vase, item #2942, *5-1/4" high, urn shape, no handles, white, Lenox wreath mark* **15.00**

☐ Vase, item #2946-1/2, *9-3/4" high, swirled rib design, tall neck, green, Lenox wreath mark* **42.00**

☐ Vase, item #2947-1/2, *10-1/2" high, hexagon shape, embossed floral design, undecorated, Lenox wreath mark* **30.00**

☐ Vase, item #2947-1/2, *10-1/2" high, hexagon shape, relief floral design, white and green, Lenox wreath mark* **50.00**

☐ Vase, item #2954-1/2, *7-1/2" high, overall pattern of small flowers (Hawthorn pattern), undecorated, Lenox wreath mark* **80.00**

☐ Vase, item #2963-1/2, *7-1/2" high, cylinder shape, embossed fruit pattern, undecorated, Lenox wreath mark* **40.00**

☐ Vase, item #3019, *7-3/8" high, embossed flowers alternating with tiny ribs, pale pink and white, Lenox wreath mark* **40.00**

☐ Vase, item number unknown, *pink exterior, creamy interior, gold trim on rim, gold wreath mark* **15.00**

☐ Vase, item number unknown, *8" high, square pedestal base, yellow with white swan handles, Lenox wreath mark* **50.00**
☐ Vase, item number unknown, *9" high, portrait of David Teniers (European artist), on shaded green and mahogany background, gold trim inside lip, signed S. Wirkner, transition mark* **300.00**
☐ Vase, item number unknown, *10" high, hand-painted poppies on shaded brown background, signed W. H. Morley, transition mark* **400.00**

Vase, *item number unknown, plume handles*

☐ Vase, item number unknown, *11" high, monochromatic turquoise picture of woman, signed W. H. Clayton, transition mark* **300.00**
☐ Vase, item number unknown, *yellow and red cabbage roses on butterscotch background, signed W. H. Morley, transition mark* **495.00**
☐ Vase, item number unknown, *11" high, hand-painted pink roses, gold trim on rim, signed W. Marsh, Lenox palette mark* **300.00**
☐ Vase, item number unknown, *8" high, pinched neck, raised gold paste and blue dot enamel work in banding around middle, pale yellow background, transition mark* **150.00**
☐ Vase, item number unknown, *approximate size 8" high, landscape in oval, background maroon, gold trim, signed Nosek, Lenox wreath mark, one vase has repair on rim, pair* **425.00**
☐ Vase, item number unknown, *12" high, white roses on green background, handles painted silver, artist signed, C.A.C. palette mark* ... **250.00**
☐ Vase, item number unknown, *13" high, plume handles, tri-color background with roses, gold inside of rim, signed Marsh, transition/Glen-Iris backstamp* **340.00**

WALL VASES *(WALL POCKETS)*

☐ Wall vase, item #2135, *bisque finish, gold outlining on embossed details, Lenox wreath mark* **90.00**
☐ Wall vase, item #2135, *glazed, undecorated, Lenox wreath mark* **80.00**
☐ Wall vase, item #2193, *glazed, undecorated, Lenox wreath mark* **75.00**

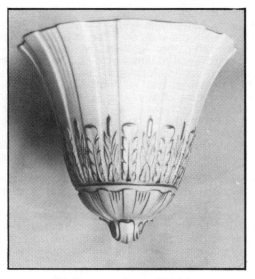

Wall vase, *item #2135*

WATERING CANS

The only Lenox watering can we have ever seen is an unmarked one which matches a catalogue picture. It was obviously a second, because the little holes in the pouring spout are flawed, with some closed off and others running together. The selling price was $100, which we consider fair for such a rare piece.

WORLD'S FAIR ITEMS

Lenox produced several items in cooperation with the Ovington's store in New York for the New York World's Fair of 1939. Most of the items are simple shapes showing embossed scenes of the fair and bearing the inscription "Officially Approved N.Y.W.F., Inc., Lic., Designed in Honor of New York World's Fair, Ovington's, New York." The Lenox wreath/Made in U.S.A. mark has the dates 1789 and 1939 on either side of it.

Although one or two samples of World's Fair items keep most Lenox collectors happy, there are collectors of just World's Fair items, Lenox and otherwise, who search for these items and who (apparently) are willing to pay more for them than Lenox collectors. We have heard rumors of Lenox World's Fair items bringing as high as $200 among such people, but have never been able to track down these stories. The prices listed below are, therefore, the prices paid by Lenox collectors only.

- ☐ Ashtray, *small, round, coral with white embossing* **28.00**
- ☐ Ashtray, *small, round, royal blue with white embossing* **30.00**
- ☐ Ashtray, *small, round, all white* **24.00**
- ☐ Cigarette box, *covered, all white* **35.00**
- ☐ Cigarette box, *covered, coral and white* **40.00**
- ☐ Vase, cylinder shape, *all white* **35.00**
- ☐ Vase, cylinder shape, *yellow and white* **50.00**
- ☐ Vase, cylinder shape, *coral and white* **45.00**

DINNERWARE

The variety of Lenox patterns is endless—counting all the variations on basic patterns, there are thousands of different patterns. Approximately 300 of the patterns were given names, while the remainder will be known forever only by their number. (Named patterns also had numbers which sometimes appear on the bottom of items along with the names.) **Table VIII** lists those patterns which had names as well as numbers.

It is possible to determine what year a given pattern was first introduced by its number. **Table IX** lists the year/letter codes, the letter in this case being the first letter of the pattern's code number. For example, Lenox Rose J300 would have been introduced in 1934.

Table X lists the more common dinnerware items by shape and/or capacity. These numbers are particularly important when trying to match a particular type of cup and saucer, for example.

Table XI is a listing of those dinnerware pattern numbers which were available only on service plates and not as general production dinnerware patterns.

Lenox dinnerware could fill a book of its very own quite easily, and we regret not being able to list more of the numbered patterns here. As a general rule, any pattern from the past can be compared to current Lenox retail prices. Following is some general information about Lenox dinnerware.

TYPES OF PATTERNS

Although it is impossible for us to describe here every pattern ever made by Lenox, we will briefly cover the different types of patterns that were made.

Transfer Decorated: Transfer-decorated patterns are the largest single group of Lenox patterns, and this group includes some of the most popular patterns ever made there (Ming, Lenox Rose, etc.). They range from overall designs to those with only a small amount of decoration, and are frequently embellished with hand work (gold trim, enamel work).

Hand-Painted: Many of the early Lenox patterns were entirely hand-painted, and the combination of the hand-painting and the early marks puts them in the highly-collectible category. This is, or course, reflected in their value. Since they were done by hand, there will be considerable variation in both color and placement of design. Much of the information listed under pattern #82 in the price guide applies to the hand-painted grouping as a whole.

Gold-Banded Patterns: Lenox patterns decorated with only gold, silver or platinum bands have always been popular, and one of them (Tuxedo) is the oldest (1912) Lenox pattern still being made today. The bands can be either acid-etched or flat gold. These patterns tend to hold up very well under use, and they have a listing appeal (unlike some of the transfer patterns which can look "dated" twenty years after they were first made). Lenox has always made a wide variety of these patterns, and they range in price from the least expensive patterns (Mansfield) to the most expensive (Westchester).

Gold trim predominated in early years, no doubt in part because the early silver trims needed polishing. The current use of platinum instead of silver has taken care of that problem, and the platinum trims seem very popular. It is interesting to note, however, that on the secondary market gold patterns almost always bring more than the platinum ones.

See following pages for illustrations of the more common gold borders.

ETCHED BORDERS

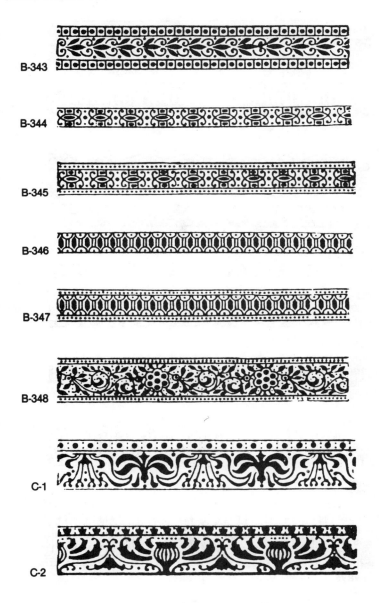

B-343

B-344

B-345

B-346

B-347

B-348

C-1

C-2

ETCHED BORDERS

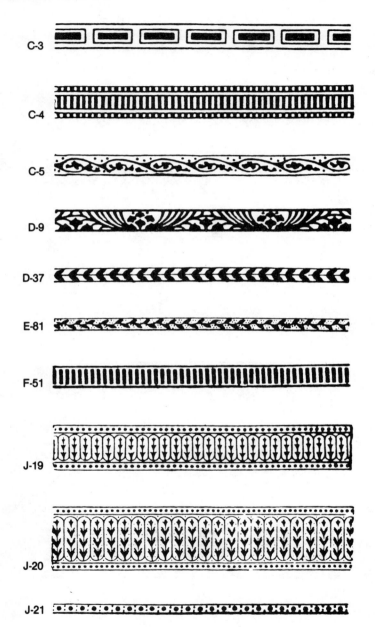

C-3

C-4

C-5

D-9

D-37

E-81

F-51

J-19

J-20

J-21

GREENWOOD POTTERY COMPANY, *semi-vitreous plate, cobalt decoration, mark D variation, 8" square.* 70.00

COLUMBIAN ART POTTERY, *creamer, gold paste trim, mark A* 150.00

COOK POTTERY COMPANY, *bottle, Belleek ware, probably had a stopper, mark A with C.H.C. variation* 350.00

(L) WILLETS MANUFACTURING, *jar, shape #6, small covered jar, hand-painted white and pink roses, ornate blue dot and gold work, signed M.J. Parker, mark B in brown, 7¼" high* 300.00
(R) WILLETS MANUFACTURING, *vase, shape #191-½, double handled crimped top, hand-painted pink roses, raised gold and blue dot enamel work, gold trim on handles and rims, signed and dated, mark B in brown, 4½" high* 250.00

(L) WILLETS MANUFACTURING, *tankard, shape #453-½, monochromatic monk scene, no artist signature, mark B in brown,
14½" high* 225.00
(R) WILLETS MANUFACTURING, *jug, shape #311, embossed and
scalloped, hand-painted pink and red flowers on shaded green and
yellow background, silver overlay work on embossed sections and on
handle, mark B in brown, 9½" high* 395.00

(L) **WILLETS MANUFACTURING**, basket, shape number unknown, spaghetti strand type, applied flowers in pastel colors, chewing gum mark, rough spots on petals, 11" long 475.00

(M) **WILLETS MANUFACTURING**, smoking combination, shape #318, includes basket for matches, tree trunk for cigarettes or cigars, and ruffled rim boat-shaped ashtray, all on rustic base, undecorated, mark B in brown 125.00

(R) **WILLETS MANUFACTURING**, jug, shape #62, shell jug, coral handle, unmarked and undecorated, 7½" high 300.00

(L) **OTT & BREWER**, teapot, dented sides, covered with grotesque coral trim, raised gold paste work on bottom half, gold trim on coral branches, spout has been repaired and there is a small crack coming down from the rim, mark I 225.00

(M) **OTT & BREWER**, parian egg, variation of mark F, signed by Broome, 1877 .... 1200.00

(R) **OTT & BREWER**, ewer, double spouted, rustic handle, top section covered with gold, bottom section has hand-painted coral colored water lilies, two small chips on top section, mark I 625.00

(L) OTT & BREWER, basket, rustic handle, raised gold paste trim in thistle pattern on beige matte finish, mark I, 6" high 500.00

(M) OTT & BREWER, vase, bulbous bottom with long neck, hand-painted yellow and brown flowers, raised gold trim, mark I, 10" high 450.00

(R) OTT & BREWER, ewer, bulbous shape, raised gold paste in thistle pattern on beige matte finish, gold trim on handle and rims, mark I, 8" high 550.00

ETCHED BORDERS

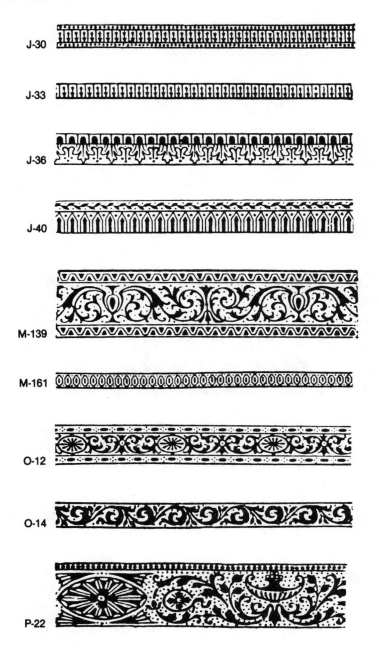

J-30

J-33

J-36

J-40

M-139

M-161

O-12

O-14

P-22

ETCHED BORDERS

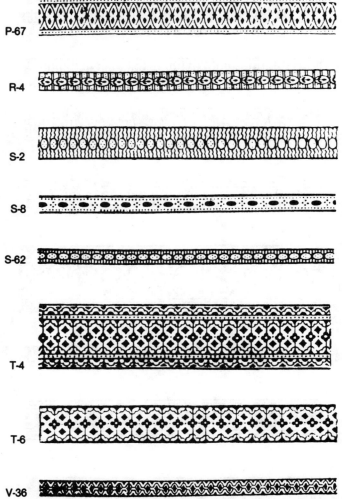

P-67

R-4

S-2

S-8

S-62

T-4

T-6

V-36

GOLD PRINT BORDERS

F-308

G-318

G-342

G-343

G-372

G-388

GOLD PRINT BORDERS

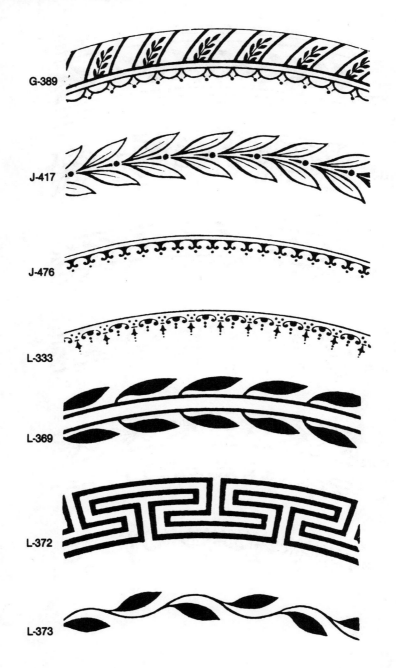

G-389

J-417

J-476

L-333

L-369

L-372

L-373

GOLD PRINT BORDERS

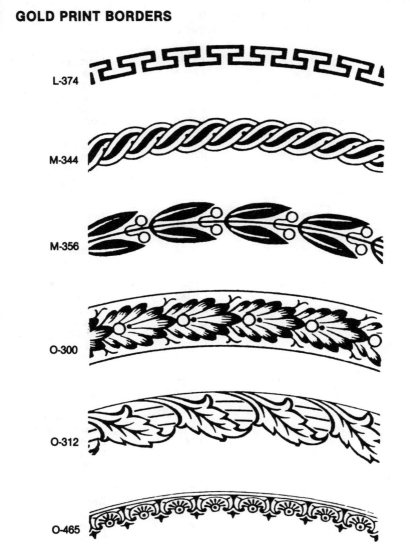

L-374

M-344

M-356

O-300

O-312

O-465

TABLE VIII
Pattern Name/Number Codes

A-300	Fountain	J-33	Tuxedo
A-300	Fountain	J-300	Lenox Rose
A-303	Pasadena	J-325A	Villa
A-557	Jewel	J-332	Rhythm
A-558	Chalet	J-374A	Chesterfield
B-300	Blue Tree	J-471B	Rhapsody
B-343A	Evanston	J-476B	Georgian
B-344A	Princeton		
B-345A	Madison	K-330	Gadroon Rose
B-346A	Springfield	K-348B	Orleans
B-347A	Carolina	K-352	Stradivarius
B-348A	Hudson	K-366B	Trianon
B-368A	Bellaire	K-367	Fountainbleu
B-369A	Lincoln	K-369A	Rock Garden
B-372A	Palisade	K-392G	Athenia
B-374A	Belmont	K-395B	Revere
B-375A	Saratoga		
B-376B	Lexington	L-300A	Normand
		L-303A	Westbury
C-300	Monticello	L-304	Vendome
C-301	Renaissance	L-306A	Chippendale
		L-315A	Minerva
D-300	Floralia	L-335	Radiance
D-304A	Floralia Ivory	L-347	Aurora
D-514	Chanson	L-355-247	Berkeley
D-515	Orleans	L-368B	Josephine
		L-369B	Platina
E-300	Grenoble	L-371B	Casino
E-300A	Grenoble Ivory	L-373B	Diana
E-301	Sheraton	L-383A	Newport
E-301A	Sheraton Ivory		
E-302	Trellis	M-3	Meadowbrook
E-302A	Trellis Ivory	M-139	Westchester
E-500	Rondelle	M-161	Windsor
E-501	Romance	M-311B	Etruscan
E-536	Symphony	M-319A	Gold Casino
		M-320	Arden Rose
F-300	Harwood	M-326	Golden Blossom
F-308A	Malmaison	M-328A	Troy
F-529	Majesty	M-356	Antoinette
		M-440	Corinthian
G-87	Virginian	M-441B	Olympia
G-345	Oak Leaf		
G-347B	Lombardy	O-12	Stanford
G-386B	Cambridge	O-300	Pembrook
G-388B	Alden	O-301	Monterey
G-510	Tableaux	O-302A	Claremont
G-511	Capri	O-312B	Royal
		O-313	Golden Wreath
H-48	Mt. Vernon	O-314B	Marlboro
H-310A	Chelsea	O-315	Lansdale
H-502	Maywood	O-316	Cretan

TABLE VIII

O-351B	Essex
O-375	Caprice
O-380	Priscilla
O-386	Pavlova
O-388	Sonata
O-389	Empress
O-394	Classic Rose
O-402A	Chantilly
O-402A	Crinoline
O-407	Pinehurst
O-430	Glenthorne
O-437	Royal Oak
O-480	Victoria
O-500	Kenmore
P-1	Mandarin
P-16	Ming
P-67	Lowell
P-302B	Savoy
P-303	Rutledge
P-306-X-26-1	Corinne
P-307	Fantasy
P-308	Carlyle
P-310R	Southern Gardens
P-314	Vassar
P-315-X-14-8-X-26	Cecile
P-316	Blueridge
P-317F	Rivoli
P-319	Cynthia
P-321-F-X-26-1	Joan
P-324	Princess
P-338	Imperial
P-341-R-X-14-1	Melody
P-349-X-26-1	Angelina
P-353	Mayfair
P-371B	Blue Bell
P-403	Addison
P-419W	Nydia
P-421-X-26-1	Romance
P-440	Bancroft
P-443	Triumph
P-454	Teresa
P-467	Springtime
P-468	Bradford
P-471	Rhodora
P-514F	Etna
P-524-247	Bellevue
P-525-247	Frontenac
P-529	Meredith
P-530	Windsor
P-533-247	Hathaway
P-539-X-15-1	Coralton
R-304B	Shenandoah
R-307	Barclay
R-311	Arcadia
R-369	Genevieve
R-400	Lenore
R-417B	Stratford
R-440	Westfield
R-441	Harvest
R-442	Wheat
S-1	Autumn
S-7A	Brookline
S-13D	Somerset
S-15F	Washington
S-40C	Westchester
S-300	Avon
S-301	Bellefonte
S-310	Springdale
S-311	Brookside
S-312	Belford
S-313	Natoma
S-314	Belvidere
S-318A	Covington
S-366A	Bellaire
T-1	Orchard
T-2	Colonial
T-3	Fairmount
T-415	Sonnet
T-417	Daybreak
T-426	Celeste
V-308	Cinderella
W-1	Florida
W-2	Golden Gate
W-3	Coronado
W-4	Maryland
W-24	Peking
W-301	Peachtree
W-306	Colonnade
W-331	Pine
X-15-6	Nautilus
X-100	Tremont
X-121	Greenwich
X-303	Olympia Gold
X-433	Dubarry
X-444	Caribbee
X-446	Trio
Y-1	Mystic
Y-37	Trent
Y-49	Festival
Z-88A	Vernon

TABLE IX
Year/Letter Codes

Numbers 1 thru 299	Numbers 300 - 500	Exceptions
A — 1904	A — 1926	W-331 Pine — 1951
B — 1905	B — 1927	W-341 Cattail — 1951
C — 1906	C — 1928	X-302 Starlight — 1952
D — 1907	D — 1929	X-304 Roselyn — 1952
E — 1908	E — 1930	X-303 Olympia — 1952
F — 1909	F — 1931	X-407 West Wind — 1953
G — 1910	G — 1932	X-421 Athenia Coupe — 1953
H — 1911	H — 1933	X-444 Caribbee — 1954
J — 1912	J — 1934	X-445 Kingsley — 1954
K — 1913	K — 1935	X-446 Trio — 1954
L — 1914	L — 1936	X-516 Princess — 1954
M — 1915	M — 1937	X-559 Glendale — 1955
O — 1916	O — 1938	A-500 Wyndcrest — 1956
P — 1917	P — 1939	A-501 Alaris — 1956
R — 1918	R — 1940	A-557 Jewel — 1957
S — 1919	S — 1941	A-558 Chalet — 1957
T — 1920	T — 1942 to 1946*	C-512 Charmaine — 1957
V — 1921	V — 1947	
W — 1922	W — 1948	*Note: The Letters I, N, Q and U were*
X — 1923	X — 1950	*not used.*
Y — 1924	* war years	
Z — 1925		

TABLE X
Lenox Dinnerware Shapes and Sizes

After Dinner Cups and Saucers

No.	Shape	Size
448	— round	2 oz.
610	— round	3 oz.
670	— round	2 oz.
813	— hexagonal	1-1/2 oz.
841	— hexagonal	2 oz.
852	— round	1-1/2 oz.
885	— round	3-1/2 oz.
895	— round	2 oz.
895-1/2	— round	3 oz.
1079	— round	2 oz.
1095	— octagonal	3 oz.
1395	— round	3-1/2 oz.
1569	— round	2 oz.
1615	— round	3 oz.
1742	— round	1-1/2 oz.
2358	— round	4 oz.
2854	— round	4 oz.

Baked Apple Dish

No.		Size
784	—	5-5/8" d. x 2-1/2" h.

Bouillon Cups and Saucers

No.	Shape	Size
557-1/2	— round	5-1/2 oz.
628	— round	7 oz.
757	— hexagonal	6 oz.
839-1/2	— hexagonal	5 oz.
846-1/2	— round	6 oz.
942-1/2	— round	5 oz.
944	— round	7 oz.
1394	— round	7 oz.

Bowls

No.	Description	Size
512	—	10-1/4" d. x 5" h.
513	—	8-1/8" d. x 3" h.
527	—	9" d. x 4" h.
553	—	6" d. x 2-1/2" h.
575	—	5-3/8" d. x 1-7/8" h.
589	—	7-3/8" d. x 2-3/4" h.
624	—	7-5/8" d. x 2-1/4" h.
690	— finger bowl	4-3/4" d. x 2-1/4" h.
715	— berry bowl	7-3/4" x 8-3/4" hexa. x 3-3/4" h.
796	— berry bowl	9-1/2" d. x 4-3/8" h.
799	—	7" d. x 2-1/4" h.
800	—	5-3/4" d. x 2" h.
811	—	5-1/4" d. x 2-1/2" h.
823	—	10-1/4" d. x 4-1/4" h.
970	—	7-3/4" d. x 5" h.
971	—	7-3/8" d. x 2-3/4" h.
1082	—	9-3/8" d. x 4-1/8" h.
1122	—	9-3/8" d. x 4-1/8" h.
1128	—	6-1/4" d. x 3-1/8" h.
1129	—	5-3/8" d. x 2-3/8" h.
1245	— berry bowl	8-5/8" d. x 3" h.
1247	— berry bowl	8-1/2" d. x 3" h.
1254	— berry bowl	9-5/8" d. x 3-1/8" h.
1261	—	5-1/8" d. x 1-7/8" h.
1667	—	9-1/4" d. x 5-1/2" h.
1722	— finger bowl	4-1/2" d. x 1-3/4" h.
1929-1/2	— berry bowl	9-5/8" d. x 4" h.
1972	—	6-3/4" d. x 1-3/4" h.
2073	—	8-3/4" d. x 3-3/4" h.

Breakfast Items

No.	Description	Size
584	— salt and pepper	1-3/8" d. x 2-1/2" h.
585	— salt and pepper	1-5/8" d. x 3-1/2" h.
933	— coffeepot	13 oz.
934	— teapot	13 oz.
935	— sugar	3-1/4" d. x 2-3/4" h.
936	— cream	3-1/2" oz.
964	— hot milk	13 oz.
1056	— egg cup	1-7/8" d. x 2-3/8" h.
1060	— coffeepot	16 oz.

1060-1/2	— hot milk	14 oz.
1061	— teapot	18 oz.
1062	— sugar	3-1/4" d. x 2-3/4" h.
1063	— creamer	4-1/2 oz.
1121	— double egg cup	2-1/2" d. x 3-3/4" h.
1125	— covered muffin	plate 7-3/8" d., cover 5-1/4" d.
1126	— covered muffin	plate 8-3/4" d., cover 6-1/4" d.
1126-1/2	— cover for muffin dish	
1337	— combination coffee set	11 oz.
1400	— combination cereal set	5-1/8"
1500	— combination cake set	8-3/4" d.
1518	— covered chop dish	4-3/8" x 6-3/4"
1610	— combination tea set	18 oz.
1628	— egg cup	2-3/4" d. x 3-1/2" h.
1774	— coffeepot	5 oz.
1775	— tray	6" x 9-3/4"
1936	— teapot	10 oz.
1946	— coffeepot	12 oz.
1947	— hot milk	11 oz.
1948	— sugar	2-3/4" d. x 2-1/2" h.
1949	— cream	3-1/2 oz.

Butter Dishes

No.	Shape	Size
932	— hexagonal	3-3/4" x 4-1/4" d. x 1-1/2" h.
1096	—	4-1/2" d. x 2" h.
1125	— covered	plate 7-3/8" d., cover 5-1/4" d.
1126	— covered	plate 8-3/4" d., cover 6-1/4" d.

Casseroles

No.	Shape	Size
640	— no handles	7-1/2" d. x 4-1/8" h.
641	— no handles	8-3/4" d. x 4-1/2" h.
642	— no handles	5-7/8" d. x 3-3/8" h.
643	— no handles	4-1/4" d. x 2-3/8" h.
716	— handled	8-3/4" d. x 4-1/2" h.
717	— handled	7-1/2" d. x 4-1/8" h.
718	— handled	5-7/8" d. x 3-3/8" h.
719	— handled	4-1/4" d. x 2-3/8" h.
2519	— handled	8-3/4" d. x 4-3/8" h.

Celery Trays

No.	Shape	Size
1599	— oval	6-1/4" x 12-3/8"
1971	— oval	5-7/8" x 11-3/4"
2012	— oval	6-1/8" x 12"
2013	— oval	5-1/8" x 10-1/4"

Cheese Dishes

No.	Shape	Size
829	— covered	7" d. x 5" h.
1396	— plate	10-3/4" d., top 5-1/2" d.

Chocolate Cups and Saucers

No.	Shape	Size
556	— round	4 oz.
600	— round	4 oz.
665	— hexagonal	1-3/4" oz.
669	— round	4 oz.
714	— hexagonal	3 oz.
815	— hexagonal	4 oz.
843	— round	4 oz.
1078	— round	4 oz.
1189	— round	4-1/2 oz.
1430	— round	5 oz.

Chocolate Pots

No.	Shape	Size
842	— round	42 oz.
905	— hexagonal	36 oz.
1367	— round	45 oz.
1429	— round	27 oz.
1960-1/2	— round	40 oz.

Cracker Jars

No.	Shape	Size
351	— round	5-3/4" d. x 5-3/4" h.
688	— round	6-1/4" d. x 6" h.
691	— round	6-3/4" d. x 6-5/8" h.
803	— hexagonal	5-3/8" x 6-1/4" d. x 7-1/4" h.
850	— hexagonal	5" x 5-7/8" d. x 7" h.
1623	— round	6-1/8" d. x 6-3/4" h.

Crescent Salad Plates

No.		Size
1314	—	6-1/4" x 9-1/4"
1414-1/2	—	5" x 7-3/4"

Horse Radish Jars

No.	Shape	Size
761	— round	2-3/4" d. x 4-3/8" h.
1288	— round	2-1/2" d. x 4-7/8" h.
1405	— round	2-1/4" d. x 5" h.

Jugs and Pitchers

No.	Shape	Size
566	— round, covered	45 oz.
567	— round, covered	32 oz.
568	— round, covered	16 oz.
666	— hexagonal	54 oz.
794	— hexagonal, covered	12 oz.
1038	— round	16 oz.
1039	— round	30 oz.
1040	— round	42 oz.
1041	— round	60 oz.
1073	— round	45 oz.
1074	— round	32 oz.

1075	— round	16 oz.
1404	— round	64 oz.
1520	— round	50 oz.
1680	— rectangular, covered	16 oz.

Luncheon Plates and Cups

These plates have indentations on one side to hold a cup, while the main part of the plate was to be used for cakes or sandwiches. In our text we have referred to these items as tete-a-tete sets to avoid confusion with the standard 9" size luncheon plates which have no place for a cup.

No.	Description	Size
943	— cup	6 oz.
1094	— cup	5 oz.
1305	— cup	6 oz.
1617-1/2	— octagonal plate	7-1/2" x 8-1/4"
1620	— cup	6 oz.
1671	— plate	7-1/2"
1684	— plate	8-3/8" d.
1755	— plate	7-1/4" d.
2069	— plate	8-1/4" d.

Marmalade Jars

No.	Shape	Size
755	— round	4" d. x 4-5/8" h.
760	— round	3-3/4" d. x 5-1/2" h.
763	— round	3-3/4" d. x 5-1/2" h.
766	— round	3-1/4" d. x 5-1/8" h.
767	— round	3-1/4" d. x 5-1/8" h.
774	— round	4-7/8" d. x 3-3/4" h.
775	— round	4-5/8" d. x 4" h.
804	— hexagonal	3-1/4" x 3-3/4" d. x 5-1/4" h.
809	— round	3-1/2" d. x 5-1/4" h.
818	— rectangular	3-1/4" x 3-7/8" d. x 4-1/4" h.
830	— round	3-3/4" d. x 4" h.
831	— round	3-3/4" d. x 4" h.
851	— hexagonal	3-5/8" x 4" d. x 5-3/8" h.
1032	— hexagonal	4-1/4" x 4-3/4" d. x 5" h.
1064	— round	4-1/4" d. x 4-3/4" h.
1274	— rectangular	3-1/4" x 3-7/8" d. x 4-1/4" h.
1289	— round	3-1/2" d. x 5-1/4" h.
2000	— round	5-1/4" d. x 2-3/8" h.

Mayonnaise Bowls

No.	Shape	Size
644	— oval	4-3/4" x 6-1/2" d. x 3-1/2" h.
745	— oval	3-7/8" x 5-1/8" d. x 4" h.
778	—	6-3/8" d. x 4-1/4" h.
779	—	5-1/8" d. x 3-1/8" h.
780	— oval	3-3/4" x 5" d. x 3" h.
781	— oval	5" x 6" d. x 3-1/2" h.
782	—	5-1/4" d. x 3-1/2" h.
783	— oval	4" x 5-1/2" d. x 3-3/8" h.
785	—	6" d. x 3-1/4" h.
795	—	5-3/8" d. x 2-3/4" h.

805	— hexagonal	4-3/8" x 5" d. x 3-1/8" h.
828	—	4-3/8" d. x 3-3/4" h.
1605	— oval	4-1/2" x 6-1/4" d. x 3-3/4" h.
2028	—	5-3/8" d. x 3-3/8" h.
2074	—	5-1/8" d. x 3" h.

Mayonnaise Underplates

No.	Description	Size
1180	— plate	6-3/8" d.
1672	— oval plate	4-1/4" x 6-1/8"

Mugs

No.	Shape	Size
754	—	6 oz.
812	—	8 oz.
1313	—	7 oz.
1493	—	6 oz.

Mustard Jars

No.	Shape	Size
679	— round	2-1/2" d. x 2-7/8" h.
680	— round	1-7/8" d. x. 3-1/4" h.
681	— round	2-1/8" d. x 3-5/8" h.
682	— round	2" d. x 3-1/4" h.
737	— hexagonal	1-3/4" x 2" d. x 3-7/8" h.
762	— round	2-1/2" d. x 3-3/8" h.
765	— round	2-1/2" d. x 3-1/2" h.
790	— hexagonal	1-3/4" x 2" d. x 3-1/2" h.
915	— hexagonal	2-1/8" x 2-3/8" d. x 4" h.
1030	— hexagonal	2" x 2-1/4" d. x 3-3/4" h.

Relish and Pickle Dishes

No.	Shape	Size
792	— oval	4" x 7-1/8" d. x 3" h.
793	— oval	4" x 7" d. x 2-3/4" h.
1106	— oval	6-1/4" x 10-1/4"
1190	— oval	3-1/8" x 6-1/4"
1191	— oval	4" x 6"
1242	— oval	3-3/8" x 4-3/4"
1246	— oval (partitioned)	4-3/8" x 7-3/4"
1366	— round	4-3/8" d.
1419	— oval	3-5/8" x 6-3/4"
1426	— oval	3-7/8" x 6-3/8"
1598	— oval	5-1/4" x 8-5/8"
2312	— compartments	9" d.

Sandwich Trays

No.	Shape	Size
1564	— cut edge, footed	8-7/8" d.
1604	— cut edge, footed	10-5/8" d.

Teacups and Saucers

No.	Shape	Size
551	— round	6 oz.
557	— round	5-1/2 oz.
654-1/2	— round	7 oz.
664	— hexagonal	4 oz.
668	— round	6 oz.
756	— round	6 oz.
773	— round	3-1/2 oz.
814	— hexagonal	4 oz.
816	— hexagonal	7 oz.
837	— hexagonal	6 oz.
838	— hexagonal	8 oz.
839	— hexagonal	5 oz.
845	— round	4-1/2 oz.
846	— round	6-1/2 oz.
853	— round	5-1/2 oz.
886	— round	4 oz.
942	— round	5 oz.
1006	— hexagonal	4 oz.
1019	— round	7 oz.
1080	— round	6 oz.
1094-1/2	— octagonal	5-1/2 oz.
1302	— round	12 oz.
1303	— round	11 oz.
1304	— round	10 oz.
1331	— round	7 oz.
1389	— round	15 oz.
1693	— round	7-1/2 oz.
1705	— round	10 oz.
1837	— round	6 oz.
2040	— round	8-1/2 oz.
2408	— round	6 oz.

Tumblers

No.	Shape	Size
378	— round	8 oz.
539	— round	10 oz.
540	— round	8 oz.
1102-1/2	— round	15 oz.
2097	— round, handled	8 oz.

TABLE XI
Lenox Service Plate Patterns

A-301	A-320-4	A-328-1	A-348-2	B-361	D-395	
A-301-1	A-320-5	A-328-2	A-348-3	B-363	D-405	F-61
A-301-2	A-320-6	A-328-3	A-348-4	B-366	D-412	F-304
A-301-3	A-321	A-328-4	A-348-5	B-379		F-305
A-301-4	A-321-1	A-328-5	A-348-6	B-390	E-51	F-309
A-301-5	A-321-2	A-328-6	A-349	B-400	E-303	F-313
A-301-6	A-321-3	A-329	A-349-1	B-410	E-304	F-315
A-302	A-321-4	A-329-1	A-349-2	B-414	E-305	F-318
A-302-1	A-321-5	A-329-2	A-349-3	C-305	E-307	F-323
A-302-2	A-321-6	A-329-3	A-349-4	C-306	E-309	F-331
A-302-3	A-322	A-329-4	A-349-5	C-316	E-310	F-334
A-302-4	A-322-1	A-329-5	A-349-6	C-318	E-311	F-334
A-302-5	A-322-2	A-329-6	A-353	C-324	E-312	F-339
A-302-6	A-322-3	A-330	A-355	C-332	E-313	F-345
A-303-1	A-322-4	A-330-1	A-358	C-339	E-314	F-347
A-303-2	A-322-5	A-330-2	A-369	C-349	E-315	F-348
A-303-3	A-322-6	A-330-3	A-372	C-350	E-316	F-349
A-303-4	A-323	A-330-4	A-375	C-358	E-317	F-351
A-303-5	A-323-1	A-330-5	A-377	C-366	E-318	F-352
A-304	A-323-2	A-330-6	A-378	C-378	E-319	F-359
A-304-1	A-323-3	A-331	A-380	C-379	E-320	F-361
A-304-2	A-323-5	A-332	A-382	C-380	E-321	F-365
A-304-3	A-323-6	A-335	A-387	C-381	E-323	F-366
A-304-4	A-324	A-344	A-388	C-386	E-329	F-367
A-304-5	A-324-1	A-344-1	A-391	C-389	E-336	F-388
A-304-6	A-324-2	A-344-2	A-392	C-392	E-386	F-389
A-305	A-324-3	A-344-3	A-394	C-395	E-344	
A-305-1	A-324-4	A-344-4	A-395	C-416	E-345	G-32
A-305-2	A-324-5	A-344-5	A-396	C-418	E-346	G-35
A-305-3	A-324-6	A-344-6	A-397	C-431	E-348	G-44
A-305-4	A-325	A-345	A-398	C-432	E-349	G-47
A-305-5	A-325-1	A-345-1	A-414	C-433	E-351	G-75
A-305-6	A-325-2	A-345-2	A-415	C-434	E-354	G-88
A-306	A-325-3	A-345-3		C-441	E-355	G-89
A-306-1	A-325-4	A-345-4	B-304	C-443	E-358	G-330
A-306-2	A-325-5	A-345-5	B-306		E-363	G-339
A-306-3	A-325-6	A-345-6	B-307	D-307	E-364	G-352
A-306-4	A-326	A-346	B-311	D-308	E-367	G-359
A-306-5	A-326-1	A-346-1	B-315	D-319	E-369	
A-306-6	A-326-2	A-346-2	B-316	D-321	E-373	H-44
A-306-7	A-326-3	A-336-3	B-317	D-325	E-374	H-46
A-310	A-326-4	A-346-4	B-318	D-326	E-378	G-53
A-319	A-323-4	A-346-5	B-332	D-327	E-382	H-341
A-319-1	A-326-5	A-347	B-337	D-330	E-388	H-342
A-319-2	A-326-6	A-348	B-342	D-338	E-389	H-343
A-319-3	A-327	A-347-1	B-349	D-347	E-390	H-344
A-319-4	A-327-1	A-347-2	B-350	D-348	E-415	H-345
A-319-5	A-327-2	A-347-3	B-352	D-351	E-420	H-346
A-319-6	A-327-3	A-347-4	B-353	D-355	E-348	H-347
A-320	A-327-4	A-347-5	B-354	D-360	E-440	H-348
A-320-1	A-327-5	A-347-6	B-355	D-366	E-347	H-349
A-320-2	A-327-6	A-348	B-356	D-370	E-441	H-350
A-320-3	A-328	A-348-1	B-357	D-386	E-443	H-351

H-352	J-339	K-325	M-316	O-364	P-388	S-333
H-353	J-340	K-328	M-317	O-365	P-389	
H-354	J-341	K-331	M-321	O-368	P-441	T-5
H-355	J-342	K-332	M-325	O-373	P-442	T-12
H-356	J-343	K-333	M-336	O-374	P-444	T-13
H-357	J-344	K-335	M-337	O-399	P-445	T-19
H-358	J-345	K-336	M-338	O-400	P-446	T-22
H-359	J-346	K-338	M-339	O-401	P-447	T-26
H-362	J-347	K-339	M-342	O-403	P-460	T-27
H-363	J-348	K-340	M-343	O-404	P-472	T-37
H-364	J-349	K-342	M-347	O-406	P-480	
H-365	J-350	K-351	M-350	O-408	P-482	V-1
H-366	J-351	K-353	M-354	O-409	P-483	V-2
H-367	J-352	K-371	M-359	O-412	P-484	V-17
H-368	J-379	K-374	M-372	O-422	P-485	V-22
H-370	J-421	K-387	M-383	O-426	P-487	V-24
H-371	J-342	K-396	M-384	O-427	P-488	V-46
H-372	J-433	K-397	M-392	O-429	P-489	V-51
H-373	J-434		M-404	O-457	P-508	V-58
H-374	J-435	L-10	M-406	O-475	P-526	
H-376	J-436	L-12	M-407	O-486	P-527	W-5
H-377	J-437	L-36	M-418	O-492	P-528	W-22
H-389	J-445	L-37		O-493		W-23
H-390	J-446	L-43	O-24	O-495	R-2	W-26
H-391	J-447	L-46	O-39	O-496	R-7	W-28
H-395	J-448	L-49	O-40		R-8	W-39
	J-449	L-49A	O-48		R-13	W-42
J-5	J-450	L-68	O-53	P-4	R-14	
J-8	J-453	L-69	O-55	P-7	R-16	X-15-8
J-22	J-454	L-71	O-56	P-9	R-300	X-17-8
J-304	J-455	L-72	O-58	P-10	R-301	X-17-9
J-305	J-456	L-81	O-50	P-12	R-377	X-19-8
J-306	J-457	L-85	O-303	P-13	R-378	X-19-9
J-307	J-458	L-310	O-304	P-24	R-390	X-22
J-308	J-459	L-311	O-305	P-25	R-392	X-23
J-309	J-460	L-312	O-306	P-26	R-414	X-24
J-310	J-461	L-322	O-307	P-29	R-434	X-25-8
J-311	J-469	L-323	O-308	P-33		X-36
J-313	J-480	L-324	O-309	P-38		X-84
J-314	J-481	L-336	O-310	P-48	S-5	X-85
J-315	J-482	L-339	O-311	P-50	S-6	X-87
J-316	J-484	L-349	O-321	P-69	S-9	X-89
J-317	J-499	L-358	O-322	P-75	S-10	X-90
J-318		L-365	O-323	P-81	S-11	X-91
J-319	K-24	L-410	O-324	P-323	S-12	X-93
J-320	K-26	L-417	O-325	P-332	S-16	X-93-1
J-321	K-28		O-329	P-333	S-18	X-93-2
J-322	K-29	M-72	O-332	P-344	S-45	X-93-3
J-323	K-31	M-89	O-334	P-375	S-47	X-93-4
J-324	K-37	M-93	O-335	P-380	S-64	X-93-5
J-326	K-42	M-167	O-347	P-382	S-65	X-94
J-328	K-47	M-300	O-348	P-383	S-66	X-94-1
J-329	K-64	M-309	O-361	P-384	S-67	X-94-2
J-337	K-65	M-310	O-362	P-385	S-68	X-94-3
J-338	K-80	M-315	O-363	P-386	S-73	X-94-4
				P-387	S-78	X-94-4

X-94-5	X-98-5	X-102-3	Y-69	Z-5	Z-61	Z-93
X-94-6	X-98-6	X-102-4	Y-70	Z-6	Z-63	Z-94
X-95	X-99	X-102-5	Y-71	Z-7	Z-74	Z-96
X-97	X-99-1	X-111	Y-72	Z-8	Z-75	Z-97
X-97-1	X-99-2	X-114	Y-73	Z-9	Z-76	Z-99
X-97-2	X-99-3	X-115	Y-75	Z-20	Z-78	Z-101
X-97-3	X-99-4	X-118	Y-76	Z-29	Z-79	Z-103
X-97-4	X-99-5	X-120	Y-84	Z-30	Z-80	Z-104
X-97-5	X-99-6		Y-85	Z-32	Z-81	Z-106
X-97-6	X-99-7	Y-18	Y-87	Z-33	Z-82	Z-112
X-97-7	X-101	Y-25	Y-89	Z-48	Z-83	Z-114
X-98	X-101-1	Y-36	Y-93	Z-53	Z-84	Z-115
X-98-1	X-101-2	Y-40	Y-94	Z-57	Z-87	Z-118
X-98-2	X-102	Y-48		Z-58	Z-91	Z-122
X-98-3	X-102-1	Y-56	Z-2	Z-60	Z-92	
X-98-4	X-102-2	Y-68				

Undecorated: Up until a few years ago, all of the various Lenox shapes were available completely undecorated. The ones most frequently encountered are Temple Plain and Coupe Plain, although the others do turn up now and then. One should be careful to differentiate between undecorated Lenox shapes with the wreath mark and those pieces of palette mark Lenox which were sold to be decorated and never were for some reason. Although all different marks can be used to fill in missing pieces, the palette mark items should be considered incomplete, and therefore not worth quite so much. Lenox is not currently making any undecorated dinnerware, and prices for these items should be figured by comparing them to the least expensive pattern in a given shape.

Embossed Dinnerware: The dinnerware discussed in previous sections is of the type where decoration was applied as the china was nearing completion. There was another type, where the pattern was actually part of the china, having been molded in as part of the production process. The proper name for this ware is embossed dinnerware, although it is commonly (and incorrectly) referred to as pate-sur-pate or as glazed jasperware.

Embossed dinnerware was available both in plain white and in colors with the white sections standing up in relief against the colored background. It is these colored pieces that gave rise to the misnomers, since from a distance they do hear a passing resemblance to other types of wares with raised designs. Those patterns with color on the rims tend to be rather heavy in appearance and feel.

Many of the embossed patterns had a limited assortment of available shapes and sizes, and some of the patterns had no serving pieces. Some of the embossed patterns are frequently seen on gift items, and there could quite possibly do double duty on the dinner table.

Below is a listing and brief description of the Lenox embossed patterns:

Apple Blossom—raised floral design (frequently mistaken for dogwood blossoms)

Beltane (sometimes seen spelled Belletaine)—crocus design in a ring around the rim.

Classic—fluting on outer part of rim (similar to Temple shape but fluting does not cover the whole rim as it does with Temple).

Fontaine—laurel wreath on outer rim.

Gadroon—gadroon border.

Hawthorn—overall design of small hawthorn blossoms.

Pagoda—Oriental motif.

Plymouth—five narrow raised bands on outer edge.

Sheffield—gentle scalloping with narrow terraced band.

Temple—fluting covering entire rim.

Terrace—five bands on rim, terraced look.

Three-Step—similar to Terrace but only three bands.

Washington/Wakefield—entire rim covered with intricate design of scrolls, cross-hatching and basketweave in a pattern described by a not-so-nice friend of ours as Revolutionary War ticky-tacky.

Many of the embossed patterns were also available in decorated versions (e.g., Gadroon Rose), but the plain versions are much more common. They have the added attraction of not showing wear, and damage is also very hard to see.

The embossed patterns do have one great disadvantage, and that is that they are very difficult to clean, particularly once food has dried in the crevises. (Try a toothbrush!)

DISCONTINUED PATTERNS

Due to production poblems or declining sales, the Lenox Company occasionally finds it necessary to discontinue a particular pattern. Although this is, of course, distressing to the people who own these patterns, it is not an insurmountable problem. Before the patterns are dropped completely, they are always available on special order for a while.

Many people have the mistaken notion that "open stock" means that a pattern will be made forever, and they become rather upset when their pattern is discontinued. (Open stock simply means that you can buy a piece at a time, as opposed to the idea of having to buy whole or partial sets at one time as is the case, for example, with many cheap sets of china.) Try to keep in mind that if the Lenox Company (or any other fine china company, for that matter) were forced to continue making unprofitable patterns, there would soon be no Lenox Company.

We would like to put to rest, once and for all, the persistent rumor that the Lenox Company will buy back your china should it be discontinued. This is definitely not the case.

If your pattern is still in production, it is a good idea to check in with your local retail outlet once a year or so to verify that the pattern is still available. It is also recommended that you purchase perhaps an extra place setting or so (or at the very least an extra cup, since they are always the first to go.)

If your pattern is one of those that has been discontinued, there are several courses of action open to you:

(1) Sell what you already have.

(2) Fill in with a similar pattern (e.g., buying current Autumn pieces to fill out a set of Trent).

(3) Use silver or crystal items to fill the void.

(4) Start looking for your pattern.

It is probably a good idea to try to complete your set only if you have at least half of what you will finally want. Looking for discontinued patterns can be frustrating and/or expensive, and it is probably not a worthwhile endeavor if you only have a few place settings of a pattern.

The place to start is with stores in your area that carry Lenox china. If your pattern has been discontinued only recently, there is a good chance you will be able to find what you need at these stores. We find it best to go in person rather than to call.

The next step is to write to the Lenox Company for a list of dealers who specialize in handling discontinued china. When writing to these dealers, be as precise as possible in your first letter, as this will save everyone a great deal of time and trouble. Give dimensions of pieces you are trying to match, as well as all the information stamped on the back (pattern names and numbers, shape numbers, and the color of the backstamp if that matters to you). It is also a good idea to enclose a self-addressed, stamped envelope since a few of the dealers will not answer you without one. Since there are waiting lists for some of the more popular patterns, do not expect immediate results. All of these matching services maintain "wants" lists, and they will let you know when they have what you need.

The prices charged by these matching services tend to be high and you will probably find considerable price variations among them, though, so don't be too quick to order from the first one to answer you.

Since we have not had personal dealings with some of the dealers on the list, we hesitate to print their names. It is our understanding that they all do business by mail order, and some have shops open to the public as well. It is a good idea to check with a particular dealer before dropping in.

If you decide to place an order, be very specific about what it is you are ordering and whether or not you will accept a partial order. Be sure to include your name and address where the package is to be shipped, since the dealer may not be able to find your original correspondence quickly, or may have more than one customer by that name. Double check your arithmetic and add in any shipping costs or sales tax.

It is important for you to know whether you are buing new or used china, and if it is used what the condition of it is. To the best of our knowledge, they all allow returns if the customer is not happy, but it is best to check on this in advance to avoid any misunderstandings.

Other sources for old china include flea markets, yard sales, auctions, antique shows, etc. The chief problem in obtaining your china this way is that you may have to buy items you don't want to obtain those you do (i.e., taking a teapot you will never use to get the sugar and creamer that are with it). Prices tend to be lower than those of the matching services, but remember to mentally add in your time and travel expenses, plus the fact that you may never find what you want.

An ad in the "china wanted" section of an antiques publication may bring results, and many dealers clip out the wanted ads and save them for future reference.

In general, the chances of finding your pattern are good unless your pattern is particularly obscure or you are being unrealistic about how much you want to spend.

CURRENT LENOX DINNERWARE

The Lenox Company presently has about fifty patterns in active production, ranging from the very formal to the informal. An additional twenty or so patterns are available only on a custom order basis.

Oxford Bone China is also produced by Lenox, and is currently available in about twenty different patterns. Since the Oxford line is still relatively new, very little of the china has shown up on the used market, and we have not included any prices for the Oxford because of this.

Lenox Temper-Ware is freezer and oven-proof, and can also be used in a microwave oven. It is guaranteed against breakage, chipping, cracking and crazing for two years of normal home use. We have not yet seen any Temper-Ware on the secondary market so cannot list prices for it.

Crystal is available in some forty patterns, many of which coordinate with Lenox dinnerware patterns. Used Lenox crystal does turn up now and then in antiques shops, and as a rule seems to be priced at about ½ to ¾ of the going retail rate.

ADDISON
☐ No recent listings.

ADRIENNE
☐ Bread and butter plate... 9.00
☐ Cup and saucer 27.00
☐ Dinner plate 18.00
☐ Salad/dessert plate 14.00

ALARIS
☐ Bread and butter plate... 5.00
☐ Cigarette lighter and urn 30.00
☐ Cup and saucer 25.00

☐	Dinner plate	15.00
☐	Salad/dessert plate	12.00
☐	Sugar and creamer	50.00
☐	Vegetable bowl, *large, open, oval*	30.00
☐	Vegetable bowl, *small, open, oval*	25.00

ALDEN

☐	Dinner plate	18.00

ANGELINA

☐	Cup and saucer	15.00

ANTOINETTE

☐	Cup and saucer	30.00
☐	Dinner plate	18.00

APPLE BLOSSOM

Apple Blossom is most commonly seen in the white and coral combination, although it was also available in other colors as well as plain white. There were no serving pieces in Apple Blossom, and the selection of place setting items was also limited. All of the following prices are for coral and white items. Other colors should be priced about the same, while the plain white should generally be slightly less. Additional listings of Apple Blossom can be found in the giftware section.

Apple Blossom, *cream soup cup and plate*

☐	Bread and butter plate	11.00
☐	Cream soup cup and underplate	15.00
☐	Cup and saucer	25.00
☐	Demitasse cup and saucer	15.00
☐	Dinner plate	18.00
☐	Salad/dessert plate	13.00

ARCADIA

- ☐ Bread and butter plate... 11.00
- ☐ Salad/dessert plate 12.00

ARDEN ROSE

- ☐ No recent listings.

ARISTOCRAT

- ☐ Current pattern

ARROWHEAD

- ☐ Bread and butter plate... 9.00
- ☐ Cup and saucer 25.00
- ☐ Dinner plate 14.00
- ☐ Gravy boat.. 35.00
- ☐ Salad/dessert plate 11.00
- ☐ Vegetable bowl, *large, oval* 35.00

ATHENIA

- ☐ No recent listings.

ATHENIA COUPE

- ☐ No recent listings.

AURORA

- ☐ Bread and butter plate... 8.00
- ☐ Cream soup cup and underplate 15.00
- ☐ Cup and saucer 25.00
- ☐ Salad plate, *square* 12.00

AUTUMN

Autumn was first introduced in 1919, and remains one of the more popular Lenox patterns. Since it is still being made, prices for the more common items can be found in a current retail list. All of the items listed below are out-of-production items.

- ☐ Baked apple dish with underplate 55.00
- ☐ Bouillon cup and saucer 20.00
- ☐ Cheese and cracker dish, *two pieces*......................... 50.00
- ☐ Chocolate pot 75.00
- ☐ Coffee cup and saucer 25.00
- ☐ Compote, *3" high, 9" diameter, badly worn* 5.00
- ☐ Fruit bowl, *double handled, 9" diameter, not including handle* 75.00
- ☐ Coffee cup and saucer 25.00
- ☐ Compote, *3" high, 9" diameter, badly worn* 5.00
- ☐ Fruit bowl, *double handled, 9" diameter not including handles* 75.00
- ☐ Platter, *16" round*... 100.00
- ☐ Ramekin, *small chip under rim* 5.00
- ☐ Vegetable bowl, *covered, double-handled* 100.00

AVON

- ☐ Bread and butter plate... 11.00
- ☐ Cup and saucer 25.00
- ☐ Dinner plate 15.00
- ☐ Salad/dessert plate 13.00

BALLAD
- ☐ Bread and butter plate 9.00
- ☐ Cup and saucer 20.00
- ☐ Dinner plate 14.00
- ☐ Salad/dessert plate 10.00

BANCROFT
- ☐ No recent listings.

BARCLAY
- ☐ Current pattern.

BARCLAY R-307 *(DISCONTINUED)*
- ☐ No recent listings.

BEACON HILL
- ☐ Bread and butter plate 10.00
- ☐ Cup and saucer 25.00
- ☐ Teapot 45.00

BELFORD
- ☐ No recent listings.

BELLAIRE
- ☐ No recent listings.

BELLEFONTE *(ALSO SEEN SPELLED BELFONT)*
- ☐ Saucer 3.00

BELLEVUE MAROON
- ☐ No recent listings.

BELLEVUE SEA GREEN
- ☐ Bread and butter plate 12.00
- ☐ Cup and saucer 30.00
- ☐ Dinner plate 18.00
- ☐ Platter, *small oval* 35.00
- ☐ Salad/dessert plate 14.00
- ☐ Sugar and creamer 60.00
- ☐ Vegetable bowl, *large oval* 35.00

BELMONT
- ☐ Dinner plate 13.00
- ☐ Salad/dessert plate 8.00

BELTANE
- ☐ Cream soup cup and underplate, *green with white* 18.00
- ☐ Dinner plate, *pale peach with white* 20.00
- ☐ Fruit saucer, *blue with white* 12.00
- ☐ Soup plate, *yellow with white* 15.00

Bellevue Sea Green, *creamer*

BELVIDERE

- ☐ Bread and butter plate... 10.00
- ☐ Cup and saucer 28.00
- ☐ Gravy boat.. 50.00
- ☐ Platter, *large oval*... 60.00
- ☐ Platter, *small oval* 40.00
- ☐ Salad/dessert plate 13.00
- ☐ Soup plate.. 15.00
- ☐ Sugar and creamer... 60.00

Belvidere, *sugar and creamer*

BERKELEY
- ☐ No recent listings.

BLUE BELL
- ☐ No recent listings.

BLUE RIDGE
☐ Bread and butter plate	10.00
☐ Cup and saucer	28.00
☐ Dinner plate	15.00
☐ Salad/dessert plate	11.00

BLUE TREE *1982 only special order. Will be discontinued 1983*
Current pattern—see retail list for prices of items.
☐ Cookie plate *(square)*	35.00

dinner plate
31.00

BRADFORD
☐ Creamer	30.00
☐ Cup and saucer	17.00
☐ Salad/dessert plate	10.00
☐ Sugar bowl and lid	35.00

BROOKDALE
- ☐ Current pattern.

BROOKLINE
☐ Cup and saucer	30.00
☐ Dinner plate	20.00
☐ Salad/dessert plate, *8-1/4" diameter*	14.00

BROOKSIDE
- ☐ No recent listings.

CAMBRIDGE
☐ Service for 6, 50 pieces	375.00

CAPRI
☐ Bread and butter plate	8.00
☐ Cream soup cup with underplate	17.00
☐ Cup and saucer	27.00
☐ Dinner plate	16.00
☐ Salad/dessert plate	12.00
☐ Vegetable bowl, *large oval*	35.00

CAPRICE
☐ Footed compote, *9" diameter*	25.00

CARIBBEE
☐ Service for 12, total of 80 pieces	1000.00
☐ Dinner plate	16.00

CARLYLE
☐ No recent listings.

CAROLINA
☐ No recent listings.

CASCADE
☐ Dinner plate 25.00
☐ Salad/dessert plate 10.00

CASINO
☐ Cup and saucer 22.00
☐ Dinner plate 17.00

CASTLE GARDEN
☐ Current pattern.

CATTAILS
☐ Bread and butter plate................................... 10.00
☐ Cup and saucer 23.00
☐ Dinner plate 16.00
☐ Fruit saucer 12.00
☐ Salad/dessert plate 12.00
☐ Teapot 35.00

CECILE
☐ No recent listings.

CELESTE
☐ Bread and butter plate................................... 8.00
☐ Cup and saucer 26.00
☐ Dinner plate 17.00
☐ Salad/dessert plate 9.00

CHALET
☐ Bread and butter plate................................... 10.00
☐ Dinner plate 17.00
☐ Salad/dessert plate 11.00
☐ Sugar and creamer....................................... 58.00
☐ Teapot 45.00
☐ Vegetable bowl, *large oval* 35.00

CHANSON
☐ Bread and butter plate................................... 7.00
☐ Cup and saucer 25.00
☐ Dinner plate 14.00
☐ Salad/dessert plate 10.00
☐ Small platter 34.00

CHANTILLY
☐ Dinner plate 16.00
☐ Teapot 45.00
☐ Vegetable bowl, *large oval* 25.00

Chanson, *bread and butter plate*

CHARMAINE

☐ Bread and butter plate	10.00
☐ Cup and saucer	25.00
☐ Dinner plate	14.00
☐ Gravy boat	45.00
☐ Platter, *small oval*	35.00
☐ Vegetable bowl, *covered*	65.00
☐ Vegetable bowl, *large oval*	30.00

CHELSEA

☐ Gravy boat	40.00
☐ Platter, *large oval, gold worn*	18.00
☐ Platter, *round buffet, gold worn*	15.00
☐ Vegetable bowl, *large oval, tiny fleck under rim and gold worn*	10.00

CHESTERFIELD

☐ No recent listings.

CHIPPENDALE

☐ Demitasse cup (no saucer)	10.00
☐ Dinner plate, *badly scratched and worn*	5.00
☐ Salad/dessert plate	8.00

CINDERELLA

☐ Sugar bowl and lid	30.00
☐ Vegetable bowl, *large oval*	40.00
☐ Vegetable bowl, *covered*	75.00

CLAREMONT

☐ No recent listings.

CLARION

- ☐ Bread and butter plate... 10.00
- ☐ Cup and saucer 30.00
- ☐ Dinner plate 16.00
- ☐ Platter, *large oval*... 50.00
- ☐ Salad/dessert plate 13.00
- ☐ Soup/salad bowl... 18.00
- ☐ Vegetable bowl, *large* 30.00

CLASSIC

Classic is very similar to the Temple shape, but the fluting does not extend as far on Classic as it does on Temple. The Temple serving pieces were used with Classic.

- ☐ Cup and saucer 14.00
- ☐ Dinner plate 14.00
- ☐ Salad/dessert plate 7.00

CLASSIC ROSE

- ☐ No recent listings.

COLONIAL

- ☐ Bread and butter plate.. 10.00
- ☐ Cream soup cup with underplate 15.00
- ☐ Dinner plate 14.00
- ☐ Service for 12, *120 pieces, badly worn, several chips*.............. 300.00

COLONNADE GOLD

- ☐ Bread and butter plate.. 9.00
- ☐ Cup and saucer 25.00
- ☐ Dinner plate 15.00
- ☐ Salad/dessert plate 12.00
- ☐ Soup plate.. 13.00
- ☐ Vegetable bowl.. 30.00

COLONNADE PLATINUM

- ☐ Bread and butter plate.. 10.00
- ☐ Cup and saucer 24.00
- ☐ Dinner plate 13.00
- ☐ Salad/dessert plate 11.00

COQUETTE

- ☐ Bread and butter plate.. 7.00
- ☐ Cup and saucer 24.00
- ☐ Dinner plate 14.00
- ☐ Fruit saucer 12.00
- ☐ Platter, *large oval*... 45.00
- ☐ Platter, *small oval* 35.00
- ☐ Salad/dessert plate 10.00
- ☐ Soup bowl 12.00

CORALTON

- ☐ Dinner plate 16.00
- ☐ Teapot 70.00

CORINNE
- ☐ Coffeepot 50.00
- ☐ Sugar and creamer... 50.00

CORINTHIAN
- ☐ No recent listings.

CORONADO
- ☐ After dinner cup and saucer 20.00
- ☐ Dinner plate 22.00
- ☐ Fruit saucer 18.00
- ☐ Serving bowl, *round, 9" diameter* 50.00

COUNTRY GARDEN
- ☐ Bread and butter plate....................................... 10.00
- ☐ Cup and saucer 24.00
- ☐ Salad/dessert plate 12.00

COUPE (PLAIN)
- ☐ Bread and butter plate... 8.00
- ☐ Cup and saucer 20.00
- ☐ Dinner plate 13.00
- ☐ Salad/dessert plate 10.00
- ☐ Salad serving bowl.. 35.00

COVINGTON
- ☐ Service for 12—8 piece place settings with several serving pieces, total of 110 pieces 690.00

CRETAN
- ☐ Bouillon cup and saucer *(current pattern)*....................... 15.00

CRINOLINE
- ☐ After dinner cup, mismatched saucer of unknown origin 12.00
- ☐ Bread and butter plate... 8.00

CYNTHIA
- ☐ Cup and saucer 14.00
- ☐ Dinner plate 27.00
- ☐ Vegetable bowl.. 30.00

DAYBREAK
- ☐ Bread and butter plate... 9.00
- ☐ Cup and saucer 25.00
- ☐ Dinner plate 16.00
- ☐ Salad/dessert plate 10.00

DIANA
- ☐ No recent listings.

DUBARRY GRAY
- ☐ After dinner cup and saucer 16.00
- ☐ Bread and butter plate.. 10.00
- ☐ Cup and saucer 27.00
- ☐ Dinner plate 15.00
- ☐ Salad/dessert plate 15.00

ECLIPSE
- ☐ Current pattern.

EMPRESS
- ☐ Dinner plate 16.00
- ☐ Gravy boat.. 45.00

ESSEX BLUE
- ☐ Soup plate, *scalloped rim* 14.00

ESSEX GREEN
- ☐ No recent listings.

ESSEX MAROON
- ☐ Dinner plate 16.00
- ☐ Sugar and creamer... 60.00
- ☐ Vegetable bowl, *large oval* 45.00

ETERNAL
- ☐ Current pattern.

ETNA
- ☐ Cup and saucer 17.00
- ☐ Dinner plate 13.00

ETRUSCAN
- ☐ Gravy boat.. 50.00
- ☐ Platter 45.00

EVANSTON
- ☐ Bouillon cup and saucer 13.00
- ☐ Ramekin 10.00

FAIRFIELD
- ☐ No recent listings.

FAIR LADY
- ☐ Current pattern.

FAIRMOUNT
- ☐ After dinner cup and saucer 16.00
- ☐ Bread and butter plate.. 10.00
- ☐ Cup and saucer 25.00
- ☐ Dinner plate 18.00
- ☐ Salad/dessert plate 12.00
- ☐ Tete-a-tete *(cup with 8-1/4" plate)*........................ 15.00

FANTASY

- [ ] Bread and butter plate.. 10.00
- [ ] Cup and saucer 22.00
- [ ] Dinner plate 14.00
- [ ] Salad/dessert plate 12.00
- [ ] Soup/salad bowl... 15.00

FESTIVAL

- [ ] Bread and butter plate.. 12.00
- [ ] Candlesticks, *8" tall* 50.00
- [ ] Cup and saucer 30.00
- [ ] Dinner plate 20.00
- [ ] Salad/dessert plate 15.00
- [ ] Vegetable bowl, *large oval* 40.00

FIRESONG

- [ ] Cup and saucer 24.00
- [ ] Dinner plate 14.00
- [ ] Gravy boat.. 50.00
- [ ] Salad/dessert plate 12.00
- [ ] Soup/salad bowl... 15.00

FLORALIA *(GREEN)*

- [ ] Soup plate.. 12.00
- [ ] Vegetable bowl, *large oval* 24.00

FLORALIA *(PINK)*

- [ ] After dinner cup and saucer 15.00
- [ ] Cereal bowl... 8.00
- [ ] Soup plate.. 10.00

Florida, *teapot*

FLORIDA

- ☐ Bread and butter plate.. 15.00
- ☐ Cup and saucer 32.00
- ☐ Dinner plate 25.00
- ☐ Platter, *round, 16" diameter, worn* 25.00
- ☐ Sugar and creamer... 60.00
- ☐ Teapot... 60.00
- ☐ Teapot, *individual size, tiny fleck on spout* 25.00

FLOURISH

- ☐ Bread and butter plate.. 10.00
- ☐ Cup and saucer 27.00
- ☐ Dinner plate 16.00
- ☐ Salad/dessert plate 12.00
- ☐ Vegetable bowl.. 40.00

FONTAINE

- ☐ No recent listings.

FOUNTAIN

- ☐ Bread and butter plate.. 13.00
- ☐ Cup and saucer 32.00
- ☐ Dinner plate 20.00
- ☐ Salad/dessert plate 15.00
- ☐ Teapot, coffeepot, sugar and creamer 200.00

FOUNTAINBLEU

- ☐ No recent listings.

FRONTENAC

- ☐ No recent listings.

FUTURA

- ☐ Bread and butter plate.. 9.00
- ☐ Cup and saucer 20.00
- ☐ Dinner plate 14.00
- ☐ Gravy boat.. 50.00
- ☐ Salad/dessert plate 11.00
- ☐ Vegetable bowl, *oval* 35.00

GADROON

- ☐ After dinner cup and saucer 12.00
- ☐ Bread and butter plate.. 7.00
- ☐ Cup and saucer 20.00
- ☐ Dinner plate 14.00
- ☐ Platter, *round, 13" diameter* 40.00

GADROON ROSE

- ☐ Bread and butter plate.. 10.00
- ☐ Dinner plate 19.00
- ☐ Salad/dessert plate 13.00
- ☐ Vegetable bowl.. 40.00

GAYLORD

☐ Bread and butter plate 10.00
☐ Coffeepot 30.00
☐ Cup and saucer 24.00
☐ Dinner plate 14.00
☐ Salad/dessert plate 12.00
☐ Soup bowl 14.00

GENEVIEVE

☐ Dinner plate 15.00
☐ Saucer (no cup) 2.00

GEORGIAN

☐ No recent listings.

Glendale, *creamer*

GLENDALE

☐ Bread and butter plate 10.00
☐ Cup and saucer 28.00
☐ Dinner plate 18.00
☐ Salad/dessert plate 12.00
☐ Sugar and creamer 70.00

GLENTHORNE

☐ Bread and butter plate 10.00
☐ Dinner plate 18.00
☐ Soup plate 14.00
☐ Vegetable bowl, *oval large* 35.00
☐ Vegetable bowl, *oval small* 32.00
☐ Vegetable bowl, *round, covered* 60.00

GOLD CASINO
☐ No recent listings.

GOLDEN BLOSSOM
☐ Cup and saucer	30.00
☐ Dinner plate	20.00
☐ Salad plate, *square*	15.00

GOLDEN GATE
☐ After dinner cup and saucer	18.00
☐ Bread and butter plate	12.00
☐ Cup and saucer	30.00
☐ Dinner plate	20.00
☐ Fruit saucer	14.00
☐ Platter, *oval, 16"*	50.00
☐ Salad/dessert plate	15.00
☐ Sugar and creamer	70.00

GOLDEN MOOD
☐ Bread and butter plate	8.00
☐ Cup and saucer	25.00
☐ Dinner plate	15.00
☐ Salad/dessert plate	10.00
☐ Sugar and creamer	50.00
☐ Teapot	45.00
☐ Vegetable bowl, *large round*	40.00

GOLDEN WREATH
☐ Bread and butter plate	9.00
☐ Cup and saucer	22.00
☐ Dinner plate	16.00
☐ Fruit saucer	12.00
☐ Salad/dessert plate	12.00
☐ Sugar and creamer	50.00

GREENFIELD
☐ Bread and butter plate	7.00
☐ Cup and saucer	25.00
☐ Dinner plate	15.00
☐ Fruit saucer	14.00
☐ Soup plate	14.00

GREENWICH
☐ No recent listings.

GRENOBLE
☐ Dinner plate	15.00
☐ Soup plate	14.00

GRENOBLE IVORY
☐ No recent listings.

HARVEST

- ☐ Bread and butter plate **8.00**
- ☐ Cup and saucer **19.00**
- ☐ Dinner plate **12.00**
- ☐ Gravy boat **50.00**
- ☐ Salad/dessert plate **10.00**
- ☐ Soup plate **12.00**
- ☐ Vegetable bowl, *large oval* **30.00**
- ☐ Vegetable bowl, *round, covered* **90.00**

HARWOOD

- ☐ No recent listings.

HATHAWAY

- ☐ No recent listings.

HAWTHORN

Items in the Hawthorn pattern were among the earliest pieces made by Lenox, and Item #1 in C.A.C. catalogues was a Hawthorn cup and saucer. In the 1960's, the pattern was briefly brought back to life as a limited edition, both in plain white and with gold trim. Earlier versions were produced in a variety of colors.

Hawthorn, *cup and saucer, small size, white*

- ☐ Bread and butter plate, *coral and white* **8.00**
- ☐ Cup and saucer, *bouillon, blue and white* **14.00**
- ☐ Cup and saucer, *covered, two-handled, white* **18.00**
- ☐ Cup and saucer, *cream soup, coral and white* **30.00**
- ☐ Cup and saucer, *full size, white, very thin* **50.00**
- ☐ Cup and saucer, *full size, white, gold trim* **25.00**
- ☐ Cup and saucer, *full size, blue and white* **25.00**
- ☐ Cup and saucer, *small size, white, C.A.C., thin* **45.00**

- ☐ Cup and saucer, *small size, white with gold trim* **21.00**
- ☐ Dinner plate, *white*... **30.00**
- ☐ Luncheon plate, *coral and white* **10.00**
- ☐ Luncheon plate, *white*.. **9.00**
- ☐ Salad plate, *white* **10.00**
- ☐ Salad plate, *coral and white* **12.00**
- ☐ Salad plate, *white, thin* **18.00**
- ☐ Salad plate, *blue and white*................................. **10.00**
- ☐ Sugar and creamer, *white, C.A.C., very thin* **150.00**
- ☐ Teapot, sugar and creamer, *coral and white*.................. **125.00**
- ☐ Teapot, sugar and creamer, *blue and white* **125.00**
- ☐ Waste bowl, *plain white*..................................... **30.00**

  Note: see the Limited Edition section for prices on the reproduction Hawthorn items.

HUDSON

- ☐ No recent listings.

IMPERIAL

- ☐ Bread and butter plate....................................... **8.00**
- ☐ Cup and saucer **20.00**
- ☐ Dinner plate **15.00**
- ☐ Gravy boat... **50.00**
- ☐ Platter, *large oval*.. **60.00**
- ☐ Salad/dessert plate **10.00**
- ☐ Sugar and creamer.. **50.00**
- ☐ Teapot **75.00**
- ☐ Vegetable bowl, *large oval* **30.00**

INTERLUDE

- ☐ No recent listings.

JEWEL

- ☐ After dinner cup and saucer **15.00**
- ☐ Bread and butter plate....................................... **10.00**
- ☐ Coffeepot **45.00**
- ☐ Cup and saucer **25.00**
- ☐ Dinner plate **15.00**
- ☐ Gravy boat... **45.00**
- ☐ Platter, *large oval*.. **50.00**
- ☐ Platter, *medium oval* **40.00**
- ☐ Platter, *small oval* **30.00**
- ☐ Salad/dessert plate **12.00**
- ☐ Soup plate... **15.00**
- ☐ Teapot **45.00**

JOAN

- ☐ No recent listings.

JOSEPHINE

- ☐ No recent listings.

KENMORE

- ☐ No recent listings.

KINGSLEY

☐	After dinner cup and saucer	**18.00**
☐	Bread and butter plate	**10.00**
☐	Cup and saucer	**30.00**
☐	Dinner plate	**18.00**
☐	Footed bowl, *small triangular shape*	**14.00**
☐	Salad/dessert plate	**13.00**
☐	Soup plate	**16.00**
☐	Sugar bowl and lid	**25.00**

LAFAYETTE

☐	Cup and saucer	**23.00**
☐	Dinner plate	**16.00**
☐	Salad/dessert plate	**10.00**
☐	Teapot	**30.00**

LAUREL
☐ No recent listings.

LAURENT
☐ Current pattern.

LENORE
☐ No recent listings.

LENOX ROSE

First introduced in 1934, this pattern enjoyed tremendous popularity and until last year was still available on a custom order basis.

Lenox Rose is perhaps the only pattern that can come close to Ming in collectibility, since both patterns were made in a huge assortment of items with a wide distribution over the years. In general, we find Lenox Rose to be superior to the Ming in that it does not show wear as quickly as the Ming does.

The Lenox Company made many variations on the basic Lenox Rose idea (e.g., Pavlova and Aurora), and most of the variations were also successful patterns.

On the used china market, Lenox Rose brings almost as much as the new. In the collecting market, giftware items with this design on them are avidly sought.

☐	After dinner cup and saucer	**15.00**
☐	Bouillon cup and saucer	**15.00**
☐	Bread and butter plate	**10.00**
☐	Cream soup cup and saucer	**20.00**
☐	Cup and saucer	**25.00**
☐	Dinner plate	**18.00**
☐	Egg cup, *large*	**20.00**
☐	Fruit saucer	**12.00**
☐	Gravy boat	**50.00**
☐	Mayonnaise bowl	**20.00**
☐	Milk pitcher	**50.00**
☐	Platter, *medium oval*	**70.00**
☐	Platter, *small oval*	**60.00**
☐	Platter, *round*	**40.00**

- ☐ Salad/dessert plate **13.00**
- ☐ Salt and pepper, *3" high* **25.00**
- ☐ Sugar and creamer... **60.00**
- ☐ Teapot **50.00**
- ☐ Vegetable bowl, *large oval* **40.00**
- ☐ Vegetable bowl, *small oval* **30.00**
- ☐ Vegetable bowl, *round, covered* **125.00**

LEXINGTON
- ☐ No recent listings.

LINCOLN
- ☐ No recent listings.

LOMBARDY
- ☐ No recent listings.

LONSDALE
- ☐ No recent listings.

LOWELL
Current pattern—all of the items listed below are out-of-production items.
- ☐ Compote, *8" diameter* **40.00**
- ☐ Teapot, *individual size*.................................. **30.00**

LUXORIA
- ☐ No recent listings.

LYRIC
- ☐ No recent listings.

MADISON
- ☐ Dinner plate **25.00**
- ☐ Mustard pot with underplate **40.00**
- ☐ Salad/dessert plate **14.00**

MAJESTIC
- ☐ Bread and butter plate.................................... **10.00**
- ☐ Cup and saucer **23.00**
- ☐ Dinner plate **14.00**
- ☐ Fruit saucer **13.00**
- ☐ Gravy boat.. **40.00**
- ☐ Salad/dessert plate **12.00**
- ☐ Vegetable bowl, *large oval* **30.00**
- ☐ Vegetable bowl, *covered* **60.00**

MALMAISON
- ☐ After dinner cup and saucer **16.00**
- ☐ Bread and butter plate.................................... **10.00**
- ☐ Creamer **30.00**
- ☐ Cream soup cup with underplate **15.00**

☐	Cup and saucer	24.00
☐	Dinner plate	17.00
☐	Salad/dessert plate	12.00
☐	Vegetable bowl, *large oval*	35.00

Mandarin, *sugar and creamer*

MANDARIN

☐	After dinner cup and saucer	20.00
☐	Bread and butter plate	13.00
☐	Coffeepot	65.00
☐	Cream soup cup with underplate	15.00
☐	Cup and saucer, *full size*	30.00
☐	Dinner plate	20.00
☐	Gravy boat	65.00
☐	Platter, *large oval*	60.00
☐	Platter, *small oval*	50.00
☐	Salad/dessert plate	15.00
☐	Sugar and creamer	70.00
☐	Tazza, *considerable gold wear*	14.00
☐	Teapot	65.00
☐	Vegetable bowl, *large oval*	60.00
☐	Vegetable bowl, *round, covered*	125.00

MANSFIELD
Current pattern. Many of the old, numbered gold-banded patterns which are not listed in this price guide can be compared against current Mansfield prices.

MARLBORO
☐ No recent listings.

MARYLAND

☐	Bread and butter plate	9.00
☐	Dinner plate	15.00
☐	Salad/dessert plate	11.00

MAYFAIR
☐ No recent listings.

MAYWOOD
☐ No recent listings.

MEADOWBROOK
☐ Compote, *gold worn*	15.00
☐ Cookie plate, *square with handles*	25.00
☐ Cup and saucer	30.00
☐ Dinner plate	20.00
☐ Salad/dessert plate	12.00
☐ Tete-a-tete set *(cup and 8-1/4" plate)*	15.00

MELISSA
☐ Bread and butter plate	8.00
☐ Cup and saucer	25.00
☐ Dinner plate	16.00
☐ Salad/dessert plate	10.00

MELODY
☐ Salad/dessert plate	11.00
☐ Saucer (no cup)	3.00

MEMOIR
☐ Bread and butter plate	10.00
☐ Coffeepot	50.00
☐ Cup and saucer	30.00
☐ Dinner plate	15.00
☐ Platter, *small oval*	35.00
☐ Salad/dessert plate	13.00
☐ Soup bowl	15.00

MEREDITH
☐ Cup and saucer	30.00
☐ Dinner plate	16.00
☐ Salad/dessert plate, *badly worn*	4.00
☐ Sugar and creamer	50.00
☐ Teapot	60.00
☐ Vegetable bowl, *large oval*	40.00

MERRIVALE
☐ Cup and saucer	24.00
☐ Dinner plate	14.00
☐ Gravy boat	50.00
☐ Luncheon plate, *9" diameter*	8.00
☐ Salad/dessert plate	12.00

MINERVA
☐ No recent listings.

MING

Ming was introduced in 1917, and was the first Lenox pattern to be copyrighted. It enjoyed immense popular appeal through the years, and has become the "in" pattern for people to collect, which has resulted in very inflated prices for the pattern. We feel Ming is a bad investment for the collector for the following reasons:

(1) It is overpriced when compared to comparable current retail prices.

(2) It is far from the finest pattern ever produced by Lenox. For example, the extra butterflies so highly prized by Ming collectors were used to hide pits on the china.

(3) It is hard to find pieces that match each other in color and shape.

(4) It does not hold up well.

Ming coloration can vary greatly from one piece to another, due both to minor variations in the original dyes and to fading from excessive or careless use. In many cases, the blue borders are faded almost completely to gray, leading many people to believe Ming was made in more than one color. Since the pattern was made for so many years, flat pieces such as dinner plates will vary somewhat in shape.

The pattern does have a certain charm, however, and the wide variety of items available in the pattern can make life very interesting for the Ming collector.

Ming was originally produced on the standard shape dinnerware, and was later also produced on coupe and temple shape items as well. We have no current listings for Ming Coupe or Ming Temple.

Ming, *covered muffin dish*

☐	After dinner cup and saucer, *footed*	25.00
☐	After dinner cup and saucer, *rounded shape*	18.00
☐	Biscuit jar, *covered*	125.00
☐	Bouillon cup and saucer	19.00
☐	Bread and butter plate, *5-3/4"*	10.00
☐	Bread and butter plate, *6-1/2"*	10.00

☐	Butter tub	50.00
☐	Cake plate, *footed, 12" diameter*	85.00
☐	Candlesticks, *pair, small*.................................	65.00
☐	Cereal bowl, *6" diameter*.................................	12.00
☐	Cheese and cracker dish, *2pieces*	75.00
☐	Chocolate pot..	125.00
☐	Coffeepot, *full size*......................................	100.00
☐	Coffeepot, *individual size*	60.00
☐	Covered muffin dish.......................................	70.00
☐	Cup and saucer, *footed type cup*	30.00
☐	Cup and saucer, *rounded bottom*...........................	24.00
☐	Cup and saucer, cream soup	20.00
☐	Decanter	100.00
☐	Dinner plate, *10"*	20.00
☐	Dinner plate, *10-1/2"*	25.00
☐	Egg cup, *large*..	25.00
☐	Egg cup, *small*	25.00
☐	Fruit saucer, *5-1/2" diameter*	12.00
☐	Gravy boat, attached underplate	60.00
☐	Gravy boat, separate underplate	60.00
☐	Luncheon plate, *9"*......................................	10.00
☐	Marmalade jar, *covered, 6-1/2" high*.......................	50.00
☐	Mayonnaise compote with underplate	60.00
☐	Milk pitcher	75.00
☐	Olive dish, *3-footed*	40.00
☐	Pitcher, lemonade	95.00
☐	Platter, *16" oval*	80.00
☐	Platter, *13" round*.......................................	50.00
☐	Platter, *12" oval*	75.00
☐	Ramekin	15.00
☐	Salad plate, *7-1/2"*	14.00
☐	Salad plate, *8-1/4"*	14.00
☐	Salt and pepper shaker, *3" high*	30.00
☐	Soup plate, *8-1/4" diameter*...............................	15.00
☐	Sugar and creamer, *full size*	75.00
☐	Sugar bowl, *individual size*	25.00
☐	Tea tile...	75.00
☐	Teapot	100.00
☐	Tumbler	30.00
☐	Vegetable bowl, *oval, open, 9-1/2" long*	40.00

MODERN PROFILE

☐	Bread and butter plate....................................	7.00
☐	Cup and saucer	20.00
☐	Dinner plate	14.00
☐	Fruit saucer	12.00
☐	Sugar, creamer, and coffeepot	100.00

MONTCLAIR

☐ Current pattern.

Modern Profile, *creamer*

MONTEREY

- ☐ Cup and saucer **25.00**
- ☐ Dinner plate **20.00**
- ☐ Sugar and creamer... **50.00**
- ☐ Teapot **35.00**

Monterey, *sugar bowl*

MONTICELLO

☐	Complete service for 12, *120 pieces, badly worn*	**700.00**
☐	Dinner plate	**15.00**
☐	Salad/dessert plate	**10.00**

Moonlight, *bread and butter plate*

MOONLIGHT

☐	Bread and butter plate, ...	**8.00**
☐	Cup and saucer	**18.00**
☐	Dinner plate	**14.00**
☐	Salad/dessert plate	**10.00**

MOONLIGHT MOOD

☐ Current pattern.

MOONSPUN

☐ Current pattern.

MORNING BLOSSOM

☐ Current pattern

MOUNT VERNON

This pattern is sometimes referred to as "poor man's Virginian, since it is so very similar yet not quite so opulent.

☐	Bread and butter plate.......................................	**18.00**
☐	Cup, *no saucer, small footed*	**25.00**
☐	Salad/dessert plate	**18.00**
☐	Sugar, creamer, teapot	**125.00**

MUSETTE

- ☐ Bread and butter plate... 10.00
- ☐ Cup and saucer 22.00
- ☐ Dinner plate 15.00
- ☐ Salad/dessert plate 12.00
- ☐ Vegetable bowl, *small oval* 25.00

MYSTIC

- ☐ Bread and butter plate... 8.00
- ☐ Cup and saucer 25.00
- ☐ Dinner plate 15.00
- ☐ Mustard pot with underplate 35.00
- ☐ Ramekin with underplate 15.00
- ☐ Salad/dessert plate 12.00

MYSTIQUE

- ☐ Cup and saucer 24.00
- ☐ Gravy boat... 45.00
- ☐ Platter, *small oval* 45.00
- ☐ Salad/dessert plate 12.00

NATOMA

- ☐ Cup and saucer 25.00
- ☐ Salad/dessert plate 10.00

NAUTILUS

- ☐ No recent listings.

NEWPORT

- ☐ No recent listings.

NOBLESSE

- ☐ Current pattern.

NOCTURNE

- ☐ No recent listings.

NORMAND

- ☐ No recent listings.

NYDIA

- ☐ Cream soup cup with underplate 20.00
- ☐ Cup and saucer 25.00
- ☐ Dinner plate 15.00

OAKLEAF BLUE

- ☐ No recent listings.

OAKLEAF GREEN

- ☐ Bread and butter plate... 10.00
- ☐ Dinner plate 15.00

OAKLEAF RED
☐ Dinner plate **15.00**

OLYMPIA GOLD
☐ Current pattern.

Orchard, *coffeepot*

ORCHARD
☐ Coffeepot **40.00**
☐ Creamer **25.00**
☐ Cup and saucer **25.00**
☐ Dinner plate **18.00**
☐ Relish tray, *9" oval* **15.00**
☐ Sugar bowl with lid.. **30.00**

ORLEANS
☐ Bread and butter plate..................................... **10.00**
☐ Cup and saucer **24.00**
☐ Dinner plate **15.00**
☐ Gravy boat.. **40.00**
☐ Salad/dessert plate **12.00**
☐ Salad serving bowl **50.00**
☐ Soup bowl **14.00**
☐ Vegetable bowl, *large oval* **30.00**

OSLO
☐ Bread and butter plate..................................... **9.00**
☐ Dinner plate **12.00**
☐ Salad/dessert plate **10.00**
☐ Saucer (no cup)... **4.00**

Orleans, *bread and butter plate*

PAGODA

☐ Bread and butter plate, *white*	8.00
☐ Cream soup cup with underplate, *white*	15.00
☐ Fruit saucer, *blue and white*	10.00
☐ Luncheon plate, *white*	10.00
☐ Salad/dessert plate, *white*	10.00

PALISADES

☐ No recent listings.

PASADENA

☐ No recent listings.

PAVLOVA

☐ Bread and butter plate	10.00
☐ Centerpiece or serving bowl, *12" long, footed, small chip on base*	30.00
☐ Cup and saucer	25.00
☐ Dinner plate	14.00
☐ Fruit saucer	10.00
☐ Salad/dessert plate	12.00
☐ Soup plate	12.00

PEACHTREE

☐ Bread and butter plate	10.00
☐ Cup and saucer	24.00
☐ Dinner plate	14.00
☐ Salad/dessert plate	12.00
☐ Salad serving bowl	45.00

Peking, *dinner plate*

PEKING

- [ ] Bread and butter plate **9.00**
- [ ] Cup and saucer, *two-handled* **10.00**
- [ ] Dinner plate **14.00**
- [ ] Salad/dessert plate **12.00**

Pine, *bread and butter plate*

PEMBROOK

☐ Cup and saucer 30.00
☐ Dinner plate 19.00

PINE

☐ Bread and butter plate..................................... 9.00
☐ Cup and saucer 25.00
☐ Dinner plate 15.00
☐ Gravy boat... 50.00
☐ Luncheon plate 8.00
☐ Platter, *small oval* 35.00
☐ Salad/dessert plate 12.00
☐ Soup plate... 14.00
☐ Teapot 50.00
☐ Vegetable bowl, *large oval* 35.00
☐ Vegetable bowl, *round, covered* 60.00

Pinehurst Blue, *dinner plate*

PINEHURST BLUE

☐ Bread and butter plate..................................... 12.00
☐ Cream soup cup with underplate 20.00
☐ Cup and saucer 27.00
☐ Dinner plate 15.00
☐ Luncheon plate 10.00
☐ Salad/dessert plate 14.00
☐ Vegetable bowl, *large oval* 40.00

PINEHURST RED

☐ Cup, no saucer 10.00

PLATINA

☐ No recent listings.

PLUM BLOSSOM
☐ Current pattern.

PLYMOUTH
☐	Bread and butter plate	**6.00**
☐	Cream soup cup with underplate	**8.00**
☐	Cup, no saucer	**10.00**
☐	Dinner plate	**12.00**
☐	Salad/dessert plate	**8.00**

Princess, *sugar bowl*

PRINCESS
☐	Bread and butter plate	**8.00**
☐	Cup and saucer	**22.00**
☐	Dinner plate	**14.00**
☐	Luncheon plate	**3.00**
☐	Platter, *medium oval*	**50.00**
☐	Platter, *small oval*	**30.00**
☐	Salad/dessert bowl	**12.00**
☐	Salad/dessert plate	**10.00**
☐	Sugar and creamer	**50.00**

PRINCETON
☐ No recent listings.

PRISCILLA
☐	Cup and saucer	**25.00**
☐	Dinner plate, *repaired*	**2.00**

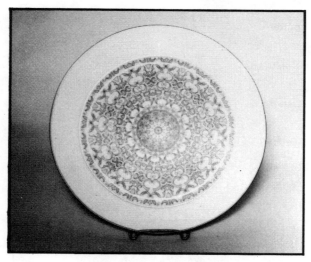

Projection, *dinner plate*

PROJECTION
☐ Bread and butter plate... 8.00
☐ Cup and saucer 20.00
☐ Dinner plate 12.00
☐ Salad/dessert plate 10.00
☐ Saucer, no cup 5.00

PROMISE
☐ Current pattern.

RADIANCE
☐ Current pattern.

RAPTURE
☐ Bread and butter plate.. 5.00
☐ Cup and saucer 15.00
☐ Dinner plate 12.00
☐ Salad/dessert plate 8.00

RENAISSANCE
☐ Cream soup cup with underplate 20.00
☐ Dinner plate 18.00
☐ Salad/dessert plate 12.00

REPERTOIRE
☐ Current pattern.

REVERE
☐ No recent listings.

REVERIE
☐ Current pattern.

RHAPSODY
☐ No recent listings.

RHODORA
☐ Current pattern.

RHYTHM
☐ Cup and saucer	20.00
☐ Dinner plate	12.00
☐ Luncheon plate	14.00

RIVOLI
☐ No recent listings.

Rock Garden, *bread and butter plate*

ROCK GARDEN
☐ Bread and butter plate	12.00
☐ Cream soup cup with underplate	20.00
☐ Cup and saucer	30.00
☐ Dinner plate	18.00
☐ Luncheon plate	15.00
☐ Salad/dessert plate	15.00

ROMANCE
☐ Bread and butter plate	10.00
☐ Cup and saucer	25.00

☐	Dinner plate	**16.00**
☐	Platter, *medium oval*	**50.00**
☐	Salad/dessert plate	**13.00**

RONDELLE

☐	Bread and butter plate	**9.00**
☐	Cup and saucer	**20.00**
☐	Dinner plate	**13.00**
☐	Salad/dessert plate	**10.00**

ROSEDALE

☐	Bread and butter plate	**10.00**
☐	Cup and saucer	**24.00**
☐	Fruit saucer	**12.00**
☐	Salad/dessert plate	**11.00**
☐	Soup bowl	**14.00**

ROSELYN

☐	Bread and butter plate	**8.00**
☐	Cup and saucer	**22.00**
☐	Dinner plate	**13.00**
☐	Salad/dessert plate	**10.00**
☐	Sugar and creamer	**50.00**

ROSEMONT

☐	Bread and butter plate	**10.00**
☐	Dinner plate	**14.00**
☐	Soup bowl	**12.00**

ROYAL

☐ No recent listings.

ROYAL OAK

☐ No recent listings.

RUTLEDGE

☐ Current pattern.

SARATOGA

☐ No recent listings.

SAVOY

☐ No recent listings.

SCULPTURE PLAIN

☐	Bread and butter plate	**8.00**
☐	Cup and saucer	**20.00**
☐	Dinner plate	**14.00**
☐	Salad/dessert plate	**10.00**

SHALIMAR

- ☐ Bread and butter plate... 8.00
- ☐ Cup and saucer 25.00
- ☐ Dinner plate 13.00
- ☐ Luncheon plate 7.00
- ☐ Salad/dessert plate 12.00
- ☐ Vegetable bowl, *large oval* 35.00

SHEFFIELD

- ☐ Cup and saucer 15.00
- ☐ Salad/dessert plate 8.00

SHENANDOAH

- ☐ No recent listings.

SHERATON

- ☐ No recent listings.

SHERATON IVORY

- ☐ No recent listings.

SNOW LILY

- ☐ Current pattern.

SOLITAIRE

- ☐ Current pattern.

SOMERSOLITAIRE

- ☐ Current pattern.

SOMERSET

- ☐ Dinner plate 20.00
- ☐ Luncheon plate 7.00
- ☐ Salad/dessert plate 11.00

SONATA

- ☐ No recent listings.

SONNET

- ☐ Bread and butter plate.. 12.00
- ☐ Cup and saucer 32.00
- ☐ Dinner plate 22.00
- ☐ Salad/dessert plate 13.00
- ☐ Sugar and creamer... 60.00

SOUTHERN GARDEN

- ☐ Cup and saucer 35.00
- ☐ Dinner plate 20.00

SPRINGDALE

- ☐ No recent listings.

SPRINGDALE *(NEW)*
☐ Current pattern.

SPRINGDALE *(OLD)*
☐ No recent listings.

SPRINGFIELD
☐ No recent listings.

SPRINGTIME
☐ Cream soup underplate 10.00
☐ Dinner plate 15.00
☐ Salad/dessert plate 12.00

STANDARD PLAIN
☐ Bread and butter plate.................................... 5.00
☐ Cup and saucer 15.00
☐ Dinner plate 10.00
☐ Luncheon plate 6.00
☐ Salad/dessert plate 8.00

STANFORD
☐ Bread and butter plate.................................... 12.00
☐ Cup and saucer 30.00
☐ Dinner plate 18.00
☐ Salad/dessert plate 15.00
☐ Teapot 60.00
☐ Vegetable bowl, *large oval* 40.00

STARFIRE
☐ Current pattern.

STARLIGHT
☐ Bread and butter plate, *worn* 2.00
☐ Cup and saucer 24.00
☐ Dinner plate 13.00
☐ Salad/dessert plate 10.00
☐ Teapot 35.00

STRADIVARIUS
☐ After dinner cup and saucer 12.00

STRATFORD
☐ No recent listings.

SUMMER BREEZE
☐ Bread and butter plate.................................... 9.00
☐ Cup and saucer 23.00
☐ Dinner plate 12.00
☐ Salad/dessert plate 10.00
☐ Salad serving bowl.. 35.00

SYMPHONY
- ☐ Cup and saucer 23.00
- ☐ Dinner plate 14.00
- ☐ Luncheon plate 8.00
- ☐ Salad/dessert plate 10.00

TABLEAU
- ☐ No recent listings.

TEMPLE PLAIN
- ☐ Bread and butter plate.. 7.00
- ☐ Cup and saucer 18.00
- ☐ Dinner plate 14.00
- ☐ Gravy boat.. 30.00
- ☐ Salad/dessert plate 8.00
- ☐ Serving bowl, *round, 9" diameter* 30.00
- ☐ Sugar and creamer... 50.00

TEMPO
- ☐ Bread and butter plate.. 10.00
- ☐ Cup and saucer 30.00
- ☐ Dinner plate 18.00
- ☐ Platter, *large oval* 60.00
- ☐ Platter, *small oval* 50.00
- ☐ Salad/dessert plate 13.00
- ☐ Vegetable bowl, *large oval* 40.00

TERESA
- ☐ No recent listings.

TERRACE
- ☐ Luncheon plate, *badly scratched* 3.00
- ☐ Salad/dessert plate 7.00

THREE-STEP
- ☐ No recent listings.

TRANSITIONAL
- ☐ Bread and butter plate.. 8.00
- ☐ Cup and saucer 24.00
- ☐ Dinner plate 14.00
- ☐ Salad/dessert plate 10.00
- ☐ Vegetable bowl, *round*.. 35.00

TRELLIS
- ☐ Gravy boat.. 40.00
- ☐ Soup plate.. 10.00
- ☐ Vegetable, *large oval* 30.00
- ☐ Vegetable, *round, covered* 50.00

TRELLIS IVORY
- ☐ Bread and butter plate.. 6.00
- ☐ Soup plate.. 8.00

TREMONT, THE

- ☐ After dinner cup and saucer 16.00
- ☐ Bread and butter plate.. 10.00
- ☐ Cup and saucer 18.00
- ☐ Dinner plate 15.00
- ☐ Luncheon plate 10.00
- ☐ Salad/dessert plate 10.00

TRENT

- ☐ Bouillon cup and saucer 15.00
- ☐ Bread and butter plate.. 10.00
- ☐ Dinner plate 20.00
- ☐ Luncheon plate 10.00
- ☐ Salad/dessert plate 12.00
- ☐ Sugar and creamer... 60.00
- ☐ Vegetable bowl, *large oval* 35.00
- ☐ Vegetable bowl, *small oval* 30.00

TRIANON

- ☐ No recent listings.

TRIO

- ☐ Bread and butter plate.. 9.00
- ☐ Cup and saucer 22.00
- ☐ Dinner plate 13.00
- ☐ Gravy boat.. 40.00
- ☐ Luncheon plate 8.00
- ☐ Salad/dessert plate 10.00

TRIUMPH

- ☐ No recent listings.

TROY

- ☐ No recent listings.

TUDOR

- ☐ Current pattern.

TUSCANY

- ☐ Current pattern.

TUXEDO

Current—the following are all out-of-production items.

- ☐ Bouillon cup, no saucer..................................... 10.00
- ☐ Coffeepot, *individual size* 30.00
- ☐ Compote, *footed, 9" diameter* 35.00
- ☐ Egg cup, *large size* 15.00
- ☐ Coffeepot, *individual size* 30.00
- ☐ Compote, *footed, 9" diameter* 35.00
- ☐ Egg cup, *large size*.. 15.00
- ☐ Sugar and creamer, *individual size* 25.00
- ☐ Teapot, *individual size*..................................... 30.00

VALERA

☐	Bread and butter plate	**10.00**
☐	Cup and saucer	**25.00**
☐	Dinner plate	**14.00**
☐	Gravy boat	**50.00**
☐	Platter, medium oval	**50.00**
☐	Cup and saucer	**25.00**
☐	Dinner plate	**14.00**
☐	Gravy boat	**50.00**
☐	Platter, *medium oval*	**50.00**
☐	Salad/dessert plate	**12.00**
☐	Soup bowl	**14.00**

VASSAR

☐ No recent listings.

VENDOME

☐ No recent listings.

VENTURE

☐ Current pattern.

VERNON

☐ No recent listings.

VICTORIA

☐	After dinner cup, no saucer	**8.00**
☐	Cup and saucer	**28.00**
☐	Dinner plate	**15.00**
☐	Platter, *large oval*	**45.00**

Virginian, *bread and butter plate*

VILLA
☐ No recent listings.

VIRGINIAN
☐ After dinner cup and saucer	**35.00**
☐ Bread and butter plate	**20.00**
☐ Coffeepot	**100.00**
☐ Compote, *9" high, scalloped rim*	**125.00**
☐ Dinner plate	**40.00**
☐ Tea caddy	**100.00**
☐ Teapot	**100.00**

WASHINGTON
☐ Bread and butter plate	**10.00**
☐ Dinner plate	**17.00**
☐ Salad/dessert plate	**13.00**

WASHINGTON/WAKEFIELD
Washington/Wakefield is a reproduction of the English salt-glazed stoneware that was found during the excavation of George Washington's boyhood home at Wakefield, Westmoreland County, Virginia. This homestead burned to the ground on Christmas Day, 1780. Excavation of the site began in 1925. Shards of pottery that were found there were taken to the Lenox Company to be reproduced, and the result was the Washington/Wakefield pattern. Advertising literature of the day indicates that a portion of each sale of this pattern was donated by Lenox to help restore the Wakefield home. Sharpness of the pattern can vary greatly, which can create problems when trying to complete a set.

Washington / Wakefield, *sugar, creamer and teapot*

☐ Bowl, cereal, *7-3/8"*	**13.00**
☐ Bowl, dessert, *6-1/4"*	**13.00**
☐ Bowl, soup, *9-1/8"*	**14.00**
☐ Bowl, soup, *8-1/4"*	**13.00**
☐ Bowl, vegetable, *oval, covered*	**125.00**
☐ Bowl, vegetable, *oval, open*	**45.00**
☐ Coffeepot	**75.00**

- ☐ Cup and saucer, *after dinner* **20.00**
- ☐ Cup and saucer, *full size* **30.00**
- ☐ Cup and saucer, *two-handled, bouillon* **15.00**
- ☐ Cup and saucer, *two-handled, cream soup* **20.00**
- ☐ Plate, dessert, 7-1/4" **14.00**
- ☐ Plate, dinner, 10-1/4" **22.00**
- ☐ Plate, luncheon, 9". **10.00**
- ☐ Plate, salad, 8-1/4" **12.00**
- ☐ Plate, salad, *square, 8-1/4"* **15.00**
- ☐ Plate, *square, two-handled (for cookies)* **50.00**
- ☐ Platter, *14" oval* **45.00**
- ☐ Platter, *large round* **100.00**
- ☐ Platter, *small round* **50.00**
- ☐ Sauce boat, attached underplate **65.00**
- ☐ Sugar and creamer, *small, open* **75.00**
- ☐ Teapot **75.00**

WEATHERLY
- ☐ Current pattern.

WESTBURY
- ☐ No recent listings.

WESTCHESTER (M-139)
Current pattern—the items listed below are out-of-production.

- ☐ Bouillon cup and saucer **20.00**
- ☐ Compote, *5" diameter* **25.00**
- ☐ Fruit bowl, *doubled handled, 9" without handles* **60.00**
- ☐ Mustard pot with lid and underplate **40.00**
- ☐ Relish tray, *9" x 6" oval* **30.00**
- ☐ Teapot, *individual size* **30.00**

Westchester, *cup and saucer*

WESTCHESTER (S40C)

- ☐ Bread and butter plate 10.00
- ☐ Cup and saucer 20.00
- ☐ Dinner plate 15.00

WESTFIELD

- ☐ Bread and butter plate 8.00
- ☐ Cream soup cup with underplate 15.00
- ☐ Cup and saucer 22.00
- ☐ Dinner plate 14.00
- ☐ Salad/dessert plate 10.00

WESTPORT

- ☐ Bread and butter plate 18.00
- ☐ Coffeepot 115.00
- ☐ Cup and saucer 40.00
- ☐ Dinner plate 30.00
- ☐ Luncheon plate 18.00
- ☐ Salad/dessert plate 20.00
- ☐ Teapot 115.00

WEST WIND

- ☐ Bread and butter plate 8.00
- ☐ Cup and saucer, cream soup 20.00
- ☐ Cup and saucer, regular 24.00
- ☐ Dinner plate 15.00
- ☐ Gravy boat 40.00
- ☐ Platter, *small oval* 30.00
- ☐ Salad/dessert plate 10.00
- ☐ Sugar and creamer 45.00
- ☐ Vegetable bowl, *small oval* 30.00

WHEAT

- ☐ Current pattern.

WINDSONG

- ☐ Current pattern.

WINDSOR

- ☐ Bread and butter plate 12.00
- ☐ Cup and saucer 29.00
- ☐ Dinner plate 18.00
- ☐ Platter, *large oval* 50.00
- ☐ Salad/dessert plate 14.00
- ☐ Soup plate 15.00
- ☐ Sugar and creamer 60.00
- ☐ Vegetable bowl, *large oval* 40.00
- ☐ Vegetable bowl, *round, covered* 75.00

WYNDCREST

- ☐ Bread and butter plate 9.00
- ☐ Cream soup cup and underplate 16.00

- ☐ Cup and saucer 20.00
- ☐ Dinner plate 14.00
- ☐ Gravy boat.. 40.00
- ☐ Platter, *large oval*... 45.00
- ☐ Salad/dessert plate 10.00
- ☐ Soup bowl.. 12.00
- ☐ Vegetable bowl, *small oval* 30.00

A-319
- ☐ Service plate... 18.00

A-375
- ☐ Service plate... 25.00

A-386FQ
- ☐ Service plate... 30.00

A-386 FQ, *service plate*

A-393G
- ☐ Large oval platter 100.00

C-318
- ☐ Service plate... 20.00

C-416
- ☐ Service plate... 15.00

D-366X11-1
- ☐ Service plate... 30.00

E-88

☐ Compote 40.00

F-40

☐ Dinner plate 15.00
☐ Cup and saucer 25.00

F-308B

☐ Dinner plate 15.00

F-372

☐ Bread and butter plate................................. 5.00
☐ Cereal bowl... 8.00
☐ Cup and saucer 14.00
☐ Salad/dessert plate 6.00
☐ Sugar and creamer, *individual size* 25.00
☐ Teapot, *individual size*.............................. 25.00

G-31

☐ Luncheon plate 20.00

G-44B

☐ Service plate.. 95.00

H-30B

☐ Dinner plate 18.00
☐ Soup plate.. 12.00

J-34

☐ Bread and butter plate................................. 7.00
☐ Coffeepot 30.00
☐ Cup and saucer 15.00
☐ Dinner plate 12.00
☐ Fruit saucer 10.00
☐ Gravy boat, separate underplate 30.00
☐ Platter, *large oval*.................................. 50.00
☐ Platter, *medium oval* 40.00
☐ Platter, *small oval* 30.00
☐ Platter, *round* 30.00
☐ Salad/dessert plate 8.00
☐ Soup bowl 12.00
☐ Soup plate.. 10.00
☐ Sugar and creamer..................................... 50.00
☐ Teapot 30.00
☐ Tray, *relish, 6" x 9" oval*........................... 15.00
☐ Vegetable bowl, *oval, open* 20.00
☐ Vegetable bowl, *round, covered* 50.00

J-319

☐ Salad plate 9.00

J-332

☐ Luncheon plate 10.00

J-417A

☐ Dinner plate **16.00**

K-1

☐ Creamer **30.00**

K-344B

☐ Bread and butter plate....................................... **12.00**
☐ Cup and saucer **30.00**

K-344B, *cup and saucer*

☐ Dinner plate **20.00**
☐ Fruit saucer **14.00**
☐ Salad/dessert plate **15.00**
☐ Soup plate.. **15.00**

M-16

☐ Cup **10.00**

M-391

☐ Cup and saucer **30.00**

M-391-X-15-1

☐ Service plate... **14.00**

O-46F

☐ Dinner plate **14.00**
☐ Sugar and creamer.. **60.00**
☐ Teapot **50.00**

O-46G

☐ Sugar and creamer... **60.00**
☐ Teapot **45.00**

P-72

☐ Demitasse cup and saucer **28.00**

P-73

☐ Service plate... **35.00**

P-73, *service plate*

P-380

☐ Service plate **30.00**

P-525W

☐ Bread and butter plate...................................... **8.00**

R-407-247

☐ Salad/dessert plate **10.00**

S-32

☐ Salad/dessert plate **18.00**

S-62

☐ Dessert plate, *7-1/2"* **10.00**
☐ Salad plate, *8-1/4"* **12.00**
☐ Sugar and creamer, *small, open*............................ **40.00**

T-372-X-196

☐ Luncheon plate **13.00**

S-62, *sugar and creamer*

W-5C
- [ ] Service plate **15.00**

W-335R
- [ ] Dinner plate **12.00**

X-54
- [ ] Service plate **15.00**

X-95
- [ ] Service plate **20.00**

Y-69G
- [ ] Service plate **20.00**

Z-32A
- [ ] Service plate **25.00**

Z-33
- [ ] Service plate **35.00**

Z-81-X-9-1
- [ ] Service plate **35.00**

#70 *(BLUE DOT)*
- [ ] Creamer **30.00**
- [ ] Muffin dish, *covered* **18.00**
- [ ] Salt dip **12.00**
- [ ] Teapot, *infuser type* **70.00**

#70, blue dot creamer

#82

Pattern #82 is perhaps the most prevalent of the early hand-painted patterns. It is found with C.A.C. marks as well as the first Lenox wreath mark, and is frequently seen with a store name as well. For whatever reason, it is often the case that the saucers are marked but not the cups. This is particularly true of those items with C.A.C. marks.

There is a large pink rose with green leaves on the front of the cups, a small rosebud on the back, and occasionally an additional rosebud on the inside of the cups. It is possible that the extra rosebud was used to hide flaws, but their rather precise placement leads us to believe that this is not the case. Earlier pieces are much more likely to have the extra rosebud. Saucers have one large rose and two rosebuds, and other flat pieces are similarly decorated.

Variations occur in the color of the artwork as well as in the placement. Although the roses are a fairly standardized shade of pink, the green leaves vary considerably from one piece to the next. Rosebuds can face left or right, apparently depending on the whim of the artist. These variations should not be considered flaws, and one should not go out of one's way to obtain pieces that match exactly.

All of the pieces of this pattern that we have seen to date have been decorated with gold trim on handles and rims.

We have never seen any dinner plates, and it would appear that the pattern was used mainly on luncheon and tea sets.

It should be noted that the roses on this pattern are quite similar to those done by Morley on vases and other items, and perhaps were indeed done by him when he was not working on more important pieces. According to the recollections of an elderly gentlemen who once worked at Lenox, this was the case. In any event, many collectors and dealers have taken to calling this pattern "Morley Rose", and the decision to place this pattern in the dinnerware section was made with a great deal of hesitation.

☐ Bouillon cup and saucer, item #175, *C.A.C. transition mark* **35.00**
☐ Chocolate cup, *double handled, transition mark* **60.00**
☐ Coffeepot, *transition mark* **125.00**
☐ Cup and saucer, item #309, *transition mark on saucers, cups un-marked* **45.00**
☐ Cup and saucer, item #309, *Lenox wreath mark, both items marked* . .   **35.00**
☐ Salad/dessert plate, *Lenox green wreath mark* **25.00**
☐ Sugar and creamer, items #372 and 373, *transition mark* **125.00**

#82, cup and saucer, transition mark

#83
Pattern #83 has small hand-painted roses and forget-me-nots and is always seen with early marks, both C.A.C. and Lenox.

☐ Salt and pepper shaker **30.00**

#86
Pattern #86 is perhaps most familiar as the pattern that was used on many of the Lenox liners for silver holders. It was also available in dinnerware, however, and was also used on a variety of other useful and/or decorative items.

☐ Bread and butter plate. **7.00**
☐ Cup and saucer, *demitasse* **15.00**
☐ Cup and saucer, *full size* **18.00**
☐ Dinner plate **15.00**
☐ Nut dish, *footed, 3" diameter* **18.00**
☐ Platter, *oval, 14" diameter*. **30.00**
☐ Platter, *round, 12"* **35.00**
☐ Salad plate **7.00**
☐ Sugar and creamer, *breakfast size*. **30.00**
☐ Teapot **50.00**

#86-1/2

Pattern #86-1/2 is a fairly common dinnerware pattern, and was also used extensively on giftware items and on liners for silver holders.

☐ Bread and butter plate... **5.00**
☐ Candlesticks, *9" tall, pair* **35.00**
☐ Compote, *miniature*.. **18.00**
☐ Dinner plate **15.00**
☐ Fruit bowl, *two-handled, 9" diameter not including handles* **40.00**

#82-1/2, sugar bowl and lid

☐ Sugar bowl and lid **25.00**
☐ Teapot **40.00**
☐ Tete-a-tete set.. **18.00**

LENOX AND METAL ITEMS

This section concerns itself with a category of Lenox unfamiliar to many collectors—those items which have been combined in various ways with an assortment of metals. These items share some or all of the following characteristics:

(1) They require special care. (This is especially true of those items combined with silver.)

(2) The Lenox collector faces stiff competition from those in other fields (e.g., silver or stein collectors.)

(3) Many of the items were finished away from the Lenox factory, and were, therefore, not necessarily subjected to the same rigorous standards as those items completed at the factory.

(4) Many of these items are pre-World War I, and they possibly represent the efforts of the then-young company to stay afloat until it had made a name for itself. It is not all that difficult to imagine Walter Lenox suppressing a yawn while listening to a silver company representative give specifications for liners.

(5) For a long time they were considered to be "illegitimate" Lenox, somehow unworthy of more than a passing glance. This has changed dramatically in the past year or two with the emergence of a whole new group of collectors for whom Lenox has no interest unless it is wrapped in silver.

(6) They are still priced far below comparable current retail prices. If a sterling silver spoon costs around $40 on today's market, surely a sterling silver demitasse cup and saucer with Lenox liner has to be a bargain at $25 or $30.

This section is divided as follows: (1) Lenox liners for sterling holders; (2) silver overlay on Lenox items; and (3) miscellaneous items.

LENOX LINERS FOR SILVER HOLDERS

Although examples of European china liners or those by other American manufacturers do turn up now and then, the overwhelming majority of these items seen today were made by Lenox. Liners were among the earliest items made at Lenox: A ramekin appears as item #151 in C.A.C. catalogues, and a demitasse liner is item #290.

Gorham and/or Mauser were probably the first silver companies to order Lenox liners for their sterling holders, with other silver manufacturers soon following suit until most major United States silver companies were producing sets. To date, no examples of foreign silver holders with Lenox liners have been seen. (The reverse is not true, however—one does see American holders with European liners.)

As a rule, the silver companies initiated the order by specifying a certain size and shape of liner, although in rare cases this procedure might have been reversed, with Lenox ordering a silver holder to fit a particular liner. The retailing of the sets was done by the silver company through jewelry stores.

These items were popular wedding gifts for many years, and usually came in velvet or satin-lined presentation cases. Few of the cases have survived to the present day, perhaps due to inexpensive construction. Most of the cases had spots for either six or eight items, and the so-called sets of twelve, so popular with today's collector, were the exception at the time they were manufactured. Gorham was the only silver company that made sets of twelve on a regular basis.

Around the time of World War II, production of liners by Lenox had just about come to an end, due to wartime production problems at Lenox and the silver companies, and also perhaps to changing life styles. The Lenox Company did make an attempt to have the silver manufacturers decide on a standard shape and size for liners, but the silver companies each wanted their own model to be the standard one. Production of liners on a special order basis must have continued for at least awhile after the war, however, since gold mark samples are seen.

The numbering system for Lenox liners seems to have been a retroactive one for the most part. For example, although bouillon liners are frequently seen with C.A.C. marks, no shape number appears on them until much later, when they were assigned #1201. Many of the items in the 1200 series of Lenox numbers were meant to be in silver holders, and it would appear that this was an attempt on the part of Lenox to make some rhyme and reason out of the rather chaotic liner situation.

Lenox collectors have ignored this aspect of Lenox for some reason, although no collection should be considered complete without a sample. From the collector's point of view, the most desirable pieces are those that have C.A.C. hand-decorated liners. These are generally found in Gorham or Mauser holders, although other marks are occasionally seen. The early

Gorham and Mauser ones are quite charming and original in that the decoration on the liner quite often carries out the design on the silver. Later versions used a more or less standard pattern on the liner regardless of what the holder looked like.

Lenox collectors should bear in mind that this category is one where they will have to battle it out with another group of collectors. Since the manufacturing of these items covered a span of some fifty years, many of this country's most collectible silver patterns are included in this period. Tiffany "Chrysanthemum", Kirk "Repousse", Unger Brothers patterns in Art Nouveau designs, and others are highly prized by silver collectors. We suggest that the would-be collector of sterling and Lenox items concentrate on the quality of the liner first and the silver second, since this will tend to eliminate a lot of the competition.

There are also many unmarked holders available, and the obvious reason for this (that the manufacturer was not especially proud of the product) appears to be wrong at least part of the time. Many of the unmarked holders are of a good quality silver, and are obviously the work of a fine company. So long as the word "sterling" appears on them, we see no particular reason to ignore them simply because the maker's mark is missing.

Roughly 99 percent of the liners made by Lenox are to be found in sterling holders, but we do occasionally see them in silver-plated holders, and also in brass or other metals. Judging from the Lenox marks, those items in silver-plated holders came much later and are probably not of much interest to collectors. It is possible they were made during World War II when precious metals were hard to obtain. Some of the shapes are interesting, but other than this there is little to recommend them. They are invariably priced close to the sterling models, and for the price difference we suggest buying the sterling ones.

The overwhelming majority of liners are in pattern #86 (a narrow gold band at the top, with a pencil line of gold beneath it both inside and out.) Others are considerably more elaborate, with hand-painted flowers, ribbons, raised gold paste work, cobalt and gold combinations, blue-dot enamel work, etc. The liners were also available in some dinnerware patterns such as Tuxedo, Lowell, Mandarin, and others. As a rule, the nicer liners were made for the better holders, although exceptions have been seen.

Altogether, at least a couple of hundred different decorations have been noted, some of which are worthy of special mention. The lovely liners for Tiffany "Chrysanthemum" holders are marked as pattern #E-45, and are done in two different shades of raised gold paste. The Mauser company specialized in the use of liners with a bright, apple-green exterior with garlands of flowers on the inside. This was known as pattern #338, although this number usually does not appear on the pieces. The same garlands of flowers, without the colored exterior, were used on a variety of liners for other companies, but we have no pattern numbers for most of these variations.

Blue-dot pattern #70 occurs on liners, and #69-B (blue-dot flowers with hand-painted, tiny gold leaves and borders) also shows up now and then. Many variations on these basic themes have been noted, but most are not numbered. Other patterns used combinations of blue-dot work with hand-painted floral designs.

Many of the designs used on liners were not used on any other Lenox items, making it difficult (if not impossible) to match them with a set of dinnerware. One exception to this would be the blue-dot liners, particularly #70, which is also found on dinnerware. For those patterns which did not have matching dinnerware, we suggest using them with one of the current Lenox gold-banded patterns.

One of the problems facing the collector is deciding if the liner and holder have been "married"—an empty holder filled with any liner that happens to fit. The following hints should help.

I. Liners marked "Made for Tiffany and Co." **always** belong in a Tiffany holder (although the reverse is not necessarily true.

2. Some silver companies, particularly Gorham, helpfully date-marked their items. Liners and holders should, therefore, match somewhat in their markings. A Gorham holder date-marked for 1926 but filled with a C.A.C. liner is probably a marriage, although a Gorham holder date-marked for 1908 and with a C.A.C. liner probably is not (items frequently sat on warehouse shelves waiting for mates.)

3. Other discrepancies can sometimes be seen with silver and Lenox marks, such as a particular silver company going out of business in 1910, yet the liner is marked "Made in U.S.A."

4. Liners which do not fit well are not necessarily married. China can shrink **approximately** 15 percent in the firing process, and this accounts for many of the misfits. In addition, the silver holders made of a thin gauge of silver can easily be bent out of shape ever so slightly, preventing the liner from fitting properly. Not all liners have to go to the bottom to be considered "right". Sometimes the silver companies used a liner from one type of holder to go in a different one, rather than special ordering a new liner from Lenox, and they are not always good fits.

5. Both liners and holders followed the fashions of the day, and liner and holder should be in keeping with each other.

For the most part, the easy days of collecting these items are gone, and collectors should be prepared to pay handsomely for prime specimens. They are still an excellent investment in our opinion, since so many liners get broken and the then-empty holders melted for scrap value.

See Table XII at the end of this section for a listing of silver company marks.

BUTTER DISHES

Small, round dishes originally meant to hold butter show up now and then, but never seem to be of exceptionally good quality. They are about 1 to 1-1/2" high, and about 4" in diameter. Some have metal holders and others have

Butter dishes

metal lids. They occasionally have small tab handles, either in the china or in the silver. We have only three listings for these dishes, all of which are shown together.

- ☐ International holder, shape #1364, pattern #86, *openwork design, Lenox wreath mark liner* **30.00**
- ☐ Watson holder #4487, shape #1364, pattern #86, *openwork design, Lenox wreath mark liner* **30.00**
- ☐ Silver lid, shape #1366, pattern #86, *mark rubbed, possibly International or Woodside, Lenox base, Lenox wreath mark, gold worn on handles* **30.00**

DEMITASSE, CHOCOLATE, AND OTHER CUPS

Demitasses, consisting of a Lenox liner, a silver holder with handle, and (usually, but not always) a silver saucer, are undoubtedly the most common of the silver and Lenox items. All of the major silver companies made them, and many lesser manufacturers produced them as well. Unlike bouillon liners, which came in only a few shapes and sizes, demis were put out in a large array, the most common of which were #1203 and #1208, both bell-shaped. There were at least ten or fifteen other bell-shaped liners, four or five barrel shaped, hexagons and octagons, and in all must have been available in at least a hundred different sizes and shapes.

Decorations on demitasse liners vary from the simple pattern #86 all the way to elaborate hand-painted specimens, and the backstamps range from the earliest C.A.C. marks right up to gold-mark samples. As it is with all of the items in the liner category, the emphasis is on early C.A.C. marks.

It is interesting to observe that although the silver makers obviously expended a great deal of time and effort in designing unique holders, in many cases they would use the same saucer with all or most of their demis. In other instances, however, the saucers show the same degree of workmanship as the holders. In rare cases the demitasse cups came without saucers.

Chocolate cups are exceedingly rare, and only a few shapes and sizes have been noted. Full-size coffee or teacups are either very rare or possibly non-existent, but a 3/4 size, somewhere between a demi and a full, was made. The punch cup shown is of a size and shape to be used as a teacup if desired.

Demitasse can vary in silver weight from a little over a troy ounce for holder and saucer all the way to five troy ounces. Three ounces would be considered a healthy weight. Those with shape #1203 liners are somewhat more popular than those with the #1208 liners, due to the larger size of the #1203.

The most expensive demitasse we have seen was a single one at an antiques show in Washington, D. C. It was priced at $125, and we unfortunately could not stay around long enough to see if it actually sold at that price. The average demi, however, will be priced somewhere around the scrap value of the silver plus an appropriate fee for the liner.

Note: An original box adds $5 to $25 to price depending on its condition.

Chocolate cup, *Wallace holder*

CHOCOLATE AND OTHER CUPS

☐ Chocolate cup, Wallace holder, *Lenox liner in pattern #86* **25.00**
☐ Chocolate cup, liner only, pattern *#338, C.A.C. mark* **60.00**
☐ Punch cup, Mauser, *3-1/2 troy ounces, ornate floral and openwork design, fancy gargoyle type handle, never had saucer, pattern #338 liner in Lenox wreath mark, set of six, owner has refused offer of $75 each.*

Punch cup, *Mauser holder*

DEMITASSE CUPS

☐ Alvin holder and saucer, *total weight 1-1/2 troy ounces, Lenox liner in pattern #86* **15.00**

☐ Alvin holder and saucer, *total weight 1-1/2 troy ounces, open work on silver, Lenox liner in pattern #86*............................... **17.00**

☐ Bailey, Banks, and Biddle holder and saucer, *no maker's mark, solid plain silver with rolled rims, hollow handle, 2-1/2 troy ounces, Lenox liners in pattern #86, set of six* **180.00**

☐ Barbour Silver Company holder and saucer, *filigree openwork design, rolled rims, total weight 2-1/2 troy ounces, Lenox liner shape*

Demitasse cup, *Charter Company holder*

#1208, rainbow set with each liner a different color (purple, pink, yellow, brown, sky blue, and tan) all with narrow gold band at rim, set of six **200.00**

☐ Charter Company holder and saucer, *weighing over 4 troy ounces, hollow handle, ornate with raised work and applied bands, Charter #SP60, possibly a special order. Lenox liner shape #1203 in pattern #P66, embossed gold band with filigree type garlands underneath, set of six* **300.00**

☐ Dominick & Haff holder and saucer, *3 troy ounces, hollow handles in an inverted "S" pattern, ornate design with raised roses, Lenox #1203 liners in pattern #86, set of 12* **400.00**

☐ Dominick & Haff holder and saucer, *plain design with hollow handle, rolled rim, 3 troy ounces, Lenox liners in shape #1203, pattern #86, set of six* **200.00**

☐ Dominick & Haff holder and saucer, *geometric openwork design, hollow handle, 2-1/2 troy ounces, Lenox liners shape #86, set of eight* **200.00**

☐ Durgin holder and saucer, *2 troy ounces, openwork design, Lenox liner #1208, pattern #86* **20.00**

Demitasse cup, *Dominick & Haff, plain design*

☐ Durgin holder and saucer, *2 troy ounces, hammered finish to silver, strap handle, Lenox #1208 liner, pattern #86, set of six* **150.00**

☐ Gorham holder, Gorham #A1224 on holder, also marked for Shreve, Crump and Low, *total weight of 2 troy ounces deceiving because so much of holder is left open, actually a good gauge of silver, Lenox liner shape number and pattern number unknown, small, hand-painted garlands of roses with gold trim, transition mark* **50.00**

Demitasse cup, *Gorham holder*

Note: This same holder has been seen with a variety of lovely liners, including blue dot designs, and all have been C.A.C. marks. This holder has turned up on occasion with china saucers as is also the case with many of the early Gorham demis.

☐ Gorham holder and saucer, *2 troy ounces, openwork design with strap handle, Lenox #1208 liner, pattern #86, set of 12 in original case*   **300.00**

Demitasse cup, *Gorham holder, openwork design*

☐ Gorham holder and saucer, *solid design with hollow handles, 2-1/2 troy ounces, Lenox #1203 liners, pattern #86, set of 12* **300.00**

☐ Gorham holder and saucer, *openwork design, strap handles, weight 2-1/2 troy ounces, pink Lenox liners in shape #1208, set of six* **180.00**

☐ Hickok-Matthews holder and saucer, *3 troy ounces, hollow inverted "S" handles, raised floral design with piercing near rim, Lenox #1203 liners, pattern J33 (Tuxedo), set of 12* **350.00**

☐ Hickok-Matthews holder and saucer, *2-1/2 troy ounces, hollow handles, plain design, Lenox #1203 liners, pattern #86, set of six* **150.00**

☐ International holder and saucer, *2 troy ounces, openwork design with hollow handles, Lenox #1208 liner, pattern #86, set of 12* **250.00**

☐ International holders, *4 troy ounces, very similar to the Charter ones shown, Lenox liners shape #1203, pattern J30 (etched gold design), set of 12, one liner missing* **350.00**

☐ Kirk holder and saucer, *"Repousse" pattern, silver weight unknown, Lenox liners #1203, pattern #86, 12 holders and saucers, 10 liners* . . .   **750.00**

☐ Kirk holder and saucer, *hollow handles, silver weight unknown, plain design, Lenox #1203 liners, pattern #86, set of eight* **320.00**

☐ Lunt holder and saucer, *2 troy ounces, hammered effect, strap handles, Lenox #1208 liners in pattern #86B, set of 12* **200.00**

☐ Mauser holder, no saucer, *stock #5711, openwork, hollow handle very ornate, beading on top and bottom, Lenox liner shape number unknown, pattern #338 (green exterior with garlands of flowers on the inside, gold trim), transition mark* **75.00**

Demitasse cup, *Mauser holder*

Note: This demi never had a saucer. Also, although the silver weight is under 2 troy ounces, this type of demi is considered highly desirable.

☐ Redlich & Co. holder and saucer, 5 troy ounces, exceptional silver work, special order for Bailey, Banks and Biddle, item #6661 (not clear whether this is Redlich's number or BB&B's), applied ornate rim, ornate hollow handle with roses and engraving, main body has lots of hand engraving and raised roses. Saucers are dated 1913 on bottom, saucer and holder both monogrammed "HMS CCC" with crown above. Probably a one-of-a-kind set. The liners are #1203, pattern E81E, cobalt exterior, etched gold rims, natural Lenox interiors. Set of six, owner has refused offer of $600.

☐ Reed & Barton holder and saucer, 2-1/2 ounces, openwork design, hollow handle, Lenox #1208 liner with pattern #86, set of eight **160.00**

☐ Reed & Barton holder and saucer, 2-1/2 ounces, plain silver with rolled rims, strap handle, Lenox #1203 liner with pattern P-1 (Mandarin), pair **75.00**

☐ Rogers holder and saucer, 2-1/2 troy ounces, openwork design with hollow handles, Lenox #1208 liner with pattern #86 . . . .   **20.00**

☐ Schofield holder and saucer, 3-1/2 troy ounces, plain design with hollow handles, Lenox #1208 liner with pattern #86 . . . .   **25.00**

☐ Tiffany holder and saucer, Chrysanthemum pattern, weight unknown but not exceptionally heavy, original liners with gold paste flowers, set of six **450.00**

Note: These also came with gold plating over the silver, and this type commands a much higher price.

☐ Tiffany holder and saucer, in Chrysanthemum pattern, replacement liners with pattern #86 trim, set of six **300.00**

☐ Tiffany holder and saucer, ornate pattern with a 1920's look to it, 4 troy ounces, Lenox liner shaped like egg cup in pattern #E88 . . . .   **60.00**

Demitasse cup, *Redlich & Co. holder*

☐ Towel holder and saucer, *openwork holder with hollow handle, Lenox #1208 liner with pattern #86B, set of six* **150.00**

☐ Unger Brothers holder only (saucers missing), *Art Nouveau flowers, Lenox #1208 liners in pattern #86, set of six* **180.00**

☐ Wallace holder and saucer, *openwork design with strap handles, Lenox #1203 liners in pattern #86B, set of 12 in original box* **300.00**

☐ Whiting holder and saucer, *plain with strap handles, Lenox #1208 liners in pattern #86, set of six* **150.00**

JARS

A nice assortment of jars and pots, usually covered, is available, although the quality of the silver is in many cases not particularly overwhelming. Note that some items have been included here which are not liners per se, but rather bases with silver tops.

☐ Honey pot, Lenox shape #894, pattern #86, *shaped like beehive with applied bees decorated in gold, silver marker's mark unreadable, bee finial, perfect* **75.00**

☐ Honey pot, *same as above but with a few minor flecks on wings of china bees.* **65.00**

☐ Honey pot, *same as above but lid has pinecone shaped finial instead of bee.* **65.00**

☐ Jam jar, *Lenox wreath mark, hand-painted strawberries, no shape or pattern number, Watson openwork holder with handle and silver lid* . **95.00**

☐ Jam jar, *Lenox wreath mark, hand-painted insects which are probably supposed to be bees but which actually resemble dragonflies, Tiffany holder and lid, no shape or pattern numbers available* **100.00**

☐ Relish pot, no shape number known, pattern #86, *silver lid by Reed & Barton* **35.00**

Honey pot

☐ Relish pot, Lenox shape #1288, pattern #86, *silver-plated holder by unknown maker* **30.0**

Relish pot

PLATES AND PLATTERS

Plates and platters with sterling rims are relatively scarce, but current prices do not seem to reflect this. Dinner and luncheon plates and one large chop plate have been seen, but no oval platters have turned up.

- ☐ Dinner plate, *Lenox Rose pattern, 3/4" sterling band, maker of silver unknown* **45.00**
- ☐ Dinner plate, *Beltane pattern, 3/4" sterling band, maker unknown* . . . **50.00**
- ☐ Dinner plate, *Ballad pattern, 3/4" sterling band, maker unknown, underpriced at* **25.00**
- ☐ Luncheon plate, *Lenox Rose pattern, 3/4" sterling band, maker unknown* **45.00**
- ☐ *Platter, round, Lenox Rose pattern, 1" ornate silver band, maker unknown* **240.00**

  This was an auction price, and we feel it represents the enthusiasm of the bidder rather than a real indication of value.

RAMEKINS

Although ramekins are not rare, they are certainly less common than soups or demitasses. As with all of the other silver and Lenox items, there is quite a difference between the best and the worst, but this is not as pronounced with ramekins as it is with, say, demitasses.

Ramekin, *Gorham holder*

- ☐ Ramekins, *very thin china with gold filigree work on rim and inside, garlands of hand-painted flowers also inside, some with transition mark and some with C.A.C. palette mark. Holders are by Gorham, weighing almost 6 troy ounces each, ornate silver with permanently attached underplate, set of six* **450.00**
- ☐ Ramekins, *same as above except gold work less elaborate on rim and outsides of ramekins are decorated in color (two green, two raspberry, two yellow). Since the monograms on this set are identical to those on the first listing, it is assumed they were originally part of the same set. Set of six* **600.00**

The difference in price does not reflect quality but rather a difference in merchandising techniques.

- ☐ Ramekins, *Lenox liners with pattern #86 trim, International sterling holders with teaspoon type handles, holders weigh approximately 2-1/2 troy ounces, set of 12* **375.00**
- ☐ Ramekin, *Lenox liner with pattern #86 liner, Tiffany holder weighing 2 troy ounces, no handle* **30.00**
- ☐ Ramekins, *Lenox liners in pattern #86, International silver holders with applied piecrust rim and small ring handles, each holder about 2-1/2 troy ounces, set of eight* **240.00**
- ☐ Ramekins, *covered, Lenox wreath mark, pattern #86, Gorham openwork holders weighing 2-1/2 troy ounces each, teaspoon handles, set of six* **200.00**

Note: The teaspoon handles mentioned above were apparently available in a variety of patterns to match flatware patterns.

SALT AND PEPPER HOLDERS

This category seems to have been somewhat neglected by the silver companies since so few types have appeared on the market. Salt and pepper shakers with silver fittings have been found in only two different designs. The first type has cruet-shaped shakers with handles, sterling caps, and snap-on sterling bases. The second type has a salt and pepper with silver caps on a small silver tray (or on a Lenox tray in rare cases.)

There are two types of liners for open salt dips, varying only slightly in size and shape. All of the salt liners we have seen were done in pattern #86.

- ☐ Salt and pepper shakers, *cruet type, maker unknown, silver caps and snap-on bottoms, pair* **45.00**
- ☐ Salt and pepper shakers, *sterling lids and tray, maker unknown* **55.00**
- ☐ Salt and pepper shakers, *sterling lids, Lenox tray, maker unknown* .. **45.00**
- ☐ Salt dip, *International openwork holder, pattern #86 liner* **15.00**
- ☐ Salt dip, *Wallace openwork holder, pattern #86 liner* **15.00**
- ☐ Salt dip, *Watson openwork holder #716, pattern #86 liner, also marked Wm. Wise & Son (retailer)* **15.00**
- ☐ Salt dip, *liner only, pattern #86* **12.00**

SHERBERTS

Identifying Lenox sherberts can be something of a problem, since they were rarely marked. (The stems are too narrow to bear a mark, and if they were marked on the body it might show through the openwork on the holder.) All sherbert liners seen thus far have been done in pattern #86.

- ☐ Liner and holder, *openwork International holder liner has straight rim in pattern #86* **30.00**
- ☐ Liner and holder, *maker unknown, Shreve & Co. name appears as retailer, scalloped rim liner with pattern #86, holder in Art Nouveau design* **50.00**
- ☐ Liner only, *straight rim type, pattern #86* **24.00**

SOUP CUPS

Two-handled cups for soup are the second most common of the silver items with Lenox liners. They consist of a china liner and a two-handled silver holder, and in 99.9 percent of the cases have no underplate. We have only seen one sample that had what was obviously an original underplate. This particular set was by the Frank M. Whiting Company, and the manufacturer's item number was the same on both silver pieces. Other bouillons that might appear to have underplates have actually been matched up with a silver bread and butter plate. None of the early presentation cases we have seen have had spots for saucers, and we conclude that the Frank M. Whiting item is a rarity.

Bouillons, although they appear to be small, hold about six ounces, roughly the same as the current Lenox rimmed soups. In addition to using them for soup, they are also a convenient size to use for desserts or as small serving pieces.

Almost all of the bouillons are item #1201, and this number can be found written or impressed on later samples. Although earlier bouillon liners are the exact same size and shape as the #1201 ones, no number appears on most of them.

Another type of bouillon, similar in size to the #1201, had a scalloped rim. All liners in this shape seen by us so far have been beautifully decorated and had C.A.C. marks on them. They had rainbow effects on the outside, with hand-painted flowers and gold on the inside. We have been unable to find an item number for this shape.

There was also a third type of bouillon, slightly larger than the #1201 but the same shape, which the silver companies also used as the liner for an assortment of small serving pieces.

Cream soups are extremely scarce, and the last set we saw was too long ago to be included in the price guide. They were rather ugly, with heavy, unimaginative holders, with liners done in pattern #86B. They held approximately eight ounces. Since the silver weight was considerable (it had to cover a large liner), we would estimate their current retail value to be about $40 each, despite their unappealing appearance. The liners for cream soups resemble cereal bowls.

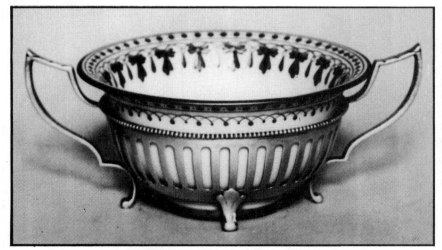

Soup cup, *Gorham holder #A21*

Bouillons should weigh at least two troy ounces to be considered respectable, and most of the better ones are better than three ounces. There are exceptions to this, of course. The Gorham A21 holder pictured in this section barely weighs in at two ounces, yet its design is unique enough to have it be considered in the top grouping.

As is the case with all items of this type, there is usually a premium price tag on sets of six, eight and twelve.

☐ Alvin holder, *1 troy ounce, pattern #86 liner, openwork design on silver* **15.00**

☐ Alvin holder, *2 troy ounces, plain silver with strap handles, pattern #86 liner, gold worn* **12.00**

☐ Barbour holders, *2 troy ounces each, openwork silver, hollow handles, pattern #86B liners, set of six* **90.00**

☐ Dominick & Haff holders, *2-1/2 troy ounces each, openwork with raised rose design on rim, pattern #86 liners, set of eight* **200.00**

☐ Dominick & Haff holder, *2-1/2 troy ounces, embossed gold rim on liner* **22.00**

☐ Dominick & Haff holders, *2 troy ounces, openwork design on silver, ornate reverse "C" handles, set of 12* **300.00**

☐ Durgin holders, *2 troy ounces each, plain silver, strap handles, pattern #86 liners, set of 12* **300.00**

☐ Durgin holder, *2 troy ounces, openwork silver, strap handles, pattern #86B liner* **18.00**

☐ Gorham holders #A21, *hollow handles, raised on four feet, vertical openwork, beading around rim, liners are transition mark, with hand-painted green and gold ribbons on inside, and gold work on rim and outside. (Note that the bottom of the liner is allowed to show through, and that there is gold trim on the bottom. This is a unique feature among Gorham items with Lenox liners.) Set of six* **360.00**

Soup cup, *Gorham holder #A2559*

☐ Gorham holder #A2559, *date mark for 1902, bent twig handles, raised on four feet, openwork design of flowers and leaves, over 3 troy ounces, liner is hand-done with a geometric gold design inside and outside, and has the transition mark. Although it does not show in photograph, the bottom of the liner shows through in this model as it did with the A21 model above, and it is also banded with gold on the bottom* **60.00**

☐ Gorham holders, *2-1/2 troy ounces each, strap handles, pattern #86 liners, set of six* **180.00**

☐ Gorham holders, *2-1/2 troy ounces each, hollow handles, openwork design resembling hearts, pattern #86 liners, set of four* **100.00**

Soup cup, *Gorham holder #A31*

☐ Gorham holder, *silver pattern #A31, strap handles, raised on four feet, openwork silver with applied ornate rim, pattern #86 liner* **40.00**

☐ International holder, *1-1/2 troy ounces, openwork design, strap handles, pattern #86B liner* **17.00**

☐ International holder, *2 troy ounces, plain, hollow handles, pattern #86 liner* **20.00**

☐ Matthews holders, *2 troy ounces each, squared-off hollow handles, pattern #86 liners, set of eight* **190.00**

☐ Matthews holders, *2 troy ounces each, inverted "S" hollow handles, bright-cut work, pattern #86 liners, set of six* **180.00**

☐ Mauser holders, *2-1/2 troy ounces each, openwork design with ornate handles, C.A.C. liners in pattern #338 (green on outside, garlands of flowers inside), set of six* **450.00**

☐ Reed & Barton holders, *2 troy ounces each, inverted "S" handles and openwork design, pattern #86B liners, set of 12* **300.00**

☐ Reed & Barton holders, *2 troy ounces each, plain, squared-off hollow handles, pattern #86 liners, set of eight* **160.00**

☐ Reed & Barton holders, *2-1/2 troy ounces each, openwork silver with band of flowers at top, set of six* **180.00**

☐ Towle holders, *2 troy ounces each, plain silver, rolled rim at top, hollow handles, pattern #86 liners, set of 12* **300.00**

☐ Towle holders, *1-1/4 troy ounces each, openwork design with hollow handles, pattern #86B liners, pair.*............................. **40.00**

☐ Unger Brothers holders, *floral Art Nouveau design, free-form hollow handles, estimated at 3 troy ounces each, pattern #86 liners, set of four* **150.00**

Soup cup, *Whiting holder, engraved*

☐ Wallace holders, *1-1/2 troy ounces, openwork design, inverted "S" handles, pattern #86-1/2 liners, set of eight.*..................... **160.00**

☐ Wallace holders, *2 troy ounces, openwork design, strap handles, pattern #86 liners, set of 10.*.. **250.00**

☐ Wallace holders, *2 troy ounces, plain silver, strap handles, pattern #86 liners, set of 12* **250.00**

☐ Watson holders, *2 troy ounces each, vertical openwork design, pattern #86 liners, set of six* **180.00**

☐ Watson holders, *2 troy ounces each, vertical openwork design, unknown pattern of flowers, set of six* **300.00**

☐ Whiting (Frank M.) holder, *ordinary openwork with strap handles, blue dot liner, possibly a married piece* **65.00**

☐ Whiting (Frank M.) holder, *2 troy ounces, plain silver, strap handles, pattern #86 liners, set of six* **120.00**

☐ Whiting (Frank M.) holder, *matching underplate, total weight 5 troy ounces, nice engraved work on silver and hollow handles, pattern #E88 liner. (Note that this is the only bouillon we have seen with a true matching underplate.)* **50.00**

☐ Whiting Mfg. Co. holders, *2 troy ounces, "Adam" silver pattern (could be matched with flatware of same name), pattern #86 liners, set of six* **180.00**

Soup cup, *Woodside holder*

☐ Woodside holders, 2-1/4 troy ounces each, openwork design, beading on rim, ornate hollow handles, liners have transition mark, and are decorated inside and out with hand-painted pink, lavender and blue flowers with raised gold paste work. The holder hides much of the design on the outside, which is not uncommon in early pieces and does not mean they did not go with each other. Set of eight **480.00**

Durgin bowl

Egg cup, *Reed & Barton*

MISCELLANEOUS

The items listed below, mainly serving pieces, represent a sampling of the large assortment of items that were available with Lenox liners. We have seen or heard of many more than these, but space allows us only this brief listing. We cannot account for why so many of these miscellaneous items were by the Watson Company.

Watson bowl, *shape #15*

Watson bowl, *shape #4043*

- ☐ Durgin bowl, *openwork holder, 5" diameter, Lenox wreath mark liner in sky blue with gold rim* **50.00**
- ☐ Gorham epergne, *center vase and four small hanging baskets on spokes coming out from center vase, Lenox wreath mark basket and vase liners. It is interesting to note that the liners for the baskets are the same small pieces that were used by Lenox as the sauce holders for their oyster plates* **350.00**

Watson bowl, *shape #311*

Watson candy dish

☐ Kirk bowl, *Revere style, plain, heavy silver, 6" diameter, Lenox liner shape #1234, pattern #86* **100.00**

☐ Reed & Barton egg cup, *4" high, R&B shape #1145, Lenox wreath mark liner, shape number unknown, decorated in pattern #86* **50.00**

☐ Watson bowl, *shape #315, two handled, 6-1/2" diameter handle to handle, openwork, Lenox liner #1234, pattern #378 (hand-painted roses), transition mark* **100.00**

☐ Watson bowl, *shape #4043, two-handled, same size as above, openwork silver, Lenox wreath mark liner shape #1234, no pattern number, garlands of hand-painted flowers* **100.00**

Watson mayonnaise

Watson covered casserole

☐ Watson bowl, shape #311, *footed with two handles, 8-1/4" across top of liner, openwork design, transition mark liner, shape and pattern numbers unknown, hand-painted flowers* **125.00**
☐ Watson candy dish, shape #3391, *6" diameter, openwork design, raised on four ball feet, transition mark liner, shape number and pattern number unknown, hand-painted flowers* **80.00**
☐ Watson mayonnaise, *silver shape number unreadable, openwork design, 5-1/2" handle to handle, footed, transition mark liner with garlands of hand-painted flowers, no shape or pattern number for liner* . **85.00**
☐ Watson covered casserole, shape #58, *openwork design, raised on four elaborate feet, 11" handle to handle, transition mark liner with cover, shape number and pattern number unkown, hand-painted flowers, crack in bottom part* **125.00**

LINERS ONLY
Following are prices for Lenox liners without holders:

☐ Pattern 69B, *transition mark (blue dot)* **60.00**
☐ Pattern 70, *transition mark (blue dot)*............................. **60.00**
☐ Pattern 86, *(plain gold)*.. **15.00**
☐ Pattern 86-1/2, *(wide gold)* **17.00**
☐ Pattern 86B, *(plain gold)* **15.00**
☐ Pattern J30, *(etched gold)* **20.00**
☐ Pattern J33, *(Tuxedo pattern)* **20.00**
☐ Pattern 338, *(hand-painted floral garlands)*...................... **60.00**
☐ Pattern unknown, *(gold filigree, transition mark)* **40.00**
☐ All pink **17.00**
☐ All pink, *gold trim on rim* **20.00**
☐ All yellow... **20.00**

The above prices apply equally to demis and soups. By adding these figures to the scrap value of the silver, it is possible to estimate the value of your items. (For example, a two ounce holder with a pink liner would be valued at $30.) Silver is currently priced at around $6 per troy ounce, but prices can change quickly.

SILVER OVERLAY

For a period of around 40 years, Lenox supplied blanks for a number of silver companies to decorate with sterling silver overlay. This overlay was applied by an electrolytic method in designs usually chosen by the silver companies, and the marketing was also done by the silver companies so far as we can determine. As was also the case with Lenox liners in sterling holders, this procedure may have been reversed occasionally, with the Lenox Company special-ordering a particular silver design.

Lenox china decorated with silver overlay is not as easy to categorize as the hand-painted items, for unlike the painted wares, which can be roughly grouped into good artwork and bad artwork, the overlay is divided into **style** of decoration rather than **quality** of decoration. This is not to say that the quality of the silver work doesn't enter into the matter, for it does, but rather that more people seem to find Art Nouveau florals more appealing than Art Deco geometrics.

Some of the silver overlay patterns are encountered over and over again, and although we do not know their official names, they have been given nicknames by collectors and dealers. The most common of these are:

(1) Cherry blossom—sprays of flowers with branches and leaves.

(2) Chinese pattern—groupings of human figures with pagodas or other Oriental motifs.

(3) Floral—any arrangement of flowers, branches and leaves which is not cherry blossom.

(4) Flying geese—scenic overlay with geese flying over a marsh. Occasionally this pattern will have hand-tinted colors in the sky and water, which adds to its value.

(5) Geometric—refers to a number of patterns with more or less straight lines or banding, usually in the Art Deco style.

(6) Ornate—an assortment of patterns with elaborate designs which cover a large part of the china.

Although a variety of marks appear on overlay items, the ones most commonly seen are the Lenox wreath and palette marks. Overlay is one area where palette mark items should not be considered inferior to wreath mark ones. They bear the palette mark because they were being sent away from the Lenox factory for the silver work, not because the final item was in some way inferior. The C.A.C. marks are still considered more valuable, particularly C.A.C. wreath marks, but this is because of their age and styling rather than because of the mark itself.

Several silver companies were actively engaged with Lenox silver overlay, including Gorham, Mauser, Reed & Barton, Wallace, Rockwell, Depasse and others. The Gorham and Mauser marks tend to increase the value of an item by their mere presence. Some of the silver companies entirely covered the bottom of the items with silver, obscuring the Lenox marks completely, which may be indicative of their feelings about American china at that time.

As a rule, the silver overlay items which are marked with the silver company's name as well as the Lenox mark are more desirable than those without the silver mark. There is a definite correlation between those items which are marked and the type of silver work done. "Name" silver companies tended to be more generous both with the gauge of silver used and the amount of territory it covered, and they also seemed to finish off the items with nice engraving work on the overlay.

The blanks supplied by Lenox to the silver manufacturers were both the regular, creamy Lenox and the early bone china as well. In fact, it is in the overlay category that a great deal of this bone china makes its appearance.

The variety of shapes used for silver overlay is not as large as it was for hand-painting, and for the most part the shapes are of the simple type. Items with lots of curves and corners made overlay work difficult if not impossible.

The infuser teapot, shape #522, turns up quite frequently with overlay on it. The infuser is a china piece with pinpoint holes in it which fits down inside the teapot. The main idea was to put the tea in the infuser and then run the hot water through it. The infuser could be removed when the tea was strong enough. Many times the infusers to these sets are missing, and the lids to the teapots will not fit properly without them. This round-bodied teaset was perfectly suited to a variety of overlay patterns, which probably accounts for the large number of them seen today.

In general, vases and teasets were made in such abundance that they must be unusual in one fashion or another in order to attract a great deal of attention.

The color of the Lenox is of great importance. The most common color is, of course, the basic Lenox color. Following this would be cobalt blue, brown, and antique ivory, all three of which seem to occur with the same degree of frequency. Green, light blue, and pink also occur, but only rarely. Some items are done in more than one color, starting out with one color and then subtly changing to another. The most common shaded colors are green, brown and orange in combination with each other.

There are some items which appear to be black, but it is hard to tell if they are indeed black or merely a very dark cobalt. A lot of these "black" items have been decorated with a great deal of overlay which tends to obscure the color. If an item is truly black and not a dark blue, it would be in the very rare class. A few pieces of turquoise have shown up, including a beautifully overlaid tea tile. There is another blue, somewhere between the turquoise and the cobalt, which turns up occasionally. In any case, there is always a premium on rarer colors. Plain white seems to go begging unless it is extravagently decorated or an unusual shape.

Some of the earlier items combined overlay with hand-painting. It appears that all of the painting was done at the Lenox factory, and then the item shipped out to the silver company for the overlay work. We have never seen a sample of a home-decorated item with silver overlay on it, and we doubt that we will, since the painting and firing had to be done before the silver overlay was put on.

The hand-painting can vary from simple, small pink roses to the finest samples of Lenox artwork. DeLan painted on items ear-marked for overlay, and Heidrich apparently made a specialty of it since his name primarily appears on overlay items. Other names crop up now and then, and many fine items are not artist signed at all.

Taking care of silver overlay can be something of a problem since the silver can be worn thin by over-zealous polishing. Many collectors allow the overlay on white or light-colored items to darken (it will become almost black with time), but this approach looks dreadful with cobalt or other dark colors. Careless handling can sometimes cause the overlay to be lifted off the china if the bond between the two materials is not perfect. We know of no one who specializes in repairing missing or lifted overlay, and can only suggest that you do what we do—carefully glue raised sections back on. This seems to work fine for vases, but on teasets the heat from the liquid will melt the glue and allow the silver to lift off again.

Copper and gold overlay are also seen in rare instances, usually on white but also on cobalt in at least one case. No prices for copper or gold overlay have been included here because none have been seen recently enough. In general, copper overlay items are worth about the same as comparable items with silver on them, and the gold would be worth more.

Run-of-the-mill overlay is still underpriced in our estimation, and even the top items still probably have some room left yet. The prices on all overlay should rise sharply in the near future as the hand-painted items become harder to find and as people realize that overlay is collectible in its own right.

In the price section, items are listed alphabetically by type of ware. Within these categories, they are in numerical order by shape number. Those items with no shape number will be found at the end of their proper grouping. Please note that the word "white" is used interchangeably to mean either natural Lenox color or the bone china color.

☐ Beehive honey jar, shape number unknown, *bees covered with silver and band of silver on base, Rockwell silver mark and Lenox wreath mark, tiny fleck on wing of one bee* **50.00**

☐ Bowl, shape #512, *filigree effect on antique ivory body, Lenox palette mark, no silver mark*.. **95.00**

☐ Bowl, shape #527, *ornate overlay on white body, green Lenox palette mark, no silver mark*.. **125.00**

☐ Bowl, shape #527, *geometric bands on white body, Lenox palette mark, no silver mark*.. **75.00**

☐ Bowl, shape #586, *10" x 3", geometric design on white body, handles covered in silver, Reed & Barton silver mark, Lenox green wreath mark*.. **100.00**

☐ Bowl, shape #586, *10" x 3", cherry blossom design on white body, handles covered, no silver mark, Lenox palette mark* **110.00**

☐ Bowl, mayo, shape #644, *mediocre overlay on white body, hand-painted small pink roses, tiny chip under rim, Lenox wreath mark*.... **40.00**

☐ Bowl, shape #793, *7" diameter, cherry blossom design on white body, Lenox palette mark, no silver mark* **60.00**

☐ Bowl, shape #793, *geometric design on pale blue body, Lenox wreath mark*.. **100.00**

☐ Bowl, shape #896, *5-1/2" diameter, strips of silver on white body, green wreath mark, Reed & Barton silver mark*.................... **35.00**

☐ Bowl, shape #896, *5-1/2" diameter, geometric pattern resembling musical symbols, Lenox palette mark, no silver mark* **50.00**

☐ Bowl, shape #922, *10-3/4" diameter, cherry blossom pattern on white, green wreath mark* **110.00**

☐ Bowl, shape #922, *10-3/4" diameter, geometric design on brown, Depasse silver mark, Lenox wreath mark* **100.00**

☐ Bowl, shape #922, *10-3/4" diameter, floral design on antique ivory, no silver mark, Lenox palette mark* **90.00**

☐ Bowl, shape #1723, *strip outlining and wreath in silver on white ground, Lenox wreath mark, no silver mark* **70.00**

☐ Bowl, shape #1723, *geometric bands on antique ivory body, Lenox palette mark, no silver mark* **70.00**

☐ Bowl, shape #1723, *ornate overlay on white ground, Gorham silver mark, Lenox palette mark* **100.00**

☐ Candlesticks, shape #930, *8-1/4" high, outlining in silver with hand-painted flowers, slight damage to silver work, Lenox wreath mark, pair*.. **80.00**

☐ Candy dish, shape #10, *5" x 7-1/4", narrow silver bands, green wreath mark*.. **30.00**

☐ Candy dish, shape #10, *5" x 7-1/4", narrow silver bands on coral body, Lenox wreath mark* **70.00**

☐ Candy dish, shape #133, *3-1/4" x 3-3/4", vertical stripes on white body, Lenox palette mark* **35.00**

☐ Candy dish, shape #510, *geometric design on white, Lenox palette mark*. **25.00**
☐ Candy dish, shape #510, *geometric design on antique ivory, Lenox palette mark* **27.00**
☐ Candy dish, shape #514, *covered, 8" x 3-3/4", geometric bandings on white, Lenox palette mark*. **100.00**
☐ Candy dish, shape #514, *covered, 8" x 3-3/4", ornate design covering most of lid, silver bands on base, C.A.C. transition mark, Mauser silver mark, white body* **130.00**
☐ Candy dish, shape #1018, *footed boat shape with handles, Art Deco silver work, green palette mark*. **50.00**
☐ Chocolate pot, shape #842, *ornate overlay on cobalt, transition mark and Mauser silver mark* **150.00**
☐ Chocolate pot, shape #842, *ornate overlay on white, Lenox wreath mark and Reed & Barton mark* **100.00**

Coaster

☐ Coaster, no shape number, *ornate overlay on brown, Lenox wreath mark*. **35.00**
☐ Coffeepot, sugar and creamer, shapes #371, #372 and #373, *square pedestal base, geometric overlay on white body, Lenox palette mark*. **175.00**
☐ Coffeepot, sugar and creamer, shapes #371, #372 and #373, *floral overlay on cobalt body, transition mark* **275.00**
☐ Coffeepot, teapot, sugar and creamer, shapes #521, #522, #523, and #524, *ornate overlay on cobalt, Lenox green wreath and Depasse marks, slight damage on inside lip of sugar bowl* **400.00**
☐ Coffeepot, sugar and creamer, shapes #521, #523, and #524, *geometric bands on brown body, Lenox wreath mark and Reed & Barton mark* **190.00**
☐ Coffeepot, sugar and creamer, shapes #597, #598, and #599, *floral overlay on cobalt, Lenox wreath mark* **190.00**
☐ Coffeepot, sugar and creamer, shapes #692, #694, and #695, *geometric bands on white, Lenox palette mark*. **150.00**

- ☐ Coffeepot, sugar and creamer, demitasse size, shapes #787, #788, and #789, *Chinese pattern on white body, Lenox wreath mark* **225.00**
- ☐ Coffeepot, sugar and creamer, all demitasse sizes, shapes #787, #788, #789, *simple banding of overlay on ivory color, Lenox palette mark*. **160.00**
- ☐ Coffeepot, sugar and creamer, individual size, shapes #933, #935, and #936, *geometrical vertical bands on white body, Lenox palette mark*. **75.00**
- ☐ Coffeepot, sugar and creamer, shapes #1013, #1015, and #1016, *ornate overlay on cobalt ground, Lenox palette mark* **175.00**
- ☐ Coffeepot, individual size, shape #1353, 5-3/4" high, *filigree overlay work on white, Lenox wreath mark*. **40.00**
- ☐ Coffeepot, individual size, shape #1353, 5-3/4" high, *ornate overlay on cobalt, transition mark* **100.00**
- ☐ Coffeepot, sugar (open) and creamer, shapes #1544, #1546, and #1547, *geometric design on white, Lenox palette mark* **150.00**
- ☐ Coffeepot, sugar (open) and creamer, shapes #1544, #1546, and #1547, *ornate overlay on ivory color, Lenox wreath mark, Gorham silver mark* **175.00**
- ☐ Coffeepot, sugar and creamer on tray, shapes #1654, #1656, #1657, *no number for tray, cherry blossom design on white body, Lenox palette mark* **375.00**
- ☐ Coffeepot, sugar and creamer, shapes #1654, #1656, and #1657, *wreath and outlines in silver on cobalt body, Lenox wreath mark and Reed & Barton silver mark*. **225.00**
- ☐ Coffeepot, sugar and creamer, shapes #1654, #1656, and #1657, *geometric pattern, Lenox palette mark, white body* **150.00**
- ☐ Coffeepot, sugar and creamer on tray, *six matching cups and saucers, flying geese pattern with hand-painting, Lenox palette mark, all items perfect* **500.00**
- ☐ Compote, shape #825, *ornate overlay on white, Lenox palette mark* . . **100.00**
- ☐ Compote, shape #825, *ornate overlay on cobalt, transition mark and Gorham mark* **150.00**

Creamer and sugar, *geometric latticework overlay*

☐ Cracker jar, shape number unknown, *6" high, ornate overlay on brown, Lenox palette mark* **150.00**

☐ Creamer and sugar (open), shapes #1063, and #1062, *geometric lattice work overlay on white body, Lenox wreath mark and Reed & Barton mark, spider crack in bottom of sugar* **35.00**

☐ Creamer and sugar, no shape number, *Art Nouveau floral overlay on brown background, Lenox palette mark* **65.00**

☐ Creamer and sugar, no shape number, *lattice work overlay on cobalt body, Lenox wreath mark* **95.00**

☐ Creamer and sugar, no shape number, *square pedestal bases, geometric overlay on white body, Lenox palette mark* **60.00**

☐ Creamer and sugar, no shape number, *fat-bodied, ornate overlay on cobalt, transition mark and Mauser silver mark* **110.00**

☐ Cup and saucer, shape #448, *square handles done in silver, silver banding on rims, Lenox palette mark* **25.00**

☐ Cup and saucer, shape #448, *square handles in silver, ornate overlay on cobalt, Lenox wreath mark* **50.00**

☐ Cup and saucer, shape #1094, *double outlining in silver, Lenox palette mark* **30.00**

☐ Humidor, covered, no shape number, *cobalt blue with ornate overlay, Lenox wreath mark* **150.00**

Inkwell, *shape #313*

☐ Inkwell, shape #313, *4", cobalt background, silver maker's mark blurred, transition mark* **150.00**

☐ Jam pot and underplate, no shape number, *straps of overlay on white body, Lenox palette mark* **50.00**

☐ Jam pot, no shape number, *thin strap overlay with hand-painted strawberries, Lenox palette mark* **70.00**

☐ Jug, shape #217, *8" high, ornate silver on brown, transition mark* **150.00**

Jug, *shape #381*

☐ Jug, shape #381, *with stopper, oval portrait on one side of Victorian lady dressed in pink gown toasting with a glass of wine. Rest of jug is a vibrant deep rose color covered with ornate Art Nouveau silver in the form of grape clusters and leaves. Gorham silver mark, dated 1896 and signed A. H. (Antonie Heidrich), minor crack in base of piece, transition mark* **450.00**

☐ Jug, shape #534, *small size, 4" high, ornate floral design on brown body, transition mark*.. **100.00**

☐ Jug, *same as above except marked with the word "Whisky", Lenox wreath mark, Depasse silver mark* **110.00**

☐ Mug, shape #251, *5" high, tankard shape, thick strap overlay on cobalt, transition mark* **95.00**

☐ Mug, shape number unknown, *4" high, tankard shape, silver banding top and bottom, silver handle, seated monk toasting with a glass of wine, monochromatic brown colors, transition mark* **150.00**

☐ Mug, shape #256, *5-3/4" high, dog holding dead bird in its mouth on air-brushed yellow and brown background, overlay in form of leaves, rim bands and handle cover, artwork signed E. A. DeLan, transition mark*.. **450.00**

☐ Mustard pot and underplate, no shape number, *footed, artwork signed E. A. Delan, transition mark, see photo*.................... **450.00**

☐ Mustard pot and underplate, no shape number, *footed pot, Art Deco overlay on white body* **40.00**

☐ Mustard pot, shape number unknown, *Reed & Barton silver mark, strap overlay on cobalt, Lenox wreath mark* **75.00**

☐ Nut dish, shape #51, *3" high, footed shell shape, outside covered entirely in silver, green palette mark, no silver mark* **35.00**

☐ Pitcher, covered, shape #270, *12" high, floral design on white, green Lenox wreath mark* **100.00**

Mug, *shape #251*

☐ Pitcher, shape #526, *6" high, geometric design on white, Lenox palette mark* **50.00**

☐ Pitcher, shape #567, *7-1/2" high, ornate overlay on white, mark obscured by silver on bottom* **70.00**

☐ Pitcher, shape #567, *7-1/2" high, ornate overlay on white, Lenox wreath mark* **75.00**

☐ Pitcher, shape #666, *sparse but nicely done silver banding, hand-painted roses, Lenox wreath mark* **75.00**

☐ Plate, *8", flying geese pattern, Lenox palette mark* **65.00**

☐ Plate, *8", hand-painted roses with strap type overlay work, Lenox wreath mark* **70.00**

☐ Plate, *9", flying geese pattern, tinted backgrounds, Lenox palette mark* **80.00**

☐ Plate, *9", plain bands of silver on rim, white, Lenox palette mark* **20.00**

☐ Powder box, shape #152, *3-1/2" x 2-7/8", ornate silver on cobalt, transition mark* **125.00**

☐ Salt dip, shape #103, *1-3/4", outside all silver, Lenox palette mark* ... **10.00**

☐ Shaving mug, shape #201, *4" high, ornate silver on brown, transition mark* **175.00**

☐ Shaving mug, shape #201, *4" high, strap banding on white, Lenox palette mark* **150.00**

☐ Swan, shape #59, *1-3/4", covered all over with silver, Lenox palette mark* **38.00**

☐ Teapot, sugar and creamer, shapes #522, #523, and #524, *fat-bodied shapes, infuser teapot, ornate overlay on white, unmarked* **75.00**

☐ Teapot, sugar and creamer, shapes #522, #523, and #524, *infuser type, ornate overlay on white, Lenox green wreath mark* **175.00**

☐ Teapot, sugar and creamer, shapes #522, #523, and #524, *infuser type, ornate overlay on cobalt, transition mark and Mauser mark* **235.00**

Mug, *shape #256*

☐ Teapot, sugar and creamer, shapes #522, #523, and #524, *infuser type, infuser missing, sugar bowl damaged, teapot and creamer perfect, geometric overlay on brown, Lenox wreath mark and Reed & Barton silver mark* **75.00**

☐ Teapot, sugar and creamer, shapes #522, #523, and #524, *infuser type, all items perfect, geometric overlay on brown, Lenox wreath mark* **195.00**

☐ Teapot, sugar and creamer, shapes #542, #543, and #544, *geometric overlay on white ground, Lenox palette mark* **150.00**

☐ Teapot, sugar and creamer, shapes #1061, #1062, #1063, *floral overlay on brown, Lenox wreath mark, Reed & Barton silver mark* **190.00**

☐ Teapot, sugar and creamer, shapes #1061, #1062, and #1063, *ornate overlay on cobalt, Lenox wreath mark and Gorham silver mark* **275.00**

☐ Teapot, sugar and creamer, shapes #1084, #1085, and #1086, *geometric overlay on brown ground, Wallace silver mark, green Lenox wreath mark* **210.00**

☐ Teapot, sugar and creamer, shapes #1182, #1183, and #1184, *ornate overlay on cobalt, Lenox wreath mark and Depasse silver mark* **200.00**

☐ Teapot, sugar and creamer, shapes #1182, #1183, and #1184, *ornate overlay on white, Lenox wreath mark, no silver mark* **150.00**

☐ Teapot, sugar and creamer, stackable variety, shape #1610, *overlay in ornate pattern on white, lid not the original one and teapot has minor damage to inside lip, Lenox wreath mark* **50.00**

☐ Vase, shape #297, *8-1/2" high, filigree design on white body, Lenox palette mark* **100.00**

☐ Vase, shape #297, *8-1/4" high, ornate design on cobalt, transition mark and Mauser mark* **135.00**

☐ Vase, shape #297, *8-1/4" high, strap banding on white, Lenox palette mark, no silver mark* **60.00**

☐ Vase, shape #314, *8" high, cherry blossom pattern on white body, green palette mark* **100.00**

☐ Vase, shape #314, *8" high, geometric design on brown, Lenox wreath mark, Reed & Barton silver mark* **110.00**

☐ Vase, shape #315, *5-3/4" high, ornate floral overlay on background which appears to be black but is possibly dark cobalt, transition mark and Gorham mark* **160.00**

☐ Vase, shape #315, *5-3/4" high, geometric overlay on white, Lenox palette mark* **60.00**

☐ Vase, shape #318, *geometric design on white body, Lenox wreath mark* **75.00**

☐ Vase, shape #318, *floral design on white body, Lenox wreath mark* .. **85.00**

☐ Vase, shape #320, *10-1/4" high, cherry blossom design on white, Lenox palette mark* **175.00**

☐ Vase, shape #320, *10-1/4" high, geometric design on antique ivory, Lenox palette mark* **100.00**

☐ Vase, shape #412, *9" high, bulbous, floral design, on white body, green wreath mark* **100.00**

☐ Vase, shape #416, *5-3/4" high, geometric design on white, green palette mark* **50.00**

☐ Vase, shape #416, *5-3/4" high, floral design on antique ivory, Lenox wreath mark* **75.00**

☐ Vase, shape #470, *18-1/2" high, flying geese pattern with no background tinting, the Lenox shape number is impressed on bottom but there is no Lenox mark* **160.00**

☐ Vase, shape #574, *ornate overlay on cobalt, Lenox wreath mark and Depasse silver mark* **85.00**

☐ Vase, shape #574, *ornate overlay on cobalt, no Lenox mark or silver mark* **40.00**

☐ Vase, shape #877, *12-1/2" high, geometric design on cobalt, Lenox palette mark* **110.00**

Vase, *no shape number*

☐ Vase, shape #877, 12-1/2" high, ornate lattice design, Reed & Barton silver mark, Lenox wreath mark **120.00**

☐ Vase, shape #879, 7" high, ornate overlay on green, Lenox wreath mark and Mauser mark **160.00**

☐ Vase, shape #880, 7-7/8" high, geometric on white body, Reed & Barton and Lenox wreath marks **50.00**

☐ Vase, shape #880, 7-7/8" high, floral design on antique ivory, Lenox palette mark **50.00**

☐ Vase, shape #897, 12-1/4" high, ornate overlay on white, Lenox wreath mark and Depasse marks **155.00**

☐ Vase, shape #1185, 10" high, vertical lines on antique ivory, Lenox palette mark **50.00**

☐ Vase, shape #1312, 8-3/4" high, ornate overlay on cobalt, Lenox wreath and Reed & Barton marks............................... **115.00**

☐ Vase, no shape number, 14" high, overall decoration with hand-painted flowering begonias. Ornate overlay in strap banding with rim and foot also banded in silver, no artist signature, transition mark ... **400.00**

MISCELLANEOUS

There seems to be no end to the ways in which Lenox and metals were combined, and a complete listing of them would fill an entire book by itself. We have chosen to ignore those items with holders that may not be original or those with metal parts which tend to detract from the value rather than add to it.

There are, however, a few more categories which remain to be discussed, and they are lumped together here in the Miscellaneous section. They are:

(1) Atomizers and perfume bottles

(2) Barometers and thermometers

(3) Bronze and Lenox items

(4) Button hooks

(5) Cigarette lighter and urn sets

(6) Clocks

(7) Jugs with silver stoppers

(8) Lenox lamps

(9) Pens

(10) Salt and Pepper Mills

(11) Steins

(12) Other

ATOMIZERS AND PERFUME BOTTLES

Early C.A.C. atomizers, which were made in at least six different shapes and sizes, are virtually unknown. Any signed sample with original fittings would be worth at least $100.

Later atomizers, with fittings by DeVilbiss, are more readily available but still not common.

☐ Atomizer, rabbit, shape number unknown, Lenox wreath mark, working condition... **75.00**

☐ Atomizer, shape #2837, top half can be used as a bud vase, working condition, Lenox wreath mark (known as the champagne bottle atomizer)... **60.00**

☐ Atomizer, shape #2817, blue with white finial (known as the fleur-de-lis atomizer), Lenox wreath mark **70.00**

☐ Atomizer, shape number unknown, Hawthorn pattern with coral dot in center of each flower....................................... **60.00**

☐ Atomizer, shape number unknown, (commonly referred to as Napoleon's hat atomizer), Lenox wreath mark **65.00**

☐ Perfume bottle, shape #28??, blue with white squirrel finial, Lenox wreath mark **50.00**

Atomizers, *assorted shapes*

*Note: All of the above have DeVilbiss fitting and the DeVilbiss mark
on the bottom as well as the Lenox mark.*

BAROMETERS AND THERMOMETERS

Both of these items are rare, and to find one with the original metal sections
is even rarer.

We have no sales listed during the past year for these items, but would
place a thermometer or barometer in original condition in the $150 range,
depending on mark and decoration.

BRONZE ITEMS

The use of gold-plated bronze mountings appears to have been a strictly early
endeavor on the part of Lenox. All of the items seen so far have been marked
with Ceramic Art Company marks. Since none of the items were sold this
year, we are giving estimated prices for them.

The first item, approximately 20 inches high, was briefly seen in the
Trenton area a few years ago. At that time, the owner rejected an offer of
$450. It had a bronze base, then several bronze the Trenton area a few years
ago. At that time, the owner rejected an offer of $450. It had a bronze base,
then several bronze and china connectors, and finally the main body of china.
There were bronze handles in the shape of women. From its general appearance, it would seem that it might have originally had a lid of some sort,
but none was present. The hand-painted decoration was of colorful orchids,
with a mottled green background, and was signed "C. Morley" (probably old
George getting sloppy with his "G" again). The china had been extensively
repaired, and dabs of green paint had been added to hide the repairs. It also
suffered from glaze crackle, a rare sight on Lenox. In spite of its many flaws,
it was a spectacular piece of early Lenox. The china itself was not marked in
any manner, and the C.A.C. mark appeared on the bronze instead.

Vase, *bronze connectors*

The second item is 18" high, and is made in four sections that are separated by gold-plated bronze connectors. There is no artist signature, and the C.A.C. mark appeared on the metal rather than the china. We would estimate its current retail value at around $400.

We have also seen a pair of candelabra, bronze plated on white metal. Each one had a miniature C.A.C. plaque wired into a window cut in the base. There were also china connectors further up on the stem, but the connectors were unmarked and of a different decoration than the plaques. The plaques did not seem to fit the window exactly and, all things considered, the items are questionable. Nevertheless, they are unique and we would have to value them at around $175 to $200 for the pair.

There are too few bronze items to allow for standard pricing structures, but keep in mind that they are surely worth more than comparable all-china items.

BUTTON HOOKS

Lenox button hooks are frequently unmarked, which makes identification and pricing difficult. We would estimate an identifiable handle with original hook to be worth in the area of $100, more if decorated.

CIGARETTE LIGHTER AND URN SETS

☐ Cigarette lighter and urn, *Alaris pattern, Lenox gold wreath mark* **35.00**
☐ Cigarette lighter and urn set, *Caribbee pattern, Lenox gold wreath mark* **35.00**
☐ Cigarette lighter and urn set, *plain pale pink, Lenox gold wreath mark* **30.00**

CLOCKS

Clocks are too rare to allow for a comprehensive pricing guide, and are very much in the pay-whatever-you-have-to category. Two shapes (at least) were made, one 8-1/4" high and the other 12-1/4" high.

Clock

☐ Clock, *probably not Lenox but decorated by Ceramic Art Company, fancy molded scroll work on top and sides, several minor chips, floral and gold trim, C.A.C. written-out wreath mark* **250.00**

Note: If the clock is not in working condition and cannot be repaired, it is sometimes possible to find a working clock and substitute it for the non-working one. If this is done, save the original clockwork.

Jug, *silver stopper*

JUGS WITH SILVER STOPPERS

The standard Lenox whisky jugs are sometimes equipped with a silver stopper. Rather than going into a lengthy listing of them here, we refer the reader to the hand-painted section and offer the advice that an original stopper adds about $25 to the value. The stoppers tend to give a rather peculiar, lopsided appearance to the jugs.

☐ Jug, *silver stopper, portrait of cavalier on one side, the interior of a tavern on the other, monochromatic green, signed WHC (William H. Clayton), transition mark* **225.00**

LENOX LAMPS

Early Lenox catalogues show a variety of lamps, few of which have survived to the present day. They varied from tiny models to a large Gone-With-The-Wind lamp. All were apparently meant to be used with kerosene.

Electrical lamps by Lenox had their heydey in the 1930's. A large assortment of models was available, many of them merely standard Lenox vase shapes turned into lamps. Others were specifically designed as lamps and came in more than one piece with metal dividers.

Identifying Lenox lamps is not always that simple, since the metal bases cover the Lenox marks, and the metal sections (which can also help in identification) are frequently covered with felt to protect table tops.

Some of the Lenox lamps had a paper label in addition to (and sometimes instead of) the familiar Lenox backstamp. If these labels are still present, they probably should not be removed, especially if there is no Lenox mark on the bottom.

On some models the standard Lenox green wreath mark was used as the backstamp, and on others will be found mark K. The metal bases, usually brass-plated rather than solid brass, are sometimes marked as follows:

Knowing the metal mark can come in very handy at a flea market or auction where it is not always possible to take a lamp apart to see if it has the Lenox mark. In addition, the little brown on/off switch will sometimes have a script letter "L" on it. (Note that if a lamp has been re-wired, this switch will have been replaced, and   sometimes have a script letter "L" on it. (Note that if a lamp has been re-wired, this switch will have been replaced, and sometimes a new brass base put on.)

Some antique shop owners get a trifle testy when customers start taking lamps apart, and it is best to get permission before doing so. A pair of pliers is usually the only tool required to disassemble a lamp, and it is not always necessary to take the lamp apart completely in order to see the mark.

Original shades were silk, and it is rare to find one in good condition. The heat from the lamp makes the silk brittle and easy to damage, and in many cases they are discolored from the heat.

If the lamp has not already been rewired, we suggest doing so if you plan to use the lamp, since forty-year-old wiring can be a very definite hazard. This, of course, brings up the old argument about altering antiques and collectibles, but we feel that a safe, usable lamp is a better investment than an unsafe one with the original wiring.

It is indeed a shame that Lenox used the brass-plated (and sometimes silver-plate) bases instead of the real thing, since the plating tends to wear off leaving owners no choice but to replace the metal parts or to hide the lamp in the back bedroom.

Table lamps are the most common, although torchier floor lamps were also made. Three different types of Lenox shades for torchiers have been noted, all worth approximately the same.

Although many of the lamps have a "dated", 1930's look to them, a new shade and rewiring can make them into usable, attractive additions to a Lenox collection. We have not noticed any price differential between those with original wiring and those that have been rewired.

Lamps are still a good buy, and are rarely priced at more than a Lenox vase of comparable size and style. Many times they can be picked up at a flea market for only a couple of dollars, since few people are even aware that Lenox made lamps. In almost all cases, they are priced lower than a new, non-Lenox ceramic lamp of similar quality.

For the most part, sizes are not listed in the price section since they tend to be somewhat misleading. The same Lenox sections were combined with taller or shorter metal sections which alters the overall size but not the size of the Lenox parts. It is the shape and color of the Lenox parts which seem to determine the value of the lamp, not the overall size.

Some of the Art Deco figures were occasionally put on metal bases with the light inside the figure. These are not included here and will be found in the figurine section instead.

The term brass has been used in the price guide to describe the overall look of the item, but it should be kept in mind that all of the items listed this way were brass-plated.

FLOOR LAMPS

☐ Torchier, *overall height 5-1/2', brass base in need of work, re-wiring needed, flared Lenox shade* **55.00**

TABLE LAMPS

☐ Brass base, *cocoa brown body with white handles, original shade, rewired* **35.00**
☐ Brass base, *forest green body with white owl's head handles, needs rewiring and shade* **90.00**
☐ Brass base, *blue with ring handles, rewired and new shade* **40.00**
☐ Brass base, *square, blue with embossed white horses, paper label, needs rewiring, no shades, pair* **100.00**
☐ Brass base, *elongated teardrop shaped body, coral color, rewired with new shade* **30.00**
☐ Brass base, *two-section white body with swan handles, rewired, no shade* **35.00**
☐ Brass base, *urn shaped body in two sections, feather handles, all white, needs wiring and shade* **30.00**

☐ Brass base, *urn shaped body in two sections, main body white, feather handles coral, rewired, new shade* **30.00**
☐ Brass base, *urn shaped body in two sections, main body white, feather handles coral, rewired, new shade* **50.00**
☐ Brass base, *one-piece white body, handles formed by multiple rings, original shade and wiring both in excellent condition* **75.00**
☐ Brass base, *fat-bodied Lenox section decorated with an overall design of oozing colors (aqua, brown, gold and green), very striking and possibly one of the earliest electrical lamps done at Lenox* **125.00**
☐ Brass base, *white cylinder body, original wiring and shade in bad condition* **25.00**
☐ Brass base, *coral body with embossed white floral design, rewired and new shade* **85.00**
☐ No metal base, *coral body with white handles, ruffled rim, probably a vase converted into a lamp at home* **30.00**
☐ No metal base, *candlestick type, hand-painted roses and ribbons, nicely decorated* **35.00**
☐ Silver-plated base, *urn shaped body in two sections, bottom section fluted and white, top section teal blue with an embossed white wreath similar to the Lenox wreath. Rewired and new shade* **100.00**
☐ Silver-plated base, *same as above except done in coral and white* ... **75.00**

PENS
Early C.A.C. pens with original metal tips are virtually unknown. Any verifiable pen in this category would be worth a minimun of $100.
  Fountain pens with Lenox bases came along much later and are also collectible. Depending on style and color, they are worth from $50 to $100.

SALT AND PEPPER MILLS
Salt and pepper mill sets are relatively recent additions, and usually have either chrome or brass lids and grinders. They are of little interest to the collectors, and as a rule should be priced somewhere in the area of similar ones still being made.
☐ Salt and pepper mill, *chrome parts, Jewel pattern, gold wreath mark* . **40.00**
☐ Salt and pepper mill, *brass parts, monochromatic brown pheasant decorations, gold wreath mark* **30.00**

STEINS
Although they are to be considered quite rare, steins are nothing more than the standard Lenox mug shapes with the addition of a metal top. The shape pictured is the most common one, and the majority of steins are monochromatic.
☐ Sterling lid and thumbrest, *soccer player in monochromatic blues, transition mark* **275.00**
☐ Sterling lid by Gorham, *hand-painted Indian in full color on pale tan background, transition mark* **325.00**
☐ Sterling lid by Gorham, *standing monk done in monochromatic browns, transition mark* **280.00**
☐ Sterling lid, *two football players, monochromatic blue, C.A.C. wreath mark* **290.00**
☐ Sterling lid, *woman golfer in monochromatic green, transition mark* . **240.00**

Stein, *inebriated monk*

☐ Sterling ribbons on copper on lid, *inebriated monk in monochromatic browns, transition mark* **250.00**

OTHER
In addition to the button hooks and pens, there were several other metal items with the C.A.C. holders. Included in this group would be nail files, letter openers, cuticle pushers, and the like. Any such item verifiable as early Lenox would be worth a minimum of $100.

TABLE XII—Silver Company Marks
In an effort to assist the Lenox collector in identifying the makers of silver items used with Lenox, following is a list of companies and their marks. Most of the companies listed here used a variety of marks on their items, but we have only included those marks likely to appear on holders or overlay.

Alvin Corporation
(Providence, RI, 1886 to present)
Few items have been seen, but all were marked in one way or another with the word "Alvin".

Bailey, Banks, and Biddle
(Philadelphia, PA, 1832 to present)
The name will either be spelled out in full or abbreviated BB&B. So far as we can tell, BB&B did not actually manufacture any of the holders, and their name appears on them as the retail store that sold them rather than as the maker. Sometimes the maker's mark will appear on the item as well.

Barbour Silver Co.
(Hartford, CT)
The company's initials, B.S.C., is seen on most items.

Caldwell, J. E. & Co.
(Philadelphia, PA)
Caldwell is a retailer rather than manufacturer. The name can be spelled out in full or sometimes seen as J.E.C. & Co.

Charter Company
(See Barbour)
Marks include: (1) oak leaf in a rectangle; (2) acorn in a rectangle; (3) the initial "C" in a rectangle flanked by oak leaves.

Depasse Mfg. Co.
(New York City, NY)
The Depasse mark was the letter "D" inside a jug shape. The name was later changed to Depasse, Pearsall Silver Co., and the mark then became "DP" inside a jug.

Dominick & Haff
(Newark, NJ, and New York City, NY)
The usual mark was a rectangle, circle and diamond close together in a row. Occasionally the initials "D&H" also appear.

Durgin
(Concord, NH and Providence, RI)
Durgin's mark was the letter "D" in an oval.

Electrolytic Art Metal Company
(Trenton, NJ)
Their name was sometimes spelled out, but more often appears as EAMCO in a rectangle with coffin corners.

Elgin Silversmith Co., Inc.
(New York City, NY)
Their mark was EL-SIL-CO in a diamond shape.

Gorham Corporation (Division of Textron)
(Providence, RI)
All marks appearing on holders thus far have had some variation of a lion, an anchor, and the letter "G" in a row. Sometimes these marks appear inside blocks and other times not. Many of the turn-of-the-century items are date-marked as well.

Hickok-Matthews Company
(Newark, NJ)
The mark was the letter "M" imposed over a scimitar.

International Silver Co.
(Meriden, CT)
The following marks have been noted: (1) some version of the word "International"; (2) the letter "W" with a quarter moon around it; (3) I.S.CO.

Kirk, Samuel and Son
(Baltimore, MD, 1815 to present)
The Kirk Company has used a number of different marks, but all using the Kirk name. Since some of the marks were used for only a short period of time, they can be used to pinpoint fairly precise dates.

Lunt Silversmiths
(Greenfield, MA)
Only a few items have been seen that were made by this company. All had the word "Lunt" somewhere on them.

Mauser Manufacturing Company
(New York City, NY, founded 1887)
The Mauser mark was a unicorn emerging from a horn of plenty.

Redlich & Co.
(New York City, NY)
The Redlich mark was a mythical creature with the head of a lion and the body of a serpent.

Reed and Barton
(Tauton, MA)
This company's mark is an eagle, the letter "R", and a standing lion. The letter "R" is sometimes enclosed in a shield.

Rockwell Silver Co.
(Meriden, CT, founded 1907)
Rockwell's mark consisted of a shield with the word Rockwell in it, or sometimes just the company's initials.

Rogers
There were several companies by this name, and we feel that the marks are too confusing to be listed here.

Schofield Co., Inc.
(Baltimore, MD)
The Schofield mark consisted of the letter "H" in a diamond, a lion in a circle, and then the letter "S" in a diamond, all in a row.

Shreve & Co.
(San Francisco, CA)
Their name usually appears as the retailer rather than maker, and is usually spelled out in full on the item.

Shreve, Crump & Low Co., Inc.
(Boston, MA)
This is a retail store, not a manufacturer. The name is usually spelled out in full.

Tiffany & Co.
(New York City, NY)
All of the Tiffany holders were marked in one way or the other with the name spelled out in full. Many items are also marked with an initial which refers to the company president's last name, which is handy for dating purposes.

Towle Silversmiths
(Newburyport, MA)
The Towle mark most frequently seen is a script letter "T" with a lion climbing up it.

Unger Brothers
(Newark, NJ)
The most frequently seen mark are the letters "UB" intertwined inside of a circle. Sometimes just the letter "U" was used by itself.

Wallace, R. & Sons Mfg. Co.
(Wallingford, CT)
They used many marks, the most common being the initial "RW&S" with a stag's head.

Watson Company
(Attleboro, MA)
Watson used a wreath (similar to the Lenox one) with a sword going up through the middle.

Whiting, Frank M. Co.
(North Attleboro, MA)
This company, frequently confused with the Whiting Mfg. Co., used the initial "W" inside a circle. Three lines branch out from each side of the circle.

Whiting Manufacturing Co.
(Providence, RI)
Their mark is a mythical creature with its paw on a circle with the letter "W" inside it. Some items were date-marked.

Woodside Sterling Co.
(New York City, NY)
Woodside used the letter "W" inside a circle. It is very close to the mark used by International and should not be confused with it.

(Note: Marks are hard to find on some items. They can be on the inside or outside of items, and in some instances can be found on the undersides of handles. On overlay items, the mark can either be somewhere on the silver or on the bottom of the item next to the Lenox mark. When the mark is found on the china itself, it would seem obvious that Lenox put the silver company's mark on the same time they put on their own, thus saving an additional firing at a later time. We occasionally see items, usually plain brown or cobalt, with the Lenox and silver company marks on bottom but having no silver on them. These are items which were ear-marked for silver overlay work but which somehow never made it to the silver company.)

FIGURINES

Lenox figurines of all types have long been popular collectibles. They probably account for less than one or two percent of total Lenox production, and this coupled with the public's fondness for them raises prices to a level which in many cases cannot be justified by size or workmanship.

The fully-detailed figurines are the ones which are probably still underpriced considering the amount of work which went into each one. Considering the lace work, applied flowers, unbelievably thin fingers, and the hand-painted outfits, they are by a far stretch still below current replacement value. Items such as the llama are on dangerous ground for they could be manufactured today for less than what people are paying for older ones.

Production problems plagued many of the figurines, and it would seem that the very qualities that make Lenox into such fine dinnerware prevent its effective use in the manufacture of figurines. Mold cracks and firing cracks are very common in the figurine line, due to the fact that a variation of more than 1/1000th of an inch in the thickness of the glaze will cause such cracks. Since it is harder to apply glaze evenly to a figure with folds and crevices than to dinnerware, this probably accounts for most of the firing cracks.

This may have been one of the reasons why so many of the figures were left in the bisque state, and is certainly the reason for the many unmarked figurines encountered today.

The lack of a backstamp on a verifiable shape does not totally kill the value as it might on other types of items, partly because in many cases the shapes can be positively identified as Lenox and partly because the public demand for the figurines is so great that they will accept unmarked items.

Minor damage is also acceptable on many of the figurines and is almost expected on the fully-detailed ones. Just how much the value is affected depends on the extent of the damage and the rarity of the figurine.

Collectors tend to refer only to the Pat Eakin items as figurines, and all others are called figurals, a rather odd choice considering that figural is an adjective and not a noun. They are in fact all figurines, and we would suggest referring to the fully-detailed figurines as Eakin type and the Deco type either by that name or as DeVegh type after the man who designed many of them. Animals can, of course, be called animals.

Neither author owns a Lenox figurine with the exception of swans, due more to personal taste than anything else. They just don't seem to fit in with the older items, and we don't like them well enough to allow a fondness for them to override other considerations. We realize we are very much alone in this matter, and that prices on the figurines of all types will probably continue to rise in the future.

Angels

ANGELS

There were two pairs of Lenox angels made, and, the smaller pair, which bend toward each other, is purely decorative. The larger pair, one with candle on the right and the other holding the candle on the left, is obviously both decorative and useful. Both angel pairs were available in plain white or with gold trim.

☐ Angel, shape #2764, 2" x 2-1/4" x 4-1/8", white, Lenox wreath mark . . . **90.00**
☐ Angel, shape #2764, 2" x 2-1/4" x 4-1/8", white with gold trim, Lenox
   wreath mark **100.00**
   The mate to angel #2764 is #2765. Both have the same dimensions
   and are priced the same.
☐ Angel, shape #2981, 2-1/4" x 2-3/4" x 6", candlestick type, undeco-
   rated, Lenox wreath mark **125.00**

☐ Angel, shape #2981, 2-1/4" x 2-3/4" x 6", candlestick type, gold trim,
Lenox wreath mark **130.00**
**Angel #2982 is the mate for #2981. Both have the same dimensions
and are priced the same.**

Birds, *jays and robins*

BIRDS

The Lenox birds are of two types, crested and not crested, and are usually
called jay and robin (in that order). The three sizes are referred to as tiny,
small and large. A further distinction is made between those with tail up and
those with tail down, with tail up being more desirable.

Color and shape affect the price somewhat, but for now all of them are in
the under $50 range. White is the most common, followed by pink and blue,
green is perhaps next and yellow is the rarest. The tail-down small jay and
robin were also available as salt and pepper shakers, and will frequently be
unmarked since the hole for the cork takes up the spot where the mark would
usually go. The birds we have seen have all been glazed. For the most part,
the birds were never decorated, and any decoration should be viewed with
some suspicion. The mark is almost invariably the Lenox green wreath/U.S.A.
one, to the point where we will not bother to list the marks in the pricing section, except to note those which are unmarked.

The large size birds came sometimes with a circle cut out of their backs so
they could be used as small planters or perhaps candy dishes. The large bird,
if we remember correctly, was always the robin type. The robin can also be
found on a base with several holes in it for use as a flower "frog", and a
Trenton collector has one of thesobin can also be found on a base with
several holes in it for use as a flower "frog", and a Trenton collector has one
of these in a cocoa brown.

Currently in production is a pair of partridge salt and pepper shakers, in a
shape and size very similar if not identical to a much older pair we have seen.

Jay Shapes

☐ Dimensions for the small tail-down jay are 1-3/8" x 3-5/8" x 1-3/4", and item numbers are #1790 for the regular and #2252 for the salt and pepper version. *It comes in the full range of colors and is usually priced at $10 or $12 for the white up to $25 for the various colors.*

☐ Dimensions for the tiny tail-up jay are not available, and item number also not available. *As a rule, priced at perhaps $15 for the white up to $30 for rarer colors.*

Robin Shapes

☐ Dimensions for tail-down one in the small size are 1-1/2" x 3" x 2-3/8", item numbers are #1788 for the regular and #2251 for the salt and pepper, *colors include coral, yellow, blue, green and white. Prices vary from $10 for white to $30 for rarer colors.*

☐ Dimensions for the tail-up robin in the small size are 1-1/2" x 2-5/8" x 3-1/8", item number is #1789, *available in full range of colors. Prices range from $15 for white to $35 for rarer colors.*

☐ Dimensions and item number for the tail-up tiny robin are not available, but the full range of colors was available. *Typically they bring as much (if not more) than the larger ones, i.e., at least $15 for white to $35 for rarer colors.*

☐ Dimensions for the tail-up large robin are 2" x 6-1/2" x 5", and the item number is #1822. *It was available in five colors, and prices range from $25 for white to $40 for hard-to-find colors.*

Covered bonbon

Other Bird Items

☐ Covered bonbon with bird finial, item #2363, *6-1/4" diameter x 5" to top of bird's tail, white with pink bottom, other colors available, Lenox wreath mark* **75.00**

☐ Covered bon bon, *same description as above but bird damaged* **45.00**

- [ ] Covered cigarette box with bird finial, item #3165, *3-1/2" x 4-7/8" x 3-1/2", white bird with pale blue box, Lenox wreath mark (other colors were also available)* **50.00**
- [ ] Flower frog bird, item number unknown, *no recent sales but owner of brown one estimates value at no less than $50.*
- [ ] Tree flower holder with bird, crested jay type, shape #2438, *2-3/4" x 2-3/4" x 3" x 5-1/4", all white, Lenox wreath mark* **50.00**
- [ ] Tree flower holder with bird, *as above but with color, add $10 to $15 depending on color combination.*
- [ ] Tree flower holder with bird, robin type, item #2434, 4" x 6-1/2" x 9", white tree with coral bird, Lenox wreath mark on nudes **75.00**
The above tree worth about $10 less in all-white, other colors worth about the same as the pink or a little more.
- [ ] Tree flower holder with bird, robin type, item #2436, 2-5/8" x 2-1/4" x 7-1/4", *all white, Lenox wreath mark* **50.00**
Add $10 to $15 for color.

To the best of our knowledge, these birds were never decorated at the factory and the occasional hand-painted one encountered today was done away from the factory. The hand-painting should not increase the value by all that much.

BOOKENDS

The so-called Trojan horse bookends, measuring 3-1/2" x 5" x 7-1/2", were available in white only and apparently in glazed only. The usual mark is the Lenox wreath mark. Among Lenox collectors, a pair typically sells for $150 to $200; however, we have heard that among Art Deco collectors the price can go as high as $400.

Women's head bookends

The woman's head bookends are 10" high and have the Lenox green wreath mark. One story we have heard about them is that they were done in honor of Amelia Earhart's flight around the world, and whether this is true or not, they are sometimes given her name. They usually sell in the $150 to $200 a pair range.

Another pair of bookends seen recently was unmarked but quite possibly Lenox, and they were shaped like books with gold trim on the pages. A signed set would be in the $200 range. Another pair of possibly Lenox bookends was shaped like a pile of stones. Very square looking plain ones, also unmarked, have been noted.

BULLDOG

The bulldog, shape #1832-1/2, measuring 4" x 8" x 5", was available in both glazed and bisque finishes, and will sometimes sport a royal blue collar. The mark can be either impressed or green wreath. The detailing is quite good, which perhaps accounts for the bulldog's popularity with collectors.

There is a hole on the bottom of his collar through which (presumably) a medallion could be suspended, although we have never seen one done in this fashion. Since it would be rather silly for the company to go to all that trouble for no particular reason, we are making the assumption that perhaps the first bulldogs were special orders for a team or organization and that each member received a bulldog with an engraved medallion.

A bulldog, glazed or unglazed, should be an easy $150 sale, more in some parts of the country. Although it is strictly conjecture on our part, a bulldog with the blue collar and the original medallion might bring $50 more.

Bulldog

DOLLS

During World War I, German bisque doll heads were unobtainable so Lenox began producing the heads for the Effenbee doll company. The Lenox heads are perhaps more prized for their rarity than for their beauty, and are avidly sought by both doll collectors and Lenox collectors. The dolls had stuffed

Doll, *hand-painted*

bodies and composition hands, and we assume that the one shown has her original clothes and wig. On the back of the head under the hairline is an impressed Lenox mark and also the Effenbee mark. The face is, of course, hand-painted, and the eyes are the non-movable type. This particular doll was purchased in 1978 for $750, and the present owner has turned down higher offers.

A 1939 **Fortune** article on Lenox china showed a picture of a pincushion doll, which once again is unexceptional in appearance but which would be a nice addition to a Lenox collection. To the best of our knowledge, the item exists only as a prototype and was not put into general production. A marked sample would probably fetch $300 or better.

Any Lenox doll should be considered a rarity and will probably be priced accordingly. The Lenox Company perhaps came on the scene a little too late to have been actively involved with dolls. Among the unanswered questions is who modeled the head.

ELEPHANTS

For the most part, elephants are middle-period Lenox items, usually with the green wreath/U.S.A. mark (if any.) They were made in several shapes and sizes, at least four different colors, and were available both in glazed and bisque. Considering the variety of elephants produced, there are remarkably few to be found, which is reflected in their prices. Interestingly, there are no known donkeys made by Lenox.

The Coxon family has in its possession what is possibly a much earlier elephant. It is very light in weight, and the detailing is exceptionally good. Although it is unmarked, it is possibly Lenox. To find such an elephant with, say, a C.A.C. mark would be exciting to say the least, since C.A.C. figurines of any sort are virtually unknown.

Of the four colors we have seen, white is by far the most common followed by gray, black and cobalt. Although most of the elephants were available both in bisque and glazed, the larger elephants usually seem to be glazed while the smaller ones are usually unglazed.

☐ Elephant, shape #2119, *7-7/8" x 4-1/4" x 6-5/8", glazed, white, Lenox wreath mark* **175.00**
☐ Elephant, shape #2120, *9-1/2" x 4-1/4" x 6-1/8", white bisque, un-marked* **100.00**
☐ Elephant, shape #2120, *9-1/2" x 4-1/4" x 6-1/8", white, glazed, Lenox wreath mark* **150.00**
☐ Elephant, shape #2120, *9-1/2" x 4-1/4" x 6-1/8", white, bisque, Lenox wreath mark* **150.00**
☐ Elephant, shape #2120-1/4, *3" x 6-3/4" x 4-3/8", white, bisque, Lenox wreath mark, good sized chip on left front foot* **125.00**
☐ Elephant, shape #2120-1/2, *3-1/2" x 7-3/4" x 5", glazed, black un-marked* **175.00**
☐ Elephant, shape #3072, *2-3/4" x 7" x 4-1/2", white, bisque, Lenox wreath mark* **130.00**
☐ Elephant, shape #3072, *2-3/4" x 7" x 4-1/2", white, glazed, Lenox wreath mark* **150.00**

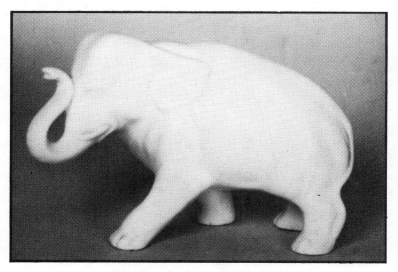

Elephant, *shape #3072-1/2*

☐ Elephant, shape #3072-1/2, *2-1/2" x 6" x 3-1/2", white, glazed, Lenox wreath mark* **150.00**
☐ Elephant, shape #3072-1/4, *2-1/8" x 5" x 3", white, bisque, Lenox wreath mark* **125.00**
☐ Elephant, shape #3074, *4" x 8-1/2" x 6-1/2", white, glazed, crack in trunk and several chips (small) on front feet, Lenox wreath mark* **140.00**
☐ Elephant, shape #3074, *4" x 8-1/2" x 6-1/2", white, bisque, Lenox wreath mark* **155.00**
☐ Elephant, shape #3074, *4" x 8-1/2" x 6-1/2", cobalt with white tusks, unmarked* **225.00**

- ☐ Elephant, shape #3222, 1-1/4" x 3" x 1-1/4", bisque, gray, both tusks broken off, Lenox wreath mark **50.00**
- ☐ Elephant, shape #3222, 1-1/4" x 3" x 1-3/4", bisque, gray, Lenox wreath mark **120.00**
- ☐ Elephant, shape #3222, 1-1/4" x 3" x 1-3/4", glazed, white, unmarked . **50.00**
- ☐ Elephant, shape #3299, 1-5/8" x 4-7/8" x 2-3/8", gray, bisque, (small elephant on white stand, dimensions include stand), Lenox wreath mark **130.00**
- ☐ Elephant, shape #3299, 1-5/8" x 4-7/8" x 2-3/8", white, glazed, one tusk broken off halfway, Lenox wreath mark **110.00**
- ☐ Elephant, shape #3301, 2-1/4" x 4-1/4" x 2-1/4", bisque, gray, (two small elephants on stand), Lenox wreath mark **160.00**
- ☐ Elephant, shape #3301, 2-1/4" x 4-1/4" x 2-1/4", bisque, white, Lenox wreath mark, (two small elephants on a stand) **135.00**
  Note: All of the elephants except #2119 are referred to as "trunk up" elephants. Obviously, #2119 is called the "trunk down" one.

FISH

- ☐ Fish, shape #2912, 1-7/8" x 3-3/4" x 4-1/2", apple green, Lenox green wreath mark **80.00**
- ☐ Fish, shape #2912, 1-7/8" x 3-3/4" x 4-1/2", white, Lenox green wreath mark **40.00**
- ☐ Fish, shape #3483, 12" long x 4-1/2" high, black with gold trim, Lenox wreath mark **175.00**

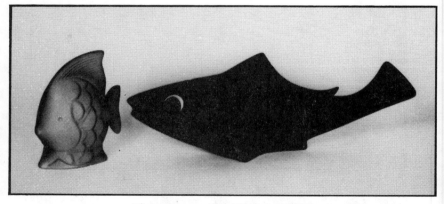

Fish, shape #2912 and #3483

FULLY-DETAILED FIGURINES

The delightful Lenox figurines are perhaps the most keenly sought Lenox collectibles of all. They are a product of the 1940's and '50's, and were primarily the work of Patricia Jean Eakin, who was later to also work for Boehm and Cybis.

Miss Eakin, who had been a ceramics engineer with the Tennessee Valley Authority, came to Trenton where she resided on Stokeley Avenue. There is at least some evidence to suggest that she originally designed the figurines long before coming to work at Lenox, but that they were the only American company capable of producing them at that time. She died only recently, in 1976, and instead of the customary funeral parlor services her family and friends gathered at a Trenton hotel for cocktails and canapes.

She made some of the original molds for the production of the Lenox figurines, and the figurines from her molds have the impressed initials PJE on the bottom (sometimes hard to read.) Although it is not yet the case, we feel that in years to come the figurines with her mark will have a higher value than those which don't. Her Lenox figurines were intended to be an American costume series.

A few of the figurines were designed after Miss Eakin left Lenox so they will never have her initials on them. The small, hand-written initials on most of the figurines are those of the artist who decorated the figurines. The Lenox backstamp can be either green or gold. A list and description of the figurines follows:

(1) **Ballerina (6")**
    (a) White dress with flowered skirt
    (b) Light blue dress with flowered skirt
    (c) Pink dress with flowered skirt

(2) **Colonial Lady (7-1/4")**
    (a) Turquoise dress, green and blue garlands on underskirt
    (b) Fawn dress, green and blue garlands on underskirt
    (c) Maroon and green dimity print, ruffled underskirt

(3) **Crinoline Miss (Name in doubt, 6")**
    Holding muff, tiny ruffle on back of bonnet

(4) **The Dandy (10-3/4")**
    Gray suit and hat, checked vest and blue cravat. He is rumored to be a likeness of Walter Lenox

(5) **Floradora (9-1/4")**
    (a) Pink blouse, black-plumed hat, lavender and pink skirt
    (b) Fawn jacket, green scallops on skirt, plumed hat

Lady Diana

(6) **Lady Diana (10")**
    White horse with rider, dressed in gray riding skirt, brown jacket and black hat

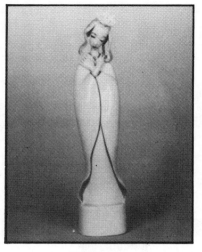

Madonna

(7) **Madonna (11")**
Blonde hair, gold trim on robe

(8) **Mistress Mary (6")**
(a) White dress, floral motifs, blue-trimmed ruffles
(b) Yellow dress, blue daisy motifs, black-trimmed ruffles

(9) **Natchez Belle (7-1/2")**
(a) Green bodice, green-trimmed skirt, white ruffles
(b) Pink bodice, aqua-striped skirt, trimmed ruffles

(10) **Prima Donna (8-1/4")**
(a) Floral hat, white coat and dress and bustle
(b) Floral hat, black coat and bustle
(c) Floral hat, pale orchid coat and bustle

(11) **The Reader (5-1/2")**
(a) Red-flowered skirt
(b) Yellow skirt

(12) **Southern Belle (6-1/2")**
(a) Blue-flowered bonnet and coat, blue dress, blue-flowered underskirt
(b) Pastel-flowered bonnet and dress, pink coat, blue underskirt

(13) **Sportswoman (6-1/2")**
Celadon green riding skirt and coat, black hat and red vest

(14) **The Twins (3-1/2")**
(a) Girls had either a blue dress, pink dress, green dress, blue polka-dot apron, or pink polka-dotted apron.
(b) The boy is usually done in brown and black.
(Note that the original twins were two girls. One of the same girls was used later with the boy, and there was never a second boy.)

Sizes vary somewhat from those listed, and two Floradoras seen recently were 3/4" different. The differences in size are due both to original assembly of the figurines and to variation in the size of platform used. Trim color can also vary considerably, probably due to the whim of the artist on a particular day.

The Reader

Damage is very common, and does not affect the value all that much if limited to minor lace damage or a missing finger. In general, damage is less forgivable on the more common figurines such as the twins or Mistress Mary.

Prices have not moved very much on the figurines in five or ten years, and they are overdue for a huge jump in value. Many dealers are justifiably unwilling to ship the figurines, creating a situation where if the collector wants a figurine and sees one locally, it might be best to pay the asking price.

In addition to the above figurines, there are several others known or thought to be products of Lenox. Jonathan Coxon's family has a figure of a woman sitting on a toilet, unmarked but quite likely a Lenox item. A private collector in New York has a large figure of a sitting Indian with beautiful detailing, which we gather is an authentic likeness of a Plains Indian. It is marked with the Lenox wreath, and additionally has the name Tollen (or possibly Toller) impressed on the side. The Lenox museum has a set of figurines modeled after famous opera characters. All of these are probably one-of-a-kind items, and should be considered treasures.

Since some of the figurines have never been sold on the open market, we will alter our usual pricing scheme somewhat to include several estimates, either ours or the owners.

- [ ] Ballerina, *perfect (actual sale)* **400.00**
- [ ] Ballerina, *badly damaged, most of crinoline skirt missing on one side (actual sale)* **200.00**
- [ ] Colonial Lady, *most of front ruffle missing (actual sale)* **225.00**
- [ ] Colonial Lady, *moderate overall damage (actual sale)* **200.00**
- [ ] Colonial Lady, *slight damage (average price from three sales)* **400.00**
- [ ] Crinoline Lady, *perfect (actual sale)* **350.00**
- [ ] Floradora, *perfect (actual sale)* **400.00**
- [ ] Floradora, *plumes missing from hat, rare decoration of green dress with embossed white design (actual sale)* **350.00**

Sportswoman

- ☐ Floradora, *hand professionally repaired (actual sale)* 375.00
- ☐ Floradora, *minor damage to hand (actual sale)* 350.00
- ☐ Indian, *owner values figure at $7,000*
- ☐ Lady Diana, *two currently on the market, both with asking price of $1,000, no other known sales*
- ☐ Lady on toilet, *unmarked, authors' estimate of $200, a marked one probably in the area of $500*
- ☐ Madonna, *perfect, owner's estimate is $500*
- ☐ Mistress Mary, *perfect (actual sale)* 350.00
- ☐ Mistress Mary, *slight damage to ruffles (actual sale)* 325.00
- ☐ Mistress Mary, *tips of fingers missing (actual sale)* 325.00
- ☐ Mistress Mary, *heavy damage (actual sale)* 225.00
- ☐ Natchez Belle, *perfect (actual sale)* 375.00
- ☐ Natchez Belle, *minor damage (actual sale)* 360.00
- ☐ Natchez Belle, *bottom ruffle entirely gone, damage to hand (actual sale)* 225.00
- ☐ Opera figures, *no known sales, authors' estimate of no less than $500 each*
- ☐ Prima Donna, *perfect (actual sale)* 375.00
- ☐ Prima Donna, *slight damage in several spots (actual sale)* 325.00
- ☐ Southern Belle, *perfect, usually priced in the $350 to $400 range, but one recently sold for $500*
- ☐ Sportswoman, *perfect (owner's estimate $350)*
- ☐ The Dandy, *perfect (actual size)* 600.00
- ☐ The Reader, *perfect, yellow dress (actual size)* 325.00
- ☐ The Reader, *perfect, flowered dress (actual sale)* 325.00
- ☐ The Reader, *damaged neck ruffle (actual sale)* 325.00

The Twins

- ☐ The Reader, *damaged on side with firing crack, undecorated, "back door" item (actual sale)* 325.00
  The Reader is the perfect example of an item which has become stuck at a certain price and just refuses to budge.
- ☐ Twin boy, *perfect (owner's estimate of $175)*
- ☐ Twin boy, *undecorated (actual size)* 140.00
- ☐ Twin girl, *perfect (actual sale)* 125.00
- ☐ Twin girl, *part of braid missing and damage to skirt (actual sale)* 100.00

FULL-LENGTH FIGURES

The full-length figures, mainly nudes, were available in a large variety of shapes and sizes.

- ☐ Woman, shape #1850, *nude, sitting with one hand behind her and the other on her head, white, glazed, Lenox wreath mark* 135.00
- ☐ Woman, shape #1851, *nude, reclining, unmarked but matches picture in old catalogues* 50.00
- ☐ Woman, shape #1852, *nude, sitting, hands behind her on the ground, Lenox wreath mark, white, glazed* 125.00
- ☐ Woman, nude, shape #2551, *sitting on top of tree vase, one arm raised to her hair, white, glazed, 2-5/8" x 3-1/2" x 6-3/4", Lenox wreath mark* 85.00
- ☐ Woman, nude, shape #2552, *sitting on top of tree vase, both arms down, 3-1/4" x 4" x 8-1/4", white, glazed, Lenox wreath mark* 100.00
- ☐ Woman and man, shapes #2682 and #2681, *12" high, glazed, white, dressed holding sheaves of wheat, Lenox wreath mark, pair* 375.00
- ☐ Woman, shape #3152, *wide skirt and fan, vase behind her, 3-5/8" x 5-1/8" x 8-1/2", bisque finish, impressed Lenox mark, called "Crinoline vase"* 140.00

Tree Vases, *woman's shape and robin's shape*

- ☐ Woman, shape #3153, *standing nude, 3-1/4" x 4" x 12-1/2", vase behind her, glazed, Lenox wreath mark, called the "Spring vase"* **175.00**
- ☐ Woman, shape #3154, *Leda and the swan, 4" x 5-1/2" x 10", vase behind her, bisque finish, impressed mark, called the "Leda vase"*..... **150.00**
- ☐ Woman, shape #3156, *kneeling nude, 3" x 3-3/4" x 10-7/8", vase behind her, glazed, Lenox wreath mark, called the "Evening vase"*..... **165.00**
- ☐ Woman with greyhound, *13" high, gold trim, Lenox wreath mark* **185.00**

Woman with greyhound, Woman's head, *shape #2138*

Similar items, without vases, typically sell in the $200 and up range. They include the "knee-up" nude which is 14" high, the standing nude which is 13" high, Leda and the swan, and the lady with the fan. The lady with fan is the exception in the pricing scheme, for it rarely brings more than $125 or $150. In addition, she causes a great deal of confusion because she is called "Crinoline Lady" in the books, "Colonial Lady" by some collectors, and probably other names we haven't heard. The terms Crinoline Lady and Colonial Lady result in confusion over the fully-detailed figurines with similar names. We suggest the use of the term "Lady with Fan" to clear up the matter. Most of the Deco figures were available with a metal base which held a light which went inside the figure, making it into a lamp. The lamp base does not seem to increase or decrease the value.

GERMAN SHEPHERD

The German Shepherd was available in three different sizes of the same shape, and came both glazed and bisque. Catalogues indicate that it was available both in white and in a fawn color, but all of those we have seen have been white. Add at least $50 to any of the following prices for a fawn-colored one.

Baby's head, Rabbit, German Shepherd, Schnauzer

☐ German Shepherd, shape #3166-1/2, 4" x 9" x 5", white glazed, Lenox wreath mark* 150.00
☐ German Shepherd, shape #3166-1/2, 4" x 9" x 5", white, glazed unmarked 100.00
☐ German Shepherd, shape #3166-1/2, 4" x 9" x 5", white, bisque, marked 140.00
☐ German Shepherd, 3166-1/2, 3-1/2" x 7-3/4" x 4-1/4", white, glazed, marked 125.00
☐ German Shepherd, 3166-1/4, 3-1/2" x 7-3/4" x 4-1/4", white, bisque, marked, damage to front paw 85.00
☐ German Shepherd, shape #3166, 5" x 10-1/2" x 5-5/8", white, glazed, marked 160.00

☐ German Shepherd, shape #3166, *5" x 10-1/2" x 5-5/8", white, bisque,
marked* **150.00**
☐ German Shepherd, shape #3166, *5" x 10-1/2" x 5-5/8", white, bisque,
unmarked* **100.00**
  * Can be seen in photo with Schnauzer

HANDS AND ARMS
The hand ashtray, shape #2759, 2-1/2" x 7" x 1-3/8", was available in white,
coral and green, and usually sells in the $30 to $35 range. An upright arm and
hand which is unmarked is sometimes sold as Lenox. The arm, as the story
goes, was used to test rubber gloves for holes.

HUMAN FIGURES, ALL TYPES EXCEPT FULLY-DETAILED
Heads and Busts. Perhaps the most spectacular Lenox bust is the one
shown of the young man with a gold turban. According to Lenox catalogues
it was available in three different sizes, but the one shown, owned by a collector in California, is the only one we know of. There are no known sales for
this item, but the owner of the one pictured states he would not sell his for
less than $2,000.

Young man with turban

Baby heads are of two different types—one type stands by itself and the
other is resting on a pair of hands (or acording to some accounts a pair of
angel's wings.) The standing type was available both in smiling and crying
versions, and is frequently called a doll's head, which is unlikely since there
are not the usual pinholes which would be used to attach the head to the
body. Regardless of this, the name persists and we see no harm in its use
since it helps to differentiate it from the other type of baby.

☐ Baby's head, shape number unknown, *smiling baby, white, glazed,
Lenox wreath mark* **125.00**
☐ Baby's head, shape number unknown, *crying baby, white, bisque
finish, no mark* **90.00**

☐ Baby's head, resting on hands, shape #2968-1/4, *3-5/8" diameter x 3" high*, Lenox wreath mark, glazed **125.00**

☐ Baby's head, resting on hands, shape #2668-1/2, 4-1/4" diameter x 3-5/8" high, bisque finish, Lenox wreath mark **125.00**

☐ Baby's head, resting on hands, shape #2968, *4-3/4" diameter x 4-1/4" high*, glazed, white, Lenox wreath mark **150.00**

Adult heads are usually of the Art Deco type, and can be either flatback or fully fashioned. They are very popular which accounts for their prices.

☐ Woman's head, shape #2138, *1-1/2" x 3-3/4" x 3-7/8"*, light green, Lenox wreath mark **125.00**

☐ Woman's head, shape #2138, *1-1/2" x 3-3/4" x 3-7/8"*, white, Lenox wreath mark **80.00**

☐ Woman's head, shape #2673 and man's head shape #2672, *both 9-1/2" high*, all codal, Lenox wreath mark, man has shock fracture on back of head, pair... **300.00**

☐ Woman's head, shape #2857, *1-1/2" x 2-1/4" x 4"*, bisque, finish, Lenox wreath mark **75.00**

☐ Woman's head, shape #2857, *1-1/2" x 2-1/4" x 4"*, glazed, finish, Lenox wreath mark **80.00**

LLAMAS

The Lenox Llama is item #3042, and its measurements are 2" x 6" x 9". It will usually be white, although gray and yellow have been seen and other colors will no doubt turn up. All of the ones we have seen have been glazed and a bisque one should be considered possibly incomplete.

Although it is really nothing more than a blob of Lenox with a long neck, it remains immensely popular both with Lenox collectors and with Art Deco collectors, and $150 should be considered as a minimum price for a white one. They are almost always perfect and backstamped, so a damaged or unmarked one should not be worth anywhere near that price.

NIPPER

Nipper

The little dog with his head cocked to one side which has long been the emblem of the R.C.A. organization was twice done in Lenox china. One version, apparently done for the opening of Rockefeller Center in New York City, was a pair of little Nippers made into salt and pepper shakers. The Lenox mark is impressed along the bottom rim. A second version of Nipper, done for some anniversary of R.C.A., is about 12" high and has a bisque finish. The bigger figure is extremely scarce, and one account has no more than a dozen of them being made. It is fully marked on the bottom.

Both versions have a decorated collar, ears, and facial features, and the larger version has "His Master's Voice" painted in as well. This one little dog manages to, at the same time, be the most common and the rarest of the Lenox canines.

The salt and pepper shakers typically sell in the $25 to $30 range (for the pair.) There were no known sales for the large one within the past year, but the owner of the one shown in the photograph values it at $350, which seems fair considering how scarce it is.

PENGUINS
Penguins are not readily available as the swans or other birds, but are still obtainable. The #1827 penguin was available only in white, while the #2678 series came in both coral and white. The white ones are occasionally decorated. Broken beaks are fairly common since the beak hits first if the penguin is knocked over.

Penguins

☐ Penguin, shape #1827, *1-7/8" x 2-1/4" x 4-1/8", white, Lenox wreath mark* **35.00**

☐ Penguin, shape #2678, *3-1/8" x 3-5/8" x 6-1/8", coral, Lenox wreath mark* **65.00**

☐ Penguin, shape #2678, *dimensions as above, white, Lenox wreath mark* **60.00**

☐ Penguin, shape #2678-1/4, *2-3/8" x 2-1/2" x 4-1/2", white, Lenox
  wreath mark* **35.00**
☐ Penguin, shape #2678-1/4, *dimensions as above, white, broken beak,
  Lenox wreath mark* **15.00**
☐ Penguin, shape #2678-1/4, *dimensions as above, coral, Lenox wreath
  mark*... **45.00**
☐ Penguin, shape #2678-1/4, *dimensions as above, decorated, Lenox
  wreath mark* **60.00**
☐ Penguin, shape #2678-1/2, *2-5/8" x 2-7/8" x 5-3/8", white, Lenox
  wreath mark* **45.00**
☐ Penguin, shape #2678-1/2, *dimensions as above, coral, Lenox wreath
  mark*... **50.00**

RABBITS

The little Lenox rabbit is item #2911, and measures 1-3/4" x 2-1/2" x 5-3/8". It is usually glazed and will have the Lenox wreath mark, and so far as we can determine was usually white, although other colors are seen on rare occasions.

The same rabbit was used as the lid for one of the Lenox atomizers, and the atomizer rabbit will be open across the bottom while the purely decorative one will be closed.

The rabbit will usually be in the $50 to $75 range, although a rare color would certainly bring more.

SCHNAUZERS

The Schnauzers were available in two styles, a sitting one and a running one, and in at least two colors, white and blue. The sitting model is considered scarcer than the running one and, of course, blue is more desirable than white. Unlike so many of the animals and other figurines, the Schnauzer is usually perfect. The 1939 catalogue indicates they were available glazed only, so perhaps a bisque one should be considered incomplete. The mark is usually the standard Lenox green wreath one. The name Schnauzer is given to the figure by collectors, since the catalogue refers to it only as "running dog" and "sitting dog".

☐ Schnauzer, shape #2877, *1-3/8" x 3-1/8" x 3", sitting, white, Lenox
  wreath mark* **60.00**
☐ Schnauzer, shape #2877, *1-3/8" x 3-1/8" x 3", sitting, blue, Lenox
  wreath mark* **65.00**
☐ Schnauzer, shape #2878, *1-1/2" x 4-1/2" x 2", running, white, Lenox
  wreath mark* **45.00**
☐ Schnauzer, shape #2878, *1-1/2" x 4-1/2" x 2", running, blue, Lenox
  wreath mark* **55.00**

SCOTTIES

A small Scottie is shown in the 1939 catalogue, and the price list accompanying it tells us it was available both in white and in black. No one we know, however, has this little dog, and we have a feeling that since they were inexpensive at the time they were made that most of them ended up being played with by children and being broken.

Another small Scottie, unmarked but belonging to a Lenox workman who says it is Lenox is up on its hind legs as if begging for food. It is perfectly adorable and is in yellow Lenox.

Since we have never seen the one in the first paragraph, our prices are estimates.

- ☐ Scottie, shape #2661, *3/4" x 1-7/8" x 1-1/4", white, Lenox mark* **75.00**
- ☐ Scottie, shape #2661, *dimensions as above, black, Lenox mark* **100.00**
- ☐ Scottie, no shape number, *perhaps 1-3/4" high, base no more than 1/2" across, yellow, unmarked* **25.00**

SEALS

Seals were made in two shapes, one shape #2727, the other unknown. Both types are very much in the "blob" category but are rare enough to bring respectable prices.

- ☐ Seal, shape number unknown, *white, Lenox wreath mark* **65.00**
- ☐ Seals, shape #2727, *white, Lenox wreath mark* **70.00**

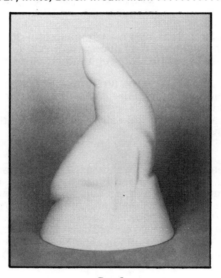

Seal

SHOES

Shoes

Lenox shoes are rather scarce, and the marks can range all the way from C.A.C. ones right up to gold wreath. Those with decoration are naturally more desirable, and a decorated one with a C.A.C. mark would probably bring an easy $150. The others with later marks bring from $60 to $100 depending on type and trim.

It is not clear at this point whether the earlier ones were meant to be pincushion holders or not, and the pincushion would probably neither add nor subtract value.

SWANS

Lenox produced their first swan in 1890, and the swan continued to be a popular item to the present day although the shape has changed. In an informal poll taken by us to determine which single Lenox item was most readily identified with Lenox better than 60 percent of those polled named the swan.

The smallest Lenox swans, shape #59, were intended to be used both as a salt dip (a small pepper shaker and a ceramic salt spoon were available with them), and as individual creamers with the #93 individual sugar.

Small swan, *shape #59*

The medium swans are also identified as sugars and creamers in Lenox catalogues, and in at least one case they are listed as flower holders. The two medium swans are of the same era, and the #68 one (generally called "wings up") is not earlier as sometimes claimed. The #68 swan is 4-1/4" high and was meant to be the sugar bowl. The #100 swan (called "wings back") is 3" high and intended to be a creamer. In addition to being somewhat impractical to use, the notion of pouring cream from the tail end of a swan seems something less than appetizing, and the overwhelming majority of these swans was used as candy dishes or decorative accessories.

The large swans, shapes #3252 and #3252-1/2, are in the "wings up" position, and are primarily used as centerpiece items. The large swans are the rarest, perhaps because of fewer sales due to the higher cost and to a

Medium swans, *shape #68 and current shape*

higher attrition rate through the years.

Swans are still being produced, and are available in 8", 6", and 4" tall versions, as well as a 2" miniature. The current shape can be seen in the middle of the photo.

- ☐ Swan, shape #59, *1-3/4" x 2-3/4", coral, Lenox wreath mark* **18.00**
- ☐ Swan, shape #59, *dimensions as above, white, Lenox wreath mark* . . **10.00**
- ☐ Swan, shape #59, *dimensions as above, white with gold trim, Lenox wreath mark* **12.00**
- ☐ Swan, shape #59, *dimensions as above, white outside, lavender lustre trim inside, gold trim on feathers, gold eyes and beak, C.A.C. green palette mark* **30.00**
- ☐ Swan, shape #59, *dimensions as above, light green with gold trim, Lenox wreath mark* **18.00**
- ☐ Swan, shape #68, *3-3/4" x 5" x 4-1/4" plain white, Lenox wreath mark* **22.00**
- ☐ Swan, shape #68, *dimensions as above, white with gold trim, Lenox wreath mark* **30.00**
- ☐ Swan, shape #68, *dimensions as above, exceptionally thin, unmarked but definitely Lenox, firing crack probably accounts for lack of backstamp* **30.00**
- ☐ Swan, shape #68, *dimensions as above, coral, Lenox wreath mark* . . **30.00**
- ☐ Swan, shape #68, *dimensions as above, green, Lenox wreath mark* . . **32.00**
- ☐ Swan, shape #68, *dimensions as above, white with Lenox Rose design and gold trim, Lenox wreath mark* **45.00**
- ☐ Swan, shape #68, *dimensions as above, all gold exterior, Lenox palette mark, not as garish as it sounds* **40.00**
- ☐ Swan, shape #100, *2-5/8" x 3-7/8" x 3" plain white, Lenox wreath mark* **15.00**
- ☐ Swan, shape #100, *dimensions as above, coral, Lenox wreath mark* . **20.00**
- ☐ Swan, shape #100, *dimensions as above, dark green, Lenox wreath mark* **28.00**
- ☐ Swan, shape #100, *dimensions as above, white with gold trim, Lenox wreath mark* **24.00**

☐ Swan, shape #100, *dimensions as above, white with Lenox Rose pattern and gold trim, Lenox wreath mark*	**35.00**
☐ Swan, shape #100, *dimensions as above, eggshell thin, C.A.C. brown palette mark*	**50.00**
☐ Swan, shape #100, *dimensions as above, baby pink, Lenox wreath mark*	**21.00**
☐ Swan, shape #3252, *6-3/4" x 9-1/4" x 8", white, Lenox wreath mark* ...	**85.00**
☐ Swan, shape #3252-1/2, *5-3/4" x 7-3/4" x 6-3/4", white with gold trim, Lenox wreath mark*	**75.00**

TOBY MUGS

The Teddy Roosevelt toby is almost always decorated, and was made for the Toby Potteries, New York. They were designed by Edward Penfield and are marked with the Lenox wreath mark and with the letter P in a shield (for Penfield.)

The 7" high William Penn toby, frequently mistaken for Ben Franklin, was produced in larger numbers, and both decorated and undecorated versions are available today. The decorated William Penn is usually found with the Lenox mark and the Bailey, Banks and Biddle store mark as well. BB&B apparently ordered several plain mugs from Lenox and had them painted by outside decorators. The undecorated William Penns are found in several color combinations (white with coral handle, all blue, etc.) The white ones are often taken and decorated, so any decorated William Penn without the BB&B mark should be compared against a BB&B marked authentic one to be sure the decoration is original with the item.

A similar situation exists with the George Washington tobies. To the best of our knowledge, the Lenox factory did not decorate their Washingtons, and sold them only in the white. The decorated Washingtons are never marked with the Lenox backstamp, and any decorated one bearing a Lenox backstamp should be viewed with some suspicion. For whatever reason, the unmarked ones were sold off as a group to a decorating company who did the painting. Since they have no markings at all, it is uncertain who did the artwork, although a possibility would be the company mentioned in first paragraph.

There are vague stories that Isaac Broome designed the Lenox tobies, and it is known that he did indeed once model a George Washington toby. What is not certain is if the one he did is the one put out by Lenox, since he supposedly did his in the 1890's, yet the Lenox models have the Lenox wreath marks and not the C.A.C. marks. Since he definitely did bring some of his earlier molds with him when he came to Lenox, it remains a possibility that the George Washington was his.

The William Penn toby has an impressed initial "B" on the back beneath the left hand (hard to see on some models.) Broome signed some of his earlier works (particularly his tiles) in just such a manner, so there appears to be some likelihood that this might be his work. Once again, however, employment dates and production dates don't match up, so our identification of Broome as the modeler will remain a tentative one. The William Penn is the most available of all the tobies, and if it is indeed a Broome it would be perhaps a not too expensive way to acquire Broome's work.

☐ Toby, George Washington, *large, undecorated, Lenox wreath mark* ..	**400.00**
☐ Toby, George Washington, *large, decorated, no mark*	**500.00**
☐ Toby, George Washington, *small, undecorated, Lenox wreath mark* ..	**300.00**
☐ Toby, George Washington, *small, decorated, no mark*	**400.00**

Toby mug, *William Penn*

- [ ] Toby, Teddy Roosevelt, *decorated, Lenox wreath mark and Penfield mark*.. **400.00**
- [ ] Toby, William Penn, *decorated, Lenox wreath and BB&B mark* **250.00**
- [ ] Toby, William Penn, *decorated, Lenox wreath mark, no BB&B mark but well-decorated* **175.00**
- [ ] Toby, William Penn, *undecorated, all white, Lenox wreath mark* **100.00**

Toby mug, *William Penn, undecorated*

☐ Toby, William Penn, *undecorated, white with coral handle, Lenox
   wreath mark* **150.00**
☐ Toby, William Penn, *undecorated, white with blue handle, no mark* .. **50.00**
☐ Toby, William Penn, *gold trim on white, probably gilded recently,
   Lenox wreath mark* **100.00**
☐ Toby, William Penn, *undecorated, white, crack in handle, Lenox
   wreath mark* **35.00**

*Note that the decorated but unmarked George Washington is
apparently more desirable than the undecorated but marked version.
Since the item is readily identifiable as Lenox, the lack of a backstamp seems to have no effect on the value.*

LIMITED AND SPECIAL EDITIONS
AMERICAN EXPRESS CHRISTMAS PLATES
Beginning in 1976, Lenox has issued a Christmas plate through the American
Express organization. The plates issued so far have been the Douglas Fir in
1976, the Scotch Pine in 1977, the Blue Spruce in 1978, and the Balsam Fir for
1979. Production has been in the area of 15,000 for each year, and the price of
the current plate is $60. We have not seen any of these plates sold on the
secondary market, so cannot give prices for any of the others.

Christmas plate

ARCHITECTS' TEA SET
This tea set is perhaps the best known of all the early Lenox limited editions.
It is a reproduction of a shape from colonial days, and is decorated with sepia
scenes of famous buildings and has copper lustre trim on handles, rims and
lids. The set includes:

☐ (1) Creamer—Mount Vernon, Virginia **35.00**
☐ (2) Cups and saucers, each **25.00**
☐   (a) Bull Pringle House, Charleston
☐   (b) Faneuil Hall, Boston
☐   (c) Library of the University of Virginia

Tea Set creamer & sugar

☐   (d) Monticello, Charlottesville
☐   (e) Santa Barbara Mission, California
☐   (f) Westover, Virginia
☐   (3) Hot water jug—Old North Church, Hartford **65.00**
☐   (4) Sugar bowl—Independence Hall, Philadelphia **40.00**
☐   (5) Tea plates—same scenes as on cups **15.00**
☐   (6) Teapot—Federal Hall, New York **75.00**
☐   (7) Waste bowl—first coat of arms of U.S.A.   **40.00**

     The tea plates, hot water jug, and waste bowl were available only as extras to the sets, and those sets without them should not be considered incomplete.

BICENTENNIAL AND SESQUICENTENNIAL ITEMS

The Lenox offering for the nation's 150th birthday in 1926 was a peacock blue cup and saucer with "1776-1926" in simple gold lettering on the front of the cup. Few are around today, and they should bring in the area of $50. Bicentennial items included the Patriots' Bowl and the Patriots' Pitcher, neither of which is being sold currently for more than issue price.

BOEHM BIRD SERIES

Issue price for the first bird plate was $35, and the issue price has risen about $3 a year to keep up with inflation. Prices vary considerably.

☐ 1970 Wood Thrush **325.00**
☐ 1971 Goldfinch **125.00**
☐ 1972 Mountain Bluebird **75.00**
☐ 1973 Meadowlark **70.00**
☐ 1974 Rufous Hummingbird **65.00**
☐ 1975 Redstart **65.00**
☐ 1976 Cardinals **65.00**
☐ 1977 Robins **65.00**

     The company does not publish production figures on these plates.

BOEHM WILDLIFE SERIES

The issue price for this series has varied from $50 in 1973 to $70 in 1978.

- ☐ 1973 Raccoons **75.00**
- ☐ 1974 Red Fox **65.00**
- ☐ 1975 Rabbits **68.00**
- ☐ 1976 Chipmunks **68.00**
- ☐ 1977 Beaver **67.00**
- ☐ 1978 White-tailed Deer **67.00**

The company does not publish production figures on these plates.

THE GOLD OF TUTANKHUMUM

The mask is approximately 6" tall, and is limited to 15,000 unnumbered pieces with an issue price of $200. It is not yet being sold on the secondary market. One word of caution—do not immerse the mask, for the water seeps up inside and is impossible to get out.

HAWTHORN TEA SET

- ☐ Cup and saucer, gold trim **25.00**
- ☐ Cup and saucer, no gold **24.00**
- ☐ Sugar and creamer, sugar lid missing **95.00**
- ☐ Teapot, gold trim **100.00**
- ☐ Teapot, no gold **100.00**

MINGA POPE PATCHIN ITEMS

These items are primarily products of the 1930's, and for the most part are sepia-tone scenics with gold trim. Series by her include the Old New York group and a set of plates done for the Colonial Dames of America which have scenes of colonial homes.

The 10-1/2" plates are the most common, but mugs, cups and saucers, and bowls are not unknown. Most of the items are in the $25 range, but the large bowl recently brought $75 at auction.

THE STATES OF THE CONFEDERACY

This series was issued in 1972 for $900 for the set, with production limited to 2,500. The most recent re-sale price we have seen was $950.

THE WALTER SCOTT LENOX VASE

This limited edition was copied from a very early Trenton item and as of April 1979, was no longer in production. It came with a wooden base and a glass dome, and was limited to 5,000 pieces at an issue price of $250.

The originals, virtually unknown except for samples in museums, were slightly larger than the copy. When and where the originals were first made is a subject of some debate, for both Willets and Ott & Brewer are thought to have manufactured the item. **The Dictionary of World Pottery and Porcelain** attributes the piece in the Newark Museum as follows: "Walter Scott Lenox, famous for founding the Trenton Pottery which has borne his name since 1896, designed this Belleek pitcher in 1887 when he was art director of Ott & Brewer. A pleasing expression of the Rococco as interpreted in the late 19th century ceramic art. Ht. 9-3/8"." It is not clear whether they are stating that the item is marked as Ott & Brewer or whether they are assuming it is Ott & Brewer from Lenox's date of employment there.

Another known sample bears the inscription on the bottom "WB 1887 to WSL", which is presumed to mean William Bromley 1887 to Walter Scott Lenox. Exactly why Bromley's name should appear on the item is not clear, but perhaps it could be taken to mean that Bromley took a sculpture by Lenox and had it fired as a surprise for him. Since it is otherwise unmarked, we do not know if it was a farewell gift from Bromley when he left O&B and Lenox was appointed art director, or whether it was a welcome aboard gift for Lenox when he started at Willets.

The origin of the Walter Lenox attribution cannot be traced, and we will probably have to take it on faith that he did indeed model the piece. Signed Walter Lenox items are unknown, but then so are signed Bromleys. Both men were art directors so both would have known their way around an art department. Although it was the custom for ceramics artists to exchange gifts, it is also possible that the initials are totally irrelevant.

That the vase/pitcher was made at Willets can be shown by page 25 of the 1893 Willets catalogue. Since the Willets one is a line for line copy of what are supposed to be Ott & Brewer ones, it would appear likely that the modeler took the molds with him from O&B to Willets. Since all the people seemed to travel from O&B to Willets and never the reverse, it would seem likely that the first ones were done at O&B and then copied at Willets, **assuming of course that the known museum samples are O&B.** If all known samples are totally unmarked, then it would be possible that Willets deserves credit for the item.

The item does not appear in either the 1891 C.A.C. catalogue or in the undated turn-of-the-century one, so we can probably safely assume that it was never a regular production item there. Perhaps Willets had better security arrangements than O&B.

The claim that this was the first piece of Belleek made in America should be amended to read the first piece of Belleek made by an American (assuming Lenox did it). If 1887 is indeed the earliest date for this item, it could not possibly be the first piece of Belleek since O&B had successfully been producing the china since 1883.

Having nit-picked at some length regarding this item, we will now tell you to go out and get one if you can find it. Regardless of its origins, it is totally delightful and the issue price of $250 may prove to be a bargain in years to come.

SPECIAL ORDER CHINA

From its earliest beginnings, the Lenox company welcomed special orders, and there is a wide assortment of such items still available today at reasonable prices. Colleges, businesses, sports groups, fraternal organizations and others all ordered Lenox with their insignias on it. In the eyes of most Lenox collectors, these markings diminish a piece and they would prefer the same items without the emblems. They bring the highest prices among members of those clubs or among collectors of, say, Masonic or Elks items. On the average, they can be valued at about the same as comparable items without the emblems.

Governments also ordered Lenox china with their State seals and the like decorating it. Here again, these items are not yet of primary interest to most Lenox collectors, and this is reflected in the relatively low prices for such items. A State of New York plate sold recently for $20, which is rather typical. As a rule, they can be rated at the replacement cost of the plate plus perhaps a 10 percent premium for having an interesting history.

Many of the more interesting hand-painted plates were special orders, but they were put in the Artware section with the other plates. Other similar special orders were put there also, since we tried to put things where beginners would look first.

PRESIDENTIAL CHINA

Three sets of Lenox china have been made for the White House, and with the exception of a Wedgwood tea service ordered during Woodrow Wilson's time, all of the china purchased for the President's use during the last sixty years has been American-made. Lyndon B. Johnson ordered a set of Castleton during his administration, but all of the other sets were made by the Lenox Company.

Woodrow Wilson was the first American president to order Lenox, through the Washington, D. C., firm of Dulin and Martin. Tiffany and Company had submitted designs which were deemed not satisfactory, and there apparently was some unhappiness with the way in which the whole order was handled. The final design was by Frank G. Holmes of the Lenox factory and the order finally placed in 1918, at a cost of $11,251,60. It was comprised of the following items:

120 Dinner plates (10-1/2")	36 Bouillon cups and saucers
120 Soup plates (8")	120 After dinner cups and saucers
120 Fish plates (8")	24 Cream soups and saucers
120 Entree plates (8")	96 Cocktail cups
120 Dessert plates (6")	24 Ramekins and underplates
120 Salad plates (7")	24 Oatmeals
84 Bread and butter plates (5")	6 Chop plates (14")
96 Oyster plates (9-1/2")	96 Service plates (11")
96 Tea Cups and saucers	

Extra gold crests were ordered at the time of the original order. Delivery of the set began in August and was completed in November. The service plates have the Presidential seal in the center, with the eagle's head turned toward the bundle of arrows since it was wartime. On the well there is a narrow, acid-etched border with stars and stripes. The rim is a deep blue, and the outer edge is done in the Westchester M-139 acid-etched border. Other piecesbto the set are done with the stars and stripes acid-etched border on the outer edge, with an acid-etched border. Other pieces to the set are done with the stars and stripes acid-etched border on the outer edge, with an ivory-colored border, and another narrow etched border on the well. The backs of the items are marked with the Lenox backstamp and "The White House, 1918".

This set continued in use through the administrations of Harding, Coolidge and Hoover, and replacements were ordered from time to time. Franklin D. Roosevelt ordered the next set of White House Lenox in 1934, at a cost of $9,301.20. These were Depression years, and the expenditure caused some criticism at that time. Mrs. Roosevelt claimed that it was cheaper to replace the entire set than to purchase individual replacements and that the order of a new set would give work to an American company. The set, ordered through William H. Plummer of New York City, was delivered finally in January, 1935, and included the below-listed items:

120 Dinner plates (10-1/2")	96 Bouillon cups and saucers
120 Soup plates (8")	120 After dinner cups and saucers
120 Fish plates (8")	24 Cream soup cups and saucers
120 Entree plates (8")	96 Cocktail cups
120 Dessert plates (6")	24 Ramekins and underplates
120 Salad plates (7")	24 Oatmeals bowls

84 Bread and butter plates (5")	6 Chop plates
96 Oyster plates (9-1/2")	120 Service plates
96 Teacups and saucers	

The Roosevelt china has a narrow outer gold band with a cobalt inside it. The cobalt band has 48 gold stars in it.

A rose and plume design in gold and the Presidential seal in color and gold complete the rim design, and there is a narrow pencil-line of gold on the well.

An additional set of china, part American-made Haviland and part Lenox, was donated to the White House in 1940 after the close of the New York World's Fair where it had been in use at the Federal Building.

The Truman Lenox, ordered through B. Altman and Company of New York City, was delivered in October 1951, and included the following items:

120 Dinner plates	120 Teacups and saucers
120 Soup plates	120 Bouillon cups and saucers
240 Entree plates	120 After dinner cups and saucers
120 Tea plates	120 Cream soups cups and underplates
120 Salad plates	12 Chop plates
120 Bread and butter plates	120 Service plates
120 Oyster plates	

The new set of china cost $28,271.40, and was done in celadon green and ivory to match the newly-decorated State dining room.

The Eisenhowers ordered some gold-banded Castleton service plates, and the Kennedys ordered no china at all. The Johnsons ordered a set of Castleton china through Tiffany and Company in 1966, at a cost of $80,000 which was raised through private donation. A set of Lenox for the Nixon administration was in the works at the time of the Watergate scandal, but was cancelled shortly before Nixon's resignation. The funds for the Nixon set were also to have been supplied by private donation. All three sets of Lenox china are put to use by the current Carter administration.

To the best of our knowledge, no Lenox White House china has come on the market, so no prices can be listed here. It is our understanding that china and silver are counted after each use to prevent the pieces being taken as souvenirs, no doubt a wise precaution on the part of the White House staff. If there is any Presidential Lenox being sold, it is certainly being done very quietly, since it is unlikely that the owner of such items would care to advertise them publicly. We would suggest paying the asking price without quibbling should a piece come your way.

LEWIS BROTHERS CERAMICS, INC.,

This company is located on the corner of Mulberry and Breuning Avenues.

Marks: *Not known*
Prices: $5 minimum for any sample.

LINCOLN POTTERY

See International Pottery.

MADDOCK POTTERY COMPANY

Beginning in 1893, Maddock Pottery produced decorated and undecorated semi-porcelain in a pottery known as the Lamberton Works, which was apparently also occupied during this time by John Maddock & Sons, and which had previously been occupied by Trenton China Company. The owners of the Maddock Pottery Company included Moses Collear, C. A. May, Thomas P. Donoher, and the Thomas Maddock & Sons Company.

M
CHINA
L

Marks: Backstamps include the one shown and at least two others, both of which incorporate the Maddock and Lamberton names.

☐ Punch bowl, *14" diameter, overall transfer cobalt decoration on out-side, scattered large flowers in cobalt on inside, gold trim on rim, very attractive for a lower level type of item, gold trim on rim in worn* **200.00** *Other items can be compared to similar items appearing elsewhere throughout this book.*

MAYER PORCELAIN MANUFACTURING COMPANY
See Arsenal Pottery.

MELLOR & COMPANY
See Cook Company.

MERCER POTTERY COMPANY
Mercer was founded in 1868 by James Moses. They made white granite, ironstone and other such wares. Under James Moses and W. B. Allen the company made sanitary wares from 1893 to 1904.

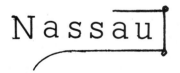

MERCER POTTERY
TRENTON, N.J.

Marks: Several backstamps are known, including those shown.
Prices: The following prices are estimates.

☐	Bowls, *serving*	20.00	30.00
☐	Bowls, *soup or dessert*	8.00	10.00
☐	Cups and saucers	10.00	12.00
☐	Dinner plates	10.00	12.00
☐	Mugs	10.00	30.00
☐	Platters, *depending on size*	25.00	40.00
☐	Smaller plates	4.00	6.00

For Mercer products made after the turn of the century, cut the above prices in half.

MILLINGTON & ASTBURY
See Millington, Astbury & Poulson

MILLINGTON, ASTBURY & POULSON
  M.A.P. was started in 1853 on Carroll Street by Richard Millington and John Astbury. Poulson entered the firm in 1859. The company made white wares, and their most famous item was a Civil War pitcher modeled by Josiah Jones. The pitcher was sold both decorated and undecorated, and the decorated ones were done by noted New York ceramics artist Edward Lycett.

Marks: As shown.
Prices: The Civil War pitcher mentioned above turns up now and then. Prices have been as follows:

- ☐ Undecorated and unmarked, *minor damage*...................... **200.00**
- ☐ Undecorated, *marked, minor damage* **425.00**
- ☐ Estimate of value for marked, decorated sample **750.00**
  Other M.A.P. products seem to have a much higher value than comparable Trenton items. Any of their items will probably have a minimum price tag of $25.

MONUMENT POTTERY COMPANY
Monument began manufacturing sanitary wares in 1896. Company officers included L. Wolff, John Clifford, J. M. Wolff, and J. M. Hoelscher.

Marks: *Not known*
Prices: A three-piece miniature bathroom set should be valued around $50. Any other items they might have made can be compared to similar Trenton items listed elsewhere.

MORRIS & WILLMORE
See Columbian Art Pottery.

NATIONAL CERAMICS
National was founded in 1906. The company is located on Southard Street and manufactures electrical porcelain.

Marks: *Not known*
Prices: $5 minimum for a sample.

NEW JERSEY PORCELAIN COMPANY
The company is located on Plum Street.

Marks: *Not known*
Prices: $5 minimum for a sample.

NEW JERSEY POTTERY COMPANY
This company was incorporated in 1869, and in 1883 the name was changed to Union Pottery Company. They went out of business in 1889. Union made some tiles and plates for the 1880 Presidential campaign. There was no connection between this company and the Union Porcelain Works of New York.

Marks: A circular mark inside a wreath, lettering "N. J. Pottery Co."
Prices: We have never seen any samples of this company's products sold on the open market. A minimum price for one of their Presidential campaign tiles or plates would be in the area of $25.

OLIPHANT & COMPANY
See Delaware Pottery.

OTT & BREWER
The company which was later to be known as Ott & Brewer was founded in May 1863 by Bloor, Ott and Booth. Bloor had the necessary technical know-how and his two partners supplied the financial backing. The building they erected was called the Etruria Pottery Works, perhaps in imitation of the Wedgwood establishment in England. During that period, however, the name Etrurian (or Etruscan) was commonly applied to wares which were copied

from ancient specimens, so perhaps the founders had something like this in mind.

Booth left the business in 1864, and his part of the company was bought by Garret S. Burroughs. Burroughs also lasted only one year, due to illness. It was at this point that John Hart Brewer entered the firm, and items which are marked "B.O.B." could mean Bloor, Ott & **Booth,** Bloor, Ott & **Burroughs,** or Bloor, Ott & **Brewer.**

The young company produced a variety of everyday wares, primarily decorated granite ware. Herman Rolege was the only decorator in Trenton at that time, and he decorated for B.O.B. as well as all the other companies. Since undecorated granite ware has not been seen, we can draw the conclusion that either the company decorated all their items or else their undecorated wares were not marked with their name.

Although Isaac Broome is generally given credit for establising O&B's parian line for the 1876 Centennial, the company did make at least two parian busts before that time. Two busts, one of Ulysses S. Grant and the other of Abraham Lincoln, are marked with the "B.O.B." mark, and since Bloor left the company in 1873, we can be relatively certain that these two parian items came before that time. It would be interesting to find out who developed the parian body and/or sculpted the figures.

Broome came to Ott & Brewer in 1875 or 1876 and greatly expanded the parian line there. Many of his items were shown at the Philadelphia exposition in 1876. Broome/O&B parian items include: Busts of Apollo, Abraham Lincoln (presumably not the same one the company did earlier), Rutherford B. Hayes, Benjamin Franklin, George Washington (two sizes), Cleopatra (a Mrs. Thompson of Trenton was the model), Ulysses S. Grant (again, presumably not the same one discussed above), Pope Pius IX (originally designed by Broome in 1858 and cast by the O&B company in 1876), William Shakespeare, and eight "races of the world" miniature heads; two vases — the famous baseball vase (two subsections of the baseball vase, the pitcher and the batter, were additionally done separately), and a pastoral vase (two sizes); a plaque of Robert Fulton; and the George and Martha Washington tea set.

Beginning around 1876 the company made a ware known as ivory porcelain. Although in color, styling and type of decoration it resembles Irish Belleek, it is not the same composition and not quite as fine. True Belleek experimentation by John H. Brewer and William Bromley, Jr., began in 1882 and was aided a year later by the arrival of John and William Bromley, Sr.

Ott & Brewer used the full range of decorating methods on their wares, including transfer decoration of various types (primarily on their nonporcelain wares), hand-painting, gold paste, Royal Worcester "cloisonne" style artwork, and Irish Belleek type pearlized glazes. Pate-sur-pate work was done there, primarily by a man named Saunders. (Where is all that pate-sur-pate now?)

Many of the better-known Trenton ceramics people got their training at O&B, including Jonathan Coxon and Walter Lenox. The company experimented with a great variety of things down through the years, and if imitation is indeed the greatest form of flattery, then Ott & Brewer must have been practically flattered to death by the other Trenton companies. O&B is generally considered to be the finest china ever made in the United States, and is certainly the most expensive of the Trenton chinas. The company folded in 1893 (or 1892) due to prolonged labor problems and the depression of the 1890's. Cook Pottery later took over the Etruria Pottery, although it is not certain whether they merely bought the building or if they also bought the O&B molds.

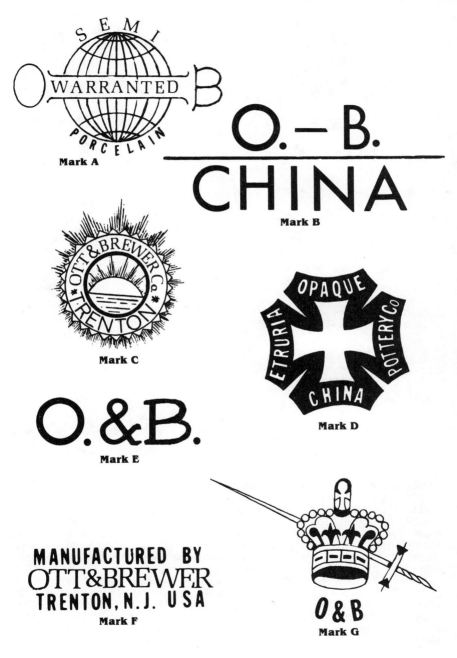

Mark A

O. – B.
CHINA

Mark B

Mark C

Mark D

O.&B.

Mark E

MANUFACTURED BY
OTT&BREWER
TRENTON, N.J. USA

Mark F

O & B

Mark G

Mark H

Mark I

Mark J

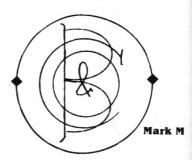

Mark K

Mark L

Mark M

Marks: Mark A is usually impressed and was used on nonporcelain items. It will frequently appear along with another mark, usually mark C. Marks B, C, and D are usually printed and are also found on nonporcelain items. Mark C is usually printed in brown, and on the rare occasions when it is found in its green version, it is usually on a nonfactory decorated item. In addition to these marks, the company used at least two different British coat of arms marks for their semi-vitreous wares. Mark A is commonly called the globe mark and mark C is known as the rising sun mark.

Marks E and F were used primarily on ivory porcelain, usually in conjunction with one of the other marks. Marks G through J were also used on ivory porcelain, with the crown marks probably predating the crescent mark. They are printed marks and will usually be reddish-brown in color. Variations of the marks are seen and include a crown with a squared-off look instead of the rounded shape shown here.

With the development of a true Belleek product, mark J was altered slightly to give us mark K. Mark K is also a printed mark, usually reddish-brown, and once again is sometimes seen along with one of the other marks. Retail store names show up now and then with Mark K, and from this we can gather that at the very least O&B had contracts with Shreve, Crump and Low of Boston, Tiffany and Company of New York, and John McDonald & Sons Company.

Pieces exhibited at the Southern Art Union in New Orleans in 1884 are marked with that information in a circle along with mark K. A cup and saucer seen recently, however, has the New Orleans mark with mark J. The use for marks L and M is uncertain.

Item numbers appear on some of the later pieces, and apparently went up at least as high as 1200. It is not certain whether this system applied to porcelain and nonporcelain items or whether different types of china had different numbering systems. O&B items are rarely if ever artist signed; however, initials occasionally are seen on the bottoms of later pieces which could very well be decorators' marks.

The Ott & Brewer marking system is not nearly as precise as the above information would lead one to believe, and although we do not have samples at hand to prove our point, we are sure we have seen ivory porcelain items with mark K and Belleek items with mark J, etc.

Prices: Ott & Brewer Belleek has never been cheap, and recent rises in price have pretty much eliminated the middle class collector. It is still possible to occasionally come across a piece of O&B at a flea market or yard sale, but for the most part now antique dealers know what they have. Most collectors do not distinguish between the ivory porcelain and the true Belleek, although most are aware that items with the crown marks can be a little heavier than those with the crescent marks, and there is little or no difference in pricing between the two types. (Remember that although the true Belleek is thinner, the ivory porcelain is older.)

Nonporcelain items still are to be found at popular prices, although this situation may not last long. As more and more O&B Belleek becomes unreachable, the granite wares and cream-colored wares will become more interesting to collectors and this is almost always followed by a rise in price.

Parian items and pieces signed by Broome are the most expensive of all. The only known sale of a Broome item during the past year was the egg shown in the color section, which was sold for $1,200. It is marked with a variation of mark F, and has the date 1877 and the Broome signature. Expect to pay a minimum of $1,500 for a marked parian bust.

NON-PORCELAIN WARES

- ☐ Cracker jar, *granite ware, oxblood color, hand-done sponged gold clouds covering jar and lid, gold trim on finial and handles somewhat worn, marks A and C* **100.00**
- ☐ Cracker jar, *as above except green background and not marked* **65.00**
- ☐ Plates, *9-1/2" diameter, hand-painted game birds, colored rims with sponged gold finish, one rim copper color and the other gray, pencil-line gold banding on outer rim and on shoulder, crazing on surface, otherwise perfect, marks A and C on one plate, mark A only on the other, pair* **100.00**
- ☐ Vase, *9" high, slightly rounded shape, hand-painted red and pink flowers on green background, probably home-done, marks A and C in green* **95.00**

Plate, *game bird*

Note: Expect to pay a minimum of $50 for any decorated piece of Ott & Brewer opaque ware. Earlier samples of this type of item are usually crazed, and this is not held against them where value is concerned.

PORCELAIN ITEMS
No attempt will be made to differentiate between ivory porcelain and true Belleek.

☐ Basket, *6" high, rustic handle, raised gold paste trim in thistle pattern on beige matte finish, mark I* **500.00**

☐ Chocolate pot, *12" high, green bottom section, top section has raised gold paste trim in several shades of gold, gold trim on dragon handle and spout and on finial and rims, mark I* **600.00**

☐ Cup and saucer, *after dinner size, gold paste trim, mark K and Tiffany & Company mark, saucer only marked, gold is not the same color on the cup as on the saucer for some reason, but it is obvious the pieces belong together* **95.00**

☐ Cup and saucer, *after dinner size, plain shape, spray of raised enamel flowers across front of cup, smaller spray on back, two sprays on saucer, pearlized pink interior, gold trim on rims and handle, mark J with New Orleans inscription, saucer broken in half and glued back together* **110.00**

☐ Cup and saucer, *Tridacna pattern, teacup size, pearlized yellow interior, gold trim on handle and rims, mark K* **125.00**

☐ Cup and saucer, *Tridacna pattern, bouillon, pearlized pink interior, gold trim on handle and rims, small fleck on underside of saucer, mark K* **120.00**

☐ Cup and saucer, *cactus pattern, teacup size, pearlized white finish, gold trim on handle and rim, crack in handle* **100.00**

☐ Cup and saucer, *after dinner size, enamel ribbon design, gold trim, mark I* **150.00**

☐ Ewer, *double spouted, rustic handle, top section covered with gold, bottom section has hand-painted coral colored water lilies, two small chips on top section, mark I* **625.00**

☐ Ewer, *raised gold paste cattail pattern, two turtle figurines applied to side of piece, turtles and coral handle decorated in green and gold, small fleck on one of the turtles, mark I* **700.00**

☐ Ewer, *bulbous shape, raised gold paste in thistle pattern on beige matte finish. gold trim on handle and rims, 8" high, mark I* **550.00**

☐ Ewer, *similar in size and shape to the one with turtles listed above, hand-painted water lilies outlined in gold, handle is formed like stem to buds and leaves which are applied near the rim, piece has been totally devastated in the back and is held together with glue, damage does not show very much in front, handle badly cracked so piece has to be picked up by the body, mark I* **175.00**

☐ Ewer, *7" high, shaped like a vinegar cruet, raised gold paste trim in chrysanthemum design on beige matte finish, mark K* **300.00**

☐ Ewer, *melon-ribbed, 8" high, white glazed background with gold paste trim in oak leaf pattern, spider crack in bottom of piece, mark I* **140.00**

☐ Shell, *raised on coral and seashell base, pearlized pink interior to shell, gold trim on rim and on base, one of the small shells that form the base has been broken off, mark I* **325.00**

☐ Shell, *1-1/2" high, 3-1/4" (handle included) wide, very delicate and thin, forked handle and two small shell feet decorated in gold, gold trim on rim, little shells are misplaced so the item wobbles ever so slightly, mark I* **75.00**

Shell, *forked handle*

☐ Shell, *similar to one above but with no handle, pearlized blue interior, mark J* **75.00**

☐ Shoe, *5" long, hand-painted small flowers in scatter pattern, gold trim, marks I and J* **325.00**

☐ Sugar and creamer, *cactus pattern, pearlized finish, gold trim on rim, bronze trim on handles, mint condition, mark I* **300.00**

☐ Sugar and creamer, *Tridacna pattern, pearlized pink inside, gold trim on handles and rims, mark J* **225.00**

Sugar and creamer, *cactus pattern*

Sugar bowl, *Tridacna pattern*

☐ Sugar and creamer, *ruffled top sugar, creamer fits inside of sugar, raised gold paste trim in oak leaf pattern on beige matte finish, mark K* **275.00**

☐ Sugar and creamer, *same shape as above, transfer print with raised enamel work, gold trim on rims, mark I* **225.00**

Note: Sugars and creamers are frequently found without their mates, and in this event a creamer is probably worth a hint more than a sugar bowl alone. The little creamer shown by itself in the photo is probably worth $10 to $15 more than a matching sugar bowl alone. The creamer sold recently for $125.

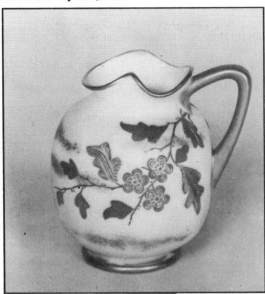

Creamer

☐ Teapot, *dented sides, covered with grotesque coral trim, raised gold paste work on bottom half, gold trim on coral branches, spout has been repaired and there is a small crack coming down from the rim, mark I* **225.00**

☐ Vase, *7" high, beautiful hand-painted orchid, raised gold paste work, openwork handles, raised on small openwork feet one of which is damaged, probably had a lid at one time which is no longer present, mark K* **325.00**

☐ Vase, *7" high, calla lily shape on rustic base, applied leaf on side helps support the lily, pearlized ivory interior, leaf pale lavender, gold trim on rim and on base section, a few small rough spots, mark I* **600.00**

☐ Vase, *bulbous bottom with long neck, 10" high, hand-painted yellow and brown flowers, raised gold trim, mark I* **450.00**

- ☐ Vase, *12" high, bulbous bottom with long narrow square neck, green background with raised gold paste trim done in at least five different shades ranging all the way from a silver color to a bronze, mark I*　**750.00**
- ☐ Vase, *12" high, bulbous bottom with long neck, hand-painted roses outlined in gold on high-glaze white finish, small repaired spot on top, mark H* **500.00**
- ☐ Vase, *10" high, double-handled, raised gold paste in three shades of gold, mark J* **450.00**
- ☐ Watering can, *7-1/2" high, raised gold paste trim on beige matte finish, damage to spout, mark I* **310.00**

PERLEE BELLEEK
Perlee was made in Trenton in the late 1920s, and possibly went under during the Depression. Their dinnerware resembles that of Lenox made during the same time.

Marks: All marks include the word Perlee in one fashion or another.
Prices: Rate against comparable Lenox items. Although Perlee is rare, there is too little demand for it at this time for prices to be very high.

- ☐ Cup and saucer, *enamel trim* **30.00**
- ☐ Cup and saucer, *gold trim* **25.00**
- ☐ Dinner plate, *floral pattern* **18.00**
- ☐ Dinner plate, *gold trim* **15.00**
- ☐ Dinner plate, *Oriental pattern* **20.00**
- ☐ Salad plate, *8¼" diameter, gold trim* **10.00**
- ☐ Tea set, *three pieces, overall decoration with teardrop shaped multi-colored enamel work* **175.00**
- ☐ Tray, *olive, oval, gold trim* **25.00**
- ☐ Vase, *unmarked but has the same enamel work as the above listed tea set* **25.00**

POOLE & STOCKTON
The name of this Trenton decorating company will sometimes appear along with that of the manufacturer.

Prices: The Poole & Stockton mark on a piece of china would probably be worth $5 beyond the basic price of the item.

POPE & LEE
Pope & Lee was a Trenton decorating establisment whose name will occasionally be found on wares decorated by them.

Prices: This decorating company's mark would probably raise the value of a given item by $5.

PROSPET HILL POTTERY
Prospect Hill was founded in 1880 by Dale & Davis. Products included semi-porcelain, white granite, and opaque porcelain. Isaac Davis ran a company prior to the partnership with Dale but it isn't certain whether or not it was called Prospect Hill Pottery at that time.

Marks: Prospect Hill marks include several using the British coat of arms. All their marks include the name I. Davis or the names of the partners, Dale & Davis. The Dale & Davis is sometimes abbreviated as D-D or D&D.
Prices: The following prices are estimates.

☐	Bowls, *dessert or soup*	5.00	7.00
☐	Bowls, *serving*	15.00	25.00
☐	Cups and saucers	8.00	12.00
☐	Dinner plates	7.00	15.00
☐	Mugs	10.00	30.00
☐	Platters, *depending on size*	20.00	40.00
☐	Smaller plates	4.00	6.00

PROVIDENTIAL TILE WORKS

Mr. James H. Robinson and Mr. C. Louis Whitehead founded the Providential Tile Works in 1885, although their first items were not produced until 1886. Isaac Broome was their first modeller and designer, and Scott Callowhill was the designer after Broome left. Although the company is best known for its embossed tiles, they also engaged in both underglaze and overglaze decorated ones, including some which were gilded and painted in a cloisonne effect.

Marks: The marks used by Providential are uncertain, but many possibly include a star. Tiles signed by Broome are sometimes marked with this star, and since none of the other companies where he worked used this mark, they are generally considered to be Providential by default. There was a Star Encaustic Tile Company in Pittsburgh, but this company used the initials S.E.T. rather than a star as a backstamp.

Prices: (All prices listed are for tiles which are 6" x 6" or smaller in size, and for tiles which are in mint or near-mint condition. The prices are estimates rather than actual selling prices, since the Providential mark is in doubt and this makes positive identification difficult.)

Embossed tiles — $50 and under for those which are not artist-signed. $100 for a signed Broome.

Decorated tiles — $50 and under for run-of-the-mill decorated tiles, either underglaze. Special or unique designs such as the cloisonne-type ones described have no established prices but they would possibly be in the $100 range.

RESOLUTE POTTERY COMPANY

Resolute was founded in 1903 by William H. Bradbury and manufactured sanitary specialties.

Marks: *Not known*
Prices: A three-piece miniature bathroom set would be in the $50 range.

RHODES & YATES

See City Pottery.

RITTENHOUSE & EVANS

See American Art China Works.

ROUSE PARIAN

No information is available about this recent Trenton company except that it is basically a one-man operation. Rouse made small ornamental items of parian, including a popular figurine of John-John Kennedy.

Marks: The word Rouse
Prices: Under $50 for most items.

SANITARY EARTHENWARE SPECIALTY COMPANY
Sanitary was founded in 1897 by Thomas Swetman and Arthur Plantier for the production of sanitary items.

Marks: *Not known*
Prices: A three-piece miniature bathroom set can be figured at around $50.

SCAMMELL
Scammell came along considerably later than many of the other companies listed here, but they did produce at least a few items which are of interest to collectors. DeVegh designed many of their Art Deco figurines, as he was also to do for Lenox, and the Scammell ones are quite a bit rarer than the Lenox ones. The company also made a great number of commemorative items, particularly plates. The overwhelming majority of their pieces, however, are lower level dinnerware items.

Marks: Most of their marks incorporated the word Scammell in one way or another. Marks can be either printed or impressed.

- ☐ Figurine, *seated woman, marked and signed DeVegh, looks for all the world like Lenox china* **125.00**
This price is three years old, and we have not seen a Scammell figurine sold since then. It is our feeling that the Scammell ones should probably keep pace with the comparable Lenox items.
- ☐ Horn-of-plenty centerpiece, *undecorated, marked Scammell and signed DeVegh* **65.00**
- ☐ Plate, *commemoration of George Washington's 200th birthday, cobalt transfer decoration, 10½" diameter* **50.00**

Lower-level wares are typically sold in the 50¢ to $1.00 range in the Trenton area. They are just too new and too common yet to bring much more than that.

SCHILLER/CORDEY, INC.
See Cordey.

SPEELER & SONS
See International.

SPEELER POTTERY COMPANY
See International.

STANDARD SANITARY POTTERY COMPANY
Standard manufactured sanitary items, and was founded in 1901. Company officials included P. H. Moohan, Richard T. Potts, Owen Healey, and John Kelly.

Prices: Three-piece miniature bathroom sets typically sell in the area of $50.

STANGL POTTERY
See Fulper Pottery.

STAR PORCELAIN COMPANY
The Star Porcelain Company, located on Muirhead Avenue, was founded in 1899 by Herbert Sinclair, Dr. Charles Britton (a drugstore owner) and Dr. Thomas H. MacKenzie (a doctor). The company manufactures electrical specialties as it has done since its founding. In 1919, Star built a plant in Frenchtown NJ, for the manufacture of spark plug insulators. The Frenchtown Porcelain Company was later sold when the automotive industry began manufacturing their own spark plugs. Star acquired the Bay Ridge Company in 1969.

STAR

Marks: As shown
Prices: To someone trying to fill out a one-from-each-company collection, one of Star's products would probably we worth at least a couple of dollars.

STEPHEN, TAMS & COMPANY
See Greenwood Pottery.

TAYLOR & COMPANY
Founded in 1865, this partnership was succeeded in 1870 by Taylor & Goodwin. See Trenton Pottery Company.

TAYLOR & GOODWIN
In 1870, Taylor & Goodwin replaced Taylor & Company. See Trenton Pottery Company.

TAYLOR & HOUDAYER
This company manufactured sanitary wares and was founded in 1883 by Taylor & Houdayer.

Marks: *Not known*
Prices: See comparable listings.

TAYLOR & SPEELER
Taylor & Speeler was the first Trenton company to manufacture pottery on a full-scale commercial basis, and their success was responsible for the huge pottery industry in Trenton that followed. They made Rockingham and yellow wares beginning in 1853, and continued in business for about 20 years. In 1858 Bloor entered the organization and provided financial backing, and the company began producing white granite ware. The Fell & Thropp Company took over the pottery at a later date.

Marks: *Not known*
Prices: We have no definite selling prices during the past year for Taylor & Speeler products. We would estimate as follows:

☐ Rockingham wares, *a minimum of* **50.00**
☐ White granite wares, *a minimum of* **25.00**
☐ Yellow wares, *a minimum of* **25.00**

Since their wares are scarce and since so few have survived in absolutely mint condition, expect to pay much more than this for anything of unusual size or shape or in particularly good condition.

TAYLOR, GOODWIN & COMPANY
Same as Taylor & Goodwin.

TAYLOR, SPEELER & BLOOR
See Taylor & Speeler.

THOMAS MADDOCK & SONS
Thomas Maddock & Sons was founded as an outgrowth of Millington, Astbury & Poulson. After Poulson died in 1861, Mr. Coughley bought his interest in M.A.P., and after Coughley died in 1869, Thomas Maddock bought Coughley's share in M.A.P. and Millington's share as well. By about 1876 the firm was known as Astbury & Maddock. At some point Maddock took sole ownership of the company and brought his sons into the business.

The company had a huge pottery on Carroll Street, and their wares included sanitary items and all-purpose stoneware. Dinnerware was included in their output, and vases and other decorative items were also made. The once-great Carroll Street pottery is now occupied by the Rescue Mission.

Marks: Backstamps include the one shown, which was primarily used on sanitary wares, and a circular mark with a crown on top which was used on dinnerware. All marks included the initials T.M.&S.

Prices: Maddock wares are rather common in the Trenton area, and this is reflected in prices for them. Some of their designs and decorations are quite attractive and we would expect to see an increase in prices shortly. For run-of-the-mill items, the following figures apply.

☐	Bowls, *dessert or soup*	4.00	7.00
☐	Bowls, *serving*	8.00	20.00
☐	Cups and saucers	5.00	10.00
☐	Dinner plates	4.00	10.00
☐	Mugs	5.00	15.00
☐	Platters, depending on size	10.00	25.00
☐	Smaller plates	1.00	5.00
☐	Three-piece miniature bathroom sets		50.00

TRENT TILE COMPANY
Trent was founded in 1882 as the Harris Manufacturing Company. Although it is not certain at what point the name changed to Trent, it was probably Harris only a short while. Chief designers and modellers were Isaac Broome (beginning in 1883) and William Wood Gallimore (beginning in 1886). The company is best known for its embossed tiles, although other types were made. At one point over 20 kilns were in operation.

Marks: Several backstamps were used, all incorporating the name Trent. The marks are usually impressed and rarely printed in ink.

☐	Embossed tile, *6" x 6", floral design, wine color, framed in wood to make a tea tile*	20.00
☐	Embossed tile, *6" x 6", boy in lace collar, gold and brown, signed Broome*	100.00
☐	Embossed tile, *4" x 4", Benjamin Franklin, golds and browns*	75.00
☐	Embossed tiles, *two, 6" x 6", peacock blue, girl and boy each with a bird, not artist signed but attributed to Gallimore due to a picture of identical tiles by him which appear in a book on ceramics, pair*	125.00

Note: Except for the first tile listed, all the tiles have been framed. Prices are for the tile only and a professional framing would add to the value.

All other tiles can be rated as follows:

Artist signed, around $100 for a human figure or face, less for other subjects.

Non-artist signed, around $75 for human subjects, down to a minimum of $10 for other subjects.

TRENTON CHINA COMPANY

This company operated from 1859 to 1891, producing both decorated and undecorated wares.

Marks: The one shown, which is impressed in the china, is the only known mark.

TRENTON CHINA CO.

TRENTON, N.J.

Prices: For a company which supposedly operated for so many years, there are remarkably few samples of their wares. The following prices are estimates:

☐	Bowls, *serving*	15.00	25.00
☐	Bowls, *soup or dessert*	6.00	8.00
☐	Cups and saucers	7.00	14.00
☐	Dinner plates	7.00	12.00
☐	Mugs...	10.00	30.00
☐	Platters, *depending on size*	15.00	35.00
☐	Smaller plates	3.00	6.00

TRENTON FIRE CLAY & PORCELAIN COMPANY

T.F.C.&P. Co. was founded in 1893 by O. O. Bowman, R. K. Bowman, and W. J. J. Bowman. They were primarily producers of sanitary wares.

Marks: *Not known*
Prices: A three-piece miniature bathroom set would be in the $50 price range.

TRENTON POTTERIES COMPANY

In 1892, David K. Bayne and William S. Hancock were able to consolidate five Trenton potteries into the Trenton Potteries Company. The five were: Crescent, Delaware, Empire, Enterprise, Equitable. At a later date another pottery, the Ideal, was built and brought into the organization. Chief products were sanitary items and hotel-type china.

Marks: A star with the initials "T.P.Co." was the primary mark of Trenton potteries. A number within the star indicated the plant where the item was made. Number 1 was Crescent, number 2 Delaware, number 3 Empire, number 4 Enterprise, number 5 Equitable. Number 6 would have been Ideal, but for the most part the 6 was not used and the word "Ideal" is inside the star instead. The star without a circle around it was typically used on sanitary wares, while the star within a circle was used on dinnerware.

Mark A

Mark B

Mark C

Mark D

Mark E

Prices: Products from Trenton Potteries are still abundant and usually sell in the under $5 range. If anything interesting was produced after the consolidation, figure it at about the same as a comparable Lenox item. (Also see individual listings for each of the constituent companies.) T.P.C. made a particularly cute three-piece miniature bathroom set which sells (as most of these sets do) in the $50 range. One of their miniature sets was designed for the toilet to hold cigarettes, the wash basin to hold matches, and the bathtub to be used as an ashtray. We haven't seen one of these sold in some time, but expect it would bring a little more than the average set of this type.

TRENTON POTTERIES WORKS
T.P.W. was founded in 1883 for the production of both sanitary wares and white granite dinnerware.

Marks: Backstamps include the New Jersey coat of arms with the word "Royal" above it, and a shield with crossed swords and the words "Porcelaine Opaque" above and "French, TPW" below.

Prices: See comparable items listed elsewhere.

TRENTON POTTERY COMPANY
Trenton Pottery Company was incorporated in 1865, and was later known as Taylor, Goodwin & Company. Fell & Thropp operated the pottery at a later date. Since Trenton Potteries Company used the same mark as Trenton Pottery Company, it is assumed there was a connection between the two.

T. P. Co.

C H I N A

Marks: The mark shown, usually printed in black, is the only one known.
Prices: The following prices are estimates.

☐	Bowls, *dessert or soup*	5.00	7.00
☐	Bowls, *serving*	10.00	20.00
☐	Cups and saucers	5.00	10.00
☐	Dinner plates	5.00	10.00
☐	Mugs...	5.00	20.00
☐	Platters, *depending on size*	10.00	30.00
☐	Smaller plates	1.00	5.00
☐	Three-piece miniature bathroom set		50.00

TRENTON TERRA-COTTA COMPANY
Trenton Terra-Cotta officers included Joseph McPherson and O. O. Bowman. Their most interesting products were garden vases and ornaments, although they also made pipes, chimney parts, and other such products.

Marks: *Not known*
Prices: Although we have not seen any sold recently on the open market, a garden vase or ornament would probably be a minimum of $100. Other items would have a base value of $5.

UNION ELECTRICAL PORCELAIN COMPANY
Union is located on Muirhead Avenue, and they manufacture electrical porcelains.

Marks: *Not known*
Prices: Electrical procelains are usually not considered to be exciting collectibles, but once again these products might be of interest to someone trying to finish out a Trenton collection. As such, any item is probably worth at least a few dollars.

UNION POTTERY COMPANY
See New Jersey Pottery Company.

WARREN KIMBLE POTTERY
No information available.

W. C. HENDRICKSON
Trenton decorating company.

Prices: Add $5 to the basic price of any item if it has the name of the W. C. Hendrickson decorating company on the bottom.

W. CORY
Cory operated in Trenton during the 1860's primarily making yellow wares. Wares by this company are exceptionally rare, and although rather clumsy in appearance, they should be considered desirable additions to any Trenton collection.

Marks: "W. CORY, TRENTON, N.J." impressed on the bottom.

☐ Mold, *2" high x 3½" diameter across the top, leaf design, marked as
above **75.00**

WENCZEL TILE
Current Trenton tile company.

WILLETS MANUFACTURING COMPANY
Willets was founded in 1879 by the Willets brothers, Joseph, Daniel and Edmund. The company was located in what had previously been the William Young & Sons pottery. Although they are best known for their Belleek-type wares, they also made opaque china, white granite ware, electrical porcelain, majolica, and sanitary wares.

The Thomas Maddock book indicates that Willets started manufacturing sanitary items in 1909, and that Joseph and Daniel Willets were the owners of the company. It is possible that Edmund had died by that time, or else that his brothers bought out his interest in the company.

The exact date when the company went out of business is not known, but 1912 seems to be the date most people accept. The year 1909, also occasionally mentioned as the closing year, was probably the year when they stopped making Belleek in favor of making sanitary wares.

The Willets Company is something of the exception in that its founders had no other known connections in the Trenton ceramics industry. We do not know where they gained their experience in making china, or what happened to them after the company closed.

Many of the better-known Trenton people worked at Willets at one time or another. William Bromley, Jr., was art director there for awhile (possibly beginning in 1886), and he was followed by Walter Lenox. There probably was no real art director there before Bromley, and we do not know who followed Lenox in that position.

A photo in the possession of George Houghton's family shows the Willets art department with four artists seated at their work spaces and one man standing, presumably the art director. He is a rather dapper man of about 35, and it is not Walter Lenox. George Houghton can be identified as one of the artists, but the names of the others remain a mystery. Since Houghton worked at Willets virtually the entire time they made decorated artware, his presence cannot be used to date the photo or to aid in the identification of the others.

Another view of the Willets art department shows Oliver Houghton at work, and the same man standing. A woman is also in the picture, which raises the possibility that Willets had a female artist at one time. Once again, the photo is undated and without names except for Oliver Houghton's. (Put down this book right now and go date all your photographs!)

Willets has only recently come into its own, and for the most part people have stopped calling it "early Lenox". As of this year, the earliest items produced there can legally be termed antiques, and there has been a great deal of activity with Willets during the past year.

Marks: Mark A is not common, but apparently was the first mark used on early Belleek-type wares. After the formula was perfected, the word Belleek was added to the backstamp, giving us mark B, which can be found in several colors. The Barber book states that red, brown and black were used for factory-decorated wares, but in our experience about 50 percent of the time, the items with mark B in brown will be home-decorated. The red version of mark B is likeliest to appear on small items decorated with, perhaps, small

Mark A **Mark B**

pink roses or scattered flower designs, although the red mark can also be found on larger, elaborately-done items. The mark in its green version is virtually 100 percent home-decorated. The black is difficult to distinguish from dark brown, and we have been unable to draw any concrete conclusions regarding its meaning.

Mark C **Mark D**

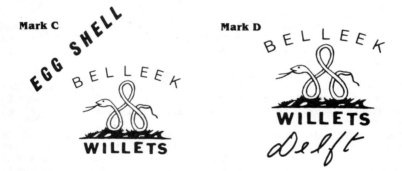

Mark C is a variation of mark B, and thus far has always been red. The items which have this mark are very fine-quality Belleek items, very much in the eggshell category, but other Willets items just as fine do not have this wording. We have been unable to make a precise dating on the use of this mark, and for now it should probably be viewed as an interesting variation of mark B and nothing more.

Mark D, always in blue, is another variation of mark B, and is found on items factory-decorated in a monochromatic blue Delft-type fashion. This line of wares may have been started in competition with the Cook Pottery Delft line, which would place mark C in the late 1890's. Except for the style of decoration, they have little in common with genuine Delft items.

Mark E is very rare, and would seem to have been used for blanks for the home artist. The body of the china is much whiter than that of the usual Willets item, and the mark probably either dates from the very early pre-Belleek days or else from the last years of the company, for it is unlikely that the company would have put out two separate white ware lines at the same time. Since so few samples of this mark have been seen, our dating and use of the mark may be way off base.

WILLETS CHINA

Mark E

Other marks used by the company include a globe mark with the initials "W. M. Co.", usually appearing with a dinnerware pattern name, and intertwined "W Co" with the wording "Opaque Porcelain". These marks usually appear on lower-level items which are of lesser importance to collectors. Another mark is sometimes called the chewing gum mark—a small pad of porcelain applied to the bottom of items such as the basket with applied flowers shown in the color section. The Willets mark is impressed into the pad. Marks of this type were generally used on items which were difficult to mark in the ordinary fashion, and the so-called spaghetti strand baskets are in this category.

Willets shape numbers will be found on many of their items, and will look like pencil-written numbers on the bottom. These numbers correspond to catalogue item numbers, and can be a great aid in positive identification of a given item. Maybe 50 percent of the items will be so marked, including both factory and nonfactory decorated pieces.

Prices: Although Willets prices can fluctuate quite a bit from one part of the country to another, as a general rule they will be somewhere between those for early Lenox and those for Ott & Brewer. This is probably about where they belong, both from an availability and an age point of view.

One of the things keeping back prices on Willets items is the inability to easily distinguish factory and nonfactory-decorated items via mail or telephone. Unlike Lenox items of the same period which are virtually 100 percent factory-decorated if they bear the wreath mark, Willets items with mark B in brown really have to be examined close up. Even then there is sometimes room for doubt since Willets did not apply quality control standards that strictly.

In the following price section, item numbers are used to positively identify the items, and the terminology from the old catalogues is also used. Although we find some of their classifications questionable, we suppose the company that made the items has the right to name them.

BASKETS

☐ Shape #121, *small ribbed basket, 5-1/2" high, twig handle, undecorated, mark B in green* **75.00**

☐ Shape #173, *rustic handle basket, 8" high, 9" wide, twig handle, outside glazed with gold trim, inside matte finish with gold paste trim on a chrysanthemum design, three shades of gold, handle speckled with gold, handle has a crack, mark B in brown* **180.00**

☐ Shape #174, *small round basket, 3-1/2" diameter, hand-painted flowers outlined in gold in a scatter pattern, gold trim on handle and rim, mark B in red* **95.00**

☐ Shape #174, *small round basket, 3-1/2" diameter, undecorated, mark B in green* **45.00**

Basket, *shape #173*

- [ ] Shape #205, 7" wide, pointed arches on sides opposite handles, undecorated, mark B in green.................................... **42.00**
- [ ] Shape #341, 5-1/4" high to top of handle, embossed design, undecorated, mark B in green.................................... **75.00**
- [ ] Shape number unknown, spaghetti strand type, applied flowers in pastel colors, 11" long, chewing gum mark, some rough spots on petals... **475.00**

BONBONS

- [ ] Shape #0, 6-1/2" diameter, 1-1/4" deep, curled handles, ruffled rim, undecorated, mark B in green.................................... **42.00**
- [ ] Shape #0, dimensions as above, hand-painted flowers, gold trim on handles and rim, artist signed and dated, mark B in green.......... **55.00**
- [ ] Shape #0, dimensions as above, pearlized pink interior, sponged gold trim on exterior, mark B in red.................................... **60.00**
- [ ] Shape #1, 6-1/4" diameter, 1-1/4" deep, undecorated, mark B in green **20.00**

Bonbon, *shape #190*

☐ Shape #1, *dimensions as above, single large pink rose in center, outside totally covered in gold, artist's initials on bottom, mark B in green* **35.00**

☐ Shape #1-1/2, *5-1/2" diameter, 1" deep, hand-painted small pink roses outlined in gold in scatter pattern, small fleck on rim, mark B in red* .. **70.00**

☐ Shape #8, *6-1/2" long, 5-1/2" wide, 1-1/4" deep, veined design in china, undecorated, exceptionally thin, mark B in green* **60.00**

☐ Shape #190, *6" diameter, covered, two rustic handles and rustic finial, pearlized white finish with bronze colored handles and finial, mark A in red* **130.00**

☐ Shape #242, *6-1/2" long, heart-shaped, covered, undecorated, mark B in green* **70.00**

☐ Shape #244, *7-1/4" long, heart-shaped with ruffled rim, small hand-painted wildflowers with gold outlining, gold trim on rim, several tiny flecks on rim, mark B in red* **72.00**

BOTTLES

☐ Shape #148, *7-1/2" high, rustic handled water bottle, fluted, matte finish with gold paste trim, mark B in brown* **160.00**

☐ Shape #148, *size as above, undecorated, mark B in green* **105.00**

☐ Shape #228, *5" high, Pilgrim bottle, glazed finish, single coral-colored orchid outlined in gold, gold trim on feet and handles, crack in one handle, mark B in red* **190.00**

BOUQUET HOLDERS

Bouquet Holder,
shape #97

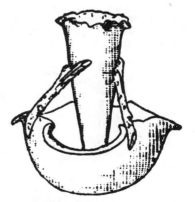

Bouquet Holder, *shape #229*

☐ Shape #97, *3-1/4" high, pyramid type comprised of five tiny jugs piled on top of each other, undecorated, handle of one jug broken, mark B in brown* **65.00**

☐ Shape #229, *4" high, small fluted-top trumpet shape vase inside a curled-edge bowl, vase part supported by three twigs connected to side of bowl, vase is pearlized pink on the outside, white on inside, trim reversed on bowl, sponged gold trim on branches, gold trim on rims, mark B in red* **125.00**

BOWLS

☐ Shape #4, *square salad, 7" square, 3-1/2" deep, undecorated, mark B in green* **40.00**

☐ Shape #4, *square salad, dimensions as above, gold paste in oak leaf pattern inside of bowl, speckled gold on outside, mark B in red* **140.00**

☐ Shape #5, *crimped salad, 9-1/2" diameter, 3-1/2" deep, chains of daisies hand-painted on outside, gold trim on trim, artist signed, mark B in green* **60.00**

☐ Shape #5, *crimped salad, dimensions as above, undecorated, mark B in green* **55.00**

☐ Shape #11, *plain salad, 10-1/2" diameter, 3-1/4" deep, hand-painted water lilies on inside, solid green exterior, gold banding on rim and base, although obviously home-done it is nonetheless a very attractive item, mark B in green* **130.00**

☐ Shape #11, *plain salad, dimensions as above, undecorated, mark B in green* **50.00**

☐ Shape #75, *handled bowl, 6" diameter, 2-3/4" deep, ruffled rim, gold trim on handles and rim, mark B in green* **45.00**

☐ Shape #165, *low crimped diamond shape, 3-1/2" high, 9-1/2" wide, pearlized yellow interior, sponged gold on outside, mark B in red* **115.00**

☐ Shape #201, *small footed bowl, 3-1/2" diameter, fishnet finish on outside, speckled gold trim on feet and gold pencil-line on rim, mark B in red* **100.00**

☐ Shape #201-1/2, *as above but with no fishnet, undecorated, mark B in green* **55.00**

☐ Shape #206, *ice bowl, 9-1/2" diameter, ruffled rim, missing its tray, hand-painted daffodils with gold trim, artist signed, mark B in green* . **85.00**

☐ Shape #240, *7" diameter, twisted ribbing, scalloped rim, undecorated, mark B in green* **75.00**

Bowl, *shape #320*

☐ Shape #320, *dragon-handled, 4-1/8" high, 7" diameter, pale green exterior, gold trim on rim and dragons, very nicely done, mark B in green* **90.00**

☐ Shape number unknown, *7" handle to handle, ruffled rim, hand-painted monochromatic blue scene, mark D in blue* **150.00**

BREAD AND MILK SETS
☐ Shape #74, *pitcher 6" high, bowl 6" diameter, ruffled rim on bowl, curly handle on pitcher, hand-painted small red roses, gold trim, mark B in brown* **115.00**

BUTTER TUBS
☐ Shape #31, *5-1/2" diameter, drainer damaged and glued together, gold trim on lid finial, gold pencil-line around mid-section, mark B in green* **50.00**

CANDLESTICKS
☐ Shape #314, *1-5/8" candlestick on trivet shaped base, undecorated, mark B in green* **45.00**

CHOCOLATE POTS

Chocolate pot,
shape #39

☐ Shape #39, *10" high, veining in china, bud finial, delicate pink tinting with brushed gold over it, gold trim on handle and finial, absolutely divine, mark B in red*.................................... **275.00**
☐ Shape #210-1/4, *10" high, gold paste on matte finish, mark B in red* **275.00**
☐ Shape #210-1/2, *10" high, undecorated, lid cracked, mark B in green* . **100.00**

CLOCKS
☐ Shape, number unknown, *7" high, embossed design on china and hand-painted roses, gold trim, replacement clockwork, mark B in red* **250.00**

Clock, *shape number unknown*

COFFEEPOTS
☐ Shape #672, 6-1/4" high, gold trim, gold handle and finial, nicely done, probably the work of one of the decorating establishments, gold too brassy looking to have been done at factory, mark B in green **100.00**

Coffeepot, *shape #672*

☐ Shape #725, 7-1/2" high, hand-painted peacocks and garlands of flowers, artist's initials E.C. (probably Edward Challinor), handle clumsily repaired and a crack in the body, mark B in brown **50.00**

Coffeepot, *shape #725*

Note: For whatever reason, the Willets Company referred to most of their pots as teapots regardless of their shape or size. For additional listings on coffeepots, see the teapot section.

COMPORTS
☐ Shape #16, 2" high, shell raised on three twig feet, pearlized blue interior, speckled gold trim on outside and on feet, mark A in red **115.00**
☐ Shape #16, 2" high, shell raised on three twig feet, undecorated, small fleck on rim, mark B in green **45.00**
☐ Shape #40, 10" diameter, shell raised on coral and seashell pedestal base, pearlized finish, base done in different shades of gold, speckled gold trim on rest of the item, mark B in red **210.00**
☐ Shape #41, 9" diameter, ruffled rim top section resting on six-footed geometric design twig base, undecorated, several flecks on rim, large hairline crack across top, mark B in green **35.00**

CRACKER JARS
☐ Shape #38, 6" high, 5" diameter, bamboo pattern, shaded pale green colors with gold highlights, lid does not fit particularly well although it is probably the original one, mark B in brown **125.00**

CROCUS POTS
☐ Shape number unknown, *two twigs form the handle, hand-painted flowers outlined in gold in scatter pattern, gold trim on rims and handle, mark B in red* **95.00**

Crocus pot, *shape number unknown*

CUPS AND SAUCERS

☐ Shape #22, *Piedmont tea, plain shape, undecorated, mark B in green*   **15.00**

☐ Shape #22, *Piedmont tea, hand-painted lily of the valley on green
  background, gold trim on handle and rims, mark B in green* **30.00**

☐ Shape #23, *Shell tea, pearlized lavender interior, sponged gold on exterior, filigree gold on handle, mark B in red* **40.00**

☐ Shape #23, *shell tea, undecorated, mark B in green* **25.00**

☐ Shape #23, *shell tea, exceptionally thin and fine, gold trim, mark B in
  red* **50.00**

☐ Shape #24, *ribbed tea, undecorated, mark B in green* **14.00**

☐ Shape #25 *(Piedmont after dinner coffee),* #26 *(Three-footed tea),* #27
  (shell after dinner coffee), and #30 *(ribbed after dinner coffee), are all
  shown in the catalogues without saucers. Since they are often
  erroneously sold as being incomplete, the prices are much lower
  than they should be. They are frequently priced around* **15.00**

☐ Shape #47, *five o'clock cup and tray, diameter of tray 7-1/2" diameter,
  veined design on tray, cup has narrow fluting and forked handle,
  shade coral coloring with sponged gold trim over it, small fleck on
  rim, mark B in red* **125.00**

☐ Shape #96, *leaf after dinner coffee, footed, pale green with embossed veining traced over in a darker green, mark B in green* **40.00**

☐ Shape #96, *leaf after dinner coffee, footed, undecorated, mark B in
  green* **30.00**

☐ Shape #99, *scalloped edge tea, undecorated, mark B in green* **18.00**

☐ Shape #99, *scalloped edge tea, small hand-painted blue forget-me-
  nots, gold trim, mark B in green* **25.00**

☐ Shape #102, *fluted bottom after dinner coffee, beige and gray with
  gold paste trim, mark B in red* **70.00**

☐ Shape #102, *fluted bottom after dinner coffee, salmon colored
  flowers outlined in gold, gold trim on handles and rims, mark B in red*   **65.00**

☐ Shape #103, *oval panel and footed after dinner coffee, undecorated,
  mark B in green* ..:.......................................   **20.00**

Cups & Saucers

shape #96

shape #102

shape #103

shape #104

shape #105

shape #126

shape #247-1/2

shape #310

shape #313, 313-1/2

- ☐ Shape #104, *square panel, square handle after dinner coffee, gold trim on handle and outlining panels, mark B in brown* **32.00**
- ☐ Shape #105, *plain top, twisted, fluted bottom after dinner coffee, pale pink with darker pink flowers, gold trim on handle and rim, mark B in green* **40.00**
- ☐ Shape #115, *doubled flowered bouillon cup and saucer, bowl 3-3/4" diameter, saucer 5-3/4" diameter, undecorated, mark B in brown* **30.00**
- ☐ Shape #126, *five o'clock after dinner coffee, embossed lily petals, forked handle, lemon yellow exterior with gold trim, mark B in red* . . . **65.00**
- ☐ Shape #126, *five o'clock after dinner coffee, embossed lily petals, forked handle, undecorated, mark B in green* **32.00**
- ☐ Shape #162, *flower handled bouillon with lid, bowl 4" diameter, saucer 5-1/4" diameter, undecorated, unmarked* **15.00**

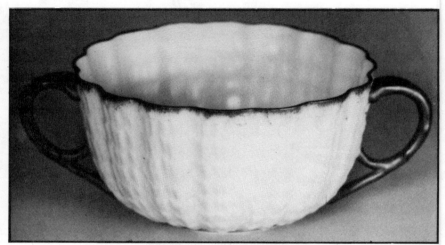

Bouillon cup, *gold trim, shape #163*

- ☐ Shape #163, *shell bouillon, gold trim, no saucer, mark D in red* **32.00**
- ☐ Shape #163, *shell bouillon, pearlized yellow interior, gold trim on handles and rims, mark B in red* **50.00**
- ☐ Shape #164, *cactus pattern covered bouillon, undecorated and un- marked* **20.00**
- ☐ Shape #164, *cactus pattern covered bouillon, gold trim, mark B in green* **30.00**
- ☐ Shape #164-1/2, *cactus pattern bouillon, outside painted in green with brown highlights, brown handles, mark B in green* **55.00**
- ☐ Shape #164-3/4, *cactus tea, undecorated, two small flecks on saucer, mark B in green* **35.00**
- ☐ Shape #164-3/4, *cactus tea, pearlized pink interior, gold trim, mark B in red* **65.00**
- ☐ Shape #182, *covered plain bouillon, saucer 6" diameter, hand- painted small poppies, gold trim on handles, rims and finial, mark B in green* **30.00**
- ☐ Shape #183, *bouillon, bowl 3-3/4" diameter, saucer 5-1/2" diameter, hand-painted yellow flowers with brown centers, green leaves, han- dles painted green with gold highlights, mark B in brown* **60.00**

Bouillon cup, *yellow flowers, shape #251*

☐ Shape #211, *footed shell tea, pearlized blue interior, gold trim, several small flecks, set of six, mark B in red* **275.00**
☐ Shape #211, *footed shell tea, undecorated, mark B in green* **50.00**
☐ Shape #212, *footed shell after dinner coffee, exceptionally thin, gold trim, mark B in red* **75.00**
☐ Shape #246, *fluted after dinner coffee with dragon handle, 2-1/2", gold trim, mark B in green* **50.00**
☐ Shape #247, *fluted chocolate, 3", no saucer, unmarked* **15.00**
☐ Shape #247-1/2, *fluted tea, set of four, each one decorated with a different flower, gold trim on rims and on dragons, artist signed and dated, mark B in green* **110.00**
☐ Shape #249-1/2, *2-1/2" after dinner coffee with dolphin handle, undecorated, mark B in green* **40.00**
☐ Shape #260, *after dinner coffee, twisted, scalloped, with dolphin handle, gold banding between scallops, gold trim on handle and rim, crack in handle, mark B in brown* **25.00**
☐ Shape #261, *chocolate cup, twisted, scalloped, with dolphin handle, pale pink exterior with small, hand-painted gold roses, exceptionally attractive for a home-done piece, mark B in green* **50.00**
☐ Shape #274, *heart-shaped after dinner coffee, forked handle, saucer missing, St. Valentine's greeting down inside, gold trim on handle and feet, mark B in green* **45.00**
☐ Shape #282, *shell tea, speckled gold trim on handle and body, mark B in brown* **60.00**
☐ Shape #308, *embossed and scalloped after dinner coffee, single large pink rose on one side of cup and three buds on saucer, gold trim, nicely done, mark B in green* **45.00**
☐ Shape #309, *embossed and scalloped chocolate cup, very thin, gold trim, no mark* **17.00**
☐ Shape #310, *embossed and scalloped tea, hand-painted lily of the valley, gold trim, mark B in green* **25.00**

☐ Shape #312, *embossed teacup, hand-painted bouquet of flowers, gold trim, mark B in green* **30.00**

☐ Shape #313, *embossed after dinner coffee, pearlized white, gold trim, mark B in red*.. **55.00**

☐ Shape #313-1/2, *embossed bouillon, undecorated, small chip on rim of saucer, mark B in green*.................................. **18.00**

DISHES

☐ Shape #29, *ice cream dish, pencil line gold around top rim, set of six, mark B in brown* **95.00**

☐ Shape #325, *strawberry dish, 8" diameter, 2" high, ruffled top, small, hand-painted gold flowers, sponged gold near rim, mark B in red* **65.00**

☐ Shape #326, *strawberry dish, 7" diameter, 1-3/4" high, ruffled rim, undecorated, unmarked* **15.00**

EGG CUPS

☐ Shape #42, *lily egg cup, 3" high, undecorated, several flecks on rim, mark B in green* **20.00**

☐ Shape #42, *lily egg cup, 3" high, pink shading on outside, two flecks on inside of rim, mark B in red* **60.00**

Egg cup, *shape #42, pink shading*

☐ Shape #42, *lily egg cup, gold trim, mark B in red* **100.00**

☐ Shape #42, *lily egg cup, coral shading with sponged gold over it, mark B in red*.. **150.00**

EWERS

☐ Shape #43, *stick handle rustic ewer, 10-1/2" high, matte beige finish with gold paste trim in chrysanthemum pattern, gold trim, on handles and rims, mark B in red* **250.00**

Ewers

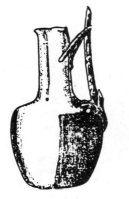

shape #43

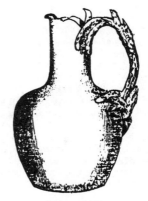

shape #44

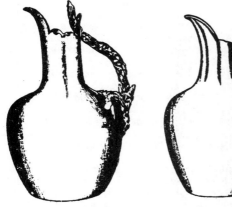

shape #45   *shape #46*

shape #81-1/2

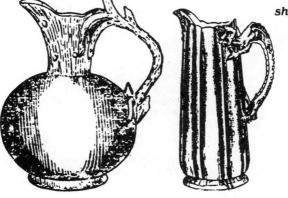

shape #231   *shape #210*

- [ ] Shape #44, *branch handle rustic ewer, 10" high, single water lily on front outliner in gold, gold trim on handle and rim, crack in handle and 1/2" chip out of spout, mark B in red* **125.00**
- [ ] Shape #45, *straight handle rustic ewer, 10-1/2" high, undecorated and unmarked* **75.00**
- [ ] Shape #45, *straight handle rustic ewer, 10-1/2" high, shaded from lavender at bottom to pea green at top, gold paste trim, gold trim on handles and rims, mark B in red* **265.00**
- [ ] Shape #46, *claret ewer, 10" high, beige matte finish, gold paste flowers, gold trim on handle and rims, spider crack in bottom, mark B in red* **130.00**
- [ ] Shape #81-1/2, *Worcester ewer, piercing on handle and neck, unmarked and piercing damaged in several places* **50.00**
- [ ] Shape #166, *small, rustic handled ewer, 8" high, hand-painted bluebird on one side, branch with pink blossom on other, gold handle, gold trim on rims, artist signed and dated, mark B in brown* **150.00**
- [ ] Shape #179, *oval, crimped top, rustic handled French ewer, 10" high, undecorated, mark B in green* **115.00**
- [ ] Shape #199, *rustic ewer, 9-1/2" high, beige matte finish, gold paste Queen Anne's lace, gold trim on handle, mark B in red* **150.00**
- [ ] Shape #202, *handled ewer, 11-1/2" high, hand-painted portrait of a little girl in bonnet, raised blue dot enamel work, about three times more gold trim than the item needs, very sloppy looking, artist signed and dated, small hairline on rim, mark B in green* **125.00**
- [ ] Shape #208, *rustic handled ewer, 7-1/2" high, undecorated, mark B in green* **50.00**
- [ ] Shape #208, *rustic handled ewer, 7-1/2" high, hand-painted red rose, gold trim, artist signed, mark B in green* **75.00**
- [ ] Shape #210, *dragon handle claret ewer, 9" high, pearlized pink with speckled gold trim, mark B in red* **190.00**
- [ ] Shape #210, *dragon handle claret ewer, 9" high, sloppy gold trim, mark B in green* **100.00**
- [ ] Shape #231, *globe ewer, 6" high, undecorated, mark B in green* **80.00**
- [ ] Shape #231, *globe ewer, 6" high, gold trim, mark B in green* **100.00**
- [ ] Shape #287, *embossed ewer, 9-1/2" high to top of spout, hand-painted cocker spaniel, gold trim, absolutely incredible, mark B in green* **100.00**
- [ ] Shape #323, *bottle ewer, 8-1/4" high, beige matte finish, gold paste in oak leaf pattern, gold trim in handle and top, mark A in brown* **180.00**

FLOWER HOLDERS

- [ ] Shape #176, *crimped edge flower holder, oval cut center, 5-1/2" high, undecorated, mark B in green* **70.00**
- [ ] Shape #224, *double handled flower holder, cut top, 6" high, hand-painted trailing vines, gold trim on handles and rim, mark B in green* **96.00**
- [ ] Shape #264, *shell globe flower holder, coral handles, ruffled top, gold paste floral decoration on beige matte background, inside glazed in pearlized yellow, mark B in red* **160.00**
- [ ] Shape #315, *low shell flower holder, 5-1/4" long, undecorated, mark B in brown* **35.00**
- [ ] Shape #316, *low shell flower holder, 4-1/4" long, hand-painted small pink roses outlined in gold, gold trim on rims, mark B in red* **85.00**

FLOWER POTS
☐ Shape #334, *cactus flower pot, 4-1/2" wide, 6" high, beige matte finish, gold trim on flower, leaves, and other high points, one foot repaired, mark B in brown* **125.00**

Flower pot, *shape #334*

GLOBES
☐ Shape #149, *rustic footed globe, 6-3/4", hand-painted red and pin, cabbage roses all around, gold trim on rim and base, artist signed and dated, mark B in green* **100.00**

Globe, *shape #149*   **Globe,** *shape #324*

☐ Shape #324, *embossed and footed globe, 5-1/2" diameter, gold trim on embossing, feet and rim, mark B in green* **87.00**

JARDINIERES
☐ Shape #268, *tall, footed jardiniere, cut and folded top, 7-1/2" high, 8-1/2" wide, gold paste chrysanthemums in three shades of gold, beige matte finish, sponged gold on feet and rim, mark B in brown* ... **225.00**

Jardiniere, *shape #268*   Jardiniere, *shape #333*

☐ Shape #333, *embossed jardiniere, 6-1/2" wide, 5-3/4" high, hand-painted mixed flowers on both sides, gold highlighting on embossing and rims, home-done but very nice, artist signed and dated, mark B in green* **135.00**

☐ Shape #333, *embossed jardiniere, 6-1/2" wide, 5-3/4" high, undecorated and unmarked* **25.00**

☐ Shape #333-1/4, *7" wide, garden scene, gold trim, artist signed, mark B in green* **125.00**

☐ Shape #333-1/2, *8" high, gold initials, gold trim on embossing and rim, mark B in green* **75.00**

JARS

☐ Shape #6, *small covered jar, 7-1/4" high, hand-painted white and pink roses, ornate blue dot and gold work, signed M. J. Parker, mark B in brown*.. **300.00**

☐ Shape #6, *7-1/4" high, hand-painted garlands of pink roses, gold trim, mark B in green* **95.00**

☐ Shape #6, *7-1/4" undecorated and unmarked* **30.00**

☐ Shape #50, *Oriental jar, 8-1/2" high, undecorated, mark B in green* ... **65.00**

☐ Shape #50, *Oriental jar, 8-1/2" high, hand-painted pink and maroon cabbage roses all around, gold trim, artist signed, mark B in green* .. **100.00**

☐ Shape #50, *Oriental jar, 8-1/2" high, hand-painted water lilies and gold trim, artist signed and dated, mark B in green* **135.00**

☐ Shape #51, *rose jar, pierced top, 11-3/4" high, gold filigree effect and gold trim on lid, lid badly damaged, mark B in green* **87.00**

☐ Shape #230, *6" high, cracker jar, hand-painted ivy with gold trim, mark B in green* **85.00**

☐ Shape #241, *7" high, twisted cracker jar, undecorated, mark B in green* **115.00**

JUGS

☐ Shape #52, *7" high, 6-1/2" diameter, gargoyle spout, shiny Chinese red with gold trim on spout and handle, mark B in green*............ **140.00**

Jars

shape #38

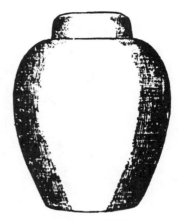

shape #50

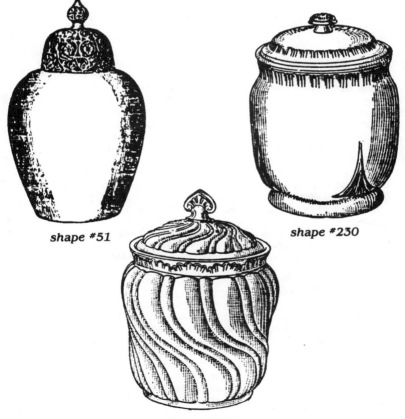

shape #51

shape #230

shape #241

Jug, *shape #56, bamboo*

☐ Shape #53, *cane jug, 7" high, decorated in natural looking colors of light brown highlighted with a darker brown, green leaf on side, dark brown handle with specks of gold, mark B in brown* 112.00
☐ Shape #54, *cane jug, 5-1/2" high, undecorated, mark B in green* 66.00
☐ Shape #55, *cane jug, 4" high, gold trim, mark B in green* 50.00
☐ Shape #56, *bamboo jug, 6-1/2" high, beige matte background, gold paste in trailing design, green bamboo leaves around handle, pinkish-beige handle, sponged gold highlights, gold trim on rim, 1-1/2" hairline on spout, mark B in red* 90.00
☐ Shape #57, *bamboo jug, 5-1/2" high, glazed finish, coral-colored flowers outlined in gold, gold trim on handle and rims, mark B in red* . 125.00
☐ Shape #58, *bamboo jug, 3" high, undecorated and unmarked* 15.00
☐ Shape #62, *shell jug, coral handle, 7-1/2" high, unmarked and undecorated* 300.00
☐ Shape #101, *5" high, small rustic jug, hand-painted blue forget-me-nots, gold trim on handle and rim, mark B in green* 75.00
☐ Shape #101, *5" high, small rustic jug, gold trim on handle, mark B in green* 55.00
☐ Shape #108, *7-1/2" high, rustic-handled ewer, hand-painted orchid, gold trim, artist signed, mark B in green* 125.00
☐ Shape #145, *globe jug, 5-1/2" high, undecorated, mark B in green* 55.00
☐ Shape #145, *globe jug, 5-1/2" high, hand-painted pansies with very pretty gold work on spout and handle, exceptionally nice for home decoration, artist signed, mark B in green* 100.00
☐ Shape #177, *oval, broad bottom, crimped top, rustic handled jug, 5-1/2" high, gold paste trim in oak leaf pattern, mark B in red* 98.00
☐ Shape #177, *description as above, hand-painted white and yellow roses in shaded brown background, gold trim on handle and rims, small chip on handle, artist signed and dated, mark B in green* 65.00

Jugs

shape #52, 52-1/2

shape #53

shape #56, 57, 58, 59

shape #210-1/2

shape #235

shape #311

☐ Shape #210-3/4, 11-1/2" high, jug, dragon handle, monochromatic blue floral design, mark B in green **150.00**

☐ Shape #218, embossed jug, 6" high, undecorated and unmarked **30.00**

☐ Shape #235, 6-3/4" high jug, dolphin handle, vertical rainbow shading, pink top and handle with speckled gold trim, crack in handle, mark B in brown **110.00**

☐ Shape #235, 6-3/4" high jug, dolphin handle, gold trim on handle and spout, mark B in green **100.00**

☐ Shape #236, 5-1/2" high jug, dolphin handle, banding of small yellow flowers around top section, gold trim on handle, rims and spout, mark B in green **85.00**

☐ Shape #311, embossed and scalloped jug, 9-1/2" high, hand-painted pink and red flowers on shaded green and yellow background, silver overlay work on embossed sections and on handle, mark B in brown **395.00**

KETTLES

☐ Shape #48, gypsy kettle, round, 4" high, hand-painted small pink roses outlined in gold, gold trim on handles and rim, mark B in red ... **150.00**

☐ Shape #48, gypsy kettle, round, 4" high, undecorated, mark B in green **45.00**

☐ Shape #49, gypsy kettle, oval, 4-1/4" long, 2-1/2" wide, undecorated and unmarked, small chip on handle **15.00**

LOVING CUPS

☐ Shape #456, three-handled loving cup, raised blue enamel flowers with gold paste trim, mark B in red **175.00**

☐ Shape #456, three-handled loving cup, hand-painted small roses and gold trim on handles and rims, marked on front "New England Sanitary Club" and on back with date and name of hotel where a meeting was apparently held, in addition to usual Willets mark also has the mark of the Trenton Potteries Company **70.00**

Loving cup, shape #456

☐ Shape #488, *three-handled footed loving cup, 9", portrait of woman, pale blue banding at top and on pedestal covered with gold filigree work, raised gold paste trim around portrait, gold trim on handles, signed Mary J. Coulter and dated 1906, mark B in brown* **425.00**

MATCH BOXES
☐ Shade #19, *3" long, shaped like treasure chest with acorn finial, undecorated and unmarked* **35.00**

MUGS AND STEINS
Shape numbers for mugs are not known, partly because catalogue pictures are too indistinct to allow us to differentiate between them.

☐ Mug, *5" high, hand-painted ears of corn on shaded brown background, mark B in green* **75.00**
☐ Mug, *5" high, hand-painted berries on shaded green background, very nicely done, artist signed and dated, mark B in green* **110.00**
☐ Mug, *5" high, hand-painted monk scene in monochromatic browns, mark B in green* **100.00**
☐ Mug, *5" high, hand-painted grapes and leaves on pale green background, artist signed and dated, mark B in green* **75.00**
☐ Mug, *5-1/2" high, monochromatic brown tavern scene, part hand-painted and part transfer, mark B in brown* **90.00**
☐ Mug, *5-1/2" high, hand-paintatic brown tavern scene, part hand-painted and part transfer, mark B in brown* **90.00**
☐ Mug, *5-1/2" high, hand-painted red berries on shaded brown background, gold handle and rim, artist's initials and date, mark B in green* **75.00**
☐ Mug, *5-1/2" high, hand-painted small white dog on brown, green and orange shaded background, signed G. Houghton and dated, mark B in brown* **350.00**

Stein, *grapes and leaves*

☐ Mug, 5-1/2" high, transfer decoration of carriage scene, gold trim on handle and rim, very sloppy, mark B in green **50.00**

☐ Mug, 5-3/4" high, covered with drippy enamel, resembles a Chianti bottle that has been used to hold candles, artist signed and dated, mark B in green **100.00**

☐ Mug, 6" high, hand-painted portrait of cavalier, shaded purple background, horrible, mark B in green........................... **75.00**

☐ Mug, 6" high, hand-painted flowers on shaded green and yellow background, very pretty, gold trim on handle and rims, artist signed and dated, mark B in green **95.00**

☐ Mug, 6" high, transfer-decorated with Masonic emblem, mark B in green **100.00**

☐ Mug, 6" high, geometric enamel designs, gold trim on handle and rim, mark B in green **50.00**

☐ Stein, hand-painted purple grapes and green leaves on shaded green background, porcelain insert in lid with hand-painted monogram, silver manufacturer unknown, mark B in green **250.00**

PLATES

☐ Shape #7, crimped edge plate, 9-1/2" diameter, pearlized yellow exterior, gold past trim inside, three small flecks on rim, mark B in red . **75.00**

☐ Shape #7, crimped edge plate, 9-1/2" diameter, hand-painted buttercups and leaves on shaded brown background, artist signed and dated, mark B in green.. **60.00**

☐ Shape #7-1/2, footed crimped edge plate, 9-1/2" diameter, 3-1/4" high, sponged gold trim on rim, gold feet, mark B in brown **85.00**

☐ Shape #65, scalloped rim plate, 8-1/2" diameter, brown lustre finish, square section on bottom part of plate with portrait of a woman, cocoa-colored enamel work around the square, raised gold paste trim over rest of plate, artist signed, mark B in brown **150.00**

☐ Shape #65, scalloped rim plate, 8-1/2" diameter, undecorated, set of 6, mark B in green **50.00**

☐ Shape #65-1/4, scalloped rim plate, banding of small blue flowers near rim, gold trim on rim, pair, mark B in green **35.00**

☐ Shape #65-3/4", scalloped rim plate, 5-1/2" diameter, gold initials in center, gold trim on rim, pair, mark B in green **6.00**

☐ Shape #127-1/2, scalloped and fluted rim plate, 6-1/4" diameter, single large pink rose in center, gold trim on rim, mark B in green **32.00**

☐ Shape #221, square plate with ruffled rim and turned-down corners, 6" across, hand-painted butterflies and flowers, gold trim on rim, mark B in green **45.00**

☐ Shape #221, square plate with ruffled rim and turned-down corners, gold paste trim in chrysanthemum design, gold trim on rim, 1/8" fleck on one corner, mark B in red **70.00**

☐ Shape #221-1/2, rectangular plate with ruffled rim and turned-down corners, 6" long, 4" wide, hand-painted small pink roses in scattered design, gold trim on rim, mark B in red **95.00**

☐ Shape #222, square plate with ruffled rim and turned-down trim on rim, nicely done, artist signed and dated, a few small rough spots on rims, mark B in green **80.00**

☐ Shape #222, square plate with ruffled rim and turned-down corners, 5" wide, undecorated, mark B in green **25.00**

☐ Shape #278, *embossed plate, 8-1/2" diameter, hand-painted small pink roses on pale green background, gold trim on rim on embossed sections, very nicely done but artwork much newer than the plate since the decoration fills in old scratch mark, set of four, mark B in green* **24.00**
☐ Shape #278, *embossed plate, 8-1/2" diameter, hand-painted single iris in center, gold trim on rim, artist signed and dated, mark B in green* **24.00**

PUFF BOXES
☐ Shape #69, *2-3/4" high, 3" diameter, embossed design, undecorated, mark B in green* **60.00**
☐ Shape #284, *4" wide, 3" high, hand-painted small flowers around outside, gold trim on rims and finial, mark B in green* **75.00**
☐ Shape #284, *4" wide, 3" high, undecorated, mark B in green* **50.00**
☐ Shape #291, *3-1/2" wide, 3" high, undecorated, mark B in green* **55.00**

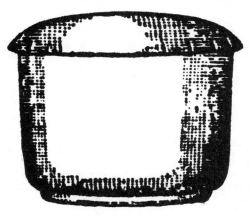

Puff box, *shape #291*

☐ Shape #291, *3-1/2" wide, 3" high, hand-painted pink and white roses on shaded yellow background, gold trim on rims, artist signed and dated, mark B in green* **90.00**
☐ Shape #291, *3-1/2" wide, 3" high, hand-painted cherubs holding up garlands of roses on pale blue background, artist's initials and date, mark B in green* **125.00**

SALT AND PEPPER HOLDERS
☐ Shape #14, *demijohn pepper, no handle, 3-1/4" high, undecorated, mark B in green* **30.00**
☐ Shape #14-1/2, *demijohn pepper, same as #14 but with handle, gold trim, mark B in brown* **45.00**
☐ Shape #15, *champagne bottle pepper, 3-1/4" high, small hand-painted flowers, gold trim, mark B in red* **65.00**
☐ Shape #18, *basket-shaped salt dip, oval, 3-1/2" long, 1/2" high, undecorated and unmarked* **20.00**
☐ Shape #21, *basket salt, rectangular, 2-1/2" long, gold exterior, artist's initials and date, small fleck on rim, mark B in green* **30.00**

- [ ] Shape #68, *pomegranate-shaped pepper with leaf base, shaded coral background covered with sponged gold, small chip on one leaf, mark B in red* **50.00**
- [ ] Shape #68, *pomegranate-shaped pepper with leaf base, undecorated, pair, mark B in green* **75.00**
- [ ] Shape #277, *individual salt dip, heart-shaped, 1-3/4" wide, hand-painted flowers and gold trim, artist's initials, mark B in green* **18.00**
- [ ] Shape #277, *individual salt dip, heart-shaped, 1-3/4" wide, undecorated, mark B in green* **12.00**
- [ ] Shape #277, *individual salt dip, heart-shaped, 1-3/4" wide, gold trim, mark B in green* **15.00**
- [ ] Shape #277-1/2, *individual salt dip, heart-shaped with ruffled rim, 1-3/4" wide, gold trim, fleck on one ruffle, mark B in brown* **14.00**
- [ ] Shape #277-1/2, *individual salt dip, heart-shaped with ruffled rim, small pink roses outlined in gold, gold trim on ruffles, mark B in red* .. **20.00**
- [ ] Shape #277-1/2, *individual salt dip, heart-shaped with ruffled rim, undecorated and unmarked* **8.00**
- [ ] Shape #286, *individual salt dip, ruffled rim, round, 2" round, small scattered flowers, gold trim on rim, unmarked* **18.00**
- [ ] Shape #286, *individual salt dip, ruffled rim, round, 2" diameter, hand-painted banding of pink roses on green background, pearlized green interior, artist signed and dated, mark B in green* **14.00**
- [ ] Shape #286, *individual salt dip, ruffle rim, round, 2" diameter, gold exterior, artist's initials, mark B in green* **10.00**
- [ ] Shape number unknown, *pedestal-type individual salt dip, all gold exterior and interior, mark B in brown* **12.00**
- [ ] Shape number unknown, *master salt on three ball feet, gold trim on rim and on feet, mark B in brown* **20.00**
- [ ] Shape number unknown, *individual salt dip on three ball feet, gold trim on rim and feet, set of six, mark B in brown* **75.00**
- [ ] Shape number unknown, *individual salt dip, three ball feet, undecorated, mark B in green* **12.00**
- [ ] Shape number unknown, *individual salt dip, scalloped rim, gold band on rim, mark B in green* **10.00**

SHELLS

- [ ] Shape #70, *small coral foot shell, 2-1/2" high, pearlized white finish with gold trim, mark B in green* **135.00**
- [ ] Shape #70, *small coral foot shell, 2-1/2" high, undecorated and unmarked* **40.00**
- [ ] Shape #71, *loaf sugar shell, 4-1/2" long, undecorated, mark B in green* **35.00**

SMOKING COMBINATIONS

- [ ] Shape #318, *3-1/2" high smoking combination, includes basket for matches, tree trunk for cigarettes or cigars, and ruffled rim boat-shaped ashtray, all on rustic base, undecorated, mark B in brown,* ... **125.00**
- [ ] Shape #318, *as above except that handle of basket is gone, mark B in brown* **50.00**

SUGARS AND CREAMERS

- [ ] Shape #13, *footed creamer, 4" high, hand-painted portrait of woman, blue enamel work and gold trim, not bad, artist signed and dated, mark B in green* **100.00**

Sugars and Creamers

shape #13

shape #35

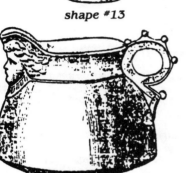

shape #36

shape #72

shape #151

shape #155

shape #216

Shell, *shape #70*

☐ Shape #13, *footed creamer, 4" high, hand-painted poppies on shaded green background, mark B in green* **55.00**

☐ Shape #35, *cane creamer, beige matte finish with raised gold paste wor, gold trim on handle, mark B in red* **10.00**

☐ Shape #36, *medallioon cream, 3" high, hand-painted dragon on shaded brown background, gold trim, small chip on spout, mark B in green* **100.00**

☐ Shape #37, *basket cream 3" high, undecorated, mark B in green* **35.00**

☐ Shape #72, *cane sugar, 3" high, mate to #35 creamer with gold paste trim, mark B in red* **100.00**

☐ Shape #73, *individual sugar and creamer, crimped rim, 3-1/2" diameter sugar, 4" high creamer, raised enamel flowers outlined in gold, gold trim on handle and rims, small fleck on rim of sugar, mark B in green* **130.00**

☐ Shape #73, *individual sugar and creamer, crimped rim, 3-1/2" diameter sugar, 4" high creamer, hand-painted daisies on pale blue shaded background, gold trim on handles and rim, artist signed and dated, mark B in green* **100.00**

☐ Shape #73, *individual sugar and creamer, crimped rim, 3-1/2" diameter sugar, 4" high creamer, raised gold paste in oak leaf design, gold trim on handle and rims, beige matte finish, mark B in red* **150.00**

☐ Shape #95, *basket sugar, oven, 3" diameter, 2-1/2" high, undecorated, mate to creamer #37, mark B in green* **35.00**

☐ Shape #118, *small, crooked neck Tuscan creamer, 5" high, hand-painted flowers outlined in gold, beige matte background, sponged gold trim, mark B in red* **110.00**

☐ Shape #118, *small, crooked neck Tuscan creamer, 5" high, undecorated, mark B in green* **30.00**

☐ Shape #151, *doubled handled, footed sugar, 3-1/2" high, hand-painted single large yellow rose on front, small yellow rosebud on back, gold trim on handles, rims and finial, artist signed and dated, mark B in green* **75.00**

☐ Shape #155, *sugar and creamer, rope handles, crimped rims on both pieces, undecorated and unmarked* **45.00**

- ☐ Shape #155, *sugar and creamer, rope handles, crimped rims on both pieces, beige matte finish with raised gold paste leaf design, gold trim on handles and rims, mark B in red* **135.00**
- ☐ Shape #170, and #171, *oval sugar 4-1/2" high, oval creamer 2-1/2" high, hand-painted bunches of violets, part of a four-piece set which includes tray and teapot, see those sections for prices on rest of set, mark B in brown* **100.00**
- ☐ Shape #170 and #171, *oval sugar 4-1/2" high, oval creamer 2-1/2" high, undecorated and unmarked* **45.00**
- ☐ Shape #210-1/2, *creamer 6-1/2" high, dragon handle, gold trim, mark B in green* **70.00**
- ☐ Shape #216 and #217, *shell sugar and creamer, sugar 4" high, creamer 3" high, raised gold paste cattail design, gold trim on rims and on coral-shaped handles, part of a three-piece set, see teapot section for matching pot* **200.00**
- ☐ Shape #216, *creamer 3" high, shell design with coral handle, decorated in a burnt orange color with gold trim, artist signed and dated, mark B in green* **45.00**
- ☐ Shape #233 and #234, *twisted sugar and creamer, sugar 3-3/4" high, creamer 3-1/2" high, gold trim, see teapot section for matching pot, mark B in green* **75.00**
- ☐ Shape #239, *fluted creamer, 4-1/2" high, dragon handle and mask spout, pearlized pink interior, speckled gold trim on handle and spout, mark B in red* **125.00**
- ☐ Shape #306 and #307, *embossed and scalloped sugar and creamer, sugar 4-1/2" high, creamer 4-1/2" high, hand-painted red and pink cabbage roses on shaded green background, gold trim on handles, rims and finial, artist signed and dated, mark B in green* **125.00**

Swan, *shape #252*

SWANS
- ☐ Shape #252, *swan salt, 2" high, undecorated, few rough spots on wings, mark B in green* **30.00**
- ☐ Shape #253, *swan cream, 4" high, undecorated, few rough spots on wings, mark B in green* **50.00**

TANKARDS

☐ Shape #453-1/4, *14" high, monochromatic monk scene, no artist signature, mark B in brown* **225.00**

☐ Shape #453-1/4, *14" high, hand-painted bunches of grapes in green and purple on shaded green background, artist signed and dated, mark B in green* **200.00**

☐ Shape #453-1/4, *14" high, hand-painted red berries on shaded brown background, very nicely done, artist signed and dated, mark Bin brown*... **250.00**

☐ Shape #453-1/4, *14" high, transfer decoration of horses on shaded brown background, gold trim on handle and rims, mark B in green* ... **175.00**

☐ Shape #572, *15-1/8" high, dragon handle, nude stepping into water, in colors of sepia, orange and green, gold band inside rim, signed George Houghton and dated, mark B in brown*.................... **450.00**

☐ Shape #572, *15-1/8" high, dragon handle, black and white St. Bernard on shaded background, signed George Houghton, dated, mark B in brown* .:................................... :.................... **600.00**

Note: The price difference between the two Houghton tankards is due to marketing variables, and the two should be priced closer together. Houghton was virtually unknown before this year and his popularity with collectors is zooming.

☐ Shape #572, *15-1/8" high, dragon handle, undecorated, mark B in green* **65.00**

TEAPOTS

Teapot, *shape #76, 77*

☐ Shape #76, *cane teapot, 5" high, beige matte finish with raised gold paste work, gold trim on handle, small fleck on spout, matches sugar and creamer listed earlier, mark B in red* **150.00**

☐ Shape #169, *oval teapot, 5" high, hand-painted bunches of violets, gold trim, part of a set, see tray section and sugar and creamer section for prices on rest of set, mark B in brown* **100.00**

☐ Shape #169, *oval teapot, 5" high, gold trim on handle and finial, mark B in green* **60.00**

☐ Shape #215, *shell teapot, 5" high, raised gold paste cattail design, gold trim on rims and on coral-shaped handle, part of a three-piece set, see sugar and creamer section for other items, damaged spout on teapot, mark B in red* **175.00**

Teapot, *shape #215*

☐ Shape #215, *shell teapot, 5" high, undecorated and unmarked, several spots of minor damage* **35.00**

☐ Shape #232, *twisted teapot, dolphin handle, 4-3/4" high, gold trim, see sugar and creamer section for matching items, mark B in green* . **75.00**

☐ Shape number unknown, *hand-painted roses in garlands held up by Cupids, gold trim on handle, rims, spout and finial, artist signed and dated, crack in handle, mark B in green* **135.00**

TRAYS
☐ Shape #17, *olive tray, 4-1/2" long, ruffled rim, small hand-painted flowers in scatter pattern, gold trim on rim, mark B in red,* **65.00**

Tray, *shape #17, small flowers*

☐ Shape #17, *olive tray, 4-1/2" long, ruffled rim, undecorated, mark B in green* **40.00**

☐ Shape #17-1/2, *olive tray, 3-1/2" long, gold exterior, mark B in green* .. **45.00**

☐ Shape #100, *diamond olive tray, 5" long, 4-1/4" wide, hand-painted yellow buttercups with green leaves, gold trim on rim, mark B in green* **50.00**

☐ Shape #100, *diamond olive tray, 5" long, 4-1/4" wide, gold trim on rim, mark B in green* **35.00**

☐ Shape #157, *oval crimped olive tray, 4-1/2" long, 3-1/2" wide, 1-1/2" deep, rustic handles, undecorated, mark B in green* **65.00**

☐ Shape #158, *triangular olive tray, 5-1/2" wide, rustic handle, small scattered pink roses, gold trim on handle and rim, mark B in red* **100.00**

☐ Shape #159, *five-sided crimped tray with handle, 7" wide, 4" high, undecorated and unmarked* **50.00**

☐ Shape #159-1/2, *same as shape #159 but with no handle, single large red rose in center, sponged gold trim on rim, not bad for home art-work, artist signed and dated, mark B in green* **115.00**

☐ Shape #213, *shell tray, 4-1/4" long, 4" wide, pearlized pink interior, outside has gold trim, mark B in red* **100.00**

☐ Shape #213-1/2, *shell tray, 3" long, 2-7/8" wide, gold paste trim, mark B in red* **95.00**

☐ Shape #214, *round tray, 1-1/2" high, 4" diameter, several flecks on rim, hand-painted small scattered flowers, gold trim, mark B in red* .. **75.00**

☐ Shape #250, *cactus olive tray, 4-1/2" long, gold trim, mark B in red* ... **95.00**

☐ Shape #250-1/2, *cactus olive tray with two handles, undecorated, several small flecks, mark B in green* **35.00**

☐ Shape #254, *heart tray, 6-1/4" long, ruffled rim, small scattered pink roses outlined in gold, gold trim on rim, mark B in red* **100.00**

☐ Shape #254, *heart tray, decorated in Valentine fashion with hearts, blue ribbon, and appropriate gold inscription, gold trim on rim, very pretty, artist's initials and date, mark B in green* **125.00**

☐ Shape #263, *pickelette tray, 7-1/2" long, undecorated, mark B in green* **32.00**

☐ Shape #285, *pin tray, five-sided, 5" wide, monogram in gold incenter, gold trim on rim, mark B in green* **40.00**

☐ Shape #285, *pin tray, five-sided, 5" wide, small hand-painted forget-me-nots and the inscription "forget-me-not" in gold, gold trim on rim, mark B in green* **90.00**

☐ Shape #295, *pin tray, 9-1/4" long, 2-3/4" wide, Delft-type monochrome blue decoration, mark D* **120.00**

☐ Shape #296, *pin tray, 6" long, 2-3/4" wide, tiny red roses, gold trim on rim, couple of flecks on ruffled rim, mark B in green* **65.00**

☐ Shape #297, *pin tray, 5" long, 3" wide, undecorated, mark B in green* . **15.00**

☐ Shape #301, *brush and comb tray, 6" wide, raised gold paste trim in chrysanthemum design, gold work done in five different shades ranging from an almost silver to a deep bronze color, exceptional work, more gold trim on ruffled rim, mark B in red* **195.00**

☐ Shape #303, *celery tray, crimped edge, 11-1/2" long, gold trim, artist's initials and date, mark B in green* ...... ∴ **65.00**

☐ Shape #327, *embossed tray, 4-3/4" long, 2-1/2" wide, undecorated, mark B in green* **20.00**

☐ Shape #328, *embossed tray, 6-1/2" long, 2-1/4" wide, transfer deco-rated with pins and needles and spools of thread, gold trim, mark B in green* **65.00**

☐ Shape #329, *harp tray, 6-1/4" long, 4-3/4" wide, gold trim on rim, mark B in green* **35.00**

☐ Shape #330, *embossed tray, 7-1/2" long, 4" wide, hand-painted pic-ture of kitten, shaded blue background, gold trim, mark B in green* ... **85.00**

TUBS

☐ Shape #340, *3-1/4" wide, embossed design, undecorated, mark B in green* **60.00**

VASES

☐ Shape #3, *small, crimped top vase, 8" high, gold paste floral decoration, beige matte finish, gold trim on rim and base, mark B in red* **150.00**

☐ Shape #3, *small, crimped top vase, 8" high, hand-painted shasta daisies on garlands around vase, gold trim on rim, very nice for home artwork, mark B in green* **125.00**

☐ Shape #3, *small, crimped top vase, 8" high, hand-painted single large pink rose, gold trim on rim, artist signed, mark B in green* **100.00**

☐ Shape #9, *water bottle vase, 10-1/2" high, undecorated, mark B in green* **70.00**

☐ Shape #9, *water bottle vase, 10-1/2" high, raised gold paste work in oak leaf pattern, beige high glaze finish, gold trim on rim, mark B in red* **200.00**

☐ Shape #9, *water bottle vase, 10-1/2" high, hand-painted little girls romping in field, artist signed and dated, so-so art work, mark B in green* **160.00**

☐ Shape #9, *water bottle vase, 10-1/2" high, hand-painted picture of cocker spaniel on shaded green background, artist signed and dated, mark B in green* **145.00**

☐ Shape #12, *long neck plain vase, 10-1/2" high, hand-painted single orchid on bulbous bottom section of vase, sponged gold trim, mark B in green but good enough to be factory-decorated* **180.00**

☐ Shape #12, *long neck plain vase, 10-1/2" high, geometric gold work on bottom section, pencil-line gold on rim, mark B in green* **125.00**

☐ Shape #28, *French flat vase, 11" high, hand-painted red and pink cabbage roses on shaded green background, artist signed and dated, mark B in green* **130.00**

☐ Shape #28, *French flat vase, 11" high, undecorated and unmarked* .. **35.00**

☐ Shape #80, *Worchester vase, pierced neck and handles, 14-1/2", high, gold trim and gold monogram, mark B in brown* **350.00**

☐ Shape #87, *small water bottle vase, 7-1/4" high, hand-painted portrait of woman, gold trim on rim, mark B in green* **110.00**

☐ Shape #87, *small water bottle vase, 7-1/4" high, raised gold paste in cattail design, high glaze white finish, mark B in red* **150.00**

☐ Shape #87, *small water bottle vase, 7-1/4" high, hand-painted monochromatic blue Delft-type scene, artist signed and dated, mark B in green* **150.00**

☐ Shape #88, *small cut top vase, 5" high, hand-painted blue and purple violets on shaded green background, gold trim on rim, nice, mark B in green* **125.00**

☐ Shape #88, *small cut top vase, 5" high, undecorated, mark B in green* **40.00**

☐ Shape #88, *small cut top vase, 5" high, transfer decoration of dog, gold trim on rim, mark B in green* **90.00**

☐ Shape #89, *small plain top vase, 5" high, transfer-decorated with horse and carriage, gold trim on rim, mark B in green* **70.00**

☐ Shape #89, *small plain top vase, 5" high, hand-painted bouquet of wildflowers, gold trim on rim, mark B in green* **80.00**

☐ Shape #89, *small plain top vase, 5" high, raised gold paste floral design, beige matte finish, mark B in red* **160.00**

Vases

shape #9

shape #12

shape #28

shape #80

shape #88

shape #89

shape #90

shape #106

shape #131

shape #132

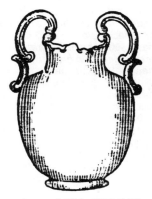

shape #191, 191-1/2

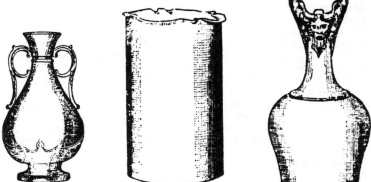

shape #204

shape #270

shape #290

- [ ] Shape #90, *long neck, crimped top, dented vase, 10-1/2" high, shaded from lavender at 'bottom to green at top with raised gold paste decoration, mark B in red* **200.00**
- [ ] Shape #90, *long neck, crimped top, dented vase, 10-1/2" high, undecorated, mark B in green* **95.00**
- [ ] Shape #106, *Mosque vase, pierced, 14" high, handles damaged and lid missing, gold trim, mark B in green* **75.00**
- [ ] Shape #131, *Vienna vase, 8" high, panels of flowers, filigree gold work between panels, gold trim on rims, artist signed and dated, not bad, mark B in green* **150.00**
- [ ] Shape #131, *Vienna vase, 8" high, hand-painted and enameled parrot, gold trim, mark B in green* **140.00**
- [ ] Shape #131, *Vienna vase, 8" high, undecorated, mark B in green* **80.00**
- [ ] Shape #132, *globe water bottle vase, 8" high, hand-painted pansies in shaded green background, artist signed and dated, pretty, mark B in green* **125.00**
- [ ] Shape #132, *globe water bottle vase, 8" high, transfer decoration of gypsy, gold trim, mark B in green* **75.00**
- [ ] Shape #132-1/2, *globe water bottle vase, 8" high, dented sides, gold trim, mark B in green* **100.00**
- [ ] Shape #138-1/2, *miniature water bottle vase with handles, 6" high, hand-painted morning glories on tan background, gold trim on handles and rim, artist signed and dated, mark B in green* **100.00**
- [ ] Shape #140, *beaded top water bottle vase, 7-1/2" high, gold trim on rims, gold banding around top section, artist's initials and date, hairline crack in base, mark B in green* **45.00**
- [ ] Shape #191, *double handled crimped top vase, 6" high, gold trim on handles, mark B in green* **80.00**
- [ ] Shape #191-1/2, *4-1/2" high, double handled crimped top vase, hand-painted pink roses, raised gold and blue dot enamel work, gold trim on handles and rims, signed and dated, mark B in brown* ... **250.00**
- [ ] Shape #203, *handled vase, pierced neck, heavily damaged in several spots, undecorated and unmarked* **15.00**
- [ ] Shape #204, *double handle vase, 12" high, hand-painted yellow and purple irises on shaded blue background, gold trim all over the thing, dreadful looking mess, artist signed and dated, mark B in green* **75.00**
- [ ] Shape #204, *double handled vase, 12" high, gold paste trim in beige matte finish, mark B in red* **200.00**
- [ ] Shape #204, *double handled vase, 12" high, hand-painted chrysanthemums on shaded yellow and brown background, gold trim, artist signed and dated, mark B in green* **150.00**
- [ ] Shape #227, *fluted Vienna vase, 8" high, raised gold paste trim on beige matte finish, repair to top, mark B in red* **100.00**
- [ ] Shape #227, *fluted Vienna vase, 8" high, hand-painted poppies on green background, gold trim, mark B in green* **150.00**
- [ ] Shape #269, *cactus handled vase, 6-1/2" high, small scattered flowers outlined in gold, pink pearlized interior, gold trim, mark B in red* .. **160.00**
- [ ] Shape #269, *cactus handled vase, 6-1/2" high, hand-painted daffodils, sponged gold trim, beautifully done, mark B in green* **125.00**
- [ ] Shape #270, *medallion vase, 9-1/4" high, gold trim on face and on rims, mark B in green* **175.00**
- [ ] Shape #290, *can vase, 4" high, 2-3/4" wide, hand-painted garlands of little roses around vase, gold trim on rim, small fleck on rim, artist signed and dated, mark B in green* **100.00**

☐ Shape #290, *can vase, 4" high, 2-3/4" wide, hand-painted birds and butterflies, gold trim on rim, artist signed and dated, mark B in green* **100.00**

☐ Shape #290, *can vase, 4" high, 2-3/4" wide, transfer decoration of horses, gold trim on rim, small hairline coming down from rim, mark B in green* **50.00**

☐ Shape #319, *foot vase, 10" high, hand-painted cabbage roses on shaded blue background, gold trim, artist signed, mark B in green* ... **140.00**

☐ Shape #319, *foot vase, 10" high, gold trim on rim and feet, mark B in green* **110.00**

☐ Shape #337, *7" high, double-handled, hand-painted water lilies on shaded green background, gold trim on handles and rim, especially nice for home work and very well suited to the vase, artist signed and dated, crack in one handle, mark B in green* **150.00**

☐ Shape #337, *7" vase, undecorated and unmarked* **100.00**

☐ Shape #481, *(or possibly 487), 12" high, beautiful portrait of woman, elaborate raised gold work, unfortunately no artist signature, mark B in brown* **600.00**

☐ Shape #550, *(or possibly 556), 15-1/4" rounded vase, shaded blue background with gold wheat, butterflies and clouds, mark B in brown*... **200.00**

☐ Shape number unknown, *two-handled 6" vase, gold paste on beige matte finish, gold wear on handles, mark B in red* **175.00**

MISCELLANEOUS

Liners in sterling holders — rate against comparable Lenox items. If Willets made anything exciting in this category, we have not seen it.

Figurines — extremely rare, so double the comparable Lenox price.

Porcelain dinnerware decorated at the factory in more or less standard patterns — rate against comparable Lenox item.

Opaque decorative ware — rate against Burroughs & Mountford or Greenwood Pottery.

WILLIAM YOUNG & SONS

William Young, Sr., began manufacturing earthenware in the Hattersley Pottery in 1853. The pottery was located on Perry Street east of the Delaware and Raritan Canal.

After they outgrew the Hattersley Pottery, Young & Sons built a new pottery in a different location. This new building, the Excelsior Pottery Works, was operated by the family until 1879 at which time it was taken over by Willets.

Marks: The first mark was an eagle, which was used until 1858. The next mark was the British coat of arms with the initials WYS underneath.

Prices: Since Wm. Young & Sons was such an early Trenton company their wares are of more than average interest. Expect to pay a minimum of $25 to $50 for their earlier items, and if something is particularly large or unusual it can go much, much higher. Some of their later very commercial products can be rated against similar items listed elsewhere in this book.

WOOD & BARLOW

See Empire Pottery.

WOODBRIDGE POTTERY COMPANY
This current company is located on Frazier Street and manufactures lamp bases.

Marks: *Not known*
Prices: To the Trentoniana collector, a sample lamp base would probably we worth a minimum of $5.

YATES, BENNETT & ALLAN
See City Pottery.

YATES & TITUS
See City Pottery.

MISCELLANEOUS
Every time we think we have finally listed all of the Trenton pottery and porcelain companies, somebody calls us with another one. Following is a general guide which can be used for either companies which are not listed or various types of items which are not listed individually under previously-mentioned companies.

BELLEEK-TYPE AND OTHER PORCELAIN ITEMS
Depending on its age, fineness and rarity, rate any item in this category against comparable items listed in the Lenox, Willets or Ott & Brewer sections.

IRONSTONE AND SIMILAR PRODUCTS
Compare against listed prices or use the following guide:

☐	Bowls, *dessert or soup size, decorated*	4.00	6.00
☐	Bowls, *dessert or soup size, undecorated*	3.00	5.00
☐	Bowls, *serving, decorated*	12.00	25.00
☐	Bowls, *serving, undecorated*	10.00	20.00
☐	Cups and saucers, *decorated*	5.00	12.00
☐	Cups and saucers, *undecorated*	4.00	10.00
☐	Dinner plates, *decorated*	6.00	12.00
☐	Dinner plates, *undecorated*	5.00	10.00
☐	Mugs, *decorated*	12.00	25.00
☐	Mugs, *undecorated*	10.00	12.00
☐	Platters, *decorated, depending on size*	15.00	30.00
☐	Platters, *undecorated, depending on size*	10.00	25.00
☐	Smaller plates, *decorated*	2.00	5.00
☐	Smaller plates, *undecorated*	1.00	3.00

FIGURINES
Consider any Trenton figurine to be worth a hint less than the comparable Lenox item if they are about the same age, or to be worth more than the comparable Lenox item if from before the turn of the century.

LAMP BASES
As a sample of a particular company's work, any lamp base should be worth a minimum of $3-$5.

ITEMS WITH SILVER HOLDERS

Figure items in this category to be worth a minimum of $10 for a small liner plus the scrap value of the silver. Add to the price for a highly-collectible silver company or pattern (see the Lenox section for further information about this) and add for a liner which is by a top company or which is particularly early.

POLITICAL ITEMS

Since you are a collector of Trenton ceramics and not of political campaign items, we would suggest not paying a premium for these items.

RAILROAD, STEAMSHIP, AND HOTEL CHINA, ETC.

The above comments about political collectibles apply to this category as well. Since all of these items have their own devoted followers already, there is no particular reason to slug it out with them over these items when a less collectible item by the same company will serve the purpose. As a general rule, you can double or triple many of the prices listed if the item is in these categories.

BIBLIOGRAPHY

Sanitary Pottery in the United States, Thomas Maddock, introductory pages missing so no date or publisher available (probably 1909).

The Dictionary of World Pottery and Porcelain, Louise Ade Boger, Charles Scribner's Sons, New York, 1971.

Encyclopedia of British Pottery and Porcelain Marks, Geoffrey A. Godden, Bonanza Books, New York, 1964.

Modern Porcelain, Alberta C. Trimble, Harper & Brothers Publishers, New York, 1962.

Encyclopedia of American Silver Manufacturers, Dorothy T. Rainwater, Crown Publishers, Inc., New York, 1975.

White House China, Marian Klamkin, Charles Scribner's Sons, New York, 1972.

The Pottery and Porcelain of the United States & Marks of American Potters, Edwin A. Barber, originally published in 1909 and reprinted in 1976 by Feingold and Lewis.

Lenox China, The Story of Walter Scott Lenox, Lenox, Inc., 1924.

The Antique Trader, "American Belleek", Nettie Goldblum, March 30, 1976.

The Antique Trader, "Collectible Lenox China", Nori and Mark Mohr, December 30, 1975.

Trenton Times and Daily State Gazette, as quoted in text.

1891 C.A.C. white ware catalogue

Undated C.A.C. white-ware catalogue

1939 Lenox, Inc., "Anniversary" catalogue

1921 white-ware catalogue

Lenox Annual Report 1977

Undated Lenox, Inc., press releases

Willets Belleek white-ware catalogue, 1893

The Southeast Trader

"News From The New South"
Published every two weeks for
Antiquers, Auctions, Shows, Flea Markets and Collectors

50 ¢
Subscription Information
(803) 359-9182